RESTAURANTS THAT·WORK

RESTAURANTS THAT WORK

CASE STUDIES OF THE BEST IN THE INDUSTRY

MARTIN E. DORF

WHITNEY LIBRARY OF DESIGN

AN IMPRINT OF WATSON-GUPTILL PUBLICATIONS/NEW YORK

TO IVONNE, MY WIFE AND PARTNER;

MY DAUGHTER, JODI; RUTH AND PHILLIP DORF;

ALFONSO AND TERESA VITERI; AND DR. AL WEISS

Senior editor: Roberto de Alba
Associate editor: Carl D. Rosen
Designer: Areta Buk
Production manager: Ellen Greene

First published in 1992 in the United States
by Whitney Library of Design,
an imprint of Watson-Guptill Publications,
a division of BPI Communications, Inc.
1515 Broadway, New York, New York 10036

Library of Congress Cataloging-in-Publication Data

Dorf, Martin E.
    Restaurants that work / Martin E. Dorf.
        p.   cm.
    Includes bibliographical references and index.
    ISBN 0-8230-4540-4
    1. Restaurant management-Case studies.   2. Restaurants, lunch
rooms, etc.—Design and construction.   I. Title.
    TX911.3.M27D598   1992
    647.95'068—dc20   92-11262
                                                                                              CIP

Manufactured in Singapore

3 4 5 6 7/ 97 96 95 94

ACKNOWLEDGMENTS

When Paul Weintraub, the former publisher of *Restaurant/Hotel Design International* magazine, suggested that I write a book about restaurants, I thought it would be a great opportunity to express my ideas about hospitality. It has been a labor of love, but it has also proven to be a task that would never have come to fruition without the support and guidance of many people.

With the deepest appreciation, I would like to thank my editor, Roberto de Alba, for the direction he gave in developing this book, and I would also like to thank Cornelia Guest, former editor of Whitney Library of Design, for her genuine support for this first-time author. A special thank-you goes to Lorraine Knapp and to my wife, Ivonne Dorf, for the research, organization, typing, and telephoning needed to produce the manuscript.

There have been many other people who contributed to this book as well that I am indebted to: Philip Langdon provided the chronological history of the American chain restaurant; Richard J. S. Gutman, a diner historian; Darrell Garwood of the Kansas State Historical Society; Nicolette Bromberg of the University of Kansas Libraries, Kansas Collection; The Museum of the City of New York, Byron Collection; The New-York Historical Society; The French National Tourist Board; John Romas of Horn & Hardart; T. Brock Saxe of TomBrock Corporation; and Robert Clinton of Clinton's Restaurant, Inc., generously supplied the photographs in the historical perspective section.

I am especially indebted to Barbara Lazaroff, whose undying dedication went into the preparation of the case studies for Spago, Chinois, Eureka, and Granita. In addition, my heartfelt appreciation goes to all the restaurateurs, chefs, general managers, architects, and designers who enthusiastically shared their knowledge, experience, passion, and vision. Without them, this book could not have been written.

CONTENTS

F O R E W O R D

BY JOSEPH BAUM

I was raised in Saratoga, New York, in a sweet Jewish family who ran a successful hotel for fifty-five years, and I grew up surrounded by juicy people who were full of humor and joy. They worked in racetracks, nightclubs, and restaurants, and I couldn't wait to get into what I thought was the wonderful world of hospitality.

What I found was quite the opposite. It was a rigid, faceless, spiritless industry filled with people who said, "You can't do this" and "You can't do that," and it appeared to me that I had the opportunity to be a light in the darkness. I thought it was time to impart my own personal feelings about the "pleasures of the table" to the public and to take the risk that people were looking for alternative dining-out experiences.

When the Four Seasons was opened in 1959, it reflected the roaring, glittering feelings of that time. People's attitudes about many things were changing, and the Four Seasons was the first elegant American restaurant that wasn't French in style, with red-flocked wallpaper. It expressed the total experience of dining, and everything from the scale of the space to the tabletop accessories was in harmony. La Fonda del Sol, The Forum of the XII Caesars, and the other theme restaurants that Restaurant Associates created made the total experience of dining accessible to a generation that never knew it was possible. It satisfied a need for a rather basic pleasure: that of self-reward.

People go to restaurants to be together, and to connect with one another. It is very important that the restaurant reinforce why customers choose to go to it in the first place. Restaurants exist to create pleasure, and how well a restaurant meets this expectation of pleasure is a measure of its success.

In the early 1980s, there was an explosion of interest in food and restaurants as entertainment worldwide. The skills and talents of chefs, purveyors, owners, architects, and designers to create sensual environments for the purpose of bringing pleasure to the dining-out public reached new heights. Celebrity chefs and award-winning restaurant spaces caught the attention of the public. At that time, there was a lot of

disposable income, and people put a lot of value on rewarding themselves by eating out. Understanding what value is and to what degree we feel we are allowed to reward ourselves very often dictates what kind of restaurant can succeed in a given location. There are 200 million people in this country who are faced with decisions about value and self-reward. This, coupled with less disposable income, creates a need to generate more consumer confidence. "Perceived value" becomes very important. Do you feel confident that you received great value when you leave a restaurant, or do you feel guilty and angry that you spent way too much for the pleasure received?

The relationship between customer and owner is crucial. It is very important that you feel that the restaurateur cares about you individually. It is expressed not only in how he or she greets you at the door, but in design issues as well. With tables a half-inch lower at the Rainbow Room lounge area, people felt more comfortable. The extra step in caring about the comfort of each detail is felt by customers individually, and they expect restaurateurs to be good citizens as well, interested in the environment and social issues. The restaurateur is no longer a distant entity because

JOSEPH BAUM. PHOTOGRAPH © DAN WYNN.

the customer expects to be much closer to the owner and the whole experience.

Good restaurateurs must have both the experience and training to develop their technique and the maturity to forget it. I don't mean to dispense with it, what I mean is it has to take second place behind the passion and element of risk that got you into this business.

The very nature of our business is individual attention to each individual customer. The owner has to be there to nourish and feed the restaurant and make sure that its success is sustained by hard work and a commitment to quality. Each restaurateur is successful because his or her persona and intellect allows the seizing of an opportunity. Restaurateurs have genuine feelings about people, food, service style, location, and the potential customer. This information grew out of genuine interest in hospitality: the business of individual attention to each individual customer. A restaurant must express each restaurateur's feelings about hospitality, and this sense of hospitality is acquired through years of experience, both positive and negative. For instance, I know not to build a Four Seasons where a Charlie O's should be located.

There is no one standard by which to measure a restaurant's success. I like large-scale, high-volume restaurants as much as I do small, intimate ones. All restaurants have to operate in a lovely way. The graceful movement and sense of style is essential in the giving of service. I think of the Rainbow Room as a place to celebrate both special occasions and everyday occasions, and I care deeply about how it conveys pleasure to our customers. I like to think of the Rainbow Room as the Statue of Liberty with one of her shoulder straps down.

Restaurants are "windows to our culture." How a restaurant expresses its time, and how it comes to life within the restaurateur's philosophy of operation and sense of style and detail has a great deal to do with its success. Today, restaurants are better than ever. Individual restaurateurs are more intellectually stimulated, and are aware of all the subtle decisions that need to be made to satisfy customer expectations.

There is a very sophisticated public right now. They are as educated and well-traveled as the smartest restaurateur. This is a dynamic, living time for the restaurant industry, and there are many opportunities for success. What is great about our democracy is that there is so much diversity and choice. People may go out less often because there is less disposable income, but they will go out to eat. They will change where they go. Take-out food, retail food, delivered food; there are so many possibilities!

There is a new generation of restaurateurs who will have the opportunity to express their feelings about the culture. Their courage, commitment to quality, and their ability to enjoy the element of risk will help them succeed. There's a lot to be cynical and skeptical about in this industry, and you have to accept the good with the bad. Above all, you have to love it, or it just isn't worth all the hard work.

INTRODUCTION

Approximately three out of four restaurants fail in the first year of business, according to recent statistics. Several reasons are cited, including undercapitalization, location, poor food and service, misunderstanding the customer base, improper management, and inappropriate design. Even if the food and service is good and the restaurant is managed properly, it can fail if it is in the wrong location or if it can't adapt to changes in the economy or shifts in demographic distribution. Some restaurateurs open in off-beat areas, spend relatively little on general construction and decor, serve well-prepared, moderately priced food, and are crowded the day they open. Others conduct in-depth demographic and market evaluations to find the best location, hire the best chef, and spend a fortune to build the restaurant and are out of business in six months.

The key to developing a restaurant concept that is a hit from the start and survives more than a few years has become more and more elusive. Competition coupled with a greater demand for value and service has made it more difficult to succeed, while changes in demographic distribution have made it even harder to define the customer base. The American population is shifting from what used to resemble a pyramid (few old and many young) to something that looks more like a pillar, with a roughly equal distribution of people in youth, middle age, and old age. For the first time, the mean age of the American population is over thirty-five. Baby boomers have aged and now have families, and, in addition, there has been a shift away from the traditional family household structures, including those of single parents, married couples with no children, and "blended households," or step-families. *American Demographics* magazine estimates that by the year 2000, married-couple households will account for barely half of all

households. Immigration is driving much of the population growth in the United States, and *American Demographics* also estimates that by the year 2000, one out of four people in the country will be a racial or ethnic minority.

These major population and lifestyle shifts, along with increased demand for affordable good-tasting food that is good for you, are shaping restaurant concepts for the 1990s, creating opportunities for a generation of restaurateurs. The questions remain: How does an inexperienced restaurateur begin to know what type of restaurant to open? Where should it be located? Who is the potential customer and competition? What food should be offered at what price, and what should it look like?

Unfortunately, there are no proven recipes for success, but the case studies and interviews in this book provide a glimpse into the hearts and minds of some of the most successful restaurateurs, consultants, and design professionals in America. Their knowledge, experience, and insights offer an approach to dealing with the hundreds of components that collectively must be in sync for a restaurant to succeed.

For the most part, the restaurants selected for the case studies have endured and prospered for several years. A few others have been created recently and are noteworthy because they have been successful since the day they opened. Several types of concepts are explored, including fine and casual dining establishments, theme and family restaurants, and low-budget projects.

There is one common thread that binds all of the people who were interviewed for this book: Their success stories are a result of their passion, vision, hard work, and, above all, their commitment to providing the highest quality food and service in environments that celebrate the joy of eating.

HISTORICAL PERSPECTIVE

EUROPE

Surprisingly, the restaurant is a recent phenomenon. Until the late eighteenth century in France, the only places for ordinary people to eat out were in inns, taverns, and cabarets. In about 1765, a Parisian "bouillon seller" named Boulanger wrote on his sign: "Boulanger sells restoratives fit for the gods." Thus, the first *restaurateur.*

The word *restaurant* first appeared in the sixteenth century and meant "a food that restores." It was used more specifically for a rich, highly spiced soup, which restored lost strength. The eighteenth century gastronome, Brillat-Savarin, referred to chocolate, red meat, and consommé as *restaurants,* and his meaning survived until the late nineteenth century, after which the word began to develop the meaning of

"an establishment specializing in the sale of restorative foods."

The French Revolution abolished the guilds and their privileges, making it easier to open a restaurant, and the first to take advantage of this situation were the cooks and servants who had lost their jobs in the great houses after their aristocratic owners lost their heads. These enthusiastic chef/restaurateurs, eager to please new arrivals to Paris, such as provincials who had no families and journalists and businessmen who were far from hearth and home, added roasts, stews, soups, patés, entrées, and side dishes to their menus. Freed from repressive guild rules, they were able to infuse their own personal stamp on the food they served. In former days,

LE RESTAURANT BLEU. PHOTOGRAPH © GUY BOUCHET PARIS, FRANCE.

innkeepers had been forced to purchase food from caterers, pork butchers, patissiérs, or the rotisseur. Grand Cuisine, hitherto reserved only for the rich, was now within the reach of the public, creating an atmosphere in which restaurants became an established institution.[1]

The first Parisian restaurant that was worthy of the name was the one founded by Beauvilliers, in 1782, in the Rue de Richelieu, called the Grande Taverne de Lourdes, who offered the novelty of listing the dishes available on a menu, and serving them at small, individual tables during fixed hours. Beauvilliers was as active in his dining room as he was in his kitchen. He could remember twenty years later the names and faces of all his customers, and he would hurry over to each table, recommending a favorite dish, suggesting a wine, giving everyone the impression that the restaurant had been opened that day just for them.[2] Beauvilliers established an ideal that has validity today: A restaurateur has a true appreciation of pleasure and has a passion for giving pleasure through food and service to his patrons.

These first restaurants were clean, even luxurious in their decor, distinguishing them from the rather spartan, often filthy inns, taverns, and public houses that preceded them. Restaurants were comfortable and quiet places where people ate alone, each having their own private dining rooms.

In the last years of the eighteenth century, the private *dining salon* had several distinct areas. The back of the room was occupied by travelers in a hurry and by large families who wished to be served quickly, pay, and leave. The middle of the room was occupied by regular customers, or the *table d'hôte*, while the remainder of the room was reserved for customers who wished to have a leisurely, elegant meal.

Cafés, which predated the first restaurants, were places that sold coffee. The first café in the world opened in Constantinople, in 1550. In 1672, a little stall selling cups of coffee was opened at the Saint-Germain fair in Paris. As soon as the French discovered the social aspects of drinking coffee in a public place combined with the delights of conversation, cafés began to open, selling brandy and sweetened wines and liquors, as well as coffee.[3]

Cafés soon became a new way of life, where people read the news, played chess or cards, exchanged ideas, talked politics, and smoked. In the seventeenth and eighteenth centuries, the

GRAND CAFÉ. LE GRAND VÉFOUR. PHOTOGRAPH © DANIEL AUBRY/FRENCH GOVERNMENT TOURIST OFFICE.

SIDEWALK CAFÉ. CAFÉ DE FLORE. PHOTOGRAPH © FRENCH GOVERNMENT TOURIST OFFICE.

cafés became highly fashionable meeting places of literary critics and politicians.[4]

The Grand Boulevard became the place where ice cream sellers and restaurateurs drew crowds with such establishments as the Café Riche and the Café de Paris. Cafés, however, survived and prospered all over Paris, especially on the left bank and Montmartre, where poets, intellectuals, artists, celebrities, dandies, and singers could be found. Cafés were richly decorated and were designed by renowned architects and designers, containing magnificently detailed walls and ceilings along with hand-carved woodwork, fine tapestries, mirrors, and the finest velvets. Renoir and Toulouse-Lautrec often illustrated the luxurious menus and tables set with elegant china, crystal, and silver.[5]

Sidewalk cafés flourished and were places to see and be seen and have survived until today. Café de Flore and Deux Magots still exist as places to sit, pause, converse, and drink coffee or an aperitif while watching the world go by.

Since the French were responsible for coining the term *restaurant*, and possibly the first to create a place that can be defined as a restaurant by today's standards, many histories, including this one, concentrate on the development of eating establishments in France. However, cafés and restaurants flourished all over Europe. In Berlin, cafés assumed the singing tradition of cabarets. In Vienna, the café became firmly established in 1683, when the invading Turks

VIENNESE CAFÉ. PHOTOGRAPH © RONALD JAQUES.

abandoned five hundred sacks of coffee. The Viennese had always considered the café to be a natural extension of their homes and offices.

They spent many hours there—in the morning to read the news, in the afternoon to discuss business, and in the evening to talk, receive guests, and play billiards. It was in Vienna that the café-concert was born. The great Viennese cafés still exist, perpetuating the traditions with their artwork, soft lights, and wooden paneling.

Italian cafés existed before the first ones opened in France, especially in Venice, where the coffee shop was part of daily life. The most famous ones date from the eighteenth century, including Café Greco, which opened in Rome in 1760, and the Florian, which opened in Venice in 1720, where public concerts were held under the arcade of Saint Mark's Square.[6] These two well-known establishments are still open today, appearing much the same as they did in the eighteenth century.

At the Café Greco or the Florian, one can still select from a variety of finger sandwiches or desserts while standing at the bar, drinking a cup of espresso. The coffee bar and dining area are alive with tourists, shoppers, and locals, each there to share the pleasure of conversation while surrounded by an interior of marble tabletops, stone floors, wood detailing, and ornate mirrors.

Bistros evolved mostly out of necessity rather than design to serve workers near or in Les Halles, in the last decades of the nineteenth

ITALIAN CAFÉ. CAFÉ GRECO. PHOTOGRAPH © CAFÉ GRECO.

century. With their honest, homemade cooking and fair prices, they became havens for struggling artists and journalists throughout Paris, whose garrets didn't have kitchens. Customers both dined and virtually lived in their favorite bistros, where grandmotherly women, or *meres*, nurtured their souls with *cuisine des meres*. The allure of these bistros is and always has been their deeply satisfying, down-to-earth cooking, served in a warm, homey, softly lighted environment.

Brasseries, originally breweries, are places that serve beer, cider, and other drinks along with garnished sauerkraut, plates of oysters, and other hot and cold dishes at any time of the day, and often fairly late at night. In Bavaria, brasseries weren't very different from inns, where people ate on wooden benches and wooden tables. In Paris, however, in the latter part of the nineteenth century, they became elegant places and were as ornately decorated as the great cafés. They were frequented by writers, artists, journalists, and politicians who played chess, argued, wrote, ate, and drank, all at the same table.[7]

The restaurants, cafés, bistros, and brasseries in Paris and other cities throughout Europe were and still remain warm, inviting, timeless places that celebrate the joy of eating, drinking, and socializing. Whether it is a homey bistro or an elegant café or restaurant, the commitment to excellence in food and service is the rule rather than the exception. This commitment to quality is reflected in the attention to detail and the use of natural materials, such as wood, marble, zinc, soft lighting, and mirrors. Artwork, fresh flowers, and abundant displays of food dot the rooms, and no one detail overpowers the senses. The focus is on people, food, and the pleasures of the table.

Restaurants in Paris and the great regional establishments throughout France continue to provide customers with luxurious surroundings, great wines, rare delicacies, and all the refinements of the culinary arts. The purpose of studying these spaces is to understand the spirit in which they were created. Each classic type—the café, the bistro, the brasserie—evolved in answer to the specific needs of its customers and owes its success to its unique symbiosis with its patrons. The "sense of place" that was created in the eighteenth and nineteenth centuries through a blend of location, scale, color, materials, arrangement of rooms and furniture, and a personal style of service can well be applied to designing twentieth century restaurants.

BISTRO. LE COMPTOIR. PHOTOGRAPH © PATRICK TRILLES DE WARREN.

BISTRO DINING ROOM. LE COMPTOIR. PHOTOGRAPH © PATRICK TRILLES DE WARREN.

In America, the restaurant became prominent during the industrial revolution of the last three decades of the nineteenth century. Urban populations were expanding, industry was booming, and Americans were away from home at mealtime. Unlike France after the French Revolution, when trained chefs left the castle to open their own establishments, the American restaurant grew from a need to serve millions of workers in a systematic approach.

There were, of course, country inns and fine dining establishments in the major American cities before the industrial revolution. These "white-tablecloth" restaurants were created by recently arrived immigrants from Europe and were mirror images of European culture; however, restaurant organizations in the last decades of the nineteenth century started and prospered as a result of the need to feed quality food in clean surroundings to an ever-growing population of

TEN MINUTES FOR REFRESHMENTS.

RAILROAD RESTAURANT COUNTER. "TEN MINUTES FOR REFRESHMENTS. THE GREAT ATLANTIC AND PACIFIC TEA COMPANY." POSTER, CA. 1886, FROM THE BELLA C. LANDAUER COLLECTION. COURTESY OF THE NEW-YORK HISTORICAL SOCIETY, NEW YORK CITY.

"HARVEY GIRLS," SYRACUSE, KANSAS, 1920. PHOTOGRAPH © THE KANSAS STATE HISTORICAL SOCIETY, TOPEKA, KANSAS.

HARVEY HOUSE, HUTCHINSON, KANSAS, 1926. PHOTOGRAPH © THE KANSAS STATE HISTORICAL SOCIETY, TOPEKA, KANSAS.

LUNCH WAGON. BROOKS CAFÉ, NATICK, MASSACHUSETTS, 1890s. PHOTOGRAPH © DINER ARCHIVES OF RICHARD J. S. GUTMAN.

DINER. EBERLING'S QUICK LUNCH, CLIFTON, NEW JERSEY, 1911. PHOTOGRAPH © DINER ARCHIVES OF RICHARD J. S. GUTMAN.

office and industrial workers on the go. Restaurants catering to these masses of people frequently sprang up at the convenient location of railroad stations.

Frederick Henry Harvey, an English immigrant, founded the first large restaurant organization in America. He developed clean, dependable, quick-service restaurants along routes traveled by the Atchison, Topeka & Santa Fe Railroad. The first Harvey House was opened in the spring of 1876 at the depot in Topeka, Kansas, and the American chain restaurant was born! The food was good, and strict standards of excellence were established and monitored, consistency being the hallmark of the Harvey House chain.

By 1901, the Harvey House operation had grown to forty-five units in twelve states, and the expansion continued into the 1930s. At first, the structures were economical and undistinguished, but as the chain grew, the architectural styles of the buildings became more decorative and sophisticated. The overall effect became more soothing, safe, and predictable, allowing the long-distance traveler to feel at home.

In the cities, the need for quick, affordable meals within walking distance from work or home was growing. Since most restaurants in these cities were too expensive for the typical worker, the lunch wagon (often a horse-drawn cart), which originated in New England in the 1870s, offered an alternative, serving sandwiches, pies, and beverages. In the 1880s, these wagons became big enough that customers could step inside, and sometimes they provided stools, counters, and tiny kitchens. The traveling lunch wagons eventually settled permanently on small urban lots and evolved into factory-made *diners*.

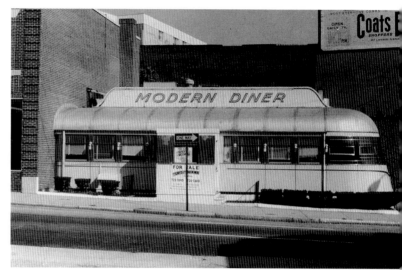

DINER. MODERN DINER, PAWTUCKET, RHODE ISLAND, 1930s. PHOTOGRAPH © DINER ARCHIVES OF RICHARD J. S. GUTMAN.

DINER INTERIORS, 1930s. PHOTOGRAPH © DINER ARCHIVES OF RICHARD J. S. GUTMAN.

SODA FOUNTAIN. MILLER & SHOEMAKER, JUNCTION CITY, KANSAS. JOSEPH J. PENNELL COLLECTION, KANSAS COLLECTION, UNIVERSITY OF KANSAS LIBRARIES.

Soda fountains, another American phenomenon, began springing up after the Civil War, spurred by the invention of the ice cream soda. This incredibly popular American drink inspired about 75,000 soda fountains by the early 1900s. *Coffee shops* and luncheonettes evolved from the soda fountain, offering an expanded menu of sandwiches and pies.

Lunchrooms—unassuming, utilitarian, small spaces—served low-priced food to working people. Many lunchrooms in the late nineteenth and early twentieth centuries were chain operations, where customers carried trays of food to chairs that had their backs against a wall and faced a noisy, bustling aisle packed with people, and no one wanted to stay any longer than necessary. These lunchrooms maximized customer turnover in a minimal amount of space.

Americans at the turn of the century were obsessed with efficiency and productivity and how they affected profitability. The *cafeteria* developed as a result of this obsession, providing a practical application for the restaurant industry's fascination with the assembly line. Cafeterias depended on large spaces and high volume, requiring a larger investment than other types of restaurants. This large space requirement narrowed the market for the cafeteria, and coffee shops developed because they could fit into small, narrow spaces where the rent was much lower.

COFFEE SHOP. EL NAVAJO, NEW MEXICO. PHOTOGRAPH © THE KANSAS STATE HISTORICAL SOCIETY, TOPEKA, KANSAS.

Counter seating at these coffee shops was conducive to quick turnover and higher profits.

The issue of profitability lead to the *standup* restaurant, where customers had no stools or chairs and leaned against a counter to eat their food. Other restaurants placed food on conveyor belts or revolving counters, and customers picked salads, fruits, vegetables, and desserts from this movable serving area while seated at a circular counter. Waiters and waitresses were not necessary, reducing operating expenses. Counter seating required less space than chairs and tables, and these space-efficient, narrow, self-service restaurants were ideal for center-city locations where there were many office workers but square foot rents were high. Thus, the self-service restaurant emerged as the central theme for the American restaurant in the twentieth century, and it was spawned out of the necessity to create restaurants that were efficient and profitable.

LUNCHEONETTE. HARVEY'S CAFÉ, LA JUNTA, NEW MEXICO. PHOTOGRAPH © THE KANSAS STATE HISTORICAL SOCIETY, TOPEKA, KANSAS.

CAFETERIA. CHILDS CAFÉ, 1899. PHOTOGRAPH © MUSEUM OF THE CITY OF NEW YORK, THE BYRON COLLECTION.

AUTOMAT. HORN & HARDART, NEW YORK, 1912. COURTESY OF HORN & HARDARDT.

AUTOMAT INTERIOR. HORN & HARDART, NEW YORK, 1912. COURTESY OF HORN & HARDARDT.

The ultimate efficient, money-making, self-service restaurant was the "Automat," a grand, glamorous, big-city idea that was started in Philadelphia at the turn of the century by Joseph Horn and Frank Hardart. These sparkling places were a combination of marble, weathered oak wainscoting, and brass trim in which precooked food was displayed in glass windows, allowing the customer to see what he or she was getting before buying it. Unlike the cafeteria, where customers waited in long lines and were served by employees behind the counter, Automats provided instant service through coin-operated machines.

In 1912, the first New York Horn & Hardart Automat opened on Broadway in Times Square; an ornate space with mosaic-tiled floors and marble tabletops. It was the pinnacle of self-service efficiency where the ordinary act of eating a quick, simple meal was glorified. These automats proliferated in New York and Philadelphia.

Disease and the need to control germs in restaurants lead to the widespread use of white,

shiny materials, such as white glass, white tile, and "Monel Metal," because restaurateurs wanted to show off how clean and sanitized their establishments were. Soda-fountain counters were made of white marble, with white porcelain enamel stools and table bases that resisted dirt, while durable "sani-onyx" tabletops looked like white glass. This obsession with cleanliness lead to the proliferation of smooth, hard flooring materials such as terrazzo, linoleum, or troweled-on substances. Exposed wood floors were out.

Competition in the 1920s and 1930s created a demand for design features that would entice customers into restaurants. Childs Restaurants stationed employees in front of the windows making pancakes in public view, and they put white tiles on the facades to make them appear more inviting. Larger expanses of plate glass allowed customers to see the sleek, modernized interiors, and restaurant fronts were angled inward to entice customers into the spaces.

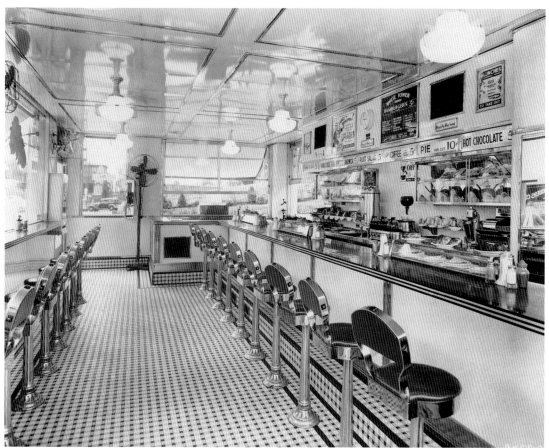

WHITE, SHINY MATERIALS. WHITE TOWER. COURTESY OF TOMBROCK CORPORATION.

FOOD PREPARATION IN PUBLIC VIEW. "GROUP OF PEOPLE LOOKING IN WINDOW OF UNIDENTIFIED RESTAURANT, N.Y.C." PHOTOGRAPH BY IRVING BROWNING, CA. 1930. COURTESY OF THE NEW-YORK HISTORICAL SOCIETY, NEW YORK CITY.

Architects and designers were retained to create storefronts and interiors that captured public attention. Rich art deco exteriors and interiors graced some restaurants in the 1930s and 1940s. Horn & Hardart used this style to reinforce the company's image and distinction, while the Childs organization moved away from its emphasis on gleaming white sanitization toward more romantic theme establishments.

In Los Angeles in the 1930s, restaurants as "fantasy" were born. Clifford E. Clinton opened Clifton's Cafeteria in 1931, and through the 1930s and 1940s, he built fantasy restaurants such as the Pacific Seas in Los Angeles. This restaurant was a tropical paradise complete with thatched huts, tropical plants, neon tubing shaped into huge flowers, and a waterfall.

The prevalent theme in the 1920s and 1930s, however, was modernism, with an increasing emphasis on the restaurant's facade, and the recognizable building became the most important element of the chain restaurant industry. The White Tower chain used its standardized facade to achieve instant recognition and to project an impression of cleanliness and speedy service. This

was one of the first examples of a restaurant organization that had a consistent architectural image for all of its locations. White Tower's recognizable image was maintained over the chain's lifespan, despite numerous modifications in materials and site adaptations.

The increasing reliance on the automobile and the vacationer's yearning for homey types of restaurants lead to the birth of the Howard Johnson chain. These symmetrical, classically shaped buildings were a model of solidarity, and the orange roofs made them easily recognizable from the highways.

Through the 1940s, 1950s, and 1960s, roadside restaurants proliferated, in some cases trying to out-do each other with such weird shapes as Indian heads, giant hot dogs, or beer barrels. Drive-ins with tall vertical pylon signs flashing information such as "Eat Here" became especially popular in the suburbs, where the automobile was an important part of daily life. Drive-ins were gathering places that allowed Americans to socialize and congregate while maintaining their privacy.

The chain drive-in restaurant prospered in the 1950s, 1960s, 1970s, and up to the present time. Ray Kroc, the second franchise agent for the growing McDonalds's chain, began an empire of standardized, safe, predictable, well-managed restaurants that still is the predominant force in the restaurant industry in America. Burger King, Wendy's, Kentucky Fried Chicken, Arby's, Hardee's, Pizza Hut, and several other large chains dominate the roadsides of America.[8]

From the industrial revolution until the late 1970s, the independently owned restaurant that served fine food was usually French in style. These quiet restaurants catered mostly to the wealthy in urban areas. Other ethnic food was served in small establishments operated by the chef/owner or families.

In the middle 1970s, the restaurant industry changed dramatically, owing in large part to major demographic shifts, disposable income, and attitudes toward food. A generation of single baby boomers had come of age and clamored for restaurant spaces that were not only spaces to dine, but to meet, see, and be seen. These baby boomers were college-educated professionals who decided to stay single, and they flooded the cities, living in small, affordable apartments. Going home alone to eat was out of the question. Restaurateurs eager to please these hordes of hungry *yuppies* began to create spaces that were extensions of their tiny apartments. These large spaces became every yuppie's living room, where they could spread out, relax, and eat and drink. Restaurateurs, in order to attract their market share, turned to young architects and designers to create spaces where young people expected to be dazzled as much by the design as they were by the food.

During this time, there was a "food revolution" as well. Nouvelle cuisine, which began in France in the late 1960s, spread to the United States in the early 1970s. Chefs, no longer bound to traditional heavy masking sauces and complicated garnitures, begin experimenting with food that was much simpler and purer in taste. This new attitude, coupled with the growing concern for proper nutrition and fitness, lead chefs to use fresh, undercooked vegetables, fish, and poultry. Natural juices, flavors, color, and the texture of these ingredients exploded on the plate in beautiful, artful presentations.

FANTASY RESTAURANT. CLIFTON'S PACIFIC SEA'S, 1930s. COURTESY OF CLINTON'S RESTAURANTS INCORPORATED.

FANTASY RESTAURANT INTERIOR. CLIFTON'S PACIFIC SEA'S, 1930s. COURTESY OF CLINTON'S RESTAURANTS INCORPORATED.

The chef, once an unknown character that hid inside the kitchen, was now a celebrity who was adored by a public eager to try new taste sensations. Wolfgang Puck, Alice Waters, Larry Forgione, and others changed America's attitudes about food forever. Americans began to realize that dining out could be a "total experience," where all the senses were stimulated. The quiet, cozy dinner that you had had once a year to celebrate a birthday was replaced by an event to be experienced several times a week.

The restaurant explosion that occurred in France after the French Revolution was occurring in the United States in the 1970s. Many American

chefs who trained in Europe came back to Los Angeles, New York, Chicago, and other cities across America to create "new regional American cuisine" at the same time that a demographic bulge had produced a hungry, educated generation eager for new gustatory sensations.

The image of the restaurant had to match the spirit and excitement of this new cuisine. In addition to the food revolution, there was an ongoing socio-cultural revolution started in the 1960s that changed our attitudes about everything, including sex, marriage, art, fashion, music, and design. Our society, bombarded with effective, seductive advertising on television and in magazines, had become more acutely aware of style and image. The restaurant, once a place to have a cozy dinner, became a place where a new generation of architects, designers, sculptors, artists, and craftspeople could express their ideas about our cultural changes. The restaurants became instant cultural museums where customers could experience exciting experiments in scale, lighting, color, form, and texture. Eating out became a night of entertainment in which one expected to experience the creative expression of the celebrity chef, as well as the celebrity designer.

Much has changed since the middle 1970s. The boom years of the 1980s have come to an abrupt halt in the recession of the 1990s. The yuppie is approaching middle age and has a family with less disposable income. Major demographic shifts are occurring, and for the first time, the median age in the United States is over thirty-five.

Formerly large, easily definable market segments are fracturing into what *American Demographics* magazine now refers to as "particle markets." It has become harder and harder to define the potential customer and create restaurant concepts that satisfy a particular "particle market." There are empty-nesters, step-families, the baby boomlet, immigrants, the disabled, savers, the affluent, the elderly, and many others, according to the National Restaurant Association.

Restaurateurs have to come up with food concepts and environments that have a high perceived-cost/value relationship to satisfy customers with less disposable income. Style and image are even more important in conveying the appropriate perception of value to the customer.

The challenges have become ever greater for the restaurateur and designer to create environments that are not confusing and inappropriate for each

MCDONALD'S, 1950S. MCDONALDS CORPORATION. COURTESY OF TOMBROCK CORPORATION.

FAMILY RUN RESTAURANT. MIKE FREY'S, JUNCTION CITY, KANSAS, 1908. JOSEPH J. PENNELL COLLECTION, KANSAS COLLECTION, UNIVERSITY OF KANSAS LIBRARIES.

of these *particle markets*. Customers in almost every market niche are seeking restaurants where value and service are provided. The relationship between food, price, service, and design are inexorably linked. Customers, value-conscious or not, are still influenced by style and image, and if the design creates a perception that there is quality and value that is compatible with the food and service, those customers will come back.

NOTES

1. *Larousse Gastronomique*, ed. Jennifer Harvey Lang (New York: Hamlyn Publishing Group, 1988), 883.
2. Ibid., 81.
3. Ibid., 170.
4. Ibid., 170.
5. Ibid., 170.
6. Ibid., 171.
7. Ibid., 135-36.
8. The chronological progression of the American chain restaurant was based on the book by Philip Langdon, *Orange Roofs, Golden Arches: The Architecture of American Chain Restaurants* (New York: Alfred A. Knopf, 1986).

CONCEPT DEVELOPMENT

Since it has become harder and harder to define the potential customer and create restaurant concepts that satisfy a particular *particle market*, how does a freshman or seasoned restaurateur decide: What type of restaurant should I open? Where should it be located? Who is my potential customer and competition? What food should I serve, and at what price? What should it look like? Why do some restaurants succeed while others close their doors soon after they open?

Unfortunately, there are no easy answers to these questions. One restaurant can succeed on a minimal investment with "sawdust" on the floor, without the benefit of professional guidance, while another $3 million, professionally planned venture with a celebrity chef fails within six months. Or, the "sawdust" concept is copied by another restaurateur eager to cash in on this hot concept and fails miserably.

Most restaurateurs and consultants would agree that the success of any restaurant depends on hundreds of factors. Some of them can be defined and analyzed, enabling thoughtful decisions to be made, while others are simply intangible. The factors that contribute to success are complex and are in a constant state of flux. The ability to create a restaurant concept that satisfies customer demand within a given time frame is difficult enough without having to contend with constant changes in demographic mix, food trends, competition, and economic conditions.

There are those who believe in in-depth market analysis and those who feel that if you don't know your concept, location, potential customer, competition, and economic conditions, you shouldn't be in the restaurant business.

Alan Stillman states, "Successful restaurants fit a particular market niche. When we built Smith & Wollensky, we felt a great new steak house concept had not been developed in the past thirty years. We looked at our competition, including The Assembly, The Palm, and Christ Cella, and decided that there was sufficient market demand for a great steak house in New York. Our concept was to provide the finest quality steak house in order to attract our share of the market. We selected Forty-ninth Street and Third Avenue for Smith & Wollensky because it was formerly Manny Wolfe's and was right smack in the middle of steak house row. We didn't need an extensive demographic analysis to determine if Forty-ninth Street and Third Avenue in midtown Manhattan was a great location for this concept. Just go out there and look at the street traffic, offices, and residential buildings. We knew this area extremely well because we had extensive experience in this area of Manhattan."

Richard Melman of Lettuce Entertain You Enterprises, Inc., a successful Chicago-based restaurant organization, states, "I have an idea file of several restaurant stories that I have developed over the years. The menu, design, general location, and potential customer are generally known before we select a specific site. You don't have to be a genius to be successful in this business. Creating and sustaining a restaurant is relatively simple. You have to understand what you want to accomplish, recognize the opportunity, and stay focused. You need to find the right location, make the best financial deal, and create a simple, "real" environment that captures the spirit of the times and fits the market niche. You have to hire, train, and develop your staff and be capable of enduring the pain of difficult times.

"Today's sophisticated diner is not satisfied with bread alone! It used to be that to run a successful restaurant, all you needed was good food. Then you needed not just good food, but good service too. Now you need to deliver great food, great service, ambience, and possess a real sense of what people want."

Joe Baum says, "Developing a successful restaurant depends on the ability to recognize an opportunity, and that ability is based on each person's persona: the sum of his or her experience, intellect, personality, and feelings about hospitality."

Artie Cutler, partner at Dock's, a highly successful seafood grill and oyster bar in Manhattan, states, "I had my eye on the location at Fortieth Street and Third Avenue for over ten years. Even though many others felt it wasn't a great site, I saw an opportunity to create a grand, affordable seafood grill for businesspeople and local residents. There hadn't been a grand seafood house in Manhattan for quite some time, and we felt a high-volume, moderately priced concept could work in this large, open space." Cutler focused on a concept, saw an opportunity, and capitalized on it, and he was able to blend all the essential elements of location, potential customer, menu, average check, and style. He also combined projected revenues, food and labor costs, operating expenses, rent, and construction costs to determine if the project was feasible.

There are restaurateurs, however, whose concepts are yet undefined and need professional guidance in order to develop successful projects, and there are several firms throughout the country that perform these services.

MARKET FEASIBILITY STUDY

Bill Eaton, vice president of Cini-Little, a full-service, foodservice consulting firm, asks potential restaurateurs, "Why do you want to open a restaurant?" Many freshman restaurateurs answer, "I need a change," or "I like people," or "I'd like a place where I can have my own table and entertain my friends." Usually, Eaton tries to talk people out of owning a restaurant if they answer in these ways.

Eaton asserts that if he can't talk the potential restaurateur out of owning a restaurant, he insists that a market feasibility study and a pro forma analysis be provided. If a client has a general concept in mind, the following items are evaluated:

1. Introduction: background and objectives; methodology.
2. Executive summary.
3. Market analysis: area description; population; average income; employment; transportation; commercial and residential development; demand generators.
4. Site analysis: positive and negative features of the proposed site.
5. Supply analysis: description of primary and secondary competitors; price comparison analysis.
6. Demand projections: by market segment; by season (if appropriate).

7. Average check calculation.
8. Estimated annual operating results: inflation; revenues; cost of goods sold; payroll (salaries, wages, and benefits); administrative and general; advertising and promotion; franchise fee (if applicable); repair and maintenance; utilities; rent.

Several concepts and general locations can be evaluated. Each concept is studied with respect to the potential customer, competition, overall menu, and price point. "We're trying to determine what each concept can do in terms of gross sales," says Eaton. A diner's success depends on high volume, and needs to be in a location that is very visible and easily accessible by car. It also needs to be in a densely populated area, hopefully next to a large shopping center.

If the site that has been chosen doesn't meet these criteria, a thematic destination concept with a higher average check, requiring lower volume, might be considered. This upscale concept, however, may require very skilled labor in an area where talent is scarce.

Once a specific concept and the general location have been selected, a pro forma analysis will be prepared, including the elements listed on the following page.

PRO FORMA STATEMENTS OF OPERATING INCOME
FOR THE FIRST THREE YEARS OF OPERATION

	May, 1992 Year 1 $	%	1993 Year 2 $	%	1994 Year 3 $	%
REVENUES						
Food & Beverage	$873,600	100.0%	$908,544	100.0%	$944,886	100.0%
COST OF GOODS SOLD	$262,080	30.0%	$272,563	30.0%	$283,466	30.0%
GROSS OPERATING PROFIT	$611,520	70.0%	$635,981	70.0%	$661,420	70.0%
PAYROLL						
Salaries	$35,000	4.0%	$37,450	4.1%	$40,072	4.2%
Wages	157,248	18.0%	163,538	18.0%	170,079	18.0%
Payroll Taxes	13,457	7.0%	14,069	7.0%	14,711	7.0%
Employee Benefits (1)	30,760	16.0%	32,158	16.0%	33,624	16.0%
Total Payroll	$236,465	27.1%	$247,215	27.2%	$258,486	27.4%
OPERATING EXPENSES						
Administrative & General (3)	$43,680	5.0%	$40,884	4.5%	$40,630	4.3%
Advertising & Promotion (2)	34,944	4.0%	27,256	3.0%	28,347	3.0%
Utilities	20,000	2.3%	20,800	2.3%	21,632	2.3%
Royalty Fee	43,680	5.0%	45,427	5.0%	47,244	5.0%
Repairs & Maintenance (4)	26,208	3.0%	31,799	3.5%	37,795	4.0%
Total Operating Expenses	$168,512	19.3%	$166,167	18.3%	$175,649	18.6%
NET OPERATING INCOME	$206,543	23.6%	$222,598	24.5%	$227,286	24.1%
RENT	$56,000	6.4%	$58,240	6.4%	$60,570	6.4%
NET INCOME (5)	$150,543	17.2%	$164,358	18.1%	$166,716	17.6%

(1) Benefits are shown as a percentage of Salaries and Wages.
(2) Reflects an upward adjustment in Year 1 to account for typical start-up costs and inventory.
(3) Reflects an upward adjustment in Year 1 because of the amount of advertising necessary to initially penetrate the market.

(4) Cost reductions of 10% and 5% respectively in Years 1 and 2 have been implemented to account for equipment warranties in effect.
(5) Income before other fixed charges such as insurance, real estate taxes, and depreciation.
SOURCE: Cini-Little International, Inc.; June 1991

PRO FORMA STATEMENT. © CINI-LITTLE INTERNATIONAL, INC.

INTERVIEWS WITH RESTAURANT CONSULTANTS

The failure rate of restaurants is very high owing to a combination of factors, including undercapitalization, misunderstanding the potential customer, location, and competition. Poor food and service, poor controls on food costs, labor costs, and staff, and poor space planning and design also contribute to this high failure rate.

Restaurant consultants can assist in developing the concept and menu, provide market and pro forma analyses, and manage the architect/designer and kitchen planner. They also can assist in hiring key personnel and training staff.

I asked two prominent restaurant consultants, Michael Whiteman and Barbara Kafka, why many restaurants don't succeed, and the following interviews present their answers.

MICHAEL WHITEMAN

Michael Whiteman is partner with Joe Baum, Dennis Sweeney, and Rozanne Gold in the Joseph Baum & Michael Whiteman Company, an international foodservices consulting firm. He has worked on projects in Japan, Australia, Taiwan, Belgium, and Spain, as well as helping to open such landmarks as Windows on the World and the Rainbow Room, of which he is part owner.

Whiteman was founding editor of *Nation's Restaurant News*, is a member of the corporation of the Culinary Institute of America, and sits on boards of directors of the Project for Public Spaces, the New York Chapter of the American Institute of Wine and Food, and the Pour la France! restaurant chain.

MICHAEL WHITEMAN, ROZANNE GOLD, AND DENNIS SWEENEY.
PHOTOGRAPH © THE JOSEPH BAUM & MICHAEL WHITEMAN
COMPANY.

Q: Why do so many restaurants fail in the first year of business?

A: Undercapitalization! No one ever believes that things cost as much as they do. And so, no one ever has enough money. Many restaurateurs are bad at budgeting because they're inexperienced. An owner sits with a designer or a contractor and says, "How much is this going to cost?," and the designer says, "Oh, the last restaurant I did cost $200 a square foot." The owner says, "Well, I can afford that." But everybody always leaves out lots of things. Nobody has a proper preopening budget. Nobody does a proper cash-flow budget. Most operators don't put together complete checklists of everything they need when they open. Suddenly, the restaurant is done, the contractor's done, the designer's done, lighting is installed, phones are hooked up, but there is still $100,000 worth of stuff that has to be bought and paid for that they all forgot about. Whether it relates to insurance, or employment agency fees, or a better wine list, or nobody budgeted for the computer, etc., etc.

Q: Why do you suppose that is? Is it endemic to the restaurant industry, or is it true in a lot of business plans?

A: I think it's true in lots of *small* businesses. The problem with restaurants is that they're capital-intensive. You can open a shoe store on a shoestring, if you'll pardon my pun. You need fixtures and a modest amount of inventory. But when you open up a restaurant, you've got exhaust requirements that a shoe store doesn't have. You have utility requirements, an enormous amount of machinery in the sense that you are building a factory in order to make the food, whereas a shoe store is not building a plant to make the shoes. There are dozens and dozens of items in a restaurant that most retail stores don't ever have to worry about.

Q: Why is the failure rate so high?

A: The high failure rate in restaurants is not necessarily confined to *new* restaurants. There is an enormous failure rate among very unsophisticated people, who get into restaurants on the coffee shop and pizzeria levels, who have no capital whatsoever. That's not to say that sophisticated restaurants that make the *New York Times* don't fail; they do. But for different reasons. They're equally undercapitalized. But also there is a lot of false glamor in this business, and people get into it because they think they would enjoy being a host. A lot of people think they are moving into a position of power, in the sense that they are controlling the restaurant and becoming very visible public figureheads. In fact, they are really entering the business of service rather than the business of power. So, they misread what they are getting into. I think that befalls rich people who made their money somewhere else, or very sophisticated people who expect to show off. They are not prepared to be paid servants in their own establishments.

Q: Let's assume for a moment that we have a particular restaurateur who has a restaurant or two, understands the business and the sacrifice, and understands the budget issues. What would you say are some of the factors that contribute to either success or failure for that person?

A: I think a major reason a restaurant fails is because the owner isn't there. Unless you have a theme restaurant, with an enormous marketing budget that allows you to create an artificial personality. If you're running an individual restaurant, and you're not there, you have no restaurant; you die.

Q: How does that compute with companies like Lettuce Entertain You? Richard Melman's an absentee owner; he's not always there.

A: Richard Melman has created, better than anybody in the last two decades, a concept for a "narrative" restaurant. Richard's restaurants tell a story. You may not be able to understand the entire story from beginning to end, but I will bet you that if you sit down with Richard and talk to him, he can tell you the story of the restaurants. Richard has made up a fictional story, in his office, with his designers, and they built the restaurants around the story. So, when you go into his restaurants, this strong, genuine design personality is a substitute for the owner's personality.

Q: It used to be that the popularity of a restaurant had to do with its food and service, not with the design. When did that change?
A: I can tell you when it really began. Well, that's not really so. I can tell you when it began in my lifetime. It began with Joe Baum, who transformed the restaurant industry.

There was a time when eating out at any kind of sophisticated level meant French. And if it were French, it meant red-flocked walls and crystal chandeliers. There was no deviation from that. If you were to have taken, in the 1950s and 1960s, all the French restaurant menus in the city of New York, torn the names off the tops and just looked at the menus, you would not have been able to tell whether you were in restaurant A, B, or C. What Joe Baum did was turn the whole thing inside out and say, "It doesn't have to be French to be good." That it is possible to have a good time in a restaurant, as well as a good meal. And so, a whole procession of restaurants was born: the Four Seasons, La Fonda del Sol, Charlie O's, Charlie Brown's; they're all narrative, dynamic restaurants that expressed very, very strong design personalities, almost on a thematic level. And that was the beginning of the substitution of design for personal ownership and personal management.

It turns out that personal ownership and good design are better than personal ownership and lousy design, or great design with no ownership. For example, Restaurant Associates was never able to make the Four Seasons a profitable restaurant when it was run as a corporate enterprise. The same people who now own and run the Four Seasons ran it at the time, but they didn't own it.

Q: What about Scoozi, for instance, in Chicago, which is a very successful enterprise? What story does that tell?
A: Well, when you walk into Scoozi, you don't walk into a restaurant. You walk into a giant environment that says, "I can almost be a small Italian village. And look over there; there's a guy making pizza. Holy smoke! Look at that platter being carried across the room." It's a major event. There are things happening everywhere; there is no room for the eye to sit down and rest. I feel like I've walked into a town, rather than a restaurant.

Q: Does every current successful restaurant have to have a sense of drama and have a strong design personality?
A: There are certain times when I use a restaurant just to have a meal and carry on a conversation, because that is the purpose for my being there. But that's rare. I think that's rare for most people. I think that, for the majority of people who are going out to eat, walking into a restaurant and just sitting down is a fairly depressing experience. There are myriads of things that should happen to you between the time you think of a restaurant and the time you get to the table.

There should be a sense of anticipation about going there. There should be a sense of anticipation about selecting something to wear. That doesn't necessarily mean dressing up, but it does mean selecting what is appropriate to the occasion. There should be something happening to you when you get to the door, when you get in the door; whether it's the greeting, whether it's what you look at, what you see, or how your date is made to feel. But the anticipation ought to grow, rather than stop. Arriving at the restaurant shouldn't be the end of it; arriving should be a continuation of the anticipation of the experience.

So, by the time you've sat down, a lot of things have happened to you, and your adrenalin should be up. It should be wonderful; welcoming. Those restaurants that just provide a mundane passage to your table will probably also provide a mundane experience throughout the entire meal. A restaurant is not purely background; a restaurant is foreground.

Q: What design elements should be considered when creating this foreground?
A: Well, first of all, most restaurants are too darkly lit. And restaurant lighting, to me, is probably the most difficult part of the design process. Fifteen or twenty years ago, the food tended to be reasonably dull. We lived in an era with food that was either brown or white, and there weren't a hell of a lot of variations. Today, food is extraordinarily dynamic. Food has become

a lot more colorful, because our chefs are roaming around looking for new ingredients. Food styling on the plate has become as important as the taste of the food. And food no longer sits flat on the plate as it once did; it stands up. Food has become architecture.

Consequently, there is a need for getting dramatic light onto the table that didn't exist before. The old cliché of a candle in a Chianti bottle for an Italian restaurant wouldn't work today, because the candle doesn't throw enough light to create the drama that food now requires. At the same time, we feel it's necessary to be very considerate about the way people look in a restaurant. Downlighting, which creates drama on the tabletop, creates shadows under the eyes. Worse than that, it accentuates wrinkles in the skin.

I think an enormous amount of time needs to be spent on having light come from a variety of sources. You need light from the side, and you need light from somewhere two feet above your head. You need light that bounces. You need light that creates highlights. You need a general glow. Fairly complicated and fairly expensive. Most people can't afford it; most people don't recognize it; most people don't deal with it.

Q: Can an independent restaurateur create his or her own restaurant without the benefit of design professionals?
A: There are thousands of restaurants around the country that have been, let's not call them "designed," but they have been put together by entrepreneurial people with a good sense of taste and style, who may not have had an architect or a designer at all. They knew what color they wanted for the four walls. And they had good instincts regarding what to hang on the walls. They didn't agonize over the quality of the china, or the design of the chair or other details, but they created a place that expressed, with warmth and affection, their own personality. And I would rather eat in one of those places, because the restaurant is still communicating all the things I said it had to, with the proviso that the owner is on the floor.

Q: Why do some highly designed theatrical restaurants lose their appeal?
A: I think "hip" restaurants usually have a very short life because they are overstated, and they "shout" too much. You know, sometimes you hear

a great joke and you love it. The second time you hear it, it sounds pretty good; the third time, you're tired of hearing the same joke. I think those restaurants that shout too loud don't endure.

There is something else to it as well: a fault of many restaurant designs is that they're too "done." They're too perfect. Too contrived. Too symmetrical. They are ultimately boring, because nothing happens. This fault is usually but not necessarily confined to hotel restaurants.

On the other hand, a guy with a sense of taste, without a designer, without an architect, manages to put together a place that has a lot of warmth, and the warmth derives from its "flaws." Its "flaws" make the personality of the restaurant.

I think also that there's too much design control in the restaurant field. It's tough to sit through lunch and have a good time in a restaurant that's too perfect. It's like walking into somebody's fancy living room and being afraid to sit down. Suddenly the propriety of the restaurant is imposing itself on your experience.

Q: How does one decide how a food concept will work in a particular area?
A: I have to tell you that after we go through all the scientific theories and analyses, studies of the demographics and all that stuff, and do all the pro formas, and all the budgets, and all the programs, it still ends up being partly a mystery. Because you can have two restaurants within shouting distance of each other, both of them fairly well-designed and both of them serving fairly good food, and one of them is successful and one is not.

You can stand there and talk to the owner of the failed one, and he's going to say, "I don't understand. My bouillabaisse is better than his, and my bread is better than his, and my steak is better than his, and he smells!" After you're all through with it, it still comes down to some indefinable mystery. That's what makes the restaurant business so wonderful.

How do you define a food concept? There is no scientific way. We've never done a market study to validate a food concept. You either feel what belongs in a location, or you shouldn't be working in the location.

Q: Can a successful concept be copied?
A: Somebody decides, having looked at a painting on the wall, "I can do that," and picks

up a paintbrush and discovers he can't do that. It's tough living out somebody else's vision. A restaurant works because it's a good expression of somebody's vision. A restaurant fails because it is a bad expression of somebody's vision. But to try to rip off somebody's vision without totally understanding it can be disastrous.

Q: How does a restaurateur learn about all the intangible elements that can contribute to success?
A: You used a nice word, because this whole business is full of intangibles. There's a spirit-like quality to creating and operating a restaurant. But I think there's a lot to be learned from people like us who worry about this all the time. The problem is getting in bed with a designer who literally will duplicate a space that he saw in Europe. Somebody has to understand what there is about the space that works, and take that part of it and use it, not to reproduce the space exactly.

Q: When do you feel a restaurant owner needs a food consultant?
A: Restaurant owners need food consultants when they don't have a strong enough sense of themselves, or a strong enough sense of their style, to be able to control the chef.

Q: But isn't that somewhat of a contradiction? If they don't have a sense of self, and they don't have a vision, how can they be successful?
A: One of the things you do as a designer and we do as a consultant, either successfully or not, depending on the job, is to get the client to believe in, articulate, and share the vision. If you can't get the client to share the vision, then nothing you do is going to work; not for very long. Because the client has to maintain the vision.

I'll give you an example of not being able to understand and share a vision. As consultants, we opened The Market Bar & Dining Rooms in the World Trade Center in 1975, with no street traffic whatsoever. In the shadow of Windows on the World, which we opened around the same time. Our busiest nights were Saturday nights, when there was nobody in lower Manhattan, and nobody in the office buildings. We ran it successfully because we had a vision of what a "market restaurant" meant. And we kept it going.

When we turned it over to another operator, they couldn't deal with the concept, although there were documents and pages and pages of words, and years of transition. It wasn't like we left on Wednesday and they took it over on Thursday. They are now, and have been for years, closed on Saturday nights, because they were never able to maintain and enrich the concept. We had a restaurant that served high-priced food in a purposely coarse, crude, rough manner, and the next operator didn't understand what that meant. He installed a corporate chef who served calf liver and blueberries. I swear. And suddenly this gutsy, big-proportioned, he-man restaurant is invaded by nouvelle cuisine dips, and there goes the business.

So, if you can't get the client to share that vision, if the client doesn't understand the vision, doesn't know how to use the machines you've made for him, then it's destined to fail. If the client is depending on the architect or the food consultant to fully create the restaurant, then there is a real problem. I mean, a theatrical producer doesn't depend on all the hired hands to create the show. The owner has to be somehow actively involved in this.

Q: What is the role of the restaurant consultant?
A: We manage the concept development and expression from beginning to end. We manage the kitchen designer. We manage the architect. We manage the lighting designers. We manage the food development process, whether we do it or someone else does. We manage the budget. We do the budgeting, so we know the breakdown to the last toothpick. We perform all the services for a client that we do for our own places, such as The Rainbow Room; including writing the menu, styling the food, scheduling labor, and helping get the place open.

BARBARA KAFKA

Barbara Kafka's most recent book is *The Opinionated Palate* (New York: William Morrow), a collection of essays, which follows *Microwave Gourmet Healthstyle Cookbook* and her bestselling *Microwave Gourmet*, both Book-of-the-Month Club main selections. She also wrote *Food for Friends* and *American Food and California Wine*. The latter four books have all been winners of the Tastemaker Award, which is now called the IACP-Seagram Award.

Most recently, as editor pro-bono for The James Beard Foundation, she compiled and edited *The James Beard Celebration Cookbook,* also a main selection of Book-of-the-Month Club. She edited *Four Seasons*—again a Tastemaker winner, *The Cook's Catalogue,* and a magazine, *Cooking,* later *The Pleasures of Cooking.*

Barbara Kafka writes a monthly opinion page for *Gourmet* and writes regularly for the *New York Times* and *Family Circle* on microwave cooking. She also writes for major food magazines, such as *Food & Wine, Eating Well, Australia Vogue Entertaining,* and, in England, *Taste;* and for newspapers. She currently writes on food issues for the *New York Times Magazine;* and previously, her work has appeared in the *San Jose Mercury News,* New York's *Daily News,* and other papers. For many years, she was a regular contributor to *Vogue.*

In the past she was active as a restaurant consultant, consultant to industry, and as a product designer. For many years, she taught with the late James Beard, and has given numerous cooking classes around the country on her own. She has won many awards and served on the boards of numerous culinary organizations, as well as educational boards. She has appeared frequently on television and has spoken on radio and at industry and professional events in the food field.

Q: What are a restaurant consultant's responsibilities?
A: One's job as a consultant of any kind in the restaurant business is to understand the capacity of the owner or the manager and explain to them what life in a restaurant is like. Many people go into this business totally unprepared for the hours, the work, the low rate of return, and many other things that they need to be aware of. Somebody may want to run a very upscale restaurant, like to go to very upscale restaurants, but not know all the elements that are involved in creating and running an upscale restaurant. And they are not going to gain that capacity quickly enough to do that, even if they have all the passion in the world. They are going to fail.

A good consultant should, ideally, not be making an abstraction. It is not like painting a picture or writing a book. And if you say this is my book or my picture, and it is perfect, or good, or marvelous by virtue of my having made it, and it is completed, it could be disastrous. And that is why I said that a consultant must have a very clear idea of what the capacities of the owner and operator are. What kind of people and how much help are they going to have to hire? Who are they going to have to hire? What is their level of sophistication? People have dreams they cannot accomplish. As a consultant, one has to be the stern voice of reality. It is not always a pleasant experience. Sometimes you have to say, "Sweetheart, I love you, but you can't afford this. You can't do this." Or, "This is a terrible location; do anything to get out of this lease."

Q: Should a restaurateur have a specific vision or overall concept?
A: I think that's good, but I think he should be prepared to modify it, to grow, to learn. If he isn't, I don't think he'll succeed. What kind of people are you going to be able to hire in the market? Will they be able to do what you envisage? Do you know enough to train them if they can't ?

Q: Let's talk a little bit about why you think restaurants fail.
A: *Undercapitalization.* Restaurateurs often forget to factor in the first year's working capital, preopening expenses, advertising, inventory, etc. Often, the income projections, computed by the amount of turns on tables and the average check amount, cannot offset the debt service incurred because of the high price of real estate and construction costs.

Misunderstanding the location. Either the location doesn't have enough foot traffic; there isn't enough natural business in the neighborhood; or the type or the restaurant concept is wrong for the location. You design a very expensive, very posh restaurant for a specific location. There are some very rich people in the neighborhood, but are there enough to support this type of restaurant?

BARBARA KAFKA.
PHOTOGRAPH
© SUSAN WOOD.

Consistency. Whatever your food is, it must achieve a certain level of consistency. That's what people come for. If they're getting good food one day and lousy food the next, the restaurant will not succeed.

Appropriateness. One of the questions I used to ask people when I was a consultant was, "What do you think people will wear when they come into the restaurant?" Because if I am going to go into a restaurant in my blue jeans, in the blue jeans part of town, the place has to be designed in such a way that I feel comfortable in that space in my blue jeans.

Am I going to get all dressed up? How many people do today? How many people come straight from work? Are we demanding too high a level of behavior from them? Is the design going to date? Is the food concept going to date? Is it too trendy, because the person says, "Oh, boy, this is a hot idea." Then they create a "hot idea" restaurant. It's hot. It's hot like crazy. For how long? You can't make back your money in two years. And if the hot crowd moves on, because they're very fickle, what are you building on? What are the people going to come back for?

Endurance. Running a restaurant is hard work. It's lethally hard. The sous chef doesn't show up. Somebody has to receive food at six in the morning. Somebody has to be there to close at one in the morning. They don't realize that come Christmas Eve, they're going to be at their restaurant; they're not going to be home with their families. Many restaurateurs are not professionals, and don't realize that running a restaurant is hard work.

Demographics. The mean age of the American population is, for the first time, over thirty-five. If a husband and wife's combined income is more than $50,000, and they have children, they will be paying for child care, so that they can both work. They have less disposable income, so they are going to seek downscale family types of restaurants, like McDonald's and Red Lobster. It would be inappropriate to locate an upscale restaurant in an area where demographics point toward family establishments.

Real estate. The high price of real estate in major cities has become a determining cause of failure. Because if my real estate is such that I am pricing not in terms of the food, or the wine, or even the labor costs, but I have to amortize a lease at a hundred dollars a square foot, or more, I'm in serious trouble.

Adapting. You constantly have to adapt, and nobody is secure. The number of people who managed to succeed for many years in this business, particularly in an upscale restaurant, is very few. As a matter of fact, I don't think it's necessarily been chef/owners that have succeeded; it's been people with good management skills, who read their customers well and are constantly adapting and moving.

Q: Why do we go to restaurants?
A: It gives us a way to explore the world. Historically, restaurants for New Yorkers, for Americans particularly, have been a way to taste many cultures, expose themselves to different styles. For some people, it's another kind of social event; a place to see and be seen, to make contacts—almost a club-like environment: The Russian Tea Room, in the old days, the Grill Room at the Four Seasons. Mortimer's certainly has that quality. And to the extent that that works, it's a very helpful formula, because it means that somebody on the floor knows the people and what works for them, and they build a kind of loyalty.

There are still places to hang out. There are still places to relax. There are places for the general cook, and that generally still means the woman, to go to avoid working all day. Increasingly, it seems to me, the woman in the demographic bulge with young children stays home more and is doing some cooking again. When she does go out, she's not going to be satisfied by the simple piece of grilled fish. She'll say, "I'm going to want something more to happen to it, because otherwise I can do it myself, thank you."

Q: What ingredients are necessary for a successful restaurant?
A: That is the great error in thinking about restaurants. There is no one statement that holds true for all restaurants. Let's take noise levels, for instance. Sometimes, people go to places that are quite noisy. The noise level at Tribeca Grill is significantly higher than at the Four Seasons, because a different kind of social event is taking place. One is a place to party. And I don't mean in the old sense, a celebration restaurant. I mean, you go in, you have a few beers or a drink, maybe see a star. There are large groups of people. It's not about intimacy. It's not really about conversation.

Then there are restaurants, and it may be more age-dependent—remember, the population is aging—in which people do want to be able to talk, as an alternative to being at home. So there are many different reasons and ways that people use restaurants, and the elements of the restaurant have to relate to that. Now, the waiter or waitress who says, "Hello, my name is . . ." or wants to talk to me, or in California is doing an audition, is almost universally terrible. It came about because we didn't want to be European. We don't have a professional label in this country, very few of us. We wanted "friendliness." But we're still tipping the people, we still want service. We still want it to be fairly clean and fairly neat, and not intrusive. So there are a few things that must be consistent, in the level of formality of the service: whether the things are carried out on a tray, whether they have domes over them, whether somebody carries four plates up his arm. All of these are style-dependent and have to be thought out.

The trouble is that people don't think things out. Like a wine list. A wine list is not good, silly, or generous. A wine list, or a glass in which to serve wine, has to be appropriate. I mean, I'm not going to put out Baccarat crystal, even if I could afford it, in a dive. Even if it has superb food; it doesn't work. Unless I think that by certain touches of incongruity I can make a statement, but that requires a great deal of sophistication.

The things that are most neglected in design are total cost and graphics. People don't realize this. They make these shells that are the restaurants, and they don't realize that people walk in and what they see, nine times out of ten, is what's on top of the table. The tabletop dominates the room, visually dominates the room. And then, of course, the people dominate the room. How do you get the people in? Do you know people?

Q: *Why is it so difficult to succeed?*
A: Many restaurants can have a beautiful space, a brilliant chef, an understanding of their customer, and still fail, because the owner didn't know how to run a business and a restaurant is always a business. The bottom line is the bottom line. When I used to be a consultant and people would say, "Well, I didn't like this, I didn't like that," the bottom line was, dear, it made money. Because other than that, you can play all the games in the world; it won't exist. As a toy, it's too expensive for anybody to afford.

You must prepare a realistic pro forma. Oh, you don't seem to have a figure here for laundry. You don't have a figure here for garbage. You don't have a figure for how much the manager or the assistant manager is going to cost you. You don't have a lawyer's fee in here. You don't have an accountant's fee. What do you think the utilities are going to cost you? There are perfectly average places that you wouldn't cross the street to look at that are making money like they're going out of style. So let us be very careful before we generalize.

Q: *How important is lighting in a restaurant?*
A: One of the gravest mistakes people make in many restaurants is underestimating the importance of lighting. They put lighting directly over people's heads, so you have terrible shadows under your eyes. People don't like to be in places where they look ugly.

I once did a restaurant years ago, this was before salmon became an in color, and there were pale salmon tablecloths, and it wasn't just the women, even the men looked younger. Everybody liked that. And it was a place for rich people, so they were older, and they really liked the beauty treatment they got. People like mirrors. There are all kinds of things people like that we have historically seen. No designer today uses good wall sconces; they put them too high. We look at historic French restaurants, you'll see that wall sconces made the lighting uneven, and gave some liveliness to the room, and the unevenness of the lighting was a frequent component.

Q: *So, there was sparkle and there was contrast?*
A: Oh, yes. Contrast. Unevenness, not flatness.

Q: *So we can learn something from history?*
A: Oh, I learn all the time. I think one of the gravest problems with many architects, and with many consultants, is that they have no sense of history. Their history is about ten years old, if that. Consequently, they don't know the richness, either of design material, or food material, or a tabletop, or of ideas, or of more styles that there are to draw on. The job of a consultant is not to give an answer; it's to give the right answer, and they can only give the right answer if they know enough different things to choose a right answer

from; a multitude of things. I am constantly reading. That's a stack of old cookbooks. These are all old cookbooks. There are art books, there are history books, there are sociology books.

Q: How can you assist an owner or architect with the design concept?
A: When we did Gotham Bar and Grill, you should have seen the first designs—good designers. I threw a fit at them. I said, "You want everybody to come into this space and say, 'Oh, another postmodern space.'" They said, "Oh, it's not postmodern." I said, "Oh, come on, kids!" I made them change 30 percent of the visual detail. First review: postmodern space.

Now, the best thing I did for that place: We were looking at this exaggerated New York storefront because most buildings in New York, most restaurant spaces, are built on the proportions of a New York storefront. Joanna's wasn't, but Gotham is just like a blown-up New York storefront, with the same problem of the incursion of the stairwell behind it, and a narrow throat at the beginning and the bigger space in the back, and so forth. And the best thing I did for them was to say, "I can't bear this." It was so rigid, so I threw a diagonal from the entrance to the rear corner, and I said, "Now, that's the axis of the design."

So sometimes, instead of going with what has been the historic way of dealing with such spaces—the bar in front, a rectangle next to it, right? And a sort of squarish rectangle in the back, which doesn't argue well when the space gets too large, or some other variable changes, a feature, like a window in the back, or whatever it may be—where the rigidity of the formula can kill you, you need to throw some other shape in there, to confuse it, to reject what is commonly done. Then you can learn a lot from what has gone on. It's not throwing out everything that's gone on, but it's also not being bound to it, and not being bound to the preconceptions of your own time.

Today, there are preconceptions about what is Italian. People aren't always conscious of them. They're truly not, but they go in with a kind of vocabulary, and you have to say, "Look, here's a picture of an Italian castle. Here's an Italian trattoria. Here are thirty different images. Now please, let's try to think this through again." No, it doesn't have to have a terra-cotta floor. First of all, they can't afford it. Second, it's too noisy. Third, everyone down the block has one. Fourth, the maintenance to make it look like it does in Italy is impossible. No little old lady's going to get down on her hands and knees with an oiled cloth and oil it every night.

So, there are infinite variables. You don't catch them all. You can't help everybody. But even the guy who's in love with his concept, and knows exactly what he wants to do, and is very lucky, might need some help.

THE DESIGN PROCESS

INFRASTRUCTURE REQUIREMENTS

Once both the market feasibility study and the pro forma analysis are completed, specific locations should be evaluated. Foodservice consultant Bill Eaton states, "Restaurateurs fall into the trap of selecting a site and signing a lease prior to the pro forma. Rent, terms of the lease, and potential construction costs for a particular site can influence price points and the entire concept. In many cases, the increased price and more sophisticated food needed to offset these operating expenses are not compatible with potential customers' pocketbooks and palates."

Undercapitalization can contribute to restaurant failures, since the initial construction costs and subsequent operating expenses affect net revenue. It is important to hire design professionals who can evaluate prospective locations to determine if a restaurant can be built on a particular site within the budget established in the pro forma analysis.

The following list has been prepared to assist restaurateurs in evaluating specific locations:

- *Kitchen exhaust, new construction:* One of the most costly elements of any restaurant is the exhaust requirements. Most codes require that the exhaust duct be 10-gauge welded black iron, in a two-hour rated enclosure (usually 2" calcium silicate or mineral wool). In most cases, the exhaust duct must terminate ten feet above the roof line, and if you're in a ten-story building and there is no exhaust shaft, the exhaust system may be prohibitively expensive, if not impossible, to provide. Many landlords assume a restaurateur who leases the space is aware of the costs and problems involved.

  Sometimes, the rated shaft is provided without 10-gauge black iron ductwork, sprinklers, smoke detectors, or fire alarms. The inexperienced restaurateur assumes the exhaust

is provided and that he or she can build the restaurant within the budget, only to find that the installation of the hood, exhaust ductwork, sprinklers, smoke detectors, and fans in a ten-story building will be prohibitively expensive. In addition to the exhaust system, make-up air must be provided, requiring ductwork and fans on the roof.

When an exhaust ductwork system is physically impossible or prohibitively expensive, alternatives are available. A rotoclone or an electronic precipitator can be placed within the space to filter grease-laden air and odors. They, however, require a substantial space for installation, and all local codes may not approve these alternative systems, and should be checked.

- *Kitchen exhaust:* Check the kitchen-range hood exhaust to determine if it is National Fire Protection Association (NFPA) Code 96 approved. Have the hood checked to determine if it can provide the proper amount of cubic feet per minute (CFM) for exhaust and make-up air required for new or existing cooking equipment. If more charbroiling or deep frying is required for the new menu, a bigger hood may be necessary. Make sure that two hoods are not connected to one exhaust system—it is not permitted in most cases.

- *Electrical systems:* Check adequacy of electric power provided at the meter room or in the panel in the space. In some cases, gas may not be available, requiring an all-electric kitchen. This kitchen may be prohibitively expensive to operate.

  Check the distance of the meter room from the space. If it is far away, it will be expensive to install wiring. Check the size of the empty electrical conduit that has been installed. It may be inadequate and should be replaced by the landlord. In many locations, if enough power has not been provided, the local power company may need to bring power from the street. This is costly and time consuming.

- *Gas service:* Approximately 1,100,000 BTUs of gas are required for an 80- to 100-seat restaurant. This reflects a total of 22 feet of cooking line.

  Check if the gas available is adequate and if the piping is sized correctly.

- *Sanitary waste and vent:* Locate the main waste line, since it is less costly to locate the bathrooms and kitchen near it. In some cases, the kitchen and bathrooms have to be located in the basement below the main sewer line. Ejector pumps are necessary to pump waste up to this sewer line. This is costly and can be an operations nightmare if the pump breaks down.

  If the restaurant is over an occupied space, plumbing connections will have to be made after hours, requiring additional cost for overtime and patching. In some cases, plumbing connections cannot be made in the center of the floor, requiring expensive trenching to the perimeter.

- *Air conditioning systems:* The size and cost of the air conditioning systems depends on the climate and the amount of exposed roof, walls, and glass area. Initial and operating costs can be prohibitively expensive in a location if there are large expanses of unprotected glass.

  Total wattage of lighting will affect the size of the unit and ductwork. Will the landlord supply enough condenser water to cool the space? What months of the year and what time during the day is condenser water supplied? When renovating a space: check the unit's age and repair record; conduct a balancing test to determine if each diffuser is supplying the correct amount of conditioned air; if more lighting is being installed, see if the existing system is capable of supplying sufficient cooling. Baseboards or other perimeter heating should be used to eliminate cold ankles.

- *Sprinklers:* A sprinkler main and adequate heads are generally supplied by the landlord in new construction. When renovating, however, additional sprinkler heads may be required to meet code requirements.

BUILDING CODE ANALYSIS

The Building Officials and Code Administrators (BOCA) National Building Code is used by many states, cities, and local construction officials. Most major cities have their own building codes, so check with your local building official to determine which code applies to your location.

There are several code-related issues that can prevent the location of a restaurant in a specific location. In addition, it may be prohibitively expensive to remove code violations. When making a site visit, there are several issues that are essential to check to determine if a restaurant use is appropriate. Use the following information as a general guide only, since codes are continually updated. It's a good idea to prepare a checklist of code requirements for use when making site visits.

Most restaurants are classified as A-3 assembly spaces. Check your local zoning resolution to make sure that a restaurant use is permitted. There have been cases when restaurants have been completed

and were prevented from opening because their use was not permitted in a specific zone.

Restaurants are very often located in commercial office buildings and shopping centers. Generally, if the building is fully sprinklered and is noncombustible construction, a one-hour rating—building with material that will delay a fire for one hour—is required. If the building is not sprinklered, a two-hour rating is usually required. Providing a two-hour fire separation has major cost implications that should be evaluated prior to selecting that location.

In some jurisdictions, if a great deal of baking is done on the premises, a three-hour separation might be necessary, since this is considered a hazardous use. Flour can ignite and explode.

Restaurants are classified as places of assembly without fixed seats. Places of assembly require compliance with many items related to safe egress. It can be expensive and sometimes impossible to have an existing site comply with egress requirements, and it is essential to evaluate whether it is economically feasible to remedy noncomplying egress issues before a site is selected.

Before construction documents are begun, and in fact during the schematic design phase, a preliminary space plan should be brought to the local construction official and fire marshal to determine if all egress issues have been resolved. Besides your local building code, the *Life Safety Code Handbook*, published by the NFPA, should be checked for egress-related issues.

The first step in determining egress requirements is to evaluate the occupant load. The BOCA code stipulates that 15 sq. ft. is required for each occupant in a dining area. One hundred sq. ft. per occupant is required for kitchen employees, and other calculations are required for standees and employees. Once the occupant load is determined, the amount and widths of the exits can be calculated.

Other important egress requirements are as follows:

1. The main exit must be capable of providing egress capacity for at least one half of the total occupant load.
2. Other exits are required and must be capable of providing egress capacity for at least two-thirds of the total occupant load.
3. A minimum of two exits is required if the occupant load is greater than 50 people, or if the travel distance from the most remote part of the space to the exit is greater than 75 feet.
4. Where two exits are required, they must be remote from each other and be placed a distance apart equal to not less than one-half of the length of the maximum diagonal dimension of the restaurant.
5. The maximum travel distance from the most remote location of the restaurant shall not exceed 200 feet in a nonsprinklered building, or 250 feet in a sprinklered space.
6. The egress width for a doorway in a space with sprinklers is computed as 0.25 inches per occupant.
7. The length of a dead-end passageway or corridor shall not be more than 20 feet.
8. The minimum required width of primary exit aisles in a restaurant serving more than fifty people is 3'8".

9. The minimum door width for a place of assembly is 36 inches.
10. Doors must swing out in the direction of egress.
11. All exit doors in restaurants where the occupant load is greater than 100 must be equipped with panic hardware.
12. Exit signs are required in all spaces required to have more than one exit.
13. Emergency lighting must be sufficient to provide floor lighting intensity equal to one footcandle.

INTERIOR FINISHES

When designing the interior of the restaurant, the following code-related interior finish requirements must be considered:

1. All materials used for interior finish and trim shall be classified in accordance with ASTM E84.
2. Interior finish includes wainscoting, paneling, or other finish applied structurally or for acoustical treatment, insulation, decoration, or similar purposes.
3. Interior wall and ceiling finish materials that have a smoke-developed rating greater than 450 when tested with ASTM E84 shall not be permitted.
4. Foam plastics shall not be used.
5. Vertical exits and passageways must have a flame spread classification of I (0-25); corridors providing exit access must be I (0-25); rooms or enclosed spaces must be II (25-75). Note that class III (75-200) materials can be used for restaurants with a capacity of less than 300 people. When sprinklers are utilized, class II or III materials are permitted in place of class I or II materials.
6. Interior trim, including baseboards, chair rails, moldings, etc., not in excess of 10 percent of the aggregate wall and ceiling areas can be class I, II or III.
7. Textile wall coverings having a napped, tufted, looped, woven, nonwoven, or similar surface shall have a class I flame spread and be protected by sprinklers. They must also pass the flame spread test specified in section 922.7 of the 1990 BOCA code.
8. Floor finish: Traditional floor finishes of wood, vinyl, linoleum, terrazzo, and other resilient floor coverings can be utilized without restriction.

9. Carpet manufactured for sale in the U.S. is required to pass the DOCFF-1 pill test.
10. Curtains, draperies, and hangings shall be noncombustible or be maintained as flame resistant.
11. The permissible amount of flame resistant decorative hangings shall not exceed 10 percent of the total wall and ceiling area.

HAZARDOUS MATERIALS AND HEALTH CODES

The Environmental Protection Agency has written minimum standards for interior pollution. Many building products, including adhesives, carpet, plywood, and other materials, can be harmful to construction workers, employees, and patrons. Proper precautions, such as ventilation and protective gear, should be used during construction. Toxins are still likely to be evident after opening day. These toxins should be tested, with appropriate action taken for their removal.

Asbestos and other hazardous materials must be removed prior to commencing with construction. Building permits cannot be issued in many cities and towns until all hazardous materials are abated.

Local health departments require all food service facilities to meet minimum sanitary standards, including: all wall and ceiling finish materials in cooking areas must be smooth, washable, nonabsorbent, and water-resistant, including fluorescent lighting diffusers; all floors should generally be nonskid, acid-proof quarry or ceramic tile with cove bases; all plumbing fixtures must be properly connected, vented, and drained; all electrical conduits and pipes should be installed within walls to minimize collection of dust and bacteria; all equipment must be NSF approved and be sealed tight to surrounding surfaces.

Kitchen equipment, range hood exhaust, air conditioning, heating, plumbing, and electrical requirements represent 65 percent of the cost for a restaurant project. Usually, budget overruns are caused by underestimating the costs for these requirements. A thorough site analysis can determine whether a specific location is economically feasible before a lease is signed.

Many restaurants fail in the first year of business because of budget overruns owed to unanticipated general construction, plumbing, electrical, and HVAC requirements. Once the lease has been signed and the project has started, it is difficult to delete any of the necessities. It is very difficult to ask investors, or the bank, to provide an additional $200,000 to $300,000 to complete a project. Even if additional funds are available, it may be very difficult, or impossible, to recover from the debt service burden.

Many restaurateurs are not aware of all the hidden costs until it's too late. The cost to modify an existing restaurant significantly can be more than starting from scratch. That is why an estimate of probable construction and operating costs should be established after a thorough site analysis is conducted by an architect and a mechanical engineer. In addition, these professionals should review the landlord's workletter, leases, and any other design criteria prior to the owner's signing the lease.

Building codes and standards for the physically disabled must be thoroughly analyzed for new construction and renovation of existing spaces in order to consider the cost implications to comply with these standards.

SPACE PLANNING

Once the infrastructure and code requirements are analyzed for a specific site, a preliminary space plan and budget should be prepared by a design professional prior to making a commitment for a specific location. If the pro forma states that 150 seats are required to net a reasonable return, it is important to evaluate whether a specific location can accommodate that seating capacity. If it can't, the average check may have to be higher, or the concept may have to change to encourage more turns on seats. The kitchen, bathrooms, and support facilities may have to be located downstairs to provide enough seating. Can this layout work with the food, style, and speed of service? Perhaps not.

Restaurateurs notoriously overestimate how much seating they can jam into a given space. Most codes permit 12 to 15 sq. ft. per person for the dining room. Another rule of thumb is 27 to 32 sq. ft. per person if you include kitchens, bathrooms, and support facilities. The rent of many restaurateurs is assessed by the amount of square footage that is leased, and the profitability of a restaurant is determined by how space-efficient the floor plan is. More seats in less square footage, without sacrificing comfort, is an essential part of planning for high-volume, low-average-check concepts. However, a fine dining establishment with a high average check may opt for fewer seats, since customer comfort is essential for its success.

Space efficiency will depend on sizes and arrangements of tables, and seating capacity will vary based on the type of operation and the style of service. Banquette seating, for example, is quite space efficient and is suitable for concepts where privacy is not essential and conversation between tables is encouraged. Booth seating for four is essential in diner concepts, but it is not efficient if there are a lot of parties of two. Quick service restaurants require small tables for two to maximize volume and speed turnover, while a steak house may require large tables and chairs to support a clubhouse ambience. A diagonal layout of tables for four is more space efficient than tables at right angles to each other.

Assuming one turn at lunch and two at dinner, seven days a week, with an average check of $30, the revenue from each seat at this restaurant is $31,500 a year. Each seat must be considered a revenue producer, and cannot be sacrificed. Several space plans that are appropriate to the concept need to be explored to determine which realizes more seating capacity. Seating capacity is, however, related to the size of the kitchen, which is in turn controlled by the complexity and style of the menu. Some kitchens may require 40 percent or more of the total space, while other concepts can only work if the kitchen is restricted to 25 percent. These are complex issues and only experienced restaurateurs and kitchen consultants can determine the delicate balance between the size of the kitchen and the seating capacity in the front of the house.

The following space planning guidelines can provide the restaurateur with a realistic assessment of the square footage breakdown and seating capacity for a particular-sized space. This thumbnail approximation, however, is not a substitute for schematic space planning layouts for a specific location, since the geometry of a specific space may reduce seating capacity or the size of the kitchen. You can often assume that in terms of square feet per seat, you will need 16 to 18 for a cafeteria, 18 to 20 for counter service, 15 to 18 for table service at a hotel club restaurant, 11 to 14 for fast food table service, 10 to 11 for banquets, and 17 to 22 for specialty formal dining. Waiting areas, coatrooms, and storage areas are not included in these figures.

In regard to service station needs, figure in one small one for every 20 seats (2'0" × 2'0") and one large central one for every 50 seats (8'0" × 2'6"). Table sizes will vary based on foodservice style, size of plates, and overall concept. Tables for two are recommended for quick service restaurants: this means a 22" × 24" for a quick service table for two; 26" × 30" for fine dining. Note that 3'0" × 3'0" square tables are sufficient for 4 people, and a 4'6" round table is sufficient for 6 to 7 people. Booth tables for four should be 2'0" to 2'6" × 4'0" and should be 2" smaller than the overall length of the seat.

When spacing tables, note that a diagonal arrangement of square tables is more space efficient and creates better sight lines in a restaurant than tables placed at right angles. Banquette seating is more appropriate for conversation and people watching, and it is also more space efficient than other table arrangements.

For bars, figure in 2'4" in bar length per bar stool. Island bars are appropriate for looking at other people and are more space-efficient than straight bars. However, island bars require bulkheads for liquor storage, and there is very little room for refrigeration.

Kitchens are usually 25 percent to 40 percent of the area allotted for the restaurant, depending on the complexity of the menu and storage needs.

As an exercise, consider the following space planning analysis for a 6,000 sq. ft. space. First, tackle the dining area. Multiply the desired amount of seats, say, 150, by 12 or 15 sq. ft. per person, which comes out to 2,625 sq. ft. for the dining room only. The square foot per occupant requirement varies, so check applicable codes. This number includes aisles and small bus stations, but does not include coatrooms, bathrooms, bar areas, and waiting areas.

For the bar area, an island arrangement seating 30 people would require a space of approximately 650 square feet (24'0" × 27'0"), as 22 sq. ft. per person is the rule in this type of space. The bar itself is 14'0" × 17'0", with 5'0" aisles all around.

A linear bar seating 30 is less space-efficient, and would require approximately 750 sq. ft.

For the bathrooms, assuming an occupant load of approximately 200 people, the National Plumbing Code requires four water closets and two sinks for women, and two water closets, two urinals, and two sinks for men. Each locality has its own regulations, sometimes requiring fewer fixtures. A bathroom that meets handicapped standards that has three water closets and two sinks for women, and two water closets, two urinals, and two sinks for men, will require approximately 400 sq. ft.

Entry areas, coat rooms, waiter's stations, and waiting areas may require another 200 to 300 sq. ft., depending on the style of the operation.

Since the entire space in the example is 6,000 sq. ft., and approximately 4,000 has been allocated for the front of the house functions listed above, 35 percent, or approximately 2,000 sq. ft. will remain for the finishing kitchen, prep areas, storage, offices, and receiving areas. The restaurateur or design professional can now decide whether this size kitchen will accommodate the desired service style and menu for the restaurant concept.

KITCHEN PLANNING

The placement and design of the kitchen is the single most important element in restaurant planning. Ultimately, it will affect the quality of the food and how many covers can be served efficiently during lunch and dinner. In addition, the cost of equipment coupled with the cost of plumbing, electrical, ventilation, and general construction represents a major portion of the overall cost of the restaurant. If planned correctly, it will contribute greatly to the success of the project; if planned poorly, it will undermine the morale of the staff and make it difficult to prepare and serve food.

The balance between the complexity and style of the menu, seating capacity, and the size and configuration of the kitchen and its support facilities is critical. An extra three feet devoted to the kitchen of a high-volume 200-seat restaurant may sacrifice 10 or more seats, but if those three extra feet are not added, it could affect the success of the entire concept.

Vic Kasner of Colonel Food Service Equipment Company has designed kitchens for Docks, Bice, Remi, and many other restaurants. He states, "A kitchen must be designed to meet the needs for the busiest period." Artie Cutler, one of the partners at Docks, states that "we work backwards in planning our restaurants. We design our kitchens first to determine how much space we need to prepare and serve our high-quality food. When you have a lunch where everyone is seated at the same time, and you're doing 400 covers within a two-hour period, you need a big kitchen, prep, and storage areas."

Barbara Lazaroff states, "The design of the kitchen comes first at all our restaurants. Forty percent of the entire restaurant at Spago is devoted to the kitchen and back of the house, because our focus is on the preparation and presentation of fine food."

The need to maximize seating for concepts that rely on high volume and a modest average check has affected the size of the kitchen for many restaurateurs. They can't devote more than 25 or 30 percent for the kitchen and support facilities and must rely on more frequent deliveries and less complex menus requiring less equipment in order to survive.

Ideally, a kitchen should be placed on the same floor as the dining room. Food can be brought to the table more quickly, preventing it from getting cold. Runners and service staff conserve energy because they don't have to walk up and down stairs. Obviously, this can lead to accidents, breakage, and lost revenue, not to mention staff attrition owing to aching feet.

In many instances, however, the need to make a profit outweighs the convenience of locating the kitchen on the first level. The profitability of a restaurant relies on how many seats it has. The costs of construction, rent, and overhead, in urban locations especially, require seating to be maximized, and, for most concepts, kitchens must be located in the basement.

Gotham, one of the most successful restaurants in New York, had to maximize seating in the dining area to make the pro forma work, and their kitchen, which is located in the basement, relies on strict coordination between the line cooks, the chef/expeditor, the manager, the wait staff, and the runners. Chef/partner Alfred Portale believes, however, that the location of the kitchen in the basement doesn't affect the quality of the food in this three-star restaurant.

Restaurants whose menus have food with relatively little density, such as pasta and thin filets of chicken or fish, should avoid having their kitchens located on another level, since these products lose heat very rapidly. Plate covers can reduce this heat loss, but in many cases food quality is not the same. Recipes and menu selections have to be carefully analyzed by the chef to minimize deterioration of food quality when kitchens are placed on another level from the dining room. Never rely on dumbwaiters or elevators as the primary expeditor of food to the dining room, because food will not stay hot while waiters wait for these conveyors. Elevators can be used as supplementary means for transporting bulk received goods to prep areas, and dumbwaiters can transport soiled dishes to the dishwasher if stairs are not available.

Most restaurant kitchens are fairly similar in nature. They all have the components described below. The size of these components varies based on the amount of seating and the extent of the menu. The following is a summary of what occurs in each component:

- *Receiving:* Meats, poultry, fish, vegetables, canned goods, and all other items are usually brought to the receiving door or loading dock. A small office is located near this receiving area, where the steward or chef can inspect the delivery. The size of this receiving area is based on the volume of deliveries.

- *Dry, refrigerated, and frozen storage areas:* Received items are unpacked and broken down in order to be stored in their proper location. Meat, poultry, and fish in some cases are cleaned and butchered before they are stored in freezers. Restaurants, however, are relying more on preportioned meats, poultry, and fish to conserve space. Vegetables are cleaned and stored in walk-in refrigerators.

- *Prepreparation area:* Vegetables are peeled and cut. Meat, poultry, lobster, and fish are further

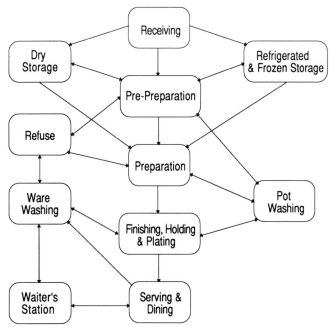

FUNCTIONAL FLOW DIAGRAM. © DORF ASSOCIATES.

trimmed and portioned. These items are placed on trays and brought to reach-in or under-counter refrigerators, which are conveniently located for use by line cooks.

- *Preparation area cold prep:* Salads and desserts are prepped in these areas before being brought to under-counter refrigeration in dessert and *garde manger* areas. Garnishes and ingredients are cut and placed in containers on the plating line.

- *Hot prep:* Stocks, sauces, and other items needed for the hot line are prepared in this area.

- *Finishing, holding, and plating:* This area is the key to the efficient preparation, plating, and delivery of food to the table. It must be designed to allow line cooks to prepare food without crossing over one another and must allow the expeditor (usually the chef) to have visual access to all parts of the preparation area. This expeditor must see every plate before it goes out to the dining room to control quality. The expeditor also controls the speed with which each appetizer, entrée, and dessert is prepared, plated, and delivered to each table.

It is not unusual for a 170-seat restaurant to prepare 300 to 400 covers in an evening. Two-thirds of these covers are usually prepared during the same 90-minute period, and the atmosphere in the kitchen during this time is very intense. Line cooks are concentrating on individual orders and instructions from the expeditor to *fire,* or cook, an entrée. This instruction to fire happens usually 10 to 15 minutes after the appetizers have left the kitchen. The expeditor receives the *dupe,* a yellow and white carbon copy of a table's order, at his computer station, and places the dupe copies on a rack in consecutive order. During the busiest times, 10 or more dupes, representing 35 or more plates, are being prepared in rapid succession. Each table may have 2, 4, 6, or 8 appetizers, entrées, and desserts, and some entrées may take longer to prepare than others, requiring the expeditor to coordinate the instructions to fire, so that all plates are delivered hot at the same time to a particular table.

It is critical that each line cook have his own conveniently located area for ingredients, sauces, and garnishes. These ingredient stations are usually located on the plating table and are approximately four sq. ft. in size. In addition, it is crucial that there is enough refrigerated storage nearby under the pick-up counter or in upright refrigerators to store *par stock* in order to meet the demands of high-volume restaurants. Preportioned meats, fish, and chicken are stored on trays or in refrigerated drawers next to each station on the line so that line cooks do not have to wait for food to be delivered from refrigerated storage in another area remote from the hot or cold lines.

During intense periods, the expeditor can best assist in plating appetizers, entrées, and desserts in a kitchen when the cold and hot section are placed at right angles to each other. This arrangement is advantageous because it allows the expeditor to see all plating activities, and to speak to all the line cooks easily. Runners assist in plating by cleaning each plate before it leaves the kitchen, and waiters only come into the kitchen to give special instruction.

The runner is responsible for putting the time on the dupe when the appetizer leaves the dining room. This gives the expeditor information on when to fire the entrée.

During this intense period, it is extremely important that the expeditor, runners, and line cooks communicate with each other and, above all, don't collide. A poorly designed and undersized kitchen can add to the already high tension level and undermine the morale of the kitchen staff.

- *Ware washing and pot washing:* Ware washing must be placed near the entrance to the kitchen, with enough circulation space to avoid conflicts with runners entering and leaving the kitchen with food. Three-compartment sinks large enough to accommodate the largest pots are located near ware washing for pot washing. Drain boards are located on either side of the three-compartment sink.

- *Refuse:* The bulk of refuse comes from receiving, preprep, and preparation areas. A small holding room should be placed near where refuse is picked up. This room needs to be cooled and under negative pressure to eliminate odors.

- *Waiter's stations:* Coffee, tea, water, and other condiments are located outside the kitchen walls in order to keep waiters out of the kitchen and increase speed of service. If kitchens are in the basement, the waiter's station would be located upstairs. If the station is on the same level, it is located near the kitchen, a distance away from the dining room, in order to reduce noise.

Four additional elements must be considered when planning the kitchen. They are:

- *Kitchen circulation:* Vic Kasner states, "There are short loops, longer loops, and invisible loops in designing kitchen circulation. The short loop, made by bus boys, is almost always from the kitchen entrance to the dishwashing area and ice machines, and out again. Placement of these functions near the entrance avoids conflicts between bus boys and runners. Runners make the long loop, entering the kitchen and proceeding to the pick-up area. The invisible loop is made within the kitchen, when clean dishes are brought back to the line by dishwashers. This invisible loop should avoid conflicts with the short and long loops."

- *Noise Control:* The noisiest part of a kitchen is where the expeditor is shouting to the line cooks to fire an entrée. The next noisiest is the drop-off area for dirty dishes. In a noisy, energized dining area, the sounds in the kitchen will not be heard. In a quiet, small dining area, it would be prudent to create a sound lock area where noise can be trapped before entering the dining room. This sound lock area should have acoustical treatment on the walls and ceiling.

- *Ventilation:* The environment in a kitchen must be kept as comfortable as possible. Most kitchens are not air conditioned, but if they are properly ventilated, they can be relatively comfortable. Uncomfortable kitchens, whether they are unbearably hot or drafty, contribute to staff defections. The amount of air that is taken out by the exhaust hoods should be replaced by make-up air. This make-up air is supplied from the roof by fans placed at least 10 feet away from the exhaust fans, so that exhaust odors are not fed back into the kitchen. Makeup air is heated or tempered to 70° before it enters the kitchen. This alleviates cold drafts that can cool the food quickly and give the line cooks colds. It

also reduces condensation on the hood surface. In warmer months, the air is supplied untempered. If the make-up air diffusers are located properly, the currents of air between the diffusers and the hood will provide comfort for the line cooks.

The amount of make-up air should be 90 percent of exhaust air in order to create negative pressure in the kitchen. This 10 percent negative pressure minimizes smoke and odor migration into the dining room. When make-up air is not tempered, the personnel tend to shut off the make-up air fan in colder months to alleviate cold drafts. Shutting off the make-up system, however, contributes to smoke and odors migrating outside the hood, creating uncomfortable conditions. The temperature and supply of make-up air is especially critical when planning "open kitchen" restaurants.

- *Lighting:* The chef, line cooks, and prep personnel need sufficient light to prepare and cook the food. Since the color of the food on the plate is critical, color-corrected fluorescent lamps or incandescent sources should be used for general lighting to minimize color distortion.

BUDGET ANALYSIS

Once the overall concept has been developed, it is also critical to the success of the restaurant that enough capital is available to construct the type of restaurant that is being considered.

A quick-service, sit-down restaurant, including equipment, acoustical tile ceilings, vinyl floors, and simple wall treatments, can be built for approximately $100 to $150 a square foot, depending on its location. A full-service restaurant (4,000 to 6,500 sq. ft.) with modest interior finishes and equipment can cost $175 to $200 a square foot. An upscale concept can cost $225 to $300 or more.

Pano Karatassos of the Buckhead Life Restaurant Group in Atlanta states, "If your concept is a quality steak house in an affluent neighborhood whose residents and businesspeople demand a richly detailed space, you'd better be prepared to open your checkbook." The

woodwork, flooring, lighting, and details must match the sophistication of your customer base.

If the restaurateur's pocketbook does not match his dream concept for a posh celebration restaurant, it should be discovered at the first meeting, not when the bids are returned and construction is about to begin. Often, the architect has to say, "This is a wonderful concept, but you can't afford this." Unfortunately, the client doesn't believe it, and thinks the architect may be inflating this estimate to justify higher fees. Thus, the budget game begins. The restaurateur says, "I can build my dream for $150 a square foot," and the design professional proceeds against his or her better judgment to design this restaurant.

The budget game is a major mistake, and it is responsible for more restaurant failures than any other issue. Realistic budgets must be established that are compatible with market realities. They must include total construction costs plus a 20 percent contingency for overruns and the cost of all equipment and preopening expenses.

Unrealistic budgets set by the owner can compromise the theme and concept of a restaurant when real prices become known during the bid process. The owner requests that the design professional proceed with construction drawings, retaining all the custom finishes, millwork, lighting, furnishings, and equipment that were estimated at $250 per square foot, because the owner feels it can be built for $150 per square foot.

The lowest bid comes back at $200 per square foot, and the owner has only borrowed money to cover costs at $150. HVAC, plumbing, electrical, general construction, and equipment requirements, which represent 65 to 75 percent of the budget, cannot be changed. In addition, this upscale concept is relying on custom finishes, millwork, lighting, and furnishings to establish a setting that will attract an affluent clientele. Guess what happens? All the interior treatments are changed at the last moment to reflect the $150 per square foot budget, thus compromising the theme and concept of the restaurant.

All this can be avoided if the owner and design professional work together to establish an appropriate budget that reflects the stated theme and concept of the restaurant. How do a restaurateur and a design professional decide what level of design will be appropriate for a given concept, location, and customer base? Pat Kuleto, a prominent restaurant designer and owner, feels that "design decisions are driven by both economic realities and market realities." A restaurateur will limit the construction budget based on projections of total revenue and the return on the investment. The pro forma might state that a restaurant that grosses $3.5 million can only afford a design that costs $175 per square foot. That budget may be appropriate for a casual family restaurant that doesn't require detailed millwork or custom lighting. The "market reality" discovered in the market analysis, however, supports an "upscale image" that will require $250 a square foot. The restaurateur's menu, average check, and the size of the restaurant may have to change in order to produce the income required for a profitable return on the investment.

The successful "upscale concept," which costs $250 a square foot, will gross $4 to $5 million a year and was the most appropriate project for that location and affluent customer base. The "family restaurant" that would have cost $175 a square foot and grossed $3.5 million might not have survived the first year.

Several budget alternatives representing varying levels of finishes, along with photos that illustrate sample images, should be presented to the restaurateur to determine if their preconceived notion about these levels of finishes matches their pocketbook.

A preliminary budget summary should be prepared along the lines of the following model, which describes a diner concept, with custom millwork in a suburban location, of 6500 sq. ft., 175 seats, and 30 bar stools. The figures include overhead, profit, and general conditions. Note that the grand total does not include architectural and engineering fees, china, flatware, and other smallwares, liquor inventory, preopening expenses, advertising, menus, or business cards.

First, give figures for the back of the house, including:

Electrical, totaling $130,000 at $20.00 per sq. ft.
Plumbing, $110,000 at $17.00
Mechanical (includes all HVAC), $210,000 at $32.30
Sprinklers, $20,000 at $3.00
Kitchen equipment, $250,000 at $38.50
Drywall, finishes, and ceramic tile in kitchen, $85,000 at $13.00

The subtotal for the back of the house is thus $805,000 at $123.80 per square foot. Figures for the front of the house should include:

Millwork, totaling $300,000 at $46.15 per sq. ft.
Finishes (including drywall, paint, ceramic tile), $85,000 at $13.00
Specialties (including glazing and doors), $60,000 at $9.25
Furniture (including booths), $50,000 at $7.70
Lighting (including dimming), $50,000 at $7.70
Signage, $20,000 at $3.00

The subtotal for the front of the house comes to $565,000 at $85.80 per square foot. The grand total for the restaurant is thus $1,370,000 at $210.72 per square foot.

Another factor that affects the success of a restaurant is time. A full-service restaurant can take 8 to 16 weeks or more to plan, design, and prepare construction documents, with another four weeks required for bidding, selecting a contractor, and obtaining permits. Approximately 16 to 24 weeks are necessary to construct the restaurant.

Once a lease is signed, a restaurateur may have very little time before rent commences. Unfortunately, this time constraint shortens the appropriate time for design and drawings, selection of a contractor, and construction.

When an appropriate amount of time is not spent on planning, design, and construction drawings, several things can happen, including:

- *Miscommunication between client and architect/designer, leading to costly changes in the field:* Not enough time to revise drawings to reduce the budget, forcing selection of the low bidder, who may not be capable of maintaining schedule or quality.

- *Lack of time to negotiate and select a contractor at an appropriate price:* This is a recurrent error on the part of many restaurateurs, since less time is spent on bidding and negotiation in the interest of starting construction in a hurry. Most bidders would be happy to solicit more cost-effective subcontractors if they had more time, and thousands of dollars can be saved if more time for this phase is permitted.

- *Forcing the contractor into an unrealistic opening date:* This usually results in costly overtime charges. It also short-circuits the shop drawings phase, which is essential for a detailed project with custom finishes and millwork. The absence of the shop drawing process leads to disputes in the field, causes delays in the schedule, and compromises quality control.

DESIGN CONCEPT

M. J. Madigan, publisher of *Hospitality Design* magazine, states, "A skilled designer can create an environment that specifically targets the market that the restaurant is supposed to attract. An experienced design professional can work with materials, color, form, and light to create a mood that can take you back in time to a 1940s diner, place you beside a Mediterranean fishing village, or create a version of a clubby steak house with a special panache that transcends kitsch. In the hands of a less skilled person, the design of a space can become an expensive failure because it misses the intended market entirely.

"An experienced designer can plug into the owner's psyche and create a space that realizes that particular restaurateur's vision. If the designer feels that vision is not consistent for the intended market niche, he or she can assist the owner in developing a concept that is more appropriate. Ultimately, however, this image must match the level of sophistication of the restaurateur, because it is important that they have a comfort level with their own space."

The combination of materials, colors, textures, shapes, furniture, and lighting communicates a particular message to the dining-out public. It must collectively represent the type of establishment and its level of sophistication and price. If it misses, even by a little, it will create a confusing message, and discourage repeat patronage.

A depressed economy and major demographic restructuring has splintered once easily definable market segments into particle markets, creating ever-increasing challenges for restaurateurs and designers who seek concepts that satisfy the needs of empty-nesters, families, the baby boomlet, newly arrived immigrants, the disabled, the affluent, the elderly, the poor, women in charge, and many other sectors of the population.

Restaurateurs are faced with formulating concepts that have a high perceived cost/value relationship in order to satisfy customers with less disposable income.

The ability to create a "hit" is elusive and difficult. The ability to create a cost-effective, innovative restaurant concept that matches market demand is even more difficult. This design-charged atmosphere places an increasing demand on the design profession to search for alternative innovative materials that convey a particular message, yet can meet budget constraints.

Very often, interior finishes and lighting are changed during design to offset budget problems, seriously compromising the intended message. On the other hand, inappropriate, expensive materials will increase construction costs, thus influencing the ability of the restaurant to survive financially.

The profitable lifespan for many restaurants in the 1980s was limited to a few years at best. The frenetic, trendy "Restaurant of the Moment" captured the sociocultural spirit of these roaring, glittering times. But M. J. Madigan states, "A retrenchment back to quieter and more sobering times has changed the type of restaurants that are being developed into more low-key spaces that have more mass appeal and look like they've always been there." More than ever, the design of a restaurant must carefully blend the location, food style, average check, and the appropriateness of the overall image to suit the intended market.

Pano Karatassos, president of the Buckhead Life Restaurant Group, states, "Our commitment to quality is reflected in the finishes, lighting, and furniture that we selected for Chops. We very rarely compromise on the look of our restaurants because our customers are expecting the best, and we give it to them. I trust the designers I work with, and I only want to work with the best. Their experience and creativity are going to help make me more successful."

Jeff Bliss, one of the partners at Mesa Grill in Manhattan, states, "Many people thought we were absolutely crazy to open a restaurant in the teeth of the recession in 1991. Restaurants were failing all over town, and the industry as a whole had experienced a substantial drop in sales. However, Jerry Kretchmer and I both felt that the reason that so many restaurants had failed recently was owed to their inability to change their menu, price structure, and overall concept to adapt to changing economic conditions. Many people felt that the restaurant industry was dead in New York, and there was no opportunity for new restaurant concepts. Jerry and I still believed, however, in the vitality of New York and were committed to develop a concept that would work despite the gloomy economic conditions.

"One friend remarked, 'I've attended the funeral for New York City several times, but the body never shows up.' We felt we could succeed if we could develop a restaurant where there was great food and service combined with a low average check in an energized, fun environment. The trick was that we needed to spend as little money as possible on the renovation and try to negotiate the best possible deal in order for this concept to work."

To try to define what style of restaurant fits a particular market segment in a particular location is futile. A restaurant in Boston that caters to an affluent over-fifty crowd will be very different in its spatial configuration, scale, choice of materials, and lighting than a restaurant in midtown Manhattan that was specifically created for an international crowd who want to see and be seen. A family style diner concept in Maryland will not have the same sophisticated informality of a wide open "exhibition kitchen" space in Los Angeles.

The casual fine dining explosion has made great food available at reasonable prices to a wide audience of people who previously only dined out on special occasions in an expensive restaurant that was usually French in style. Dining out usually meant finding a place that served consistently good food. Now people expect the level of design to match the level of food and service. These spaces, however, cannot be one-note overbearing environments that wear thin in a year and compete with the need to enjoy the dining experience. They require a sense of timelessness that allows them to endure and prosper for many years. Materials need to be selected that last and require relatively little maintenance, since the constant repair, replacement, and refinishing of materials can be costly.

The "total experience" of dining that Joe Baum created for a generation of Americans is a harmonious blend of materials, color, form, space, light, uniforms, napery, glassware, flatware, china, and menu graphics that all combine to reinforce why we choose to go to a particular restaurant. The psychosocial reasons we choose a particular dining experience that confirms our self-concept change according to our age, how we feel about the food we eat, and how much we can afford. One day we can be quite satisfied with a hot dog at the ballpark or sampling dim sum in Chinatown. A noisy, energized, see-and-be-seen environment feels good because we get to put on our best casual clothes and meet friends, while another night, we need a space that is more intimate where we can relax.

Morris Nathanson of Morris Nathanson Design of Pawtucket, Rhode Island, believes in "selecting materials that are familiar, warm, and friendly, that create a sense that a place has been around for a while, and is going to be around for quite some time. The planning of the space takes into account the need for privacy and intimacy as well as the need to peoplewatch and gather with friends to schmooze at the bar. It is important that customers are not given confusing messages, and know how to dress and feel comfortable. I recently walked past a hot new Caribbean-style restaurant and didn't walk in because I wasn't dressed in a bright shirt or shorts."

Pat Kuleto feels "the most crucial element in the design of Chops or any of my high-end casual dining restaurants is the tremendous sense of arrival upon entering the space. I want people to immediately sense the excitement and drama of the entire space. At Chops, as soon as you enter, you can see the bustling cooking line, the bar, and a good portion of the dining room. It dazzles the senses and heightens expectations. Chops was conceived as a quintessential macho steak house.

It was designed to convey a men's club image, but had to be appealing to women as well. The materials selected, such as marble floors, mahogany woodwork, etched glass, and the lighting are all organic "real" materials to compliment "real" organic food."

Jim Biber, architect and designer, took the approach that the design of Mesa Grill on lower Fifth Avenue in Manhattan had to match the exuberance an color of the food. "It's a very cranked-up palette, with vibrant colors that are alive with energy and were inspired by the color and exuberance of the food. The space, with its high ceilings, large columns, funky Southwestern-style lighting fixtures, and space-expanding black-and-white photos, was created for a hip young crowd of design professionals, photographers, and people in the visual arts. The design was specifically suited for this client, this space, this menu, and this customer base. I'm sure the next restaurant I do will look quite different."

Another restaurateur eager to cash in on this hot new concept may not succeed, because the confluence of the customer base and location can never be quite the same. That's what makes the restaurant business so special, risky, and tantalizing, all at the same time.

LIGHTING DESIGN

Perhaps the single most important design feature in a restaurant is the lighting. People are phototropic and are drawn to the light in a space more than any other feature, and we form our impressions of a restaurant based on our emotional and metaphorical responses to the color, brightness, and shape of the light in the room. The quality of light can stimulate our senses and add high drama and exuberance to a space or it can create a soothing, relaxed, comfortable mood. Done poorly, it can make us look ghoulish and old, with dark circles under our eyes. Done well, it can make us look and feel wonderful.

Carroll Cline of Cline, Bettridge, Bernstein, Lighting Designers in New York states, "The light in a restaurant should try to embody the spirit of light outdoors by incorporating directional light (sunlight), overall or ambient light (skylight), and sparkle (the kind of light we see reflected on water or leaves).

Directional light is accomplished from a variety of sources in the ceiling that focus light on artwork, food displays, tables, and major architectural features like columns or ceiling breaks. Directional light also guides us to our table and allows us to see our menu and the food on the table. Skylight can be accomplished by uplighting the ceiling with cove light, pendants, or wall sconces, while sparkle is created through a combination of the finish materials like mirror, reflective surfaces, glassware, and lighting fixtures that by themselves create a point source of light that glistens."

Michael Whiteman, a leading restaurant consultant, feels that "many restaurants are too darkly lit. Fifteen or twenty years ago, food tended to be dull, and we lived in an era when food was either brown or white. Today, food is extraordinarily dynamic, and has become a lot more colorful, while the food styling on the plate has become as

BLOOM'S. DORF ASSOCIATES. WALL SCONCES AND PENDANT FIXTURES CREATE A WARM GLOW AND ARE THE APPROPRIATE METAPHOR FOR THIS FRIENDLY DELI/CAFÉ. PHOTOGRAPH © MASAO UEDA.

BLOOM'S. DORF ASSOCIATES. ACCENT LIGHTING HIGHLIGHTS MEMORABILIA, CREATES SPARKLE ON THE REFLECTIVE CLOCK AND PORCELAIN SURFACES, WHILE COVE LIGHTING PROVIDES AMBIENT "SKYLIGHT." PHOTOGRAPH © MASAO UEDA.

important as the taste of the food. It is as much a part of the space as any other architectural treatment or object, and consequently, there is a need to dramatically light the table in order to see the color and presentation on the plate. As important as it is to light the food, it is equally important to make sure that this lighting doesn't create shadows under the eyes or worse than that, accentuate wrinkles in the skin."

Jerry Kugler, a lighting designer in New York who was responsible for the lighting at Gotham, China Grill, and many other restaurants, feels, "simplicity and having a strong single idea is a key factor for a lighting scheme. Too often, restaurateurs will see lighting fixtures in other restaurants, lighting showrooms, and catalogs, and say, "Oh, that's a good idea," and, "Over there, that's a good idea," and when they all come together, all you have is a very bad bouillabaisse. What's even more problematic is the ubiquitous contemporary wall sconce that was chosen from a catalog that may look good as an object, but is totally the wrong metaphor for the space. Slick, trendy sconces and pendants tend to connote a sense that this is a place where I get small portions of well-decorated food. Our impression of the restaurant is quite opposite to what the owner had in mind, and sometimes I wish I had an aerosol can of Sconce-Away."

Bloom's, a delicatessen/cafe designed by Dorf Associates on Fortieth Street and Lexington Avenue in New York City, provides a good example of lighting that is properly tailored to the contemporary yet timeless spirit of the space. The fixtures are consistent in style with each other, and combine to create a unified impression that reinforces the friendly deli message. The cove-lit ceiling coffer supplies "skylight" or ambient light, while directional light emanates from sconces and recessed accent lights, and "sparkle" reflects off the many shiny surfaces such as marble tabletops, copper trim, and decorative displays of memorabilia and pickle jars.

Michael Whiteman states, "I think an enormous amount of time needs to be spent on having light come from a variety of sources. You need light that bounces off walls, that creates contrast, highlights, and sparkle, and light that creates a general warm glow. Most people can't afford it; most people don't recognize it; most people don't deal with it."

Not only should lighting be appropriate for each setting, it also has to be appropriate for each individual restaurateur. A plethora of adjustable low-voltage accent lights highlighting objects in the space can be an operations nightmare for unskilled and unsophisticated maintenance personnel, since fixtures that are aimed and focused on opening night will probably be shining in someone's face three months later, when the lamp is changed. Expensive lamps that are not easily obtainable can also present a problem for an unsuspecting owner.

Since incandescent light is the most appropriate source of illumination for restaurants because it is most flattering to food and people, the amount of energy it consumes and the heat that it generates must be controlled. Well-lighted spaces can be accomplished by using light sources that don't generate more than 3 to 4 watts per square foot. Watts produce heat, and that affects the size and operating costs of the air conditioning system. An additional watt per square foot can add thousands of dollars in operating costs per year. In addition, the amount of energy consumed by an overlit restaurant will contribute to much higher electrical bills.

Contrary to popular belief, low-voltage lighting neither saves energy or prolongs life. Its virtue is the control of the beamspread, which enables light to be focused on a particular object. Energy-saving PAR lamps or the new HIRs do conserve energy and provide more light with less wattage. Their application, however, is limited to spaces with high ceiling and more theatrical, dramatic environments, because they tend to create harsh, bright spots of light when used too close to objects. Simple A lamps in wall sconces, pendants, and recessed downlights can provide much of the illumination for a restaurant. They are easy to obtain, simple to change, and produce a warm glow of light that is friendly to people and food.

A computerized, user-friendly, easily programmable dimming system with four or more presets for lunch, cocktails, dinner, and cleanup can be purchased for as little as $3,000. Dimming systems allow the restaurateur to vary the mood of the room easily, while conserving energy and prolonging lamp life. A press of a button will automatically alter all the lights for a given time period, alleviating the need to constantly control a multiple of conventional slide or rotary dimmers. Once the program is set, it can be locked into place so that personnel cannot play with the lighting levels.

Pam Morris of Exciting Lighting has designed and hand-crafted light sculptures and fixtures for some of the most successful restaurants in the country, including Postrio, Splendido's, Chops, The Buckhead Diner, Fog City Diner, and most recently she has translated Barbara Lazaroff's underwater concept for Granita in Malibu, California, to create breathtaking fixtures.

Morris studied at the Art Student's League in New York City and has a degree in fine arts. She was a finalist in General Electric's Edison Awards and was honored as a Designer on Parade in San Francisco. She has lectured and been published nationally.

Pam Morris feels that "light has the ability to create states of mind, and as you view it, you are involved with it. Often, when people are creating a mood with lighting, they just think in terms of dimming the lights. Instead, I create light sculptures and fixtures that stimulate the senses and evoke magical, mysterious, whimsical, or comforting feelings that are appropriate for a specific environment."

The following is an interview with Pam Morris, who discusses individual projects and their lighting solutions.

Q: How did the architecture influence your design solutions for the Postrio Bar?
A: It was a very difficult space, architecturally, because the bar entry is a long room like a bowling alley. Beyond this there is a step-down mezzanine with some dining, then a very steep stairway down into the main dining room. In other words, the dining is three rooms away and two elevations away from where you come in. So

PAM MORRIS.
PHOTOGRAPH © KEN ALTSHULER.

the architect had to entice people to move through the space to get into the dining room. He did this by inlaying a ribbon pattern in the marble floor ("follow the yellow brick road"). I echoed this up in the ceiling with a shadow design that becomes visual stepping stones. On a secondary level, there is a sense of a party with the ribbons in the floor and these little shadows that are like balloons. Also, since the floor was white marble, I needed to put a reflector underneath the lamp so that the halogen light used would reflect off that and up into the ceiling and not glare onto the white marble floor—yet there is a little sparkle that you can see reflected in the floor, so it adds a festive glistening. Also, because of the room's bowling alley shape, I was concerned that the diners in the bar might feel that they were in a hallway, so the wire system marks the perimeter of the room and collects them under a canopy. This makes the room smaller, brings the ceiling down a little bit, and gives a more human scale to the room (see photograph, p. 54 top).

Q: Tell me what the neon is doing at the end of the room.
A: Well, it's the light at the end of the tunnel, again for the purpose of giving direction. In this way it is guiding people; they are drawn to the brightest source of illumination. We are drawn to light. It is a brainstem phenomenon that we have no control over. It's similar to moths drawn to a porch light, or to fish that are drawn into nets with the fishermen's lights at night, and we're not immune to that, we're animals too. Lighting, you know, is not just a decorative element, it's a primal element. It's at the core of all life itself. There's water, air, and light!

And on the secondary level of decor, this fixture is creating color—a lavender light, which is speaking of an exotic and sublime space. It's exciting and calming at the same time. I wanted to say, "You are some place special and unique." And doing it with lavender light is very effective. Lavender is also complementary to skin tones without being the too common "bordello red."

Q: It's a very unusual color. How did you come up with that?
A: This neon color doesn't exist. To create it I had to mix three individual neon tubes placed side by side: a red, a white and a blue to get this lavender color.

Q: Are there other colors coming from the fixture?
A: The way I placed the neon, there's a hollow, curved metal arch. It's like a rectangular box that's been curved, and the neon is placed inside. On the top there's a piece of edgelit glass. This glass is being lit with the white neon, then the blue neon is coming down from an opening in the bottom. All three colors are hitting the back of the wall and reflecting into the room. It would not be the same if the wall had been painted lavender. Light emanates an energy. It is alive.

Q: What were the challenges in the main dining room?
A: The little lights in the bar were like fireflies. The main dining room is an open, two-story room with the upper part huge and empty. So I needed to create a very large-scale fixture that would fill the space, sort of like floating clouds, without being heavy or ominous. What I wanted to do with them was to make them so intriguing that you wouldn't be distracted by the empty ceiling and air conditioning ducts, or by people looking at you when you're at the top of this grand stairway ready to enter. I wanted to create something that was so visually strong and immediate that people would be drawn away from those feelings. I wanted to say, "Come in and have a party!" *Gourmet* magazine said they were "the wildest party favors in town!"

I believe that lighting should be something that you are comfortable with. It is similar to food in that it's something you can love. I think the easiest way to understand this idea would be to remember when you were a small child sleeping in your bedroom and trembling that there were alligators under your bed, or the bogeyman was going to get you and who knows what was in your closet. Just having a little nightlight soothed that fear. Light has a very soothing, calming, humanizing effect on us. A lot of lighting that we see today is designed with a ruler and is square and hard. I don't think this has a place in restaurant design. We don't eat square food; it isn't comfortable to hug things with sharp edges. I think that lighting needs to have a softness and a friendliness. I think of light as a friend. Light is from an early age our comfort, and I'm remembering that, in bringing it into these environments. When we work, we can tolerate discomfort, but when we eat, I think it is very important to be comfortable.

Q: How did you determine the scale of this space? How did you decide that this was the right size for the area so that it would neither be overpowering nor get lost?

A: I took a template that was made out of plywood and had two assistants on tall ladders—they were very tall; I think they may have been twelve-foot ladders. We tried a diameter of both 28 and 36 inches. And truthfully, I originally thought that 28 inches would be sufficient, but it wasn't at all; it needed to have the full 36 inches. So sometimes you actually need to mock it up in the environment to know (see photograph, p. 54 bottom).

Q: I would think the mounting height would make a big difference in that very tall space.

A: Yes, it needed to be close to the ceiling to fill up that space and not let the ceiling be flat and empty. Yet it had to be low enough in the room to be with you while you were sitting down so far away.

Q: One of the things that I find interesting is the sense of depth that the fixtures have. Something seems to be emerging from within—the way that you have shadows inside. Was there a reason for that?

A: You know, I'm really glad you asked that question, because this is one of my favorite stories. When I design, I don't design to match things—like little pink socks with a little pink dress. I was asked to put ribbons on these fixtures to match the ribbons in the floors. But I couldn't see any purpose for putting them on, other than just gratuitous decoration. The ribbons in the floors were justified architecturally—they had a purpose: to tie the rooms together visually, as a common element running through the marble and then the carpet. So I had to find a reason to put them on the fixtures, and the story I came up with is that these are the ribbon eggs, and they split in half. The ribbons that are inside, which are shadows, are unborn ribbons. The ribbons on the floor fell out of the crack created when these two halves split open.

Q: These same pieces combine fluorescent and incandescent in the same fixture; that is a bit

unusual. Actually, I think it's groundbreaking! Why did you do this?

A: Well, you know, I like the combination of white light and warm light. I notice that in my kitchen in the morning when I have low sunlight coming through the redwood trees, it filters through the green leaves and makes the light a cool color. Then I have a little stove light above my antique white porcelain stove. This is incandescent, and thus a warm, yellow light. It's a magical combination. It's hard to describe, but you can instantly feel it. It's also refreshing to the eye, because if you only take in yellow light then you blank out yellow. White light refreshes the retina, so it can reinterpret the yellow again. Visual sorbet!

Q: Tell us about Chops Bar. Was there a reason to use portable fixtures along the bar?

A: Yes, two reasons. White marble was used on this bar top to lighten the space a little bit, but it simultaneously created a sterile feeling right under your elbows. I put these fixtures on the bar to create intimacy, a sense of a friend being there with you so you weren't left alone on this white marble slab. They have a fun sense about them. There's a collapsing design here in the metal and to me it feels like a businessman would feel after work—he's just letting down, relaxing. I felt that men come here after working hard, being focused, being directed all day and that seeing this melting shape would identify with them. It's hard to describe, but they would attune themselves to that and then just relax more. It would also be a source of conversation, because whenever there's something stunning to look at, people tend to get into more interesting conversations than if they have nothing other than the weather or what they do for work to help them as a topic. So this stimulates lively bar conversation.

Q: I was noticing that underneath those fixtures, and on the edge of the wall sconces, you've put a magenta color that is very different from the overall feeling of the space. What was some of the reasoning behind that?

A: Well, I suppose a little bit of horseradish in the cocktail sauce—it's the unexpected, "Whoops, what was that! Who was that masked man?" It's just a tickle. Not strong enough to compete, but it's one of those things you see out of the corner

BAR/ENTRY. POSTRIO. PHOTOGRAPH © DENNIS ANDERSON.

MAIN DINING AREA. POSTRIO. PHOTOGRAPH © DENNIS ANDERSON.

of your eye, and you just look twice and don't even know if you really saw it. Also, the fuchsia color that's oozing out the bottom here on the bar is to warm up that icy white marble. And it's a fantasy color because if it had been red, I think it may have had that bordello connotation that bars so often have. And it would have just gone flat. This way, it becomes exciting! It's a stimulating color because it's so unusual.

Q: *The top part of the glass is very intriguing, it has a crystalline quality to it. What is that made of?*
A: It's actually cast from the original molds that were used on the schooners in the 1800s. It's a deck prism. Back in those days, the men would be out to sea for three months, and they couldn't bring enough kerosene to see below, so they would insert these prisms into the decks and the sunlight would be magnified down below so they could see. Again, it's a masculine image, down in the hole of the ship, in dark spaces.

Q: *What's the source of illumination inside that's lighting the glass?*
A: It's an incandescent tubular bulb. It's used in exit signs and instrument panels in aircraft. It's a 145-volt lamp run on a 120-volt circuit, so in effect, it increases the lamp life by a factor of maybe ten to twenty. And the reason I needed that was because it is a difficult lamp to change. I made it as easy as I could, but it takes a little bit of trouble, so this way, they will have to change it maybe only every four years.

Q: *Coming from Postrio, which has a feminine feel to it, Chops seems very strongly masculine. Were you trying to work with that, or was it something that may have stood in your way?*
A: The reason my work is so different each time is because I become part of the project at hand, so I will do what is uniquely right for it. I found it to be a fascinating voyage to go from the soft, pink, cloud-like fluffy floating forms at Postrio to these very solid, angular, compact forms in a dark space. It is a masculine place. It's a place where men have power lunches. There was no interest in wanting women here at all. So it was a challenge, but it was a compelling challenge. I found myself thinking of spaceships and military images and shields and arrows and spears, but not in terms of pain or destruction, more in terms of sculpture. I saw them as masculine sculptures,

and I saw them as shapes that men devise, perhaps for a function, but the shapes themselves were actually sculptures.

It's very interesting to make something that could hurt you, and yet turn that into something that's friendly. And truthfully, I think that's what the source of masculine energy is, and that's what I was working with in this restaurant. It's a power, a force, a raw, crude energy that, when put to good, can serve, and can be tremendously useful. I think this piece may speak about that masculine aspect.

Q: At Splendido's Restaurant, how did you come up with a fixture that worked with this architecture?
A: One of the main concepts was creating a fishing village that would be in the Mediterranean. It, of course, would be near the water, and as in a culture that would span, say, six or seven generations it would have been added to and worked on, so maybe one section of the restaurant might be a little more modern and another part might be really ancient.

There are heavy beams, the whole place is clad with real stacked rock walls that are much heavier than a brick wall would be. That, of course, was

BAR FIXTURE. CHOPS RESTAURANT. PHOTOGRAPH © KEN ALTSHULER.

LARGE VESSEL FIXTURE. SPLENDIDOS. PHOTOGRAPH © DENNIS ANDERSON.

WALL SCONCE. SPLENDIDOS. PHOTOGRAPH © DENNIS ANDERSON.

done in Mexican restaurants in the 1960s quite a bit, so to ask San Francisco to accept this concept and not just write it off as passé was taking a big risk. I needed to figure out how I could let people know immediately that this is a special place and there are some special experiences to have there. So when I was thinking of what I could do to support this new old place in San Francisco, and help it to work, I had to ask myself, "What kind of fixtures do you make for a place like this?" You can't make anything that looks like a light fixture anybody has ever seen anywhere, because it will just be mistakenly thought of as an old-fashioned place. And I couldn't just slap some modern stuff on either, because it would be a pastie and would really be out of place. My answer was to create sculpture, and have it bridge over time, have it be a relic of the future from the past.

Q: The large vessels have a real sense of age to them—they almost look like they have been recovered or reconstructed.
A: I was thinking of what was unique about an old fishing village culture—one of the things that was unique were the containers they used to hold their food that were called *amphorae*. (We use Tupperware and baggies.)

One of the purposes of these fixtures is to be a room divider. So that they would have the magic effect of appearing ghost-like, I decided to make them out of glass. When I was in Turkey, Greece, and Italy, I noticed that almost everything I saw was a relic. It was a broken fragment of something. And museums were full of these reconstructed pieces. So I decided that the way to make them appear and feel the most ancient would be to assemble them as if the fisherman had gone down and collected them on the beach. The pieces were held together in a crude sort of way to make this spirit vessel.

I put sand on the bottom rather than enclosing it, as it would have again that reference to being dug up. Also the light coming through sand is a wonderful color.

Q: When you've got light coming through regular glass it has a somewhat greenish glow to it. On people's skin, that's not very complimentary. How were you able to create this fixture but also make the people that were sitting near it feel comfortable within that light?

A: That was a challenge. I loved that green quality because it looks liquid and watery. The Mediterranean is an incredible turquoise green color and yet this very wonderful color doesn't look good on faces. I took a piece of copper cloth and put it around the bulb, so the bottom would have a peach color and would reflect onto the faces soft skin colors. Then, it would fade into a green watery color. Also, the pink makes the green appear greener.

Q: You were talking about generation to generation—recipes used to be passed through families.
A: It is a very personal concept for me and simply stated it's a bestowal. And it is the idea of being handed something very precious and very sacred by someone who was very close to you. It is something that we in this culture miss out on quite a bit. That feeling that our great grandfather or grandmother has given us something hand-to-hand, touching. Feeling the warmth of her hands. The memory of her perfume. And we often don't know our older people. So again, this restaurant was encompassing generations, it was creating an old place to be and these fixtures are remembering what would happen if we had those generations with us at one time, and they could give us something in a direct, very intentional, very personal presentation. It would be, in fact, our heritage.

Q: Whose hands were the models for the fixtures with hands?
A: I used my own on several and then I used a metalworker's hands. I liked his knuckles quite a bit. They had a kind of earthy quality to them.

Q: Is there a reason for the choice of color for these fixtures? They have, for me, a flame-like quality.
A: Well, again this goes back to those primal memories of antiquity—embers and coals, hearth and heart. The colors being as warm as they are, they are torches on the wall. Embers on the wall, fires on the wall. Again, the idea of being in an ancient place with a flickering flame. And there are also many little creatures swimming in the glass, a little decorative element that looks somewhat like little amoebas. I put those in to capture the idea of a primordial soup, the beginnings of life, the stirrings of the

unconscious. Just some random bits that make us who we are and what we were.

Q: Is there something about the type of food that was being served that had an influence on the sort of offering feeling of these fixtures?
A: Yes, in a sense. There were actually several inspirations for these fixtures. And in a place that is spanning six generations, each generation will probably make up their own interpretation and their own story. Normally, I have one concept. But for these, there are quite a few. One of the concepts was a feast. The food here has a peasant nature to it, as if you could forget the silverware and eat with your hands.

It also has a feeling of bounty. The way the food is presented, and the way it is ordered, so you can imagine patting your stomach after a full meal. The other thing I am working with in these fixtures is the idea of, again, the amphora, a container, a vessel, rather than something that is cut in half and put on the wall like so many sconces today—they are half of something—I wanted this to be all of something.

And in fact, one of the main purposes of my work is to transport people into another time and into another place. If you think about our modern society today, five minutes before a dinner reservation people can be rushing to be on time, they can be cutting people off at lights, stealing parking places, they can be ruthlessly competing to get to the restaurant. And then the minute they walk in the door they have to slow down, stop, and start enjoying themselves. If they were to stay in that mode, they would try to eat their dinner the fastest to win. Well, you don't win anything because you ate your dinner the fastest! You win if you enjoy it the most. So my work is transporting people into this fantasy, where we are just feeling, not thinking, not understanding, not figuring anything out, just there. Just enjoying and just being.

Q: I notice you have names for the fixtures at Granita Restaurant.
A: Yes, they are no longer just fixtures, they are sculptures and they are not just objects, they are creatures. I think the most interesting thing is, although they have no eyes, they seem alive. It is very unusual to be able to relate to or recognize life without the "windows to the soul" as a way

in. The light is the life. I am not working with just pretty things that match the decor. I am working with energy, and forces and power that come with emotion and vital essence. I want people to feel, to react. I don't want them to analyze, or comprehend with their mind alone. I want them to receive beauty viscerally. I want it to be a physical-emotional experience. It is the same difference as eating canned or overcooked vegetables versus fresh garden-grown, vine-ripened tomatoes.

Q: So you are doing with light what Wolfgang Puck has done with the food.
A: Yes, I'm asking how wonderful can it get? And I don't have a cookbook!

Q: The materials are so unusual, what are they?
A: Cast bronze with chemical patinas (no paint), hand-blown glass inset crystals and ivory bubbles. My work for Granita embodies some of the principles most important to me. We're in a very awkward position of appearing very advanced technically and paradoxically, feeling very inadequate and insecure in that technology on an individual basis. I feel design needs to provide a touchstone to the human—to craft, to art, to something that is understandable, that has a footprint of a human being having been there and having touched it, and felt it, and having made it.

Q: The way these are mounted is also quite unusual.
A: Yes, the dancing pods in the bar are tilted sideways as if swimming to the surface and the coral flutes in the private dining room are in diagonal groups of two and three, so they have direction and movement and seem alive rather than geometrically positioned. Granita is an aquatic realm—movement and undulation are how you know you are in an underwater environment. But using real movement can be unsettling. Overstimulation is like overspicing, it interferes with true enjoyment and satisfaction.

Q: The one called "dancing pod" is green; that's not a color you normally use.
A: Ordinarily, I would never have that color near people's faces. But the salmon walls are so hot in color, they reflect the warmth to keep the people

looking tan. Also, the contrast value would have been too low if the pods had been a warm color; they would have disappeared. Rules are meant to be understood, not followed!

Q: And the three fixtures over the bar?
A: I call these the tippy-toe fish. They are sized to be a presence over the bar, yet not block the

view. I made them vertical, like a wine bottle, to accomplish this. The fun is that fish swim sideways, so maybe when they have too much to drink, they get vertical. It is very important at the bar to have some very interesting features, because this stimulates interesting conversations. The more positive the experience, the sooner they will return.

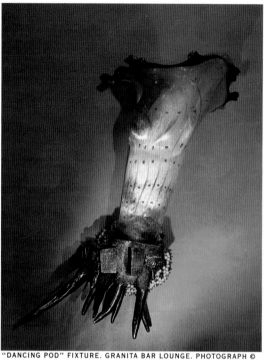

"DANCING POD" FIXTURE. GRANITA BAR LOUNGE. PHOTOGRAPH © MARTIN FINE.

"CORAL FLUTES" FIXTURE. GRANITA PRIVATE DINING AREA. PHOTOGRAPH © MARTIN FINE.

"TIPPY TOE FISH" FIXTURE. GRANITA BAR. PHOTOGRAPH © MARTIN FINE.

"FISH BLOSSOMS" FIXTURE. GRANITA DINING ROOM. PHOTOGRAPH © MARTIN FINE.

RESTAURATEUR'S INGREDIENTS FOR SUCCESS

As Joe Baum states, "Good restaurateurs must have both the experience to develop their technique and the maturity to forget it." The success of any restaurant depends on the vision, focus, passion, and commitment to excellence of the owner and emanates from genuine feelings about people, food, service, and style. "The very nature of our business is individual attention to each individual customer and each owner must nourish and feed the restaurant and make sure that it's success is sustained by hard work." The persona of each restaurateur, the sum of his or her intellect and feelings about hospitality, must be conveyed to the management team and staff to insure success.

Creating and sustaining a hit restaurant depends on hundreds of ingredients that must blend to satisfy customer expectations. Each restaurateurs' recipe for success is based on years of experience both positive and negative, resulting in the ability to recognize an opportunity and respond to it. Most restaurateurs would agree that creating a successful restaurant is part experience, part knowledge, mixed with more than a pinch of magic. The ability to create a restaurant concept that satisfies customer demand is extremely elusive with constant changes in demographic mix, food trends, competition, and economic conditions.

In the interviews that follow, Richard Melman, Wolfgang Puck, Barbara Lazaroff, and Alan Stillman share their insights regarding their overall concepts—on location, menu, service style, design, staff selection, training, and management philosophy—that contributed to their successes.

Although they each readily admit that their concepts are no proven recipe for success, each of them share an essential ingredient: an overwhelming commitment to provide great food, service, and value and to insure that each customer feels special.

LETTUCE ENTERTAIN YOU ENTERPRISES, INC.

The credo of Lettuce Entertain You Enterprises, Inc. (hereafter referred to as Lettuce Entertain You), is, "Deliver great food, great service, value, and fun while making each customer feel special."

It's a credo and concept that Richard Melman, president of Lettuce Entertain You, his partners, and a team of nearly 4,000 employees have fine-tuned since Lettuce Entertain You's first restaurant, RJ Grunt's, opened in 1971 with an investment of $17,000.

Since that time, Melman, "the man with the golden touch," and his partners have created a string of the most successful restaurants in the country, including: Café Ba Ba Reeba!, Scoozi, Shaw's Crab House, Ed Debevic's Short/Orders Deluxe, Avanzare, Ambria, The Pump Room, Un Grand Café, Hat Dance, Bub City, Tucci Benucch,

and the Eccentric. Recently, Lettuce Entertain You has opened the Corner Bakery, Maggiano's Little Italy, and Pappagus, a Greek restaurant.

A Chicago native, Melman was born into the business of restaurants (his father owned a delicatessen) and was raised in the city's Logan Square neighborhood. As a boy, Melman would rather have played baseball than worked, yet he found himself turning to the foodservice industry when he needed to earn money for school expenses and entertainment. Melman did everything from grilling burgers to selling Good Humor bars to peddling hot dogs.

After high school, Melman tried college. In fact, he tried several! He never could, however, settle down at any particular school long enough to earn his degree. Next, he decided to spend some time in the family business, and for four years, he immersed himself in every detail of foodservice.

Finally, Melman felt he had found something he excelled at and enjoyed. Based on the numerous vacations his father and his partner were taking, and their increased reliance on his efforts in the restaurant, he believed he had earned a deserved partnership in the family business and asked his father for one. Says Melman, "When I asked them if I could buy into it, they said no, claiming that I wasn't ready. When that happened, something inside me changed and I knew I could not stay in their business any more and work with the same level of interest."

Frustrated and a little disheartened, Melman left town and sought his fortune elsewhere. He worked at other restaurants, but later returned to Chicago, where he became a manager at a popular eatery. Melman, however, was not satisfied—he wanted to open his own restaurant and experiment with new food concepts, styles of service, and decor.

In 1970, Melman took his first step toward making the dream of his own creation a reality when he met Jerry A. Orzoff, a successful real estate developer. Melman regarded Orzoff as a savvy businessman, and Orzoff soon became and remained a mentor of Melman. Orzoff in return liked Melman's offbeat ideas. They decided to pull together, combined and raised the necessary funds, and opened their first restaurant, RJ Grunt's, in Chicago's Lincoln Park on June 10, 1971.

Melman poured every creative idea he had into the restaurant. He added a bit of deli because he knew it and Jerry liked it. He put in a dash of macrobiotic and even added a new concept, a gigantic salad bar, but nothing appeared to work in those early weeks. Almost a month after opening, there were no sales in sight and Melman had to face the fact that the restaurant might not succeed and he might have to take several extra side jobs to pay back the loans.

Throughout those difficult days, Orzoff supported Melman and encouraged him to believe what he was hearing from his friends and on the street: that RJ Grunt's was fun and unique and would catch on soon. Says Melman, "Those first weeks at RJ Grunt's taught me something very important that I will never forget. No matter how much work we put into a new restaurant and no matter if we think everything is perfect, there is no guarantee of success, and we must never take that for granted.

"There were two people who were important in my life in terms of male figures. One was my father and the other was Jerry. Without Jerry, this never would have happened," says Melman of his late partner and friend, who died in 1991. "He taught me how important a good partnership can be to success."

The eventual success of RJ Grunt's helped build Melman's confidence and gave him energy. His and Orzoff's ideas were beginning to be realized. Throughout the 1970s, they opened a string of exciting and popular restaurants. And today, Melman, with his family of partners, owns and manages more than thirty restaurants nationwide and in Japan, with annual sales in excess of $100 million.

RICHARD MELMAN

Q: *How do you develop the concepts for your restaurants?*
A: The ideas for most of Lettuce Entertain You's restaurants are developed from an initial story line prepared by me. These stories define the style, food, decor, and location for each space. A team of seven to twelve people is assembled, consisting of chefs, architects, artists, a managing partner, a staff trainer, and other support personnel. Using this story as a basic canvas, the team then layers and develops the initial idea.

The development of each concept after a story has been written is the key to the success of Lettuce Entertain You's concepts. At Lettuce, opening a restaurant—especially in the past five years—is like producing a film. I begin with a storyboard and write a description of a proposed restaurant to express my feelings and associations about the concept and to keep the team focused. I'm interested in creating "real" spaces that customers can associate with, that create a "sense of place."

The script of Ed Debevic's Short/Orders Deluxe revolves around a crazy, fun-filled, and irreverent story line. The year is 1952. Returning from the Korean War, a young man dreams of building a small business, something dear to his heart and framed in his memory—a diner, all booths and countertops and brushed chrome appliances, where waitresses serve up simple stick-to-the-ribs food and a little big-sister friendliness and advice. A place just like his favorite diner alongside a country highway in his hometown of Talooca, Illinois, where he once worked.

Ed, the fictitious star of this hit production, is a big guy in his early fifties with an impressive gut who likes to bowl and drink beer. He's the kind of guy who makes sure Pulaskis (translation: a shot and a beer) are on the menu in the company of highballs and Rob Roys. His Brunswick "Black Beauty" bowling ball is on display with a half-dozen trophies.

Q: *How do you choose the locations for your restaurants?*
A: I have an idea file of restaurant concepts that I have compiled over the years. When I feel the time is ripe for a particular concept, I try to find a location that is compatible with this concept.

I knew Scoozi wanted to be a large, fun, festive Italian restaurant, and I began to look for a large open building in an industrial area of Chicago. I narrowed it down to the River North area, a district that had many art galleries, but was somewhat out of the way. I sensed that this area was improving and selected a building suitable for the concept. The space felt "real" for the kind of restaurant I had in mind. This "real" quality is one of the most important factors in selecting a site. Scoozi could not work in a downtown office building.

Bub City was a concept that I had for over three years before finding a location. Bub City is a crab shack, barbeque, country-western, hillbilly kind of place that couldn't work in an upscale location. I wanted the yuppie to feel a little nervous walking to this place and found a location in an industrial area of Chicago.

The compatibility of the location and the concept must occur if my idea for a particular restaurant is to succeed. A county-western, shit-kicking space just wouldn't feel right on Michigan Avenue. It wouldn't be real, have an edge to it, and be unique.

I feel that my instinct for picking a location for a specific concept negates the need for in-depth demographic analysis. If the location doesn't fit my image, it won't work. The location must make economic sense as well before it is selected. Patience is the key to finding the right location for a particular concept, and I don't dilute a concept I've had in mind for several years just to suit a location.

I know Chicago extremely well and I don't need a demographic survey to tell me where to locate a particular concept. I suspect, however, as we expand outside of Chicago, we will need to rely more on demographic analysis.

Q: *How important is the design of each concept?*
A: The difference between a great restaurant and a good restaurant is attention to detail. We assemble a team of architects, interior designers, and artists to create "real" environments. The overall design concept and all the decorative details are essential in order for the story that we've created to be perceived as real by the customer.

Q: *Is a budget prepared for each project?*
A: Most of the time we do not exceed budgets by very much. We have an experienced team who visits the site, analyzes problems, and prepares a detailed estimate of the entire cost of the project. Once the overall theme of the restaurant is established, we are interested in maintaining its integrity. Again, I feel the decor must be "real," and we try not to sacrifice any important finishes, lighting, furniture, or artwork. The story we've created must be maintained or else the customer will be confused.

Q: *Do you prepare a pro forma for each concept?*
A: Yes. Much of the success of Lettuce Entertain You comes from strong company discipline. Like the old Green Bay Packers, we know how to win. We're known for our fun, creative side, but I feel much of the credit for our success goes to our accounting and analytical departments.

A team analyzes each space and prepares a thorough pro forma. Problem areas are identified that could increase the budget and are factored into the pro forma. As many as twenty pro formas are prepared for different concepts and locations each year. Only two or three of these concepts are developed. A preliminary space plan is developed to determine seating capacity before a space is selected.

Each of these concepts must provide quality and value for the customer or else it won't work. We structure each deal financially in order to provide this quality and value.

Q: *How are the menus developed?*
A: A great deal of research goes into determining a menu for our restaurants. If we're doing a Greek restaurant, we will evaluate what's currently being served at other establishments. We will travel to Greece and taste as many dishes as we can. We then develop our own recipes and taste-test them. Each week, we'll taste a component of the menu. One week we'll try appetizers; another week we'll

taste soups or entrées. This taste-testing process takes a lot of discipline and time, but is an essential reason why we are successful. At many of our restaurants, we offer foods that are low in fat and sodium because so many of our customers are health conscious.

During the menu-testing phase of the project, we test for taste and presentation to determine how appealing the menu item will be to the customer. All the items selected have to taste wonderful and look great on the plate in order to create a sense of value. We sometimes select an item whose food cost may be very high, but overflows on the plate and captures the attention of the customer. We also try to imagine what the first hundred customers will eat to determine what will be on the menu. We are committed to providing value and quality for our customer, which are reflected in higher food costs. These higher food costs can be mitigated by better control of labor, operating expenses, or volume.

Q: How is staff selected and trained?
A: We try to select appropriate staff to suit the personality of each of our projects. A profile of the type of person required for a particular restaurant is established, and a staff is selected that fits that profile.

At Café Ba Ba Reeba!, we chose staff members who could speak a smattering of Spanish to serve up the small-portioned foods, and found a Spanish-born chef/partner with extensive experience in Spanish cooking. At Ambria, it might be someone who is impeccably knowledgeable, yet very friendly. At Ed's, the requirement might be someone who can keep things going with the flow of a Mel's Diner. The ability to pop bubble gum with a loud snap doesn't hurt either.

One of our strengths is the ability to "hire right" and "train right." We spend a lot of time selecting, training, and developing our staff—three to four weeks are spent training the staff prior to each restaurant's opening. We are now serving 140,000 to 150,000 customers per week in over thirty restaurants, and our service staff is our most important asset. We have to work with them every day to develop their skills, since you can't expect to train them in a three-week period. In addition, we have to provide a pleasant working environment and attend to their emotional needs. We have flexible schedules, generous health insurance benefits, vacation pay, and psychological counseling for those who need it. We also help employees find an apartment or buy a car.

Job applicants are judged 49 percent on skills and experience and 51 percent on strength, confidence, leadership ability, and what kind of person they are. We try to find enthusiastic, bright people who have a positive attitude, aren't easily offended, and genuinely care about making people comfortable and happy. Twice a year, groups of employees are encouraged to meet with the partners in strict confidence to assess their bosses, their restaurants, and the company at large.

I am a firm believer in teamwork, and I reward good managers by making them partners.

Q: Why is Lettuce Entertain You so successful?
A: You don't have to be a genius to be successful in this business. Creating and sustaining a restaurant is relatively simple:
1. You have to understand what you want to accomplish, recognize the opportunity, and stay focused.
2. You need to find the right location and make the best financial deal.
3. You have to hire, train, and develop your staff.
4. Create a simple, "real" environment that captures the spirit of the times and fits the market niche.
5. Be capable of enduring the difficult times.

We've hit a lot of home runs with the bases loaded and have also hit a lot of singles and doubles. We feel we succeed when we stretch a single into a double and sustain it. Scoozi, Café Ba Ba Reeba!, Bub City, and several others were home runs, but some others were singles over the past twenty years. We succeed because we recognize the danger signals, have patience, and know how to adapt and deal with the rough times.

I'd say that the fear of screwing up has also contributed to our success. We concentrate on what we're doing, stay very focused, and we carefully review food costs, menu selections, level of service, construction costs, location, rent, staff selection, and the fifty other factors that contribute to the restaurant's success before committing to a project.

People have gotten more sophisticated. It used to be that to run a successful restaurant, all you needed was good food. Then you needed not just good food, but good service, too. Now you need to deliver great food, great service, ambience, and possess a "real" sense of what people want!

Barbara Lazaroff and Wolfgang Puck together have revolutionized the restaurant industry. Spago, Chinois, Eureka, and their latest endeavor, Granita, are all magical places where food and design combine to treat all the senses.

Barbara Lazaroff, president of Imaginings Interior Design, Inc. and co-owner of the four restaurants, designed Spago, where she helped introduce the exhibition kitchen; Chinois On Main, a Fellini-esque rendition of Asia; Eureka, inspired by the mechanics of the brewer's art and the classic films *Metropolis* and Chaplin's *Modern Times*; and Granita, in Malibu, a dynamic and wildly unique "abstract interpretation" of the quality of light and sense of movement underwater. In addition, Barbara Lazaroff has designed projects in Japan and Los Angeles, including Spago Tokyo, The Playboy Club in Japan, and Shane Hidden on the Glen Restaurant.

Wolfgang Puck, one of the most innovative and influential chef/restaurateurs in America, is credited with the innovation of a multicultural cooking style, using only the freshest of ingredients, in what is widely known now as *California cuisine*. His cooking style has been imitated from Tokyo to Paris. Puck is also president of the Wolfgang Puck Food Company, which manufactures and markets a line of frozen gourmet pizzas nationwide and is in the process of expanding the initial pizza outlet at Macy's San Francisco throughout the country. In addition to the four restaurants, which are examined in this book, Postrio Restaurant in the Prescott Hotel was opened in 1989, has been praised as a culinary masterpiece, and is indeed a phenomenally successful enterprise. Wolfgang Puck has also been a regular guest chef for more than seven years on "Good Morning America," and his culinary talents can be enjoyed at home via his video "Cooking with Wolfgang Puck" (scripted and designed by Barbara Lazaroff). He is also the author of *Modern French Cooking for the American Kitchen* (New York: Houghton Mifflin), and *The Wolfgang Puck Cookbook* and *Adventures in the Kitchen*, both published by Random House. Spago Las Vegas is slated to open in the fall of 1992.

Lazaroff and Puck take a true mom-and-pop approach with regard to the development, management, and day-to-day operations of each of their restaurants. They also believe that "if you want the community to be interested in your restaurants, you must be interested in the community." The innumerable charities they have dedicated their time and talents to is a testament to their commitment to this tenet. The American Wine and Food Festival, which Spago organized in 1983 to support Meals on Wheels to aid elderly and all homebound individuals, has raised more than $1.6 million. Additionally, they are deeply committed to the American Cancer Society with an annual event, as well as various AIDS organizations. Wolfgang Puck has contributed enormously to various programs and events for the support and education of young culinary and hospitality students. Barbara Lazaroff is a dedicated supporter of various social issues, including the advancement of women as a member of the Network of Executive Women in Hospitality, the Women's Hollywood Political Committee, and as a lecturer within her field of design and as a member of such budding organizations as California Women in Environmental Design.

Puck and Lazaroff feel that "the moment you believe 'you've made it' is the moment you better prepare for the 'ride down the hill'!" They are constantly reexamining their methods, goals, and opportunities and believe they are learning all the time. They are also hoping that Puck's brother Klaus, a student of Cornell's School for Hotel and Restaurant Management, and their three-year-old son, Cameron, will prove to be assets in their restaurants and make it possible for them to take a few more vacations!

BARBARA LAZAROFF

Q: Why do you think your restaurants are so successful?
A: They are each individual, spirited, stimulating, nurturing environments that celebrate the sensual act of eating. Their focus is on the creative, spontaneous preparation and presentation of food. Customers keep coming back because great food is served at reasonable prices in a comfortable, casual environment where each person feels special. The restaurants are successful because we work very hard to please our customers. The restaurant business is about people and service.

Wolf and I truly enjoy making people happy with food, design, and service. Our customers know that we care about them, and the quality and value of the food served. We make each customer feel appreciated and welcome in our restaurants, which keeps them coming back. We know our market and understand our customer extremely well. We know how to treat them and what makes them happy. People feel that each of our restaurants is an extension of their home.

Each of our restaurants has chefs who are stars in their own right and are managed by experienced people who are committed to quality and excellence in food and service. I've long believed that the harder you work, the more luck you have. Spago was very much a hit from the beginning, but the initial funding, development, and subsequent managing of all of the restaurants was never a *given*. I think much of our success is owed to how we treat our employees, and how in turn how they treat our customers. In addition, careful management and cost controls are of the utmost importance.

Q: Why do you feel so many restaurants fail in their first year?
A: Perhaps the biggest reason is undercapitalization. Not having enough money to complete the project as conceived, and not having enough working capital for the crucial first year. Funds must be reserved for opening inventories, public relations, start-up salaries, and utilities. Ninety percent of restaurants fail in great part because of poor management. Some great chef/restaurateurs have failed because they are not good businesspeople. They can't control food costs and in some cases, they can't command respect from their staff.

Q: How do you select and train your staff?
A: You can make a nice person a good waiter, but you can't make a good waiter a nice person. We try to hire happy, friendly people who are passionate about food and service. All of our wait staff are extremely knowledgeable about the food and wine served. Frequently, wine seminars, cooking classes, and regular tastings at staff meetings help keep the wait staff and management informed. At Granita, all of the wait staff rotate and work in the kitchen once a week in order to understand how the food is prepared.

We need a staff that knows our customer. Many people dine at our restaurants three to four times a week, at the same time, year after year. It is very important that we know the people in the community where the restaurant is located. Many of our staff who work the door at our restaurants have been with us for many years. They know each customer and make them feel special. If a customer is on a Pritikin diet, or is allergic to walnuts, our staff can advise them to order an appropriate dish. We want our staff to be friendly, but don't want them to be effusive with remarks like, "Hi, I'm Tracy, and I'm your waitress today." Service at all of our restaurants is amiable but professional.

There is always a waiting list of well-qualified people looking for an opportunity to work at all of our restaurants, because of the opportunity to learn and advance within the organization. Wolfgang attracts many young chefs who are eager to learn his techniques, and, in fact, over the years many have gone on to open their own successful restaurants. Additionally, the employees are compensated well, not only in salary, but we provide good health care benefits and a sense of stability. Also, people enjoy working in an environment that is energized and fun.

A large portion of our staff, including management, at all of our restaurants is female. Wolf was one of the first chefs to have women cooks in the kitchen, and I wanted them on the waitstaff and in management positions. It is also very important that we maintain discipline; however, we must also sustain a high level of morale. Without the support, loyalty, and integrity of the staff, we ultimately fail.

Each restaurant has an executive chef and a sous chef. Many people think that Wolfgang is chef at all these restaurants. While he hires and gives direction to all his chefs, and cooks in one of the restaurants every night, each restaurant could not succeed unless each chef were totally dedicated and fully involved on a moment-to-moment basis within each aspect of the daily operations of the kitchen. They also add their own accents and personality to Wolf's direction. I believe that behind every great legend are a lot of little legends. Each of our chefs is a star in his or her own right. They are in control and have, as they must, the power to hire and fire.

Q: How important is the kitchen design to the success of the restaurant?
A: Paramount. In all of our restaurants, the design of the kitchen comes first. Forty percent of the

entire restaurant at Spago is devoted to the kitchen and back of the house, because our focus is on the preparation and presentation of fine food. Appropriate space has to be set aside for equipment, storage and prep areas, and staff circulation.

Each chef, line cook, and wait staff works incredibly hard for long hours where deadlines occur every few minutes. It is truly athletic work and requires intense concentration. There must be enough space so that people aren't colliding with each other constantly. In addition, the cooks must have sufficient light and efficient ventilation so that they can work comfortably.

The finish materials used in the kitchen must be easily maintainable and durable, so that they don't self-destruct.

Q: How has the exhibition kitchen contributed to your success?
A: The exhibition kitchen is not a new idea. There have been exhibition kitchens in Europe and in the United States. Wolfgang wanted everyone to see the fresh, locally grown ingredients he was using in the preparation of the food. The exhibition kitchen allowed customers to share in the excitement of this new cooking style. It also created a sense of warmth by allowing customers to feel like they were eating in a big eat-in kitchen.

The energy and excitement of seeing wonderful food prepared in a dramatic setting created a sense of participatory theater that has become a trademark for our restaurants. It works for us, but it doesn't work for everyone. Many chefs feel uncomfortable in an exhibition kitchen. Additionally, there are lighting and ventilation problems as well as maintenance issues.

Q: Why do you think the sense of whimsy and fantasy have become so important to the restaurant experience?
A: Fantasy is so important to me because I grew up in a little apartment in the Bronx, and my dream was to travel around the world and see everything there was to see. I had an inner fantasy life and then later, having the opportunity to travel, I collected an additional array of visual imagery. When I had the opportunity to design restaurants, nothing could be more fun than to share my visual experiences by creating visually rich environments. I'm actually quite analytical, but my initial designs are spontaneous and come from the heart. It is in the later phases of refining the work that I become quite technical and exacting. But my true excitement about my work is that I can touch people by creating environments that are stimulating, nurturing, and seductive.

Eating is a sensual experience. Our first contact with hunger and pleasure as a child creates a love affair with food—I understand that even further now that I am a mother. A restaurant that stimulates all of our senses heightens the pleasure of eating and makes it enjoyable. The diaphanous glow from the lighting at Granita, the sensual forms and colors at Chinois, and the fantasy of being inside a brewery at Eureka make dining in each of them an event.

If people feel, however, that the space is more important than they are, they're diminished by it. They have to feel they're completing it.

Q: How important is lighting as a component in the design of your restaurant?
A: Lighting is the most important element in the design of a restaurant environment. You can take the same room and light it differently and create an entirely different mood. The quality of light in a room is so visceral and affects the senses very deeply. Light affects the nervous system and emotional responses to the degree that deprived of it, people withdraw and feel depressed.

Color and light are interrelated and when blended properly make food and people look their best. Because our kitchens are exposed, however, I have to make sure that there is enough light for the chef to see the food and work surfaces. This creates brightness and glare problems because the kitchen is part of the dining room. It can destroy the mood in the space entirely. To overcome this problem, I use large aperture fixtures to produce an even wash of light in the kitchen behind a soffit that doubles as a fire curtain. I also place shielded small Halogen lights directly over the display counter to illuminate the food. These small focused light sources allow the waiters to see the food without letting light spill into the dining room.

The ambient and decorative lighting in each of our restaurants has become more sophisticated. Granita has a plethora of light sources for general illumination and special effects. I choose the best source for each design application I can find and adapt them to suit each area of the space. Title 24, the state energy code in California, restricts the amount of energy we can use in a restaurant environment. Because Granita is also a "gallery," and the brew tank areas at Eureka are considered "display," we were able to use more light. The lighting in Granita had to abstractly evoke the mystical, mysterious, primordial quality that one associates with the sea. The only way to accomplish that was with blown glass that had a great deal of depth and color. The fixtures that Pam Morris created are soothing and evoke a diaphanous, mystical fantasy.

Q: How long should a restaurant design endure?
A: If it is designed with the proper ingredients of space, scale, color, texture, and form, and has energy and style, it could last indefinitely. Spago and Chinois have been open for many years and have yet to be remodeled. The materials used at all of our restaurants are easy to maintain and are enduring. The materials utilized at Chinois have held up extremely well over the last nine years. I think that if they self-destructed within the first two years, when we were struggling financially, and we had had to remodel, we might not have made it.

Q: What is the future for the restaurant industry?
A: People will always need to go to a restaurant to have fun and eat wonderful food. We have become intoxicated as a culture with the creations of a generation of young, incredibly talented chefs. "Casual dining" has made great food affordable to the millions of Americans that are working harder and harder to make a living. Two-career families find it difficult to make time to prepare food at home, and even though one would surmise that dual salaries would create more disposable income, the present economic conditions are making it less affordable for the middle and working classes to dine out.

Restaurants, however, are not getting cheaper to build. Taxes, food, and labor costs are continually rising, and therefore restaurateurs face the challenge of keeping rising costs under control. We, however, have never strived to have the lowest operating costs in town; our goal has always been to provide great food and ambience and great service at a great value. It is a constant balancing act. Perhaps we will continue to see more and more upscale establishments where the chair that was once occupied for the entire evening needs to be turned twice or more. There is also a growing interest in dining at home, and

especially in well-prepared take-home food; but nothing will ever replace the experience of going out to a great restaurant. Customers, however, must feel that they've received real value. The future of the restaurant industry? I am certain Wolfgang would say that the general direction is toward a greater number of smaller chef-owned and -operated restaurants with ethnic influences becoming increasingly prominent. As for a comprehensive answer, well, entire books can and have been written regarding trends for the future, and no one seems to agree. Perhaps we're not the ones to ask; we don't predict—we **do**!

WOLFGANG PUCK

Q: Why do you think all of your restaurants are so successful?
A: Restaurants are a *people* and service business. If you're going to be successful, you must hire happy, friendly people . . . . The wait staff must have the same passion for food and wine as the chef. If they're a vegetarian and don't like wine, it's going to be hard to convey a sense of excitement about a wonderful quail or a good chardonnay to the customer. Wait staff must be good psychiatrists and actors as well. If they are not happy, it's important to still convey a feeling of warmth and friendliness to the customer. The patrons must still think everybody in the restaurant is there to make them happy.

Q: Can a restaurant be successful if the owner is not there?
A: I think so. It really depends on the style of the restaurant. Spago is a much better restaurant now than it was when it first opened. I was there every day for the first year and we had many operational problems. Thank God we had so many customers. I think it is a more profitable and better-organized restaurant now because we have trained a staff that is extremely capable of operating the restaurant by itself.

We have several restaurants, and our customers don't expect us to be at each restaurant every night. They are coming because they like the food, the ambience, the spirit, and the service. Our persona is in each restaurant even if we are not there in person. Our menu is balanced, so customers can eat very well and spend $30 or splurge and spend $100.

Q: How do you keep staff morale high?

A: The kitchen in all of our restaurants is part of the dining room. The chefs and line cooks get to know the customers. Food journalists often write about each chef in our restaurants. This praise helps contribute to keeping morale high. Customers come up to the counter and talk to the cooks, telling them how they loved the food. It's much better than working in the "basement," like I did when I was at Maxim's in Paris. Waiters and door staff know most of our customers, so there's a certain family spirit. Since we have several restaurants, there is a lot of opportunity for promotion. Through years of experience and advancement, a dishwasher may, as at Spago, become a line cook. A busboy can, as at Granita, become a floor manager. Frequent staff meetings help to clear any bad feelings and keep employees involved in decision making.

Q: Do you have to go to school to become a chef?

A: No. You don't have to go to school to learn how to cook. It is not a science. It's very straightforward. You learn by practicing. Some people have more innate talent than others, but if you have interest and passion, you will be able to spend sixteen hours a day in the kitchen and think this is your hobby. I feel people pay me for what I really love to do—what can beat that feeling in life?

Q: How many hours do you work each day?

A: From 8:00 in the morning 'til 1:00 A.M. About seventeen hours. I am trying to work out a schedule where I work three weeks and take three or four days off.

Q: What advice would you give a new restaurateur?

A: To work hard and be patient. Success does not come overnight. It takes a lot of time and dedication to be successful in this business. All of our restaurants have been a struggle. Success has not come easily.

Q: Where did you receive your training?

A: I started when I was fourteen as an apprentice in a small hotel restaurant in Austria. For the next seven years, I worked in several restaurants in France, including the L'Oustou de Baumaniere in Provence, Maxim's in Paris, and the Hotel de Paris in Monaco. Jean de Noyer, a restaurateur from New York, brought me to the States in 1973, but I never worked in New York. My first job in the United States was at La Tour in Indianapolis, where I worked for a year. In 1974, I moved to Los Angeles, and after six months in a miserable downtown eatery, I became the chef and partner at Ma Maison restaurant and Ma Cuisine cooking school until I left in 1981 to open Spago.

Q: What has influenced your style of cooking?

A: I have been in love with food and cooking since I was a young boy. My mother was a chef and I was surrounded by wonderful aromas in the kitchen. I was trained in France and I have been inspired by the different cultures in this country. Fifteen years ago, a restaurant had to serve French food to be great. Now restaurants have become much more diverse, and so have people's taste buds. Heavy, complex, masking sauces have been replaced by the natural flavors of the ingredients.

A new cuisine has evolved with chefs experimenting with a variety of foods and spices from the Far East, South America, and Europe. Our food is simpler and healthier, with more fish and poultry, salads and fresh vegetables, and less red meat. Sauces are lighter, with grilling and roasting replacing heavier types of cooking.

Q: Who purchases the food for your restaurants?

A: I go to the fish market in downtown Los Angeles four times a week. It's important to touch and feel the food you're going to cook. If you were going to buy a car, you wouldn't purchase it and call the salesman to send it over without test driving it. You'd go there to look at many cars before you made a selection. Our produce is selected from quality local farms, such as the Chino Ranch in Rancho Santa Fe. Lamb and quail are purchased from specialty farms in Sacramento. Fish is procured directly from fishermen in Nantucket, Florida, and Alaska.

Q: Who is involved in selecting the items for the tabletop?

A: Both Barbara and I feel that what people touch and see is very important. Our wine glasses are crystal, and are made by Riedel of Austria. When you drink fine wine, you expect it to be served in fine crystal. Our china is manufactured by Villeroy and Bosch, and our flatware is silverplate from Oneida.

Q: Do you need to prepare a pro forma and market analysis for each restaurant?
A: No! We know west L.A. very well. Experience has taught us about food costs, our potential customer, and location. Our gut feelings tell us if a restaurant should have 80 or 200 seats, and what the average check should be. People are not discouraged if they have to drive 10 minutes or 30 minutes. We are fortunate to have a very loyal following. If we built a restaurant in East Los Angeles, I'm not sure how well we would do.

Q: What is the organizational structure for all the restaurants?
A: All the restaurants are autonomous; we don't have a corporate structure. At Spago, we have a general manager, Tom Kaplan, who is also our partner. Ultimately, I think it would be best to have a managing partner at each restaurant.

We promote from within and each general manager and chef is responsible for hiring and firing at each restaurant. Our staff contributes greatly to our enduring success.[1]

THE NEW YORK RESTAURANT GROUP

The New York Restaurant Group is one of the most successful restaurant organizations in the United States. It owns and operates some of New York's best restaurants, including Smith & Wollensky, Manhattan Ocean Club, La Cité, and The Post House. The group consists of twelve people who are responsible for marketing, public relations, accounting, concept development, and operations. Alan Stillman, president and founder, created The New York Restaurant Group in 1972. He owned and operated fifteen restaurants, among them TGI Friday's, prior to starting this organization.

ALAN STILLMAN

Q: How are the concepts for your restaurants developed?
A: When I opened TGI Friday's in 1965, I didn't know much about the restaurant business. Its success was owed in large part to luck. I had no idea what I was doing. Since then, I have created twenty-nine successful restaurants that have depended on experience, careful planning, and sound business principles.

We are in the business of creating 200-plus seat restaurants with an average check of $40, and we must provide environments that justify spending that kind of money, because 50 percent of our business is corporate and the other 50 percent individuals. Most of our customers are "upper income bracket," and are on expense accounts, while 80 percent of the checks are picked up by men.

We build one restaurant a year that we hope will be around for many years, since we are not in the business of creating trendy restaurants. Our goal is to develop restaurants that gross $7 to $15 million a year.

Many of the storyboards for these restaurants were changed before, during, and after the restaurants were built. Manhattan Ocean Club started out without tablecloths. We had antique copper table bases and beautiful wood tabletops, and after six months of complaints, we switched to tablecloths. The original wooden tabletop selection didn't work for a fine seafood restaurant in midtown Manhattan.

The original idea for Manhattan Ocean Club was to create an informal Soho-like seafood restaurant that felt like an art gallery. It didn't work. We needed to create an upscale look for the kind of customer we were attracting, so we bought more Picasso sculpture, included finer linen service, and the space began to suit its customer base.

In Cité, we went to the flea market in Paris and purchased incredible antique chandeliers that came from a twenties movie theater. Six months later, we discovered that they don't work for what we are trying to do in New York. We were trying to do a tongue-in-cheek informal french restaurant, and we thought the chandeliers were funky. Although similar chandeliers are used routinely in Parisian brasseries, they were perceived as formal by some of our patrons, and it made the restaurant look uptight. Down came the chandeliers, which cost $30,000.

Cité was to be the "Brasserie for the Eighties," but didn't anticipate the recession of the 1990s. You must be flexible enough to change the environment and menu to suit changes in the economy. Now the restaurant is a grand café that serves higher-priced, more sophisticated French food, and the decor had to be more informal.

Remember, we plan to have Cité around for the next twenty years, and we can afford to break even for a few years until the economy turns around.

It used to be that "location, location, location" was the most important factor in determining a restaurant's success. I think that's old. People now say it's "service, service, service." That's old. I think you need good food, not great food. You need a good environment, not a great environment. You need good service, not great service. Then you have to find your niche and determine how you need to improve to meet your customers' expectation levels.

Q: How are the design concepts developed?
A: We design our restaurants for the long haul. Each of our spaces is a classic that can withstand the test of time, and Arnold Syrop and I choose quality materials, artwork, and lighting to create environments that are visually rich and convey an image of quality.

For Manhattan Ocean Club, we bought sixty-five antique column capitals. For La Cité, the railings were purchased in a flea market. The bar rail in Cité is from the original Bon March Department store, and there is $400,000 worth of art on the walls of Manhattan Ocean Club. Does this make a difference? I'm not sure. Does the customer notice? I don't know.

We feel the commitment to quality is understood unconsciously by our customers and contributes to the appeal of our restaurants. It reflects the expectations of the customer we are trying to attract, namely the businesspeople.

Q: How do you select locations?
A: We spent two and a half years looking for a space for La Cité that could seat 250 people on one floor in midtown Manhattan. There were not that many spaces that large available. Manhattan Ocean Club, Cité, and Smith & Wollensky are not site specific; they would work anywhere in midtown Manhattan.

Q: How are budgets developed?
A: Cité cost $5 million to build. The original budget was $4.4 million, and not one single design compromise was made, since everything that was originally designed was included. We have a world-class location in the Time/Life building in Manhattan, seating 300 people, and have an opportunity to gross $15 million, so we

made a commitment to design the best restaurant we could, and let it rip.

Q: How do you select and train your staff?
A: The key to running many restaurants is finding and keeping key personnel. We believe strongly in delegating a great deal of responsibility to the chefs, managers, and key wait staff of each of our restaurants, and we tell them that they are on their own. The chefs, after they have worked with us a year or two, are better be able to create their own menus and call us on the phone once a month and tell us the menu is available for tasting. The chef at Manhattan Ocean Club changes the menu without consultation. He is on his own. We know he understands food cost and the customers' expectations.

We interview hundreds of applicants for each of our restaurants before selecting them, and we usually allow three weeks for front-of-the-house staff training. Training is a continuous kind of program, since one year after opening you might have five waiters left from the fifty you hired.

The New York Restaurant Group has created a "farm system" of personnel that are trained within the organization and promoted as they acquire experience. The manager at Smith & Wollensky's grill, who has been there for three years, has been transferred to La Cité to run the grill there. He has developed experience in running a grill with an average check of $27.

The general manager for each restaurant is a managing partner and must consult with the other partners before making changes to the menu, price, and decor."

Q: How important are public relations, advertising, marketing?
A: We do more public relations, advertising, and marketing than any other chain operator in the country. It is immensely important to the success of the organization, because we try to establish the widest possible base of customers. We draw from all over the country and want to be the place to go for business people and tourists. This customer base could not be established without spending over a million dollars in advertising a year.

We are criticized by other organizations for how much advertising we do. I'm not sure why. I think it's ludicrous not to tell people what you have to offer and where you are. Every other product in the U.S. is advertised. Why not high-end restaurants?

Q: Could your restaurants have failed?

A: Each one of my restaurants were brought back from the brink of disaster. Smith & Wollensky opened in the middle of a recession in 1977 and was almost destroyed by fire three months after it opened. We got a review four months after it opened from the *New York Times* that was terrible, and overcame this negative review by serving better food and beginning an aggressive advertising and marketing program. We raised additional capital from the limited partners to accomplish this goal. Unlike a bad movie that can't be fixed after it's released, a restaurant can change and improve with better service and food.

Q: What is the future for the restaurant industry?

A: You can open a restaurant with four white walls with great food prepared by a great chef and serve a hundred covers a night and be successful. But you're not in the restaurant business, you're running a restaurant. You are a restaurateur, not a businessman!

The future for creating and maintaining great restaurants over the next twenty years will depend on people who understand the restaurant business, specifically, organizations that operate several restaurants, since these organizations have experience and purchasing power that enable them to provide consistent quality in food, service, and decor. They can afford it.

It has happened in the hotel business. The chain operators have created the best hotels in the world. The Four Seasons is the best hotel in many cities. The same thing will happen in the restaurant business. Chain operators can pay chefs more and provide the best benefits for their employees. If I buy a million pounds of fish a year, I will be able to provide the best fish available and the lowest prices to my customer. Chain operators who have experience can provide the best service, best dining environment, and best food because they can afford to do so.

NOTES

1. The section on Barbara Lazaroff and Wolfgang Puck is copyright 1992 by Barbara Lazaroff.

CASE STUDIES

The eighteen case studies that follow concern restaurants that have endured and prospered. Two of the restaurants, Mesa Grill and Granita, are newcomers that have achieved instant acclaim from the day they opened.

Each of these in-depth case studies contains information concerning the hundreds of ingredients that contribute to a restaurant's success, starting with each restaurateur's personal approach and ending with invaluable information on average covers sold at lunch and dinner, the average check, liquor and wine sales (usually a percent of the average check), food cost (relative to menu price), labor cost (relative to total sales), rent, and yearly sales. In between, there are sections on restaurant concept and menu development, construction budget analysis, space planning, kitchen design, the design concept, and staff selection, training, and service. Also included are detailed floor plans, kitchen plans, and source lists.

The case studies were chosen to represent a cross-section of restaurants from around the country that responded to a combination of key factors, including customer demand, location, competition, and ever-changing economic conditions. Some restaurants achieved enduring success only after overcoming initial setbacks, while others have continually flourished because they were able to maintain consistency.

The restaurant business is not an exact science. The key to developing a restaurant that is a hit from the day it opens and that survives more than a few years has become more and more elusive. This section, however, explores proven, successful examples that can give the freshman or seasoned restaurateur ideas about what type of restaurant to open, what food to serve and at what price, where to locate a restaurant, how staff should be selected, and what a restaurant could look like and what it should cost. There are no easy answers, but it is hoped that the information and insights contained in these case studies will aid restaurateurs in making important decisions that will allow them to succeed.

S C O O Z I

Scoozi is another hit concept of Lettuce Entertain You Enterprises, Inc., and is owned by Marv Magid and Rich Melman. Marv Magid recently passed away in a tragic helicopter crash.

DESIGNERS

Scoozi was designed by Aumiller/Youngquist, PC, an architectural and interior design firm located in Mount Prospect, Illinois. In addition, Jordan Mozer and Associates and Trudy Glossberg were involved in the design.

Aumiller/Youngquist is widely recognized for its outstanding architectural and design accomplishments in the restaurant and hospitality field. In addition to Scoozi, they have designed America's Kitchen, Hat Dance, The Eccentric, Skipjack's, Tucci Benucch, Tucci Milan, and Ed Debevic's.

SOURCES

ARCHITECT: Aumiller/Youngquist, PC,
    Jordan Mozer & Associates, Glossberg Associates
GENERAL CONTRACTOR: Capitol Construction
ENGINEERING CONSULTANT: Desi Engineering
PHOTOGRAPHER: Steinkamp/Ballogg Chicago
DINING TABLES, CHAIRS: Shelby Williams
BOOTHS, BANQUETTES, BAR TABLES: Edelman Jankow
BARSTOOLS: Vitro
MURALIST: Made In Chicago
MILLWORK: Emco
CUSTOM LIGHT FIXTURES: Wilmer Snow, Emco, designed by
    Jordan Mozer & Associates
TILE INSTALLATION: Acorn Tile
PENDANT LIGHTING: Atelier International, Artemide, Robert
    Sonneman for Kovacs, Mel Brown, Foscarini
LOW-VOLTAGE TRACK LIGHTING: Trak
DOWNLIGHTS: Halo

RICHARD MELMAN. PHOTOGRAPH © LETTUCE ENTERTAIN YOU ENTERPRISES, INC.

BILL AUMILLER. PHOTOGRAPH © LAURY YOUNGQUIST.

KEITH YOUNGQUIST. PHOTOGRAPH © LAURY YOUNGQUIST.

Scoozi is a 12,800 sq. ft. full-service restaurant located in a warehouse/loft area of Chicago at 410 West Huron Street. Opened in 1986, Scoozi is a wide-open, exuberant trattoria serving Italian food. It was a success from the day it opened and continues to be one of Chicago's favorite restaurants.

Rich Melman describes the story line for Scoozi as follows: "The year is 1926. Two restaurateurs in a village just south of Milan stumble upon an aging artist's studio. It's one of those mammoth halls, popular during the Renaissance, where painters and sculptors pursued their art. The plaster is crumbling, the marble floor scuffed. Some walls are covered with charcoal sketches by long-forgotten masters; others are filled with faded, curling remains of art posters. Into this, the restaurateurs bring the polished mahogany and chrome trappings of a trattoria."

Rich Melman says that he chose the location for Scoozi because the space fit his image for a big, fun, festive Italian restaurant. "We chose the River North section because I sensed the neighborhood was about to grow with artists and young professionals purchasing loft space. I like to find an area just before it peaks. That way, I can usually negotiate a more favorable deal. Because this space was surrounded by a lot of artists' studios, it fit the story line for the concept. I looked at this space and knew it was right and not to long after that, we made a deal for the space.

"It is extremely important to us to negotiate the best terms for our restaurants. The average check is directly influenced by how good we are as site selectors and negotiators. We believe we're going to be successful if we offer great food at reasonable prices, and if we make a great deal on the building, we can translate these savings into higher quality food.

Bill Aumiller states, "This off-beat industrial location adds to the allure by creating a sense of mystery and suspense. It's just a little scary walking down the street, and this gets your juices flowing so that the experience of walking into the space is just that much more exciting.

"We brightly lit the exterior to give a sense of security and secured the parking area. The big red tomato, the yellow awnings, and the enlarged label art on the outside of the building suggest the excitement within and raise expectations." Rich Melman continues, "We saw an opportunity and were able to make it work."

EVERYONE IN CHICAGO SAYS, "MEET ME AT THE RED TOMATO." PHOTOGRAPH © STEINKAMP/BALLOGG CHICAGO.

Rich Melman states, "We spent a great deal of time in Italian restaurants and trattorias in the United States and Italy to determine the menu. We decided to offer a widely diverse menu where large portions were served at affordable prices.

"When I was developing the menu for Scoozi, I had tunnel vision, and ate at every Italian restaurant I could, and read as many cookbooks as possible. I talked to the people sitting next to me in the restaurants I visited to find out what they were eating. Often, I got ideas and recipes from the people I spoke with and incorporated them into the menu."

410 WEST HURON CHICAGO, ILLINOIS 60610 (312) 943-5900

SCOOZI MENU COVER. © LETTUCE ENTERTAIN YOU ENTERPRISES, INC.

APERITIVI

NEGRONI	4.50	PORTO ROSSO	3.75	MANGIAM
IL GABBIANO	3.75	SPAZZATURA	4.50	E BERE.
BELLINI SCOOZI	4.50	AMERICANO	3.75	

ANTIPASTI FR

INSALATA CAPRESE HOMEMADE MOZZARELLA, SLICED
CARPACCIO MIMOSO SLICED RAW SIRLOIN, ARUGUL
GAMBERONI ALLA CALIFORNESE SHRIMP, AVOCADO, SA
MELANZANE GRIGLIATI GRILLED EGGPLANT, PEP
IL CANTINONE PROSCIUTTO, TOMATO, MOZZARELLA, GR
SALMACCIO SMOKED SALMON, MELON, CHIVES
INSALATA DEL CONTADINO TOMATOS, RED ONION

PIZZA SENZA F
PIZZA WITHOUT C

ESPINOZA TRADITIONAL TOMATO SAUCE, WOODLAND
♥ **PORTO TICINESE** CHARRED TUNA, GREENS, BALSA

PIZZA

MARGHERITA TOMATO, BASIL, HOMEMADE MOZZARELLA	6.25	12.25	INSALATA Mixed green
SOFISTICATA BACON, ARUGOLA, RED ONION, MOZZARELLA	6.75	12.75	MONTE SO goat cheese
IL BIANCO ALFREDO SAUCE, ONIONS, SAUTEED ARTICHOKES	6.25	12.25	INSALATA watercress,
NOSTRA ITALIAN SAUSAGE, PEPPERS, FONTINA CHEESE	6.50	12.50	tomato, oliv
EMILIA·ROMAGNA ASPARAGUS, MUSHROOMS, THREE CHEESES	6.95	12.95	CALAMARI calamari, mi
PIZZA SPACCATA LARGE SPLIT PIZZA		13.50	

MINESTRO

PAST

PENNE ALL'ARRABBIATA TOMATO, BASIL, GARL
SPAGHETTINI ALLE VONGOLE FRESH CLAMS, H
MEZZALUNA BANDIERA CHEESE FILLED, ALFREDO, PESTO
ORECCHIETTE "GRAN SUCCESSO" PROSCIUTTO, ASPA
MOSTACCIOLI AI FORMAGGIO BROCCOLI, WALNU
FUSILLI RUSTICA SAUSAGE, EGGPLANT, MOZZARELLA, S
RAVIOLI CON FONGHI MUSHROOM FILLED, MARSALA,
LINGUINE DEL GOLFO SHRIMP, MUSSELS, CLAMS, SQUID,
GNOCCHI DELLA NONNA SPINACH GNOCCHI, AURORA OR

PIATTI DEL
PLATES OF THE H

POLLO PAESANO HOME STYLE ROASTED CHICKEN & VEGETAB
PETTO DI POLLO RIPIENO CHICKEN BREAST STUFFE
POLITO E SEMPLICE BREADED VEAL CHOP, TOMATO, ONI
SCALOPPINE AI FUNGHI VEAL SCALOPPINE, WOODLAND
PAPERINO AGRO DOLCE DUCK BREAST, ROAST PEPPERS,
FEGATO ALLA GENOVESE SAUTEED CALVES LIVER, SAUSAG

18% gratuity added to a party of eight or more

In consideration of all our guests, cig
smoking is permitted only at the bar.

© 1988 Jessica's High Ceilings, Inc.

DA PIÚ SAPORE A' LA VITA

A N T I P A S T I   C A L D I

| | | PORZIONE | |
| --- | --- | PICCOLA | GRANDE |

ZUCCHINI FRITTI	FRIED ZUCCHINI STICKS, LEMON		4.95
COZZE ZINGARELLA	STEAMED MUSSELS, TOMATO SAUCE		5.75
VONGOLE ALLA SASSI	BAKED CLAMS, OREGANO, GARLIC, BREAD CRUMBS		5.75
SALSICCIA E FASULL	GRILLED SAUSAGE, ESCAROLE, WHITE BEANS		5.75
FAGIANO CON FUNGHI	SMOKED PHEASANT, WILD MUSHROOMS, POLENTA		5.50
CARCIOFI "BUONAROTI"	FRIED ARTICHOKE LEAVES STUFFED WITH SHRIMP		5.75
FUNGHI AI FERRI	GRILLED WOODLAND MUSHROOMS, TOMATO GARLIC BUTTER		5.50
♥ MUSCOLI ALLA GIUSEPPE	STEAMED MUSSELS, VEGETABLE BROTH, GARLIC TOAST		5.75

P I A T T I   G A S T R O N O M I C C I

LA CUCINA FA DEL SUO MEGLIO, CERCATE DI
FARE DEL VOSTRO MEGLIO ANCHE VOI

A L L A   G R I G L I A
FROM THE GRILL

		PICCOLA	GRANDE
GAMBERONI DELICATI	GRILLED SHRIMP, ARTICHOKE, TOMATO, GARLIC BUTTER	8.95	14.95
♥ TONNO ALLA FINOCCHIO	TUNA, FENNEL, ORANGE, GLAZED RED ONION	7.95	13.95
♥ POLLO STEPHANO	MARINATED GRILLED CHICKEN BREAST, STEAMED VEGETABLES		8.95
COSTADA DI VITELLO	GRILLED VEAL T-BONE, MUSTARD ROSEMARY SAUCE		14.95
♥ FILETTO DI MANZO	IN REALTA..... HEART HEALTHY !!!		12.95
♥ CANNESTRELLI FESTOSI	SEA SCALLOPS, ARUGULA, TOMATO RELISH		12.95
SPIEDINI MISTI	GRILLED SKEWER OF VEAL, SAUSAGE, CHICKEN, QUAIL		13.95
POLLO DEL MATTONE	GAME HEN COOKED UNDER A BRICK !!		9.95

R I S O T T O

Piatti di Pazienza

RISOTTO DEL CAPO CUOCO
RISOTTO MADE FRESH ON THE HALF HOUR
served from 6-10 p.m

V E R D U R E   E   C O N T O R N I

PATATE E FORMAGGIO	SLICED POTATOES, GORGONZOLA CHEESE	2.95
SPINACI AGLIO ED ACCIUGHE	SPINACH, ROAST GARLIC, ANCHOVY	2.75
BROCCOLI AI NOCI	BROCCOLI SAGE BUTTER, WALNUTS	3.25
ASPARAGI CON PARMIGIANO	GRILLED ASPARAGUS, PARMIGIANO	3.95

D O L C E

SEMIFREDDO AL CAFFÉ	1.95
VANILLA GELATO, ESPRESSO	
GELATI ITALIAN ICE CREAM	3.25
PROFITEROLE CREAM PUFFS	4.25
STUFFED WITH GELATI	
MILLE CALORE MASCARPONE	
CHEESECAKE, APRICOT RAISIN COMPOTE	
TIRAMISU	4.50
FRUTTA FRESCA FRESH FRUIT	3.50
IN SEASON	

B E V A N D E

CAFFÉ AMERICANO	1.50	LIMONATA	1.50
DECAFFEINATED	1.50	S. PELLEGRINO	2.50/3.75
ESPRESSO	2.00	CHINOTTO	1.50
CAPPUCCINO	2.25	BITTERINO	1.50
TE	1.50	ARANCIATA	1.50

♥ These items are prepared from recipes that meet the fat and cholesterol guidelines of the American Heart Association of Metropolitan Chicago for healthy adults.

Partial left column (trimmed page edge)

		PORZIONE	
---	---	PICCOLA	GRANDE
...ASIL			3.95
...IVE OIL			4.95
			5.95
...mic. VINAIGRETTE			4.80
...O			5.25
...L			5.50
...E, ANCHOVY			3.95

...AGGIO

...S, SAUSAGE		6.25	12.25
...RETTE		7.95	13.95

...LATE

...MISTA		3.25
...grette		3.95
...nuts		4.25
...ugula,		
...sun dried		
...Spicy fried		6.95
...sar dressing		

...PPE

...E Vegetable soup, pesto		2.95

...CHILES		6.25	9.25
...C, OLIVE OIL		6.75	9.75
...SAUCES		6.95	9.95
...HROOMS, CREAM		6.50	9.50
...CHEESES		6.50	9.50
...TO SAUCE		6.75	9.75
...O		6.95	9.95
...SAFFRON		7.95	10.95
...SAUCE		6.50	9.50

...CASA

...NDANZA		12.25
...OAT CHEESE		9.95
...RBETTE		14.95
...S, PORCINI BROTH		13.95
...ALSAMIC VINEGAR		11.95
...BACON		9.25

There will be times when quality will not meet our specifications, and an item on the menu will not be served.

4/91

Bill Aumiller states, "The total budget for Scoozi was $2.3 million, including kitchen equipment. The project took six months to plan, design, and create construction documents, and it took approximately four months to build.

"Since this space was formerly a garage, it didn't have adequate electrical service, plumbing, or HVAC. These utilities had to completely demolished and rebuilt, adding to the cost of the project. The bow trusses in the space made it difficult to mount HVAC equipment and run ductwork. We had to build a one-story addition on the rear of the restaurant where we added a 3,000 sq. ft. prep kitchen. It also allowed us to mount all of our air conditioning equipment on this new flat roof. This addition, however, forced us to add a series of three self-closing fire shutters, compartmentalizing the new addition and the dining room.

"Lettuce Entertain You is committed to quality and detail in their restaurants. Usually, we have to hold back the client from spending more money rather than the other way around."

Rich Melman states, "There is a limit to how much we will spend on a given project, but if a wall mural or trompe l'oeil work will determine if the design matches the story line, I usually will spend the money."

Bill Aumiller states, "the storyboard created for Scoozi by Rich Melman and his partners greatly influenced the design of Scoozi. This large, wide-open space suited the story that an aging artist's studio where painters and sculptors had pursued their craft had been converted by restaurateurs into a bustling trattoria.

"We picked up on this theme by detailing sepia tone sketches on the walls that could have been done by artists before they went out to the floor to paint or sculpt. We also have sculptures in various locations throughout the dining room, because we felt strongly that this space had to have a sense of history. It's not necessarily the kind of space you would find in Italy, but it feels Italian.

"In Italy, restaurateurs very rarely get a beautiful historic interior to create a restaurant. They may add a contemporary layer onto a richly detailed space or one with stone barrel vaults, and it was this adaptive reuse of an aging space that inspired us. We didn't want people to walk in and have it be obvious that this was a garage; we wanted to create a space that seemed real and wasn't a superficial stage set that would lose its appeal after a few visits.

"The lighting in the space is traditional near where people are seated, and becomes contemporary where the ceiling is higher. This eclectic combination of fixtures creates energy and

THE BAR WITH ITS COLORFUL WINDOW DISPLAY IS A GREAT GATHERING PLACE. PHOTOGRAPH © STEINKAMP/BALLOGG CHICAGO.

BOW TRUSSES, FUNKY LIGHTING, CRACKED FLOOR TILE, AND A VARIETY OF CHAIRS CREATE A FUN, FESTIVE, "REAL" ITALIAN TRATTORIA. PHOTOGRAPH © STEINKAMP/BALLOGG CHICAGO.

excitement. We wanted the space to be bright, so we provided a grid of high-intensity track fixtures that provide ambient light. The pendant light fixtures add vitality and interest and we also introduce pin-spots to illuminate artwork and floral arrangements.

"The finish materials used are traditional and include warm oak, cracked tile, and painted cracked plaster. Like Café Ba Ba Reeba!, none of the chairs match and the space has a timeworn appeal. Again, we wanted the space not to appear perfect, so that customers got the impression that this space had developed and grown over time.

"Lettuce Entertain You's restaurants are planned for the long haul, and materials are selected that will age well over time. We wanted to see the traffic pattern in the hardwood floors and intentionally patched the floors with mismatched woods. In the main dining room, we have installed eighteen varieties of 'rubble tile' and three varieties of marble, all broken into pieces and set in a dark filler.

"Wall treatments consist of precracked plaster that covers the building's brick interior. Pipes and layers of stone come through the cracked wall. Murals and faux treatments cover some of the walls, while others have a time-worn fresco.

THE FINISH MATERIALS GIVE THE IMPRESSION THAT THIS SPACE HAS GROWN AND DEVELOPED OVER TIME. PHOTOGRAPH © STEINKAMP/BALLOGG CHICAGO.

SPACE PLANNING

Bill Aumiller states, "Scoozi is built on several levels in order to create a series of intimately scaled rooms within one huge space. Everyone has a view of the door and the activities surrounding the kitchen. The people in the main dining room near the bar are comfortable on this raised platform because drinkers are not hovering over them, and the people seated at the two smaller raised dining rooms on each side of the restaurant have a great view of all the goings on. It's a little like the Spanish steps and a Greek theater all rolled into one.

"The banquettes in the middle of the main dining area are divided into four quadrants to provide separate distinct identities, and in order to avoid the trap of symmetry and repetition, we laid out the booth seating on the right platform in standard rows along the wall, while the booth seating on the left platform is U-shaped.

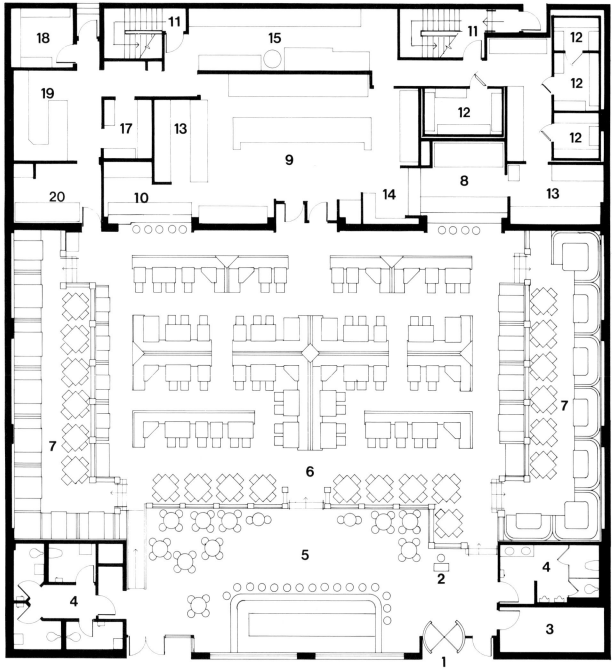

SCOOZI FIRST FLOOR PLAN. COURTESY OF AUMILLER/YOUNGQUIST.
REFERENCE TABLE: 1. ENTRY; 2. HOSTESS; 3. COAT ROOM; 4. MEN'S ROOM (RIGHT SIDE); WOMEN'S ROOM (LEFT SIDE); 5. BAR/WAITING; 6. MAIN DINING;
7. UPPER DINING; 8. PIZZA PREP/OVENS; 9. COOKLINE/PICK-UP; 10. SERVICE BAR; 11. STAIRS TO OFFICES AND LOCKERS; 12. WALK-IN COOLERS;
13. PASTA/PASTRY PREP; 14. CASHIER; 15. KITCHEN PREP; 16. SALAD/DESSERT; 17. POT WASH; 18. DRY STORAGE; 19. DISHWASHING; 20. ICE MACHINES

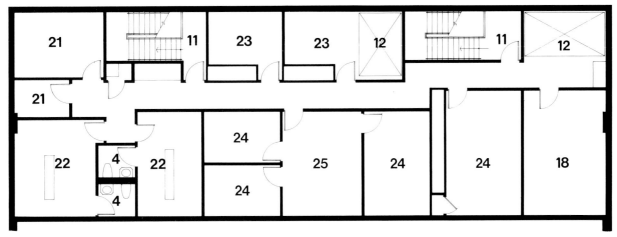

SCOOZI SECOND FLOOR PLAN. COURTESY OF AUMILLER/YOUNGQUIST.
REFERENCE TABLE: 18. DRY STORAGE; 21. MECHANICAL; 22. EMPLOYEE'S LOCKERS; 23. LIQUOR & WINE STORAGE; 24. OFFICES; 25. OFFICE

"The bar is located immediately adjacent to the entrance and was planned as a linear bar rather than an island because the back bar is lined with windows. There are 325 seats in this space, and we didn't want to leave too much open space, since people want to eat near each other in this exuberant environment. It's more intimate. They don't come here to dine alone. The men's and women's bathrooms are located on opposite sides of the restaurant just to break with the norm." Scoozi's 12,800 sq. ft. are divided up as follows:

DINING ROOMS, BAR AND REST ROOMS:
  6,450 sq. ft.
FIRST FLOOR KITCHEN: 3,200 sq. ft.
SECOND FLOOR OFFICES, LIQUOR STORAGE,
  EMPLOYEE BATHROOMS AND LOCKERS:
  3,150 sq. ft.

KITCHEN DESIGN

This high-volume, fast-turnover space places great demands on the kitchen, and approximately 6,000 sq. ft. is allocated for the kitchen, storage, and prep spaces at Scoozi, which represents nearly 50 percent of the space. Early on in the process, Bill Aumiller and the project team decided that it did not want the kitchen to be the main attraction, so on the rear wall, windows offer a partial view of the kitchen to "give a hint of what is going on."

Rich Melman states, "The kitchen was originally planned to be the headquarters for our Italian division, and that's why it is so large. We make some of our pastas and prepare all of our own pastries in the bakery at Scoozi."

COST OF OPERATIONS

Scoozi serves approximately 900 covers daily. It continues to be a very popular and successful restaurant. Its cost of operations are as follows:

SEATING CAPACITY: dining area, 325; bar, 25
AVERAGE WEEKLY COVERS: lunch, 1,400;
  dinner, 5,300
AVERAGE CHECK: lunch, $15.75; dinner, $22.00
YEARLY LIQUOR AND WINE SALES: $2.245 million
FOOD COST: 27.3%
LABOR COST: 20.8%
TOTAL EMPLOYEES: 170
RENT: 6.0%
YEARLY SALES: $7.2 million

Scoozi is a larger-than-life abstraction of an Italian trattoria. Its time-worn materials, including mahogany-stained oak, painted cracked plaster, cracked tile, and funky lighting fixtures evoke an Italian flavor without its being like any other Italian restaurant. Several levels assist in creating an intimate scale in this wide open space that bursts with energy and excitement.

Dining at Scoozi is an absolute surprise. It is located in an industrial building in the River North section of Chicago. You can't miss the big red tomato with the tattered yellow awnings. Once inside, the grand scale of the space explodes with excitement.

Once again, Rich Melman found a wonderful space on the fringe of an up-and-coming neighborhood that suited his original storyboard, and he converted this former garage into an extraordinary Italian trattoria that overflows with quality food, service, and fun at affordable prices.

CAFÉ BA BA REEBA!

OWNER

The owner is Lettuce Entertain You Enterprises, Inc., which is partnered by Richard Melman, Gabino Sotelino, and Jennie Smith.

DESIGNER

Café Ba Ba Reeba! was designed by the firm of Aumiller/Youngquist, PC, located in Mount Prospect, Illinois.

SOURCES

ARCHITECT: Aumiller/Youngquist, PC
CONTRACTOR: Capitol Construction
MECHANICAL CONSULTANT: G&C Consulting Engineers
REFRIGERATION UNITS: Custom Bar-Crafters
TILE, MARBLE: Acorn Tile
CHROME TUBE STOOLS: Vitro
WOODEN STOOLS: L&B/Empire
CHAIRS: Shelby Williams
LIGHT FIXTURES: A-Lamp & Fixture
CHINA: Homer Laughlin
FLATWARE: Meridional
GLASSWARE: Arcoroc
MURALS AND ARTWORK: Made in Chicago (Paul Puncke and Corkie Neuhaus), Vicki Tessmer, Mark Wingo/Grambauer, Tom Zoroya
PHOTOGRAPHER: Mark Ballogg, Steinkamp/Ballogg

RICHARD MELMAN. PHOTOGRAPH © LETTUCE ENTERTAIN YOU ENTERPRISES, INC.

BILL AUMILLER. PHOTOGRAPH © LAURY YOUNGQUIST.

KEITH YOUNGQUIST. PHOTOGRAPH © LAURY YOUNGQUIST.

Café Ba Ba Reeba! is an 11,350 sq. ft. full-service Spanish/tapas restaurant that seats 340 people in the winter and 400 in the spring and summer and is located at 2024 North Halsted Street in Chicago, Illinois. It has been one of the most popular and successful restaurants in Chicago since it opened in 1985.

Richard Melman states, "For Café Ba Ba Reeba, the story goes like this: It's 1962 in a picturesque older section of Madrid. Music is cooling the sun-parched day as office buildings empty businessmen and workers into the winding streets. Instead of heading home, most stop at Spanish taverns called *tascas* for a pre-dinner drink and tapas. Leaning into burnished wood bars, patrons sip wine and beer and nibble at portions of Jamon serrano, mussels, tortilla espanola, sardines, and anchovies. Huge smoked hams hang above the bar, and brightly painted tiles and cooking utensils adorn the walls."

Architect Bill Aumiller states, "Rich Melman and his partners Gabino Sotelino and Jenny Smith had always wanted to open a traditional Spanish restaurant that served full dinners and tapas, those delicious 'little dishes from Spain.' It couldn't be a typical tapas restaurant because tapas traditionally is served at the bar. The space had to reflect a Spanish, not Mexican image, and had to convey a comfortable neighborhood quality. The neighborhood selected for this restaurant was just to the south of the DePaul University area where many young professionals lived, and it was a vibrant residential neighborhood that was getting stronger. These young professionals for the most part were single, and if they were married, had no children. Since they worked long hours, they didn't have time to cook and needed an affordable, comfortable, yet energetic place to eat.

"Ideally, Rich likes to find sites where the neighborhood is just starting to grow so that he can secure the best deal. If he waited until everyone moved in and the property values went up, the deal for the restaurant would not be as attractive. He also likes to lease or buy the buildings where the restaurants are located.

The three-story building that houses Café Ba Ba Reeba! was built in 1920, and did not have a whole lot of character. What it did have was an enclosed outdoor patio area with some interesting trees.

The previous restaurant that occupied this location was successful during the warm months, but did poorly during the winter because it was dingy inside. The key to Café Ba Ba Reeba!'s success was that it was surrounded by a strong residential neighborhood that allowed it to build a strong walk-in crowd, and from that foundation it grew, because it became a destination restaurant as well. This colorful, themed restaurant drew an enthusiastic crowd year 'round.

THE COLORFUL, FAMILIAR PALETTE OF TILEWORK, ARTIFACTS, FOOD DISPLAYS, AND WARM WOODS CREATES LAYERS OF DETAILS THAT PEOPLE DISCOVER OVER A PERIOD OF TIME. PHOTOGRAPH © STEINKAMP/BALLOGG CHICAGO.

Rich Melman states, "The Spanish/tapas menu concept for Café Ba Ba Reeba! came first, before the location was selected. In fact, the idea for a neighborhood tapas bar/restaurant was developed as a story years before the restaurant was built.

"Tapas originated centuries ago in Spanish taverns where glasses of sherry, wine, or beer were covered with bread, cheese, or sausage. The intention of this practice, as it states on our menu, was to keep the flies out of guests' drinks. These *lids* proved to be so tasty that people would often choose their favorite bar by the quality of its tapas.

"Café Ba Ba Reeba! offers both cold (*frias*) and hot (*calientes*) dishes. Spanish paella and larger portions of selected regional specialties are offered. All the menu items served are quite reasonably priced. Since we are a high-volume, casual dining restaurant, we can offer great value to our customers."

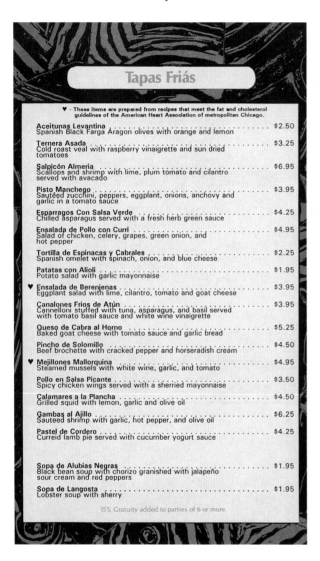

Tapas Friás

♥ - These items are prepared from recipes that meet the fat and cholesterol guidelines of the American Heart Association of metropolitan Chicago.

Aceitunas Levantina Spanish Black Farga Aragon olives with orange and lemon	$2.50
Ternera Asada Cold roast veal with raspberry vinaigrette and sun dried tomatoes	$3.25
Salpicón Almeria Scallops and shrimp with lime, plum tomato and cilantro served with avacado	$6.95
Pisto Manchego Sautéed zucchini, peppers, eggplant, onions, anchovy and garlic in a tomato sauce	$3.95
Esparragos Con Salsa Verde Chilled asparagus served with a fresh herb green sauce	$4.25
Ensalada de Pollo con Curri Salad of chicken, celery, grapes, green onion, and hot pepper	$4.95
Tortilla de Espinacas y Cabrales Spanish omelet with spinach, onion, and blue cheese	$2.25
Patatas con Alioli Potato salad with garlic mayonnaise	$1.95
♥ **Ensalada de Berenjenas** Eggplant salad with lime, cilantro, tomato and goat cheese	$3.95
Canalones Frios de Atún Cannelloni stuffed with tuna, asparagus, and basil served with tomato basil sauce and white wine vinaigrette	$3.95
Queso de Cabra al Horno Baked goat cheese with tomato sauce and garlic bread	$5.25
Pincho de Solomillo Beef brochette with cracked pepper and horseradish cream	$4.50
♥ **Mejillones Mallorquina** Steamed mussels with white wine, garlic, and tomato	$4.95
Pollo en Salsa Picante Spicy chicken wings served with a sherried mayonnaise	$3.50
Calamares a la Plancha Grilled squid with lemon, garlic and olive oil	$4.50
Gambas al Ajillo Sauteed shrimp with garlic, hot pepper, and olive oil	$6.25
Pastel de Cordero Curreid lamb pie served with cucumber yogurt sauce	$4.25
Sopa de Alubias Negras Black bean soup with chorizo granished with jalapeño sour cream and red peppers	$1.95
Sopa de Langosta Lobster soup with sherry	$1.95

15% Gratuity added to parties of 6 or more.

Tapas Calientes

Pincho de Pollo y Chorizo Chicken and chorizo brochette with garlic cumin mayonnaise	$3.95
Pollo en Salsa Picante Spicy chicken wings served with a sherried mayonnaise	$3.50
Caracoles Alioli Sauteed escargots served on garlic croutons topped with alioli	$4.50
Pincho de Solomillo Beef brochette with cracked pepper and horseradish cream	$4.50
Croquetas de Pollo y Jamón Chicken and ham croquettes served with tomato sauce	$2.95
♥ **Pasta con Setas** Pasta with wild mushrooms in a mushroom port wine broth	$4.95
Gambas al Ajillo Sauteed shrimp with garlic, hot pepper, and olive oil	$6.25
Champiñoñes Rellenos Stuffed mushrooms with spinach, garlic and cheese	$3.95
Queso de Cabra al Horno Baked goat cheese with tomato sauce and garlic bread	$5.25
Calamares a la Parrilla Grilled squid with lemon, garlic and olive oil	$4.50
Pastel de Cordero Curried lamb pie served with cucumber yogurt sauce	$4.25
Verduras Asada Baked zucchini, eggplant, peppers, mushrooms, onions, and tomato with fresh herbs	$3.95

Salads

Ensalada de Casa Mixed greens with vinaigrette dressing garnished with eggs	$2.95
Ensalada de Espinacas Spinach salad with bacon, eggs and balsamic vinaigrette	$3.25
Ensalada Mixta Mixed greens with ham, tuna, onion and cucumber served with a vinegar and oil dressing	$3.95

Soups

Sopa de Alubias Negras Black bean soup with chorizo granished with jalapeño sour cream and red peppers	$1.95
Sopa de Langosta Lobster soup with sherry	$1.95

Beverages

Café o Te	$1.25	**Refrescos**	$1.25
Espresso o Cappuccino	$2.00	**Agua Mineral**	$2.00

Specialties From The Oven

Paella

Paella a la Valenciana . . . . $8.95 per person
A traditional Spanish rice dish with chicken, pork, shrimp,
mussels, squid, monkfish, green beans, tomatoes, and saffron

Paella de Mariscos . . . . $11.95 per person
A traditonal Spanish rice dish with lobster, shrimp, mussels,
squid, monkfish, garlic, tomato, and saffron

Regional Specialties

	Raciones	Entradas
Steak Encebollado . . . . Grilled beef tenderloin with onion marmalade, manchego cheese, and topped with crispy onions	$7.50	$14.95
Ternera al Jerez . . . . Sauteed veal escalopes with an almond, roasted garlic, and sherry sauce	$7.95	$15.95
Cordero a la Parrilla . . . . Grilled escalope of lamb marinated with garlic and paprika	$5.95	$11.95
Pollo Glaseado . . . . Half chicken marinated with honey and cumin, grilled and served with potatoes.		$6.95
♥ **Salmon al Aroma de Mostaza Zalacain** . . . . Baked salmon with a mustard topping and a vegetable vinaigrette	$6.50	$12.95
Lomo en Adobo . . . . Sauteed pork loin rubbed with garlic, paprika, and oregano served with yellow rice	$5.95	$11.95
Cazuela la Ba-Ba-Reeba! . . . . Casserole of shrimp, mussels, clams, fish, and angel hair pasta in spicy sauce		$9.95
♥ **Brocheta de Pollo** . . . . Chicken breast brochette marinated with garlic, paprika, cumin, and onion with yellow rice	$5.50	$10.95

Desserts

Profiteroles al Chocolate-puffs with banana ice cream and hot fudge $3.95

Bizcocho Borracho-lady fingers soaked with espresso, rum, kahlua,
and brandy layered with marscarpone custard $3.95

Platanos al Carmelo-bananas with carmel sauce $2.95

Tarta de Chocolate-flourless chocolate tart $3.50

♥**Pastel de Chocolate**- Healthy Heart chocolate cake
served with raspberry sauce $3.95

Flan-Spanish caramel custard $2.95

There are times when quality will not meet our specifications
and an item on the menu will not be served.

Bill Aumiller states, "Café Ba Ba Reeba! took approximately four and a half months for the development of the design and the preparation of the construction documents and five months for construction. The total cost for the project, including kitchen equipment, was $1.8 million.

"The project was costly because there were code restraints that had to be overcome. There were three separate structures that housed Café Ba Ba Reeba! Two apartment buildings were attached, and a one-story addition had been added to the previous restaurant. Because there were three stories, the size of the dining areas was limited owing to fire separation restrictions. We had to compartmentalize the two three-story buildings and the one-story building into three separate fire zones, which we accomplished by providing self-closing fire shutters between the buildings. Two exits had to be provided from each one of the buildings.

"Each of the five fire shutters required $12,000, while the additional exits cost an additional $40,000. Even though this was an existing restaurant and we weren't changing its use, the Building Department wouldn't let us grandfather this project.

"One additional hit to the budget initially was providing sprinklers for the restaurant and the apartments on the third floor. However, because of substantially reduced insurance premiums, this investment was paid for within one year.

"There was a severe leak in the building coming from the rotted waste lines. In addition, the roof was leaking because of the patching and repatching of penetrations. The basement only had an inch and a half concrete slab, and it was not sufficient for the weight of kitchen equipment. We had to dig out the floor and pour a new 4" slab.

"All of these costly base building issues might have been avoided if we were retained to provide a survey prior to the lease being signed. These hits to the budget came as a surprise, and since this unfortunate occurrence, we provide Lettuce Entertain You with a code survey as well as a budget analysis regarding major utility and structural requirements."

THE CARTOONISH MURAL TITLED "THE LAST TAPAS" PROVIDES A TOUCH OF WHIMSY. PHOTOGRAPH © STEINKAMP/BALLOGG CHICAGO.

Bill Aumiller states, "The design of Café Ba Ba Reeba! had to look like it had been there for a long time, so we used familiar materials such as wood and tile to convey a sense of warmth and permanence. We don't want to design a one-joke restaurant where people chuckle once and don't come back. We layered and layered Café Ba Ba Reeba! with details, so that people would continually discover them over a period of time.

"Typically, we sit with Rich and his partners and brainstorm with them to develop a concept statement. This statement emanates from Rich's storyboard and provides us with a strong central focus. These parameters developed from the storyboard really help in the design process.

"We started with familiar, comfortable tones of wood as the foundation for this neighborhood concept, and we added a colorful palette of tilework, artwork, artifacts, and food displays. The wood is red-stained oak, and we used yellows, reds, teals, and aquas to reflect the Spanish influence.

"The murals and artwork are two- and three-dimensional, cartoony, and whimsical, providing a lot of the energy in the space. One is titled *The Last Tapas*. Another, titled *Picasso's Chicago Guernica*, is Picasso-ish and conveys a Spanish influence. We used some of the existing wood on the floor and patched where it was needed to create a well-worn, established look.

"We wanted to see the traffic pattern in the floor so the space looked like it had been lived-in. We didn't want the restaurant to look too perfect, slick, and designed. Every pore of this restaurant smells like garlic, and if this space had been given a sophisticated image, it would have failed.

"The chairs are not all the same, and patches in the floor and the mismatch of materials make the space comfortable, fun, and real. In addition to the Spanish metaphors, there are subtle 1950s references in the furniture and lighting, with square, overstuffed red or turquoise bar seats and chrome moldings that are purely American.

"The lighting in Café Ba Ba Reeba! takes on a supporting role and is used primarily to illuminate the artwork, artifacts, and food displays. A variety of pendant fixtures are placed throughout the space to create a sense of spontaneity and fun."

THE VARIETY OF DINING ROOMS PROVIDES AN ALTERNATIVE FOR REPEAT CUSTOMERS. PHOTOGRAPH © STEINKAMP/BALLOGG CHICAGO.

Café Ba Ba Reeba! seats 290 people in the winter and 350 in the summer, in addition to the 50 people seated at the bar.

The 11,350 sq. ft. of the restaurant is located on two floors as follows:

DINING AREA WITH BARS, INCLUDING BATHROOMS:
6,025 sq. ft.
KITCHEN, 1ST FLOOR FINISHING: 1,625 sq. ft.
BASEMENT PREP: 3,700 sq. ft.

Bill Aumiller states that "the small finishing kitchen and dishwashing area is on the ground level in order to maximize seating capacity, with cold prep, storage, bathrooms, the coat room, and administrative functions located in the basement. Handicapped restrooms are on the ground level.

"We prepared several alternative plans and settled on the one that was built, even though it was more expensive. It was chosen because it maximized views to the garden and created a centralized exhibition kitchen. The entry corridor was planned to act as a buffer to temper the air because this is such a high-volume restaurant.

"Upon entering the space, the customer is dazzled by the cold tapas displays to the right and the hot tapas displays to the left. Once inside, there is a sequence of spaces starting with the rotating oven, another cold tapas display, another bar, and a series of intimately scaled dining rooms. We wanted to offer customers a variety of spaces that would be discovered on successive visits. During slow periods or when there is a need for private parties, the front of the restaurant as well as the other smaller dining rooms can be separated.

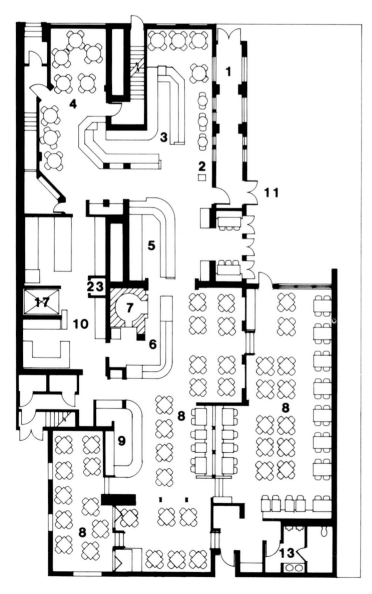

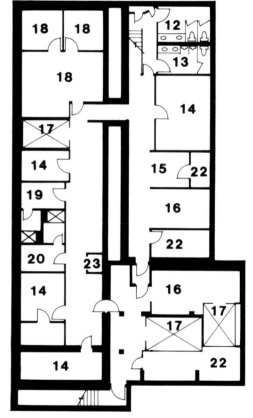

LEFT: CAFÉ BA BA REEBA FIRST FLOOR PLAN.
COURTESY OF AUMILLER/YOUNGQUIST.
REFERENCE TABLE: 1. ENTRY; 2. HOSTESS; 3. BAR;
4. BAR/LOUNGE; 5. HOT TAPAS COOK LINE; 6. COLD TAPAS
& DESSERTS; 7. WOOD BURNING OVEN; 8. DINING; 9. BAR;
10. DISHWASHING; 11. OUTDOOR DINING; 13. MEN'S
BATHROOM; 17. WALK-IN COOLER; 23. DUMBWAITER

ABOVE: CAFÉ BA BA REEBA BASEMENT FLOOR PLAN.
COURTESY OF AUMILLER/YOUNGQUIST.
REFERENCE TABLE: 12. WOMEN'S ROOM; 13. MEN'S
ROOM; 14. WINE STORAGE/DRY STORAGE; 15. PASTRY
PREP; 16. COLD PREP; 17. WALK-IN COOLER;
18. OFFICES; 19. EMPLOYEE LOCKERS; 20. RESTROOMS;
22. MECHANICAL; 23. DUMBWAITER

"Early on, we knew we needed to fit in as many seats as we could to make this high-volume, low-average-check concept work economically. Bar and dining areas are not as clearly defined as other restaurants since the bars are also used for food service. We wanted to infuse a lot of energy throughout the space.

"Because of the style of food, many small dishes are brought to the table and shared family style, encouraging groups of four or six, rather than tables for two. Diagonal square four-tops are Rich's favorite kind of table. He feels more comfortable at this type of table than any other. We used 34" × 34" tables to make the tabletop more cozy, since it is more compatible to the small dishes and the style of service.

"Because this is a casual restaurant, tables floating in the space rather than booths or banquettes are more appropriate. This table arrangement also makes it much more flexible for private parties."

KITCHEN DESIGN

Bill Aumiller states, "In order to maximize seating capacity, the kitchen on the main level was kept to a minimum. All of the cooking is done here along with the dishwashing functions, and the cold prep, walk-in freezers and refrigerators, dry storage, receiving and administrative functions, are located in the basement.

"A dumbwaiter was originally planned, installed, and abandoned within the first two weeks of the project, since one hundred pounds of live lobsters were destroyed because the dumbwaiter malfunctioned. I had warned that dumbwaiters don't serve much of a purpose because you can't get in there with the load. Instead of walking up and down the stairs to load and unload the dumbwaiter, it's easier and more efficient to carry things manually.

"We design the kitchens in our restaurants, and we specifically designed the kitchen at Café Ba Ba Reeba! so that no one in the finishing area had to go back to the prep area. The flow is from back to front. The brick oven and the hot food preparation is done on display for the customer to see.

"The cooking facilities in the prep kitchen are for the preparation of the cold tapas. The hot line in the front prepares about fifty percent of the items on the menu, and the brick oven prepares the roasted items and the paella.

"Kitchens are getting smaller, with restaurateurs relying more and more on frequent deliveries to cut down on the amount of space required for storage. Equipment that prepares only one appetizer on the menu is being eliminated. At one time, we allocated 40 percent of a space to the kitchen and bathrooms; now it's more like 30 percent."

COST OF OPERATIONS

Café Ba Ba Reeba! currently serves approximately 600 covers daily to people from throughout Chicago. It continues to be a very popular and successful restaurant. Its cost of operations are as follows:

SEATING CAPACITY: dining areas, 290; 50, bar
AVERAGE WEEKLY COVERS: lunch, 500; dinner, 3,700
AVERAGE CHECK: lunch, $14.75; dinner, $21.00
YEARLY LIQUOR AND WINE SALES: $1.3 million
FOOD COST: 28%
LABOR COST: 26.7%
TOTAL EMPLOYEES: 124
RENT: land and building owned
YEARLY SALES: $4.4 million

Café Ba Ba Reeba! is a patchwork of motifs from Spain with some 1950s references that create a comfortable, yet energized and whimsical environment. The colorful palette of materials, along with worn floors, chairs of every style, and pungent cooking aromas, conveys a festive neighborhood quality. Garlands of garlic, basil, and dried peppers hang in front of a wood-burning oven where traditional roasts and paella are prepared. Hot and cold tapas are displayed throughout the space so that customers salivate before reaching their tables. The inexpensive array of tapas are served family style at cozy tables.

Brightly colored murals add color and humor to this "imperfect" space where floors, tiles, and lighting don't match. Café Ba Ba Reeba! is pure Rich Melman. This high-volume, low-average-check concept is located in a neighborhood bursting with young, hard-working professionals seeking a place to hang out where they can also afford to eat.

S P A G O

Spago, which opened in 1982, is a 6,500 sq. ft. full-service restaurant that seats 160 people and is located on Sunset Boulevard in West Hollywood, California. It serves a variety of wonderfully prepared pastas, pizzas, and other signature entrées created by Wolfgang Puck. Barbara Lazaroff's quintessential California café, with its open dining area and exhibition kitchen, is one of the most popular restaurants in the world.

Barbara Lazaroff states that "Wolf wanted a very casual restaurant with red-and-white checkered tablecloths and sawdust on the floor. He wanted to serve great pizza and pasta at reasonable prices in a friendly atmosphere. I wanted very much to make Wolf feel comfortable in the space. If the owner feels uncomfortable, as though he is wearing an ill-fitting suit, he or she cannot put the customer at ease. I didn't give him the checkered tablecloths or the sawdust, however!

"Initially, Spago received a lot of press, and was supported by a celebrity crowd. These celebrities attracted a strong star-struck share of the market. However, only a third of our customers are celebrities. People came to Spago because the food was wonderful and the prices were extremely reasonable. The check averages of L'Orangerie, Michael's, and l'Hermitage were $75 at the time we opened Spago. Our average check was $32.

"Many food critics and friends thought we were out of our minds to open a *pizza parlor,* as they then called it. Many nights, Wolf woke up in a cold sweat thinking he would have to leave the country if it didn't work out! The design of Spago, with its open kitchen and dining area, seemed to click from the beginning. It had the right balance of zeitgeist and magic. This magic energy and excitement was created by Wolfgang and the line cooks in the open kitchen. The pizza oven and food displays made it obvious that this restaurant's focus was on food and the joy of preparation.

"At the time Spago was opened, fine dining meant expensive nouvelle French. Wolf revolutionized the restaurant industry with his style of cooking. The exposed kitchen, although not a new concept, was new in the United States for fine dining establishments. The freshest ingredients combined with herbs and spices, served in an upbeat, friendly environment at prices that the average person could afford, was a refreshing new approach.

"Wolfgang certainly elevated the pedestrian pizza to a new level of appreciation and creativity. His philosophy about cooking is quite direct; he says, 'buy the best quality possible, and don't screw it up!' Translated, it means, don't overcook or mask food in heavy sauces that hide rather than enhance the dish, and don't present food in a fashion that makes it too precious to eat.

"The impact of Spago on the style of American dining was so far-reaching that the *Los Angeles Times* featured a cover story on the 'Spago-ization of America.'

"We looked at several sites before we selected the final one. In fact, we looked at a site in Santa Monica, south of where Chinois is located. We wanted to purchase the land and the building, but couldn't afford it.

"The building on Sunset Boulevard where Spago is now located had been on the market for almost six years and was then occupied by a Russian-Armenian restaurant called Kafka's. It was a conglomeration of tiny rooms, narrow corridors, and low ceilings. Before we signed the deal, I went there to dinner to survey the possibilities, and felt we needed to gut the space in order to make it work. We wanted a casual place, and didn't want to spend a lot of money on the renovation, but I could see that most of the interior had to go, even one of the central bearing walls!

"This area on Sunset Boulevard was not very desirable, and we were afraid that even though Wolf had already built a following at Ma Maison, no one would come to this part of town. The deal the landlord offered was extremely attractive. There was a straight rent per month with no percentage attached, and a long-term lease. We felt we couldn't afford to pass it up. However, we only had $3,500 between us, and no bank in Los Angeles would personally loan us any money; we had to have a friend cosign our $60,000 loan.

"Thank goodness Wolf's reputation encouraged some people, most of them from his cooking class, to invest their money and others to come to this otherwise undesirable location. Several years ago, we had to spend $800,000 to purchase land for more parking. If that land had not been available and we could not have gone to the bank to borrow the money, Spago would have been a 30-seat restaurant; in other words, Spago possibly would not have survived.

SEEING THE COLORFUL ARRAY OF FOOD, THE WOOD BURNING PIZZA OVEN, AND THE COOKS HAVING A GREAT TIME ALLOWS EACH DINER TO BE PART OF THE COOKING EXTRAVAGANZA. PHOTOGRAPH © MICHAEL MONTFORT.

"Spago, say in Kansas City, would certainly have been a much different restaurant. Initially, the West Hollywood location in large part contributed to its success. We attract celebrities, studio heads, and producers because Hollywood is our neighborhood. If we were located in Washington, D.C., we would be entertaining congressmen, senators, and perhaps the President, on a weekly basis. I think our Hollywood location was a boost initially, but enduring success must be earned every day, day after day."

MENU DEVELOPMENT

The menu at Spago is the creation of chef Wolfgang Puck. He describes the origins of the Spago menu as follows: "First I decide what the overall direction of the cuisine will be. For example, is it primarily a fish restaurant, or a Chinese restaurant, or Mediterranean-inspired? Then the design develops, most importantly incorporating the equipment needs and the flow of the kitchen. Then Barbara adds her personality and distinct style, and I've learned not to get too involved at that juncture!

"It is only in the last two weeks before opening that the final elements of the menu are clarified. After the restaurant opens, the energy of the people fills the space, and the cuisine continues to be defined and redefined.

"My fond memories of Chez Gu, a rustic pizza café in Provence, motivated me to experiment with new versions of the pizzas and calzones that I had always savored on my nights off from work. Spago favorites include duck (or lamb) sausage pizza with goat cheese and smoked salmon pizza with caviar. Pasta and bread have always been two of my favorite foods; I knew I wanted to create many homemade varieties, and indeed we produce several fresh pastas and breads at Spago daily. Angel-hair pasta with broccoli and goat cheese and lobster ravioli with spicy dill butter, and warm loaves of olive sourdough and six-grain breads, are standard fare for Spago regulars. Over the years, the head chefs have contributed their personal influences with such recipes as Spago's first chef Mark Peel's roasted lamb with rosemary and thyme. Along with chefs Francois Kwaku and Makoto Tanaka, we try to introduce new variations, such as Francois' seafood risotto and Makoto's sauteed abalone served on a crispy noodle pancake, and indeed we have daily specials and change the menu seasonally.

"My 'regime' downfall has always been my great passion for wonderful pastries, cookies, and ice creams. Our first pastry chef Nancy Silverton and the current pastry chef Mary Bergin (who has been here since Spago's inception) have created such Spago classics as individual apple tart served warm with caramel ice cream, and raspberry chocolate mousse cake."

BUDGET

Barbara Lazaroff states, "The budget was $700,000, with nearly $200,000 being utilized for making the structure comply with the earthquake codes and other mechanical and structural requirements. Besides our personal loan of $60,000 and two other initial partners of $30,000 each, we also raised $15,000 per share from over twenty investors. One hundred fifty thousand dollars of that money went toward key money. Other requirements, such as the liquor license, a

SPAGO WINE LIST. PHOTOGRAPH © WOLFGANG PUCK/BARBARA LAZAROFF.

CHEF
MAKOTO TANAKA

APPETIZERS

Chino Farm sweet corn chowder with light jalapeño cream	9.75
Sauteed Pacific oysters with spicy salsa	12.00
Cold asparagus with whole grain mustard cream	12.75
Smoked lobster spring roll with sweet and sour sauce and arugula leaves	17.50
Sauteed shrimp with Thai cucumber salad and spicy tomato relish	12.50
Home smoked salmon with dill cream and toasted brioche	14.75
Chopped Chino Farm vegetable salad	12.50
Marinated fresh tuna with avocado, kaiware and sweet onion	14.75
Field greens with balsamic vinaigrette and goat cheese sauteed in olive oil	12.00
Sauteed foie gras with mango and cinnamon plum wine sauce	15.50
Pistachio duck sausage with Chinese mustard glaze and new potato salad	11.50
Tempura lemon sole with three color tomatoes and basil vinaigrette	12.50

PASTAS

Angel hair pasta with clams and mussels in garlic and black bean sauce	12.50
François' wild mushroom risotto with sweet peas	17.50
Steamed half lobster with spicy linguini and tomato basil fondue	17.50
Sonoma lamb ravioli with tomato curry sauce	13.50
Roasted vegetable and potato half moon ravioli with grilled baby chicken and sage parmesan butter	15.00

FROM OUR WOOD-BURNING OVEN

Grilled Chino Farm vegetable pizza with marinated tomatoes, basil and buffalo mozzarella	13.50
Calzone with roasted peppers, sun dried tomatoes, wild mushrooms and goat cheese	12.50
Pizza with duck sausage, tomatoes, basil and shiitake mushrooms	13.50
Pizza with prosciutto, goat cheese, thyme and red onion	13.00
Pizza with artichokes, shiitake mushrooms, eggplant and caramelized garlic	13.50
Pizza with peppered Louisiana shrimp, sun dried tomatoes and leeks	14.50
Pizza with spicy chicken, roasted peppers and sweet onions	13.50

ENTREES

White Atlantic sea bass with a pistachio herb crust and wild mushroom vinaigrette	19.50
Roasted farm-raised chicken breast with goat cheese and oriental style ratatouille	22.50
Seared scallops with spinach bow tie pasta with saffron, tomato and black olive sauce	22.50
Roasted Cantonese duck with Chino Farm melon, watercress salad and caramelized lime tangerine sauce	24.50
Grilled calf's liver with potato puree and port wine mustard glaze	22.50
Grilled free range chicken with double blanched garlic and Italian parsley	19.50
Roasted whole black bass with fennel salad and lemon herb vinaigrette	24.50
Grilled squab with polenta and a Cabernet niçoise olive sauce	23.50
Mandarin quail with crispy vegetables and ginger orange sauce	24.50
Grilled salmon with spinach puree and sweet Maui onions with balsamic vinegar butter	22.50
Roasted Sonoma lamb with gratin of potatoes and rosemary green peppercorn sauce	24.50
Grilled vegetable plate with basil lemon vinaigrette	18.50

Split 2.00

Our olive sour dough and six grain breads are made daily

Water will be served upon request due to state drought conditions

GOOD FRIENDS DON'T LET FRIENDS DRIVE DRUNK

BARBARA LAZAROFF - INTERIOR DESIGN
The art in the restaurant is on consignment and is available for purchase

reserve for start-up costs, legal fees, etc., reduced the final monies available for the design budget to well under $275,000.

"We used the existing tables and scraped the bubble gum from underneath. Wolf wanted to spend $49 on simple chairs. I knew they'd be 'timber' in a year and held out for chairs that cost three times as much. They've lasted ten years and are just now being replaced for aesthetic reasons.

"Because Spago was conceived as a casual, friendly, unpretentious café, it would have been inappropriate to spend a lot of money to create an environment that would not reflect this image. We also simply could not afford it!"

DESIGN CONCEPT

Barbara Lazaroff states, "As simple as Spago is, Wolf wanted a space that was much simpler. When people first walk into Spago, they are surprised to see how casual it is. There is so much hype and publicity surrounding Spago that it is difficult to imagine how comfortable it is inside. Spago has a very homey, friendly, welcoming atmosphere. Entering Spago, customers are drawn to the lush, exotic floral displays, the bustle of activity and divine aromas emanating from the open kitchen, the sounds of laughter and lively conversation in the dining room—the animated rhythm of the restaurant. As the patrons further examine the room, they may be surprised by the simplicity of the decor. Spago is a rather humble design, but all the elements seem to work to put people happily at ease, and help even first-time diners feel as though they are part of an intimate club.

"It was one of the first open and bright dining rooms where everyone could see and be seen. The tables are very close together, encouraging people to talk with their neighbors. Utilizing blonde woods and other natural materials, I wanted to create the relaxed feeling of a California beach house in the midst of the city. The decor is a backdrop for the changing displays of contemporary art, the floral arrangements, for the expansive view of Hollywood through the windows along Sunset Boulevard, for the tempting display of pastries, and especially for the guests and the food, which should always be center stage!"

SPAGO DINING ROOM. SPAGO HAS A HOMEY, FRIENDLY, WELCOMING AMBIENCE. PHOTOGRAPH © FIROOZ ZAHEDI.

Barbara Lazaroff states that "the space planning began with the placement of the kitchen and the entrance. The kitchen, as with all the other restaurants, was considered first. The preparation and plating of the food for 360 dinners each night at 2.25 *seatings* [which is another term for *turns* or amount of times a chair is used at lunch or dinner] required a substantial amount of space. There's always a tug and pull between the amount of seats needed to be profitable and the space required in the kitchen to serve those seats. The open kitchen, and specifically the double wood-burning ovens, were placed in the direct line of sight from the entrance in order to maximize its appeal. Additionally, these ovens are a substantially large piece of equipment, with a 7'-deep foundation and a fairly large footprint. The oven placement, which abuts an exterior wall, was optimum because the depth of the wood-burning ovens could be projected outward and not into the limited interior space.

"The entrance was placed on Horn Avenue, set back from Sunset Boulevard, in order to provide a buffer between the entrance and the 'ladies of the night' and other dubious folk. The small bar to the left of the entrance is a waiting area reserved for diners with room for twenty people comfortably, but invariably it is always packed sardine-style. We decided early on not to have a bar crowd at Spago because of the undesirable element on Sunset.

"A large portion of the dining room was placed parallel with the windows to take advantage of the views of West Hollywood and Sunset Boulevard. Almost all of the diners in this area have a clear view of the exposed kitchen area and the entrance as well.

"The dining area directly adjacent to the kitchen allows a complete, more intimate view of the entire exhibition kitchen throughout the dining experience.

"Patrons that will be dining in the rear and patio areas walk past the exhibition kitchen, which I believe is a tantalizing and salient introduction of what is to follow. Some patrons request the patio because it is quieter and more intimate; others prefer the more animated dining room. The patio can also be sectioned off and is a wonderful room for private parties up to sixty.

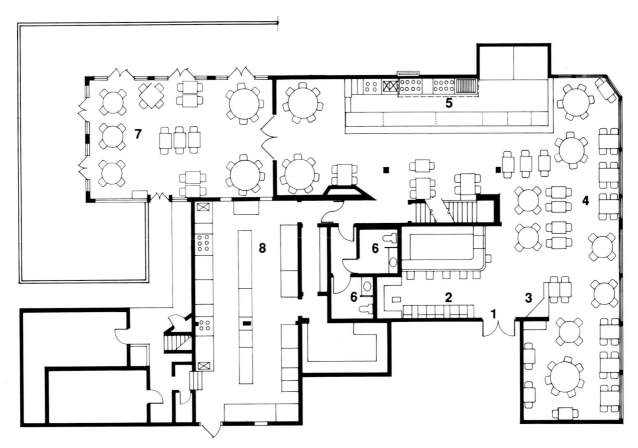

SPAGO FLOOR PLAN. COURTESY OF IMAGININGS INTERIOR DESIGN, INC. REDRAWN BY IVONNE DORF.
REFERENCE TABLE: 1. ENTRY; 2. BAR/WAITING AREA; 3. RECEPTION; 4. DINING AREA; 5. EXHIBITION KITCHEN; 6. BATHROOMS; 7. PATIO DINING; 8. KITCHEN

And, for over ten years, we've had our share. Celebrations that run the gamut from serious wine tasting to the most amusingly kooky!"

"When we first opened," Lazaroff recalls, "we were very limited for space, and the building requirements for handicap accessibility caused the facilities to be larger than we had initially planned. I decided to make them *unisex:* they alternated as male or female (one person at a time, of course). The comical situations that arose owing to the lack of adequate facilities to accommodate the crowds at Spago became an inside joke. Lines were often so long, it was bandied about town that the best place to meet a potential spouse was waiting for a lavatory at Spago."

The 6,500 sq. ft. of Spago and is located on three levels as follows:

MAIN DINING ROOM (110 SEATS): 1,600 sq. ft.
PATIO DINING AREA/GARDEN (50 SEATS):
    1,100 sq. ft.
BAR AREA (8 BARSTOOLS, 10 LOUNGE SEATS):
    400 sq. ft.
BACK KITCHEN: 1,000 sq. ft.
OPEN KITCHEN LINE: 3241 sq. ft.
EXTERIOR WALK-IN: 130 sq. ft. (since 1988)
DRY STORAGE: 200 sq. ft.
SUBTERRANEAN LIQUOR STORAGE: 100 sq. ft.
SUBTERRANEAN WINE STORAGE: 550 sq. ft.
SECOND LEVEL: offices, 585 sq. ft.; employee
    room, 225 sq. ft.; linen/glass/china, 150 sq. ft.
BATHROOMS: first level, 42 and 56 sq. ft;
    second level, 72 sq. ft; employee/second level,
    40 sq. ft. (added in 1991)

KITCHEN DESIGN

"The exposed kitchen builds a level of trust between the chef and the customer," according to Lazaroff. "It reminds you of hearth and home, since you get to see and smell the preparation of the food. The diner nods approval and can interact with the chef as though the dining room were a big family style kitchen. This homey, friendly atmosphere was and still is part of the magic at Spago.

"Seeing the colorful array of produce, the wood-burning pizza oven, and the cooks having a good time preparing the food heightens expectations and allows each diner to be part of this cooking extravaganza. For the first time in a fine dining establishment, they were able to see a master chef preparing a dish just for them."

"The kitchen was designed in a long, straight line to minimize crossover among the line cooks. Wolf planned to widen the kitchen to provide more prep area behind the line. However, this expansion proved much too expensive, because the building cantilevered in this location over a receding hill area; the shoring-up costs were prohibitive. We did, however, add an additional five feet of linear space in 1987 and realigned the front counter in 1990, adding an additional ventilation hood to accommodate more equipment and a larger work area. In total, we have increased the work space on the front line by 30 percent since the restaurant opened.

"One could argue that a disadvantage of having an exposed kitchen can sometimes be the additional noise contribution to the dining area. However, our customers never seem to mind the sounds of waiters calling their orders, 'fire it!,' or the sizzle of fish on the hot mesquite grill."

"The attitude and application of lighting at Spago jostled the public's sensibilities almost as much as the food. Europeans were much more accustomed to a higher light level. For the first time, part of the reason you came to a restaurant was to see the color and texture of the food on your plate. People were shocked to see how bright it was; they were used to candle-lit, dark restaurants.

"Special lighting was selected to illuminate the artwork on the walls and flower arrangements. Track lighting was selected because it reinforced the casual and theatrical quality of the space. It also was selected because I chose to remove the ceiling drywall for a warmer, rustic look, and a two-foot higher ceiling height. Structurally, I could not have used recessed lighting, so track lighting was viable and could be easily and fairly inexpensively installed. I created angled drywall housings for the large-aperture fixtures over the cooking area. These units provided a bright even light, while high-intensity track fixtures were utilized that could be adjusted to attractively light the food on the display counter without creating glare into the eyes of the customers. But above all, it was the amount of lumens per square foot that was causing the controversy and debate."[1]

COST OF OPERATIONS

Spago currently serves dinner daily to local and regional residents, businesspeople, tourists, and

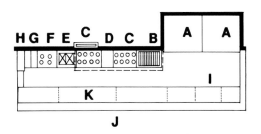

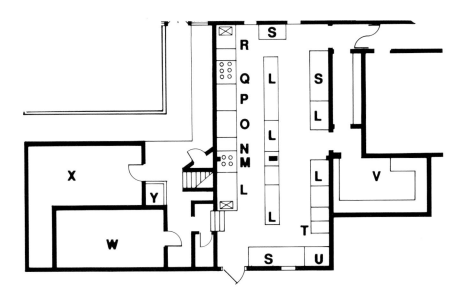

celebrities. It continues to be one of the best and most celebrated restaurants in the world. Its cost of operations are as follows:

SEATING CAPACITY: 160
AVERAGE COVERS: dinner, 360
AVERAGE CHECK: dinner, $32
LIQUOR AND WINE SALES: 35%
FOOD COST: 34%
LABOR COST: 30% (payroll tax and worker's comp. add 3% to 4%)
TOTAL EMPLOYEES: 100
RENT: 2% of gross (unique)
YEARLY SALES: $6 million

Ten years ago, Barbara Lazaroff and Wolfgang Puck revolutionized the restaurant industry by creating the "quintessential California restaurant." Most fine dining establishments at that time were dimly lit, stuffy, expensive environments. Spago's lively, open, brightly lit dining area with the open kitchen visible to every customer focused attention on the preparation and presentation of food.

It became a landmark overnight, home to legendary agent Irving Lazar's annual Oscar Night party, and is many customers' home-away-from-home because it is comfortable and unpretentious. Customers can dress casually and relax. Another big surprise was that great food prepared by master chef Wolfgang Puck was not expensive. A variety of gourmet pizzas prepared in a wood-burning oven, and now-classic dishes such as grilled free-range chicken with double-blanched garlic and Italian parsley and Sonoma lamb ravioli with tomato curry sauce altered and expanded the American palate.

Wolfgang Puck's commitment to use fresh, locally grown ingredients in dishes that delighted the eye as well as the palate has greatly influenced a generation of chefs and restaurateurs. Similarly, Barbara Lazaroff's "playground for adults" greatly influenced a generation of restaurant designers. It offered diners, designers, and owners a new perception of, and expanded possibilities for, the type of environment appropriate to fine cuisine. Together, because of their continuing commitment to quality and excellence and their passion for making each customer feel special, they have created one of the most successful restaurants in America.

NOTES

1. © 1992 by Barbara Lazaroff.

C H I N O I S

OWNERS

Wolfgang Puck and Barbara Lazaroff

DESIGNER

Barbara Lazaroff, Imaginings Interior Design, Inc.

SOURCES

ARCHITECTURAL DESIGN, INTERIORS, AND OVERALL LIGHTING: Barbara Lazaroff, Imaginings Interior Design, Inc.
CONTRACTOR: Robert Krumpe Construction
PHOTOGRAPHERS: Penny Wolin and Mark Adams
CARPENTRY: James Douglas Carpentry
PENDANT FIXTURES IN KITCHEN: Flos, Italy
LIGHT FIXTURES OVER BAR: Oluce, Italy
TRACK LIGHTING: Stilnova, Italy
RECESSED LIGHTING: Lightolier
SPOTLIGHTS: Capri
TRACK CANS: TrakLiting, Inc., and Lightolier
IRON AND COPPER WORK: Art in Iron, Los Angeles
VENTILATION HOOD: Advanced Engineering & Construction Corp.
DOORS AND WINDOWS: design by Barbara Lazaroff
CHAIRS: Alias through ICF, Inc.
TILE WORK (EXCEPT FLOORS): Payne & Bartels, design by Barbara Lazaroff
FLOOR TILE: Import Tile Center, installed by Frank Rodriguez
TABLE BASES: Falcon
ELECTRICAL AND NEON WORK: Tri-Star Electrical

PLASTER WORK: Ralph Wyatt
BLACK SLATE COUNTERTOPS AND BUS STATION TOPS: S. H. Radack & Associates
LACQUER WORK AND STAINING: Oscar's Painting
MIRROR AND GLASS: S & H Glass
SKYLIGHT: Semco, design by Barbara Lazaroff
ORCHID AND BROMELIAD GARDEN: Melinda Taylor & Douglas Raglin
FLOWER ARRANGEMENTS: Barbara Lazaroff
BRICK WOODBURNING OVEN: design by Barbara Lazaroff
FAN-SHAPED ARTWORK: Miriam Wosk
CONTEMPORARY VASES: Anna Silver, Henry Zeringue, Platt
ENAMELED METAL SCULPTURE: Dorothy Gillespie/Gallery West
EPOXY RESIN DEVIL SCULPTURE ON DINING COUNTER: Eugene Jardin
PAINTING ON BAR COUNTER: Danny Alonso, design by Barbara Lazaroff

WOLFGANG PUCK AND BARBARA LAZAROFF. PHOTOGRAPH © PAUL HARRIS.

Chinois is a 3,700 sq. ft. jewel box of a restaurant that seats ninety people. (900 sq. ft. of office and storage space were added in 1990.) It is located on Main Street in Santa Monica, California, and was completed in 1983. It serves an eclectic blend of Asian-French food in a wonderfully exuberant and colorful environment, and it is considered by many as their favorite restaurant in the world.

Barbara Lazaroff states, "The concept of Chinois arose from Wolfgang's and my need to challenge ourselves creatively.

"Spago was a very simple visual expression, and I wanted to create a new restaurant that reflected my feelings about space, color, and texture. Chinois started as a result of a dare. The investors at Spago told us we couldn't open another Spago-type restaurant within the Los Angeles metropolitan area. So Wolf and I decided to open an Asian-French restaurant. Wolf loved the challenge of creating a new menu that he wasn't familiar with.

"However, I told Wolf that I absolutely had to spend more money on Chinois than we spent at Spago in order to convey to customers in this area that we were in fact a fine dining establishment. Chinois had to be visually more refined than the bars on the block to send a message out that we were a restaurant, not a "watering hole." This area of Main Street was the home of many new wave nightclubs and was somewhat rough around the edges. Chinois softened and redefined this hard-edged image. Because of its location, we knew it could potentially attract customers from Brentwood, Pacific Palisades, and Malibu, and indeed they come from all over the world."

Chinois is located on Main Street in Santa Monica in a building that was formerly occupied by a notorious new-wave nightclub called Blackies. Lazaroff says that "when Chinois first opened on Main Street, there were not as many antique shops and avant-garde boutiques as there are now. In fact, the popularity of Chinois was in part responsible for the resurgence of that area of Main Street.

"We chose this site simply because it became available. We always thought Main Street was a good location because it had so much foot traffic. In addition, many high-end condominiums were being built in this area, adding to the already affluent customer base. Since Los Angeles is a town where everyone drives, this location could draw from Malibu, Pacific Palisades, Brentwood, Westwood, and Beverly Hills.

CHINOIS. AS ONE WALKS OR EVEN DRIVES BY, THE ENTIRE RESTAURANT IS IN FULL VIEW, ALL THE WAY BACK TO THE DRAMATIC KITCHEN. PHOTOGRAPH © PENNY WOLIN.

"The menu development for Chinois resulted from the need to create something very different from the menu at Spago," explains Lazaroff. "The original investors at Spago did not want us to open a similar restaurant nearby that could compete, so one night Wolfgang came home and jokingly said, "Let's open a Chinese restaurant." And I said, "You know, Wolf, that's a great idea."

"Wolfgang, however, didn't know a thing about Chinese or Asian cuisine, and the night before Chinois opened, hadn't tested even half the recipes. He feels cooking is a spontaneous act of creativity, and claims he was waiting to see what the restaurant looked like before he planned the menu. Considering the dishes that came out of the kitchen the first few weeks, I could tell he had been thinking about the cuisine very seriously for a long time! He says he gets extremely bored if he knows exactly what he's going to serve and it's planned months in advance. His commitment to the freshest and most intriguing ingredients at the market each day inspires him."

Wolfgang Puck adds, "We are also committed to offering our food at reasonable prices in order to convey a sense of value to our customer. The average check at Chinois was $35 when we opened, and our food costs for lobster and lamb were quite high. We spent a year and a half experimenting with the food cost of certain menu items before we began to see a profit. The food cost at Chinois is over 35 percent; the highest among all our restaurants, because of the high cost of the primary ingredients we use in our cooking. I experimented with ingredients and menu items at Chinois for a long time before I could make the food on the plate taste as delicious as it did in my imagination!"

Collaboration with executive chef Kazuto Matsusaka has produced such trend-setting dishes as whole sizzling catfish with ponzu sauce, which has raised the once-lowly catfish to gustatory stardom. Grilled Mongolian lamb chops with baby greens and cilantro vinaigrette, and Shanghai lobster risotto with spicy ginger and green onions served on a bed of deep fried baby spinach leaves exemplify the blend of Asian and European cuisines that is Chinois' signature. A delicate trio of creme brules—ginger, mandarin orange, and chocolate mint—provides a variety of taste sensations."

On the subject of transition and growth, Puck states, "After ten years with us, Kazuto will be venturing out to open his own establishment. The executive chef of Spago, Makoto Tanaka, will guide Chinois' kitchen through the nineties. I believe this introduction of new spirit provides very positive change and inspiration for both the restaurant and the individual chef."

FIRST FLAVORS

Oriental shrimp cakes with Thai cucumber salad	$16.75
Chatham scallops in rice paper sauteed with brunoise of garden vegetables with oil and vinegar dressing	$15.50
Crispy potato pancake with Chinois smoked salmon and black caviar	$19.50
Duck sausage with Mandarin plum glaze and spring roll	$12.75
Stir-fried lamb with wok-fried Maui onion rings in radicchio leaves	$11.50
Chatham clams and mussels with peppered linguini and garlic black bean sauce	$18.75
Lobster tempura with warm watercress and sweet mustard sauce	$19.25

RICE AND VEGETABLES

Chinois vegetable fried rice	$7.50
Duck fried rice	$8.50
Stir-fried baby eggplant	$7.75
Stir-fried vegetables	$7.50

BARBARA LAZAROFF - Architecture and interior design. The "on consignment" art at Chinois is available for purchase.

Lazaroff states that "$280,000 had to be spent on providing structural changes in order for the building to comply with California earthquake requirements. The space was a long, narrow shoe box and needed several essential elements in order to create a comfortable and exciting sense of space and scale. The roof was virtually removed and four feet of frontal footage were added, as were an additional five feet to the rear. Seventeen feet of a brick bearing wall were removed to create the orchid garden on the south wall.

"I wanted to create a chic casual restaurant with a kick and realized that we had to spend more money per square foot than we had at Spago to create this environment. Luckily, the banks knew us better, and we were able to raise the money. Initially, the entire budget for Chinois was $550,000; three

---

CHINOIS ON MAIN

DINNER

KAZUTO MATSUSAKA - CHEF

CHINOIS CLASSICS

ST FLAVORS

rried oysters with and salmon pearls	$9.75
th marinated ger cinnamon	$19.00
bs with	$14.75
ith potato nd Chinois	$17.50
with hrooms	$17.00
salad	$12.75
tuna sashimi i sauce	$18.75

ENTREES

Cantonese duck with fresh plum sauce	$23.75
Barbecued salmon with marinated black and gold noodles, oba vinaigrette	$21.75
Grilled Mongolian lamb chops with baby greens and cilantro vinaigrette	$27.75
Whole sizzling catfish with ginger and panzu sauce	$23.00
Shanghai lobster risotto with spicy ginger and julienne of green onions	$27.75
Charcoal grilled Szechuan beef, thinly sliced, with hot chili oil and cilantro shallot sauce	$27.50

ENTREES

Mille-feuille of squab with wild mushroom sauce	$28.50
Charred pork chop in Thai paste and apple fennel chuttney	$23.00
Crisp Mandarin quail with sweet and sour star anise sauce	$27.00
Grilled Atlantic striped bass with summer vegetables and saffron garlic oil vinaigrette	$24.75
Charred rare tuna with port and sweet pepper sauce	$22.75
Grilled chicken with sesame tahini sauce and Matsusaka's marinated vegetables	$21.50
Whole steamed scorpion fish in oriental broth (for 2 persons)	$22.00

In cooperation with California's emphasis on water conservation we are happy to serve water upon request.

CHINOIS DINNER MENU. PHOTOGRAPH © WOLFGANG PUCK/BARBARA LAZAROFF.

months into construction, we knew we would exceed the allotted funds. Items not originally scheduled, such as the $25,000 cloisonné cranes, and approximately another $50,000 for one-of-a-kind Asian artifacts such as our Buddha head and 400 60-year old Chinese plates, added significantly to the overall costs. We also closed the jobsite for over one month to travel to Japan for the opening of Spago Tokyo; and we incurred other time delays relating to our investment deal, which of course translates into cost overruns as well. We raised an initial $200,000 from the investors, and by the end of the project, our bank loan totaled $450,000 with a three-year repayment plan. We also acquired a $150,000 equipment lease. Our 6 percent rent, repayment loan, and equipment lease taught us very quickly how to operate on a tight budget. Here is a strong example where long-term commitment by ownership and our management team of Micky Kanolzer and Bella Lantzman played a key role in the eventual success of the restaurant. Chinois developed from a slow start to achieve its full stride after four years."

DESIGN CONCEPT

Barbara Lazaroff states, "The design of Chinois, like all of my designs, comes from the heart, and very personal experiences. When Wolf came home one night with the idea to create an Asian-French restaurant, I began to sketch the yin and yang logo, and the 'energy waves' I added along with the emotional ideas of balance and flow were the inspiration for many of the forms at Chinois, including the curvilinear entrance partition, undulating bar top, flowing door and window mullions, and the tile motifs. I wanted to create a relaxed, yet exotic environment. I refer to my design as 'my five-year-old fantasy of what China would look like'; it doesn't look like this, but who cares—all the better!

"Perhaps it was a reaction and an evolution of growing up in the Bronx, in an environment where the world around me wasn't physically beautiful. I turned to books, movies, museums, and my inner fantasy life for beauty. There is a growing movement toward an international style, particularly in hotel-restaurant design. But I analyze the feelings and message I'm trying to convey with each project, and each one is a very individualized singular expression. Obviously, some people prefer the ambience of one of the restaurants more than the others. We are often asked which one is our favorite; I think that is like asking a parent which of their children they love the most. Each restaurant has its assets and shortcomings, its special memories and unique emotional history. I spent my wedding night on the concrete floor of Chinois, the night before opening. I nursed my son in the Spago office in between rounds of 'meeting and greeting.' Eureka and Granita allowed me, and indeed forced me, to really stretch artistically and as a businesswoman. I've learned good (and hard) lessons."

The use of color, including fuchsia, celadon, and black, is Lazaroff's subliminal expression of a Chinese palette. Contemporary wood and paint constructions by Thai artist Kamol, an oversized painted and jeweled fan by Miriam Wosk, and exquisite vases commissioned from Anna Silver are counterpointed against antique Asian artifacts, such as a Buddha head from a Chinese temple, hand-embroidered and painted Japanese obis, moon-cake molds, and a kabuki fan Lazaroff procured in Kyoto. This sensual explosion of texture, form, and color heightens expectations and sets the stage for an exuberant dining-out experience.

There isn't a bad seat in the house at Chinois. Either you're sitting next to the entrance watching people come and go, or you're sitting next to an orchid garden ablaze with color and light. You may sit right next to the chef, sharing in the excitement of preparation. Wherever you're seated, you're part of the experience where inspired food is served in an equally inspired visual extravaganza. This space has a timeless quality and will never go out of style.

Lazaroff states that "the lighting at Chinois was selected to light objects and important focal points within the space, including the entry partition, the exposed kitchen area, the floral displays, artwork, and artifacts. Special effects include fuchsia neon concealed in the perimeter of the skylight soffit, which reflects off the solar reflective glass and creates a mirror at night. The patrons gazing upward are treated to kaleidoscope visions of the reflected dining room. The lighting reinforces the interior shapes and forms, and highlights the tile mosaics, art, and exotic flower arrangements, and generally heightens the sense of drama and allure.

The 'coolie-hat'-shaped pendant fixtures over the bar define this space and add sparkle, illuminating the handpainted bar top. The custom copperplated pendants adjacent to the exposed cooking area follow the line of the performance seating counter and spotlight the food presentation. The lacquered Italian track lighting running the length of the dining room was specially selected to provide the best color rendition for the artwork and floral displays, and its profile reminds one of pop-art fans."

"During the day," says Lazaroff, "the natural light is diffused by the abundant window display of vivid orchids and bromeliads, and additional light pours through a 20' by 6' skylight. In the evening, the lighting creates a mystical and inviting glow, drawing passersby to peer through the expansive French doors at the activity within."

THE SKYLIGHT IN THE CEILING AND THE ELABORATE ORCHID WINDOW DEFLECT THE EYE UPWARD AND OUTWARD, VISUALLY BREAKING UP THE "RAILROAD CAR" FORM. PHOTOGRAPH © PENNY WOLIN.

SPACE PLANNING

Barbara Lazaroff says that "Chinois was a long, dreary rectangle of a space. By adding five feet in the rear, I could provide greatly needed kitchen space, and by extending the frontal footage another four feet, I could create seating for up to twelve additional customers and a small but adequate reception area. The space planning for the kitchen came first, and we were able to set aside a total of almost 35 percent of the overall space for storage, prep, and cooking areas. We prepared a projection of profit and loss and determined that we needed at least 90 seats for successful operation. This seating capacity was based on the average check and the amount of covers we expected to do during each service.

"I determined early on in the space planning phase that I had to make each table 2" smaller than normal, and the chair width could not exceed 18" in order to fit in 90 seats. I also wanted round tables, but didn't want to turn away large parties, so I designed tables with flaps that converted into squares.

"In order to alleviate the long narrow feeling, I created a sequence of spaces that tricked the eye. The undulating, curvilinear tiled partition at the entrance guides the customer to the right and focuses attention on the array of colorful, highly textured surfaces, such as bamboo, curved and lacquered window mullions, and custom tile. The skylight in the ceiling and the elaborate orchid garden window deflect the eye upward and outward, visually breaking up the railroad car form. In addition, the exposed kitchen with its reflective hammered copper hood and high-

MANY PEOPLE RESERVE THE COUNTER ADJACENT TO THE EXHIBITION KITCHEN TO ENJOY THE FLOOR SHOW AS CHEFS PREPARE FOOD IN THE SIZZLING WOKS AND ON THE GRILL. PHOTOGRAPH © PENNY WOLIN.

intensity lighting is the high-energy focal point at the end of this animated rectangle. Adjacent to the open kitchen is the 'performance seating' counter, which allows people to feel very comfortable dining alone. Many people reserve the counter to enjoy the 'floor show,' as chefs prepare food in the sizzling woks and on the grill.

"The curvilinear bar is an 'energy wave' that again allows the eye to focus on an object rather than on the geometry of the space. There is no divider between the dining room and the bar

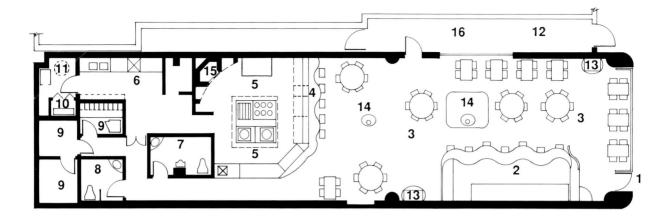

CHINOIS FLOOR PLAN.
PLANS ON THIS PAGE COURTESY OF IMAGININGS
DESIGN, INC. REDRAWN BY LORRAINE KNAPP.
REFERENCE TABLE: 1. ENTRY; 2. BAR; 3. DINING
AREA; 4. COUNTER DINING; 5. EXHIBITION KITCHEN;
6. BACK KITCHEN; 7. MEN'S RESTROOM; 8. WOMEN'S
RESTROOM; 9. STORAGE; 10. ELECTRICAL PANEL;
11. HOT WATER HEATER; 12. EXIT PASSAGE; 13. BUS
STATION; 14. STATUE; 15. OVEN; 16. BROMELIAD
DISPLAY

CHINOIS KITCHEN PLAN.
REDRAWN BY LORRAINE KNAPP.
REFERENCE TABLE: A. GRILL; B. 6-BURNER STOVE
WITH OVEN; C. WATER-COOLED WOKS; D. OVEN,
ROTISSERIE; E. SALAD AND COLD APPETIZER PREP;
F. PICK-UP; G. COUNTER SEATING; H. UNDERCOUNTER
REFRIGERATION; I. UNDERCOUNTER FREEZER;
J. WORK TABLE AND UNDERCOUNTER REFRIGERATOR;
K. WALK-IN REFRIGERATOR; L. STORAGE;
M. ELECTRICAL PANEL; N. TRASH COMPACTOR;
O. OFFICE; P. DISHWASHING

because the space is so narrow. This worked to our advantage, because of the positive energy created between people at the bar and the tables. It is a people-watching space where individuals seated at the bar can see the diners, and vice-versa. Everyone seated in the space has a view of the exposed kitchen and the entrance.

"Design details include tile walls, which are adorned with swooping, interwoven 'energy waves' spliced into a background of unevenly broken tiles that have been arranged to create a dynamic of visual dimension. Tubular soffits and lacquered compound curves meld into the sandblasted ceiling joists. The uninterrupted expanse of eight 8' high doors reveals the activity on Main Street and adds a sense of depth. Indeed, as one walks or even drives by, the entire restaurant is in full view, all the way back to the dramatic kitchen. The space has a very seductive, inviting glow. After nine years, I'm still stimulated as I approach and enter Chinois."

Chinois is 3,700 square feet and is on one level (900 sq. ft. were added in 1990):

BAR AREA: 200 sq. ft.
DINING ROOM: 1,125 sq. ft.
EXPOSED KITCHEN: 425 sq. ft.
PREP KITCHEN: 350 sq. ft.
STORAGE: 180 sq. ft.
BATHROOMS: 130 sq. ft.
OFFICE: 50 sq. ft.
EXTERIOR PASSAGEWAY: 380 sq. ft.

KITCHEN DESIGN

"The kitchen design was the initial consideration at Chinois," states Barbara Lazaroff. "It would have been easier if the kitchen could have been a bit larger. In fact, we extended the kitchen on the plans a number of times, and finally Wolf wanted to extend the exhibition kitchen an additional three feet into the dining area. However, this would have substantially reduced the number of seats, which we needed to make Chinois a profitable venture. The kitchen at Chinois occupies 30 percent of the entire space. The storage and prep areas as well as the kitchen itself have to be sufficiently sized to enable the staff to prepare and execute the food properly. We have now acquired the space next door, moved the employees' dressing rooms and our office there, and now utilize the formerly occupied area for a new pastry prep area. This has made operations much more efficient and has also brought down food costs, since we no longer have to purchase and transport any of our desserts from Spago.

"The peninsula arrangement of the kitchen conserves space and works because the food is served family style. Because of the narrowness of the restaurant, a straight cooking line would not have been feasible. Also, people love to sit at the counter adjacent to the kitchen: the performance seating reminiscent of a sushi bar counter is like participatory theater. People can connect with the chefs, and the height of the counter actually allows people to peer into the sizzling woks as they are perched on their stools.

"The ventilation hoods had to be extremely efficient to handle the heat and potential smoke rollout. The charcoal grill, 8-burner Wolf Range stove with a convection oven, and 3-bowl water-cooled woks all produce a great deal of BTUs and smoke. The make-up air had to be strategically placed to avoid cold air circulation across the food pick-up areas.

"The compact Chinois kitchen is probably one of the most efficient and highly productive kitchen designs, considering the space constraints that challenged us."[1]

COST OF OPERATIONS

Chinois currently serves approximately 180 dinners daily and 60 lunches (Chinois is open only Wednesday, Thursday, and Friday to lunch customers) to local and regional residents, businesspeople, tourists, and celebrities. Chinois is primarily a dinner destination restaurant, and because there are not large office buildings in close proximity to the restaurant, lunch is not Chinois' primary source of business. It continues to be many customers' favorite restaurant in the world. Its cost of operations are as follows:

SEATING CAPACITY: 90 (including counter
    seating); bar, 10
AVERAGE COVERS: lunch, 60; dinner, 180
AVERAGE CHECK: lunch, $28; dinner, $50

LIQUOR AND WINE SALES: 25% of sales
FOOD COST: 34%
LABOR COST: 22.5% (payroll taxes and worker's
    comp. add 3.5%)
TOTAL EMPLOYEES: 55
RENT: 6%
YEARLY SALES: $3.5 million

Chinois is a true collaboration between two people who are committed to excellence. Barbara Lazaroff and Wolfgang Puck have created a restaurant that is pure magic. When one walks into this space, there is a sense that something wonderful is about to occur. The sensual explosion of Fellini-esque form and hue, and the creative use of light in this space heightens expectations and sets the stage for the wonderful food that tantalizes the palate.

The link between artful expression in both food and design is at its height in Chinois. Each reinforces the other to create a very memorable dining-out experience. Everyone in the restaurant feels special and is witness to visual and culinary brilliance. The food and design express their crosscultural influences from both East and West. Wolfgang Puck uses French style and technique blended with Asian ingredients to create signature Chinois dishes.

Wolfgang Puck was influenced in large part by Barbara Lazaroff's masterful blending of European style and Asiatic influences. Lazaroff wanted to created a showplace for Puck's highly interpretive version of Asian-French cuisine. Customers are treated to a dazzling show, on the walls as well as the plate, and leave feeling that they have received great value. Chinois is successful because of this wonderful blend of design, reasonably priced yet excellent food, and knowledgeable yet amiable service. The unique and friendly atmosphere and inimitable cuisine keep people coming back for more.

The commitment to quality in both food and design raised food and construction costs, causing Lazaroff and Puck to struggle somewhat through the first four years. Chinois never suffered from lack of customers, however. The consistently wonderful food and the timeless, enduring environment will never lose their freshness and have made Chinois a runaway hit.

NOTES
1. © 1992 by Barbara Lazaroff.

EUREKA

OWNERS

Wolfgang Puck, Barbara Lazaroff, and the Los Angeles Brewing Co.

DESIGNER

Barbara Lazaroff, Imaginings Interior Design, Inc.

SOURCES

ARCHITECTURAL DESIGN, INTERIORS, AND OVERALL LIGHTING: Barbara Lazaroff, Imaginings Interior Design, Inc.
CONTRACTOR: Pacific Southwest Development
ADDT'L RENDERING AND DETAILING: Deborah Forbes
SHELL ARCHITECT: Peter Devereaux
PHOTOGRAPHY: Penny Wolin and Toshi Yoshimi
METALWORK, GLASS, DOORS, AWNING FABRICATION: Venice Glass/Ali Harati, Principal
LIGHTING: Diva collection, CSL Lighting, Lightolier, Poulsen Lighting, Bishops Lighting, LSI
CUSTOM CERAMIC TILES: Mike Payne & Associates/Architectural Ceramics
ETCHED GLASS BLOCK: Polly Gessel
KITCHEN AND BAR EQUIPMENT: Avery Restaurant Supply/Shel Brucker and Lee Elster
VENTILATION HOOD: Avery Restaurant Supply, design by Barbara Lazaroff, Imaginings
BAR: Venice Glass, design by Barbara Lazaroff
KITCHEN AND KITCHEN EQUIPMENT DESIGN: Wolfgang Puck, Barbara Lazaroff, and Lee Elster/Avery Restaurant Supply

BACK BAR/KITCHEN CONSULTANT: Lee Elster/Avery Restaurant Supply
CUSTOM BRICK OVEN: Eugenio Chiusaroli
BREWING EQUIPMENT: A. Steinecker Machinenfabrik, GmbH
BOOTH AND TABLE FABRICATION: Kress Industries
TABLE DESIGN, BOOTH DETAILING: Barbara Lazaroff, Imaginings
BOOTH COVERING: Like Leather
CHAIRS, STOOLS/CAST ALUMINUM, AND MAHOGANY: Bob Josten
CARPET: Harbinger
MAIN DINING ROOM CHAIRS: Cappellini "Xan" chairs/Diva Collection
LANDSCAPING: E. P. T. Dave Thoms
TEXTURED SILICA GEL AND METAL FILING WALL FINISH: Tim Harris
PAINTED CEILING TREATMENT AND OTHER SURFACES: Lencon Painters
ARTWORK: Barbara Lazaroff, Judy Stabile, Oscar Pumpin, Susan Venable

WOLFGANG PUCK AND BARBARA LAZAROFF. PHOTOGRAPH © PAUL HARRIS.

Eureka Restaurant and Brewery is an 8,000 sq. ft. full-service restaurant (with an additional 2,000 sq. ft. for brew tanks), brew pub, and charcuterie that seats 170 people in the dining room and serves twenty at the "elbow bar." The beverage bar seats up to thirty-four for drinks. The restaurant is attached to an additional 20,000 sq. ft. structure that houses a brewery with the capacity to produce 175,000 cases a year of Eureka beer for national and international distribution.

The complex is located in an industrial area of Santa Monica, California, and was completed in 1990. It serves a crosscultural blend of food in an energized, industrial-themed environment. It is another visual and culinary delight from the team of Barbara Lazaroff and Wolfgang Puck.

According to Wolfgang Puck, "The idea for Eureka revolved around the concept of creating a brewery for production of beer to be sold to retail outlets. The original idea for a microbrewery was the long-time dream of Mark Scott, Jerry Goldstein, and Andrew Hoffman and had been in a preliminary development stage for several years before they approached Barbara and me to combine it with a restaurant."

The large public space that is the restaurant is a very modern version of the old-fashioned beer hall. Wolfgang Puck and Barbara Lazaroff wanted to create a reasonably priced menu geared toward the neighborhood, which includes postproduction studios, computer think-tank companies at lunch, and people from the West Los Angeles area at dinner. Because the home-brewed beer is the beverage of choice at Eureka, the average check for many diners is approximately ten dollars lower than at the other Puck/Lazaroff restaurants. Investors in Eureka were buying shares in both the brewery and the restaurant in one package.

The location for Eureka was critical to its success. Since a brewery is an industrial/manufacturing use of real estate, Eureka needed to be located in an area where mixed use of land was acceptable.

The only industrial park on the west side of Los Angeles was the Santa Monica/Olympic corridor. There were industrial areas in East Los Angeles, but Wolfgang and Barbara did not feel they would be suitable for the restaurant. The site selected would draw its dinner crowd from nearby Westwood, Brentwood, and Greater Los Angeles. Wolfgang

Puck states, "In Los Angeles, everyone has to drive anyway, and an extra five or ten minutes on the freeway is not considered an inconvenience." Barbara Lazaroff feels that "the slightly out-of-the-way location in an industrial park added to the allure and mystery of Eureka. The neighborhood is very modest and unassuming, the structure is quite imposing with its expansive windows exposing the enormous brew tanks. As you turn the corner and slowly approach—it suddenly appears."

Wolfgang Puck states, "What was surprising is how well we are doing at lunch. The post-production film studios that surround us, such as Skywalker, George Lucas' Sound Studios, and Big Time, Inc., where people like Oliver Stone sound edit their movies, create a great lunch crowd."

MENU DEVELOPMENT

The menu developed by chef Wolfgang Puck and Jody Denton is an eclectic blend of Asian, Latin, and European cuisines with an American flair. The emphasis is on fresh, locally produced ingredients.

Specialties include pizzas baked in a wood-burning oven, homemade cheeses, innovative sausages, prosciutto, and cured and smoked meats, which are made on the premises and displayed in the charcuterie and are thus highly visible from the dining room. Fresh pastas and mesquite-grilled

AS YOU ENTER THE DRIVEWAY, YOU ARE STRUCK BY THE DRAMATIC IMPACT OF THE BREW TANKS AND THE ENTRANCE. PHOTOGRAPH © PENNY WOLIN.

fish and meats are seasoned with Oriental or Latin herbs and spices. In addition, a large assortment of breads and rolls are baked fresh daily. Pastries, ice creams, and cookies are also homemade.

Eureka California Lager, Eureka Pilsner, and Eureka California Dark are produced at the brewery and served together with other domestic and imported beers. An extensive wine list is also offered. The average check is reasonably priced at $20 for lunch and $32 for dinner.

BUDGET

Eureka was a technically and financially complex project that combined a brewery and a restaurant. Unforeseen sewer and drainage problems, as well as other costly infrastructure necessities, required using money set aside for marketing the beer to complete construction. The project was also delayed for over four months during construction, primarily because of such technical mishaps.

Barbara Lazaroff states, "A variety of other issues contributed to delaying the project for another year. The community surrounding Eureka was against the project because they feared it would encourage drunk drivers on their streets. We were forced to hire legal assistance and lobby the city to retain our industrial use permit, which the building was already zoned for. The partners also had to lobby Sacramento for a law that would allow us to own a wholesale liquor license while retaining our retail liquor licenses.

"In addition, prior to commencing construction, parking requirements necessitated making costly changes to the building and surrounding land. These contingencies led us to the decision to tear down the existing warehouse structure and build from the ground up. A second prospectus was prepared and issued, which caused a further time delay. All of these budget overruns required an additional $1.5 million investment. Much of this money was needed to complete the brewery, not the restaurant portion. There was not adequate funding for the building of the restaurant, which came into full swing after the brewery was three-quarters of the way completed, and we elected to borrow an additional $400,000 to complete the restaurant interior.

"The initial problems with the beer and the fact that money was not available for marketing have not made the brewery a highly profitable venture as of yet. The restaurant, however, has exceeded its projections. We projected $4.5 million, and the restaurant is grossing over $5 million annually.

"Our goal is for the beer to eventually take off in the marketplace so that the brewery can one day support the restaurant. Presently, the restaurant is the money-making venture. Obviously, no savvy businessperson would spend the huge sum of money we did for the entire complex for just a restaurant alone. The restaurant is fabulous as a separate entity, but it was created in large part for the promotion of Eureka Beer. We are presently in a restructuring phase with some of our original major investors, such as J. P. Jones Dejoria of John Paul Mitchell Systems and Maurice Marciano of Guess? Jeans, to provide adequate monies for the proper and large-scale promotion of the beer."

JODY DENTON · CHEF

HOT AND COLD APPETIZERS

HOUSE SMOKED SALMON WITH GRILLED FENNEL VINAIGRETTE AND ONION LAVOSH

JAPANESE BARBEQUED EEL AND RARE TUNA WITH CUCUMBER-RICE SALAD AND TOASTED SESAME DRESSING

LAMB CARNITAS EMPANADA WITH A ROASTED CORN-POBLANO CHILI SAUCE

CRAB FALAFEL SALAD WITH A SAFFRON PITA AND RED PEPPER TAHINI

TANDOORI CHICKEN SALAD WITH LENTIL CHIPS AND SPICY MANGO RELISH

BABY ROMAINE WITH SUMMER TOMATOES AND FRESH BREADSTICKS

TAMARI SEARED YELLOWTAIL WITH SAUTEED ASPARAGUS AND LEMON SAKE CREAM

MIXED GREEN SALAD WITH GRILLED VEGETABLE VINAIGRETTE AND FETA CHEESE

PIZZA FROM OUR WOOD BURNING OVEN

ITALIAN SAUSAGE WITH ROASTED PEPPERS AND BASIL

THAI SHRIMP WITH STIR FRIED VEGETABLES AND PEANUTS

GRILLED VEGETABLES WITH PLUM TOMATOES AND PARMESAN CHEESE

WILD MUSHROOMS AND GOAT CHEESE WITH CARAMELIZED SHALLOTS

GRILLED CHIPOTLE BEEF WITH SMOKED MOZZARELLA AND CILANTRO

PASTA

BAMBOO STEAMED LOBSTER DIM SUM WITH BLACK VINEGAR PONZU

BLUE CHEESE-POTATO RAVIOLI WITH A BABY CHICKORY SALAD AND PEAR SAUCE

SPINACH LINGUINI WITH MANILLA CLAMS, SUMMER VEGETABLES AND A ROASTED GARLIC-TOMATO BROTH

SEARED SCALLOPS, SHRIMP AND BASS WITH BLACK OLIVE GNOCCHI AND OREGANO-ROASTED TOMATO PESTO

"Originally, the investors wanted an old-fashioned brewery with traditional wood finishes," states Barbara Lazaroff. "I said I thought it would be more appropriate to create a brewery for the 1990s. A brewery is a factory for the production of beer, and I felt that the restaurant should reflect this industrial aesthetic. The environment had to be fun, whimsical, and energized in order to appeal to a young crowd, as well as our established clientele.

"As a child, I was mesmerized by the film classics *Metropolis* by Fritz Lang and Charlie Chaplin's *Modern Times*. The image of the big gears turning is etched in my memory and provided the inspiration for Eureka's visual theme. The whimsical combination of gears, bolts, and rivets throughout the space is a testament to the brewmaster's art and to twentieth century industry.

"As you enter the driveway (guided by elegant bollard light standards) you are struck by the dramatic impact of the entry, with its industrial copper and etched glass doors covered by a copper awning that sweeps toward the sky. Glass block, a traditional industrial material, is used under the brewhouse windows. These glass blocks are etched with gears, levers, bolts, and rivets, and provide the first hints that you are about to enter a whimsical space. The narrow entryway to Eureka adjacent to the vaulted brewhouse contains an 8' by 5' glass block wall etched with an abstract interplay of oversized gears with mechanical devices.

EUREKA DINNER MENU.
PHOTOGRAPH © WOLFGANG
PUCK/BARBARA LAZAROFF.

FROM OUR CHARCUTERIE

WILD BOAR BRATWURST WITH HORSERADISH CREAM AND APPLE WALNUT CHUTNEY	9.00
SPICY JAMAICAN CHICKEN SAUSAGE WITH BLACK BEANS AND TAMARIND CREAM	8.50
SMOKED ALMOND DUCK SAUSAGE WITH SOBA NOODLE CAKE AND BLOOD ORANGE-GINGER SYRUP	9.50
BARBEQUED PORK SAUSAGE WITH GRILLED PINEAPPLE RELISH	9.00
SHELLFISH PAELLA SAUSAGE WITH SHRIMP-TOMATO COULIS AND SALSIFY CHIPS	10.00

ENTREES

ROASTED SALMON WITH BLACK BEAN-GOAT CHEESE SAUCE AND GRILLED ONION RELLENO	18.00
SEARED MEDALLIONS OF LAMB WITH CURRIED GREEN ONION NOODLES AND TOASTED PEANUTS	18.50
ACHIOTE GRILLED CHICKEN WITH YELLOW TOMATO MOLE AND TORTILLA LASAGNA	16.50
WOK CHARRED DUCK WITH TOGAROSHI-PLUM BROTH AND MUSHROOM WONTON STICKS	19.00
LEMON-THYME SWORDFISH WITH ASPARAGUS AND WILD MUSHROOM POLENTA	19.50
CORN BATTERED SHRIMP WITH GUAJILLO CHILI SALSA AND WARM COUNTRY POTATO SALAD	18.50
CHINESE ROASTED PORK CHOP WITH SHIITAKE FRIED RICE	16.50
GRILLED MAHI MAHI WITH TOASTED MACADAMIA NUT SAUCE AND LOMI SALMON RELISH	17.50
PEPPER GRILLED RIBEYE STEAK WITH SMOKED TOMATO KETCHUP AND FRIED ONIONS	22.50

ARCHITECTURAL AND INTERIOR DESIGN AND LIGHTING BY BARBARA LAZAROFF
Imaginings Interior Design, Inc.

Selected works of art are on consignment and are available for sale.

COMPLIMENTARY MENU COPIES AVAILABLE FROM HOST

"As you enter the dining room, you are met by the elegant curved maitre d' station and the unusual structure made of perforated pewter panels, copper, and stainless steel that stands directly behind it, which functions as coat storage and houses the audio system and master computer panel for the kinetic art. This structure is lit from within, and the light emanating through the perforated panels combines an artistic element with its true function.

"To the right, you observe the commanding 40'-long hand-hammered copper bar top, the front face of which is accented with perforated

THE DINING ROOM INCORPORATES TWO LEVELS, DIVIDED WITH A LOW WALL OF INTERIOR-LIT ETCHED GLASS BLOCKS. PHOTOGRAPH © PENNY WOLIN.

YOU CAN OBSERVE THE ENORMOUS BREW KETTLES FROM THE ENTIRE RESTAURANT. PHOTOGRAPH © PENNY WOLIN.

pewter panels in an interplay of copper pipes and oversized stainless steel nuts and brass bolts. Behind the bar, framed by 15' by 12' copper-clad windows, you can observe the enormous brew kettles warmed with twenty large fresnel lights, which provide an intense copper glow to the tanks, which overflow onto the bar top, creating an almost fluid illusion.

"At the back of the restaurant is the showcase exhibition kitchen. Incorporating a gear motif to continue the industrial theme, I framed the counter with slate shaped in the form of sawtooth gears and placed glazed wall tiles mimicking gears behind the cooking line. In addition, custom copper and stainless hoods are bordered with massive stainless steel nuts and bronze bolts.

"Off to one side of the exhibition kitchen is the charcuterie, in which homemade sausages, salamies, and prosciuttos are produced and aged. The window to the charcuterie is framed with glazed tiles in the shapes of the various sausages.

"The dining room incorporates two levels, divided with a low wall of interior-lit etched glass blocks, topped by a brushed-stainless hand rail atop bands of copper and stainless steel. The metal is clad with more nuts and bolts.

"A glance at the copper glow of the vaulted skylights over the dining room provides a sense of a gold mine and provides a warmth as a counterpoint to the general use of metals.

"I continued the gear motif throughout the entryway to the dining room by utilizing granite and Chinese slate cut in the shape of sawtooth gears; even the carpeting has been cut to accommodate the jagged teeth of these slate gears.

"Additional unique accents include the custom-crafted striated wood tabletops, which are accompanied by artist Bob Josten's unique cast-aluminum and hand-carved hard rock maple wood chairs and the companion barstools made expressly for Eureka. The recessed dining room sports handsome Cappellini "Xan" chairs from Italy, with chrome and cherry wood frames with a finely patterned black and white upholstery.

"Eureka's lighting is one of its grace points. Various small points of light imbue the space with a warm glow, particularly those areas where the lights reflect off the orange hue of the polished copper and the apricot textured walls. Lighting is the most challenging yet rewarding device available to the designer, for lighting has the potential to provide the drama that ties all other elements of design together. By installing numerous and varied light sources, each focused on a specific area of the restaurant, I was able to accent the details of the underlying design. I combined Ingo Maurer's cable system with German-made Grau fixtures. These units seem to be floating above the main dining room, and their forms are themselves conversation pieces. The imported wall sconces and torcheres are pieces of sculpture as well as light points. I utilized billboard lighting inside the brew house to provide strong, even light that diffuses through the etched block walls below the large glass panels that expose the brew kettles. The 300-watt LSI fresnels with copper gels are angled to best illuminate the brew kettles and produce a nighttime illusion of them being made of copper. The reflected glow from the tanks cascades onto the hand-hammered copper bar top, producing a fluid effect. The elegant solid copper Poulsen pendants over the bar provide a soft glow, define the bar counter, and were selected for their harmonious form. The charcuterie lights are gelled to provide a flattering light to the hams, sausages, and other meats displayed in this area. The overall light level at Eureka is kept somewhat lower than our other restaurants because of all of the reflective surfaces and to set off focal points, such as the brew tanks, artwork, the orange neon in the skylight soffits, kitchen, and charcuterie areas, and such elements as the kinetic art, which has its own art display.

"I have also installed a programmable computerized dimming system by Lightolier that handles the 106 dimmable circuits. With it, one can preset various combinations of lighting and thereby have the capability of altering the environment and mood of the restaurant. I have provided a different setting depending on the time of day, the weather, and the type of event at the brewery. It also allows the staff and myself the ease of controlling a very complex lighting system efficiently before every service, so that we may spend the time attending to our customers. It is also comforting to know that I can walk into the restaurant and be assured that it is lit the way I originally intended it to be."

SPACE PLANNING

Barbara Lazaroff states that "the functional components of the brewery came first in the space planning of Eureka. The brew tanks and all other support space generally dictated the size of the restaurant. The restaurant is 8,000 sq. ft., with an additional 2,000 sq. ft. display area for the brew tanks. The kitchen prep area is quite large because we have a bakery that produces all the bread for Eureka and half of the bread for Granita. All of the sausages that we serve on premises are prepared in the charcuterie.

"The brew tanks became the visual focus for the restaurant and had to be visible from the exterior entry, the bar area, and the dining room. We had the open kitchen concept; now we had the open brewery. We also knew we needed a very large bar because one of the main features of the restaurant was the beer. We only have a beer and wine license.

"The elbow bar that runs parallel with the bar is a great place for people who come alone to have a meal and a drink. At Chinois, as well as at Eureka, people who come alone love to sit at the counter to watch the action. The exhibition kitchen was placed opposite the entrance area and the bar to maximize its dramatic setting. I also placed a window between the dining room and

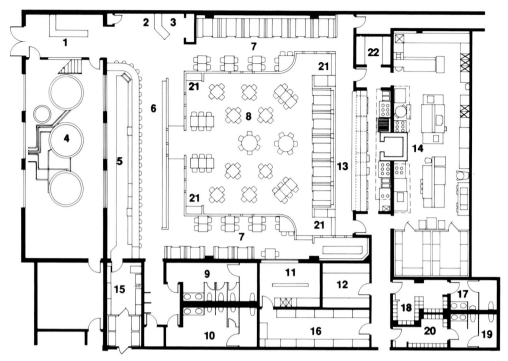

EUREKA FLOOR PLAN. PLANS ON THIS PAGE COURTESY OF IMAGININGS INTERIOR DESIGN, INC. REDRAWN BY IVONNE DORF. REFERENCE TABLE: 1. ENTRY/CASHIER/WAITING; 2. MAITRE D'; 3. COAT CHECK; 4. BREW HOUSE; 5. BAR; 6. ELBOW BAR; 7. DINING; 8. LOWER DINING AREA; 9. WOMEN'S BATHROOM; 10. MEN'S BATHROOM; 11. CHARCUTERIE; 12. OFFICE; 13. EXHIBITION KITCHEN; 14. KITCHEN; 15. BEVERAGE STORAGE; 16. STORAGE; 17. MALE EMPLOYEE'S BATHROOM; 18. MEN'S LOCKERS; 19. FEMALE EMPLOYEE'S BATHROOM; 20. WOMEN'S LOCKERS; 21. BUS STATIONS; 22. COFFEE, WATER STATION, ICE MACHINE

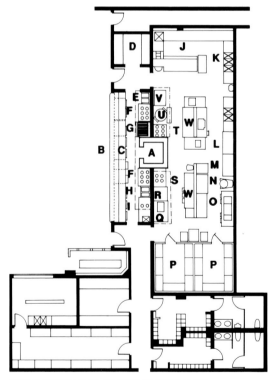

EUREKA KITCHEN PLAN. REDRAWN BY IVONNE DORF.
REFERENCE TABLE: A. OVEN; B. WAITSTAFF PICK-UP;
C. UNDERCOUNTER REFRIGERATOR; D. COFFEE, WATER, ICE STATION;
E. FRYERS; F. 6-BURNER STOVE WITH CONVECTION OVEN BELOW;
G. BROILER; H. PASTA COOKER; I. WORK TABLE WITH 2-BURNER
OVEN; J. DISHWASHING; K. POT WASHING; L. REFRIGERATOR;
M. FREEZER; N. 60 QT. MIXER; O. DOUGH SHEETER; P. WALK-IN
COOLERS; Q. TRIPLE BAKE OVEN; R. DOUBLE CONVECTION OVEN;
S. 4-BURNER OVEN; T. 6-BURNER OVEN; U. 40 GALLON KETTLE;
V. SMOKE OVEN; W. PREP COUNTERS

the charcuterie so people could peer in to see the preparation and display of the sausages. This left one wall for a 'kinetic computer-animated sculpture' that I envisioned from the beginning of this project. This Rube Goldberg-like piece is a tongue-in-cheek folk art relief map of Los Angeles with the Eureka Brewery at its central focal point. It is a whimsical work that infuses a sense of humor into this otherwise modern palette of metallic surfaces and nuts and bolts."

The parking garage for this site had to be placed on the top of the building, restricting the height of the ceiling owing to site-line restrictions from street level. This restriction mandated that the dining room be lowered in the center to create a grand scale for this space.

BREWERY: 20,000 sq. ft.
ENTRY/RECEPTION: 650 sq. ft.
BAR AREA: 800 sq. ft.
BEER STORAGE: 200 sq. ft.
DINING AREA: 2,750 sq. ft.
BATHROOMS: 550 sq. ft.
TELEPHONE AREA: 100 sq. ft.
EXHIBITION KITCHEN: 450 sq. ft.
DISHWASHING: 280 sq. ft.
PREP KITCHEN STORAGE: 1,000 sq. ft.

CHARCUTERIE/STORAGE: 500 sq. ft.
OFFICE: 150 sq. ft.
EMPLOYEE'S LOCKERS/BATHROOMS: 500 sq. ft.

KITCHEN DESIGN

Lazaroff explains, "The exhibition kitchen is a 35' straight line design with the wood-burning oven taking center stage. The kitchen is directly opposite the three prominent brew kettles with the dining room directly between. As one enters the restaurant, the kitchen is the most obvious focal point. The 35' ventilation hood in the exhibition kitchen appears to be three separate units joined together. They are designed to emulate and reinforce the design element of the three brew kettles directly across the room.

"The wood-burning oven was placed center on the cook line for personal reasons of symmetry of design. It was the major point of contention between Wolfgang and myself because with regard to traffic flow and chef visibility, it was not the optimum point of placement, but it is certainly workable."

Wolfgang Puck states, "The Eureka kitchen line consists of a six-burner stove for hot appetizers and sausages. Next on line is the pasta cooker, which is adjacent to another six-burner stove utilized for finishing the pasta and cooking the various pasta sauces. The wood-burning oven follows, which is utilized for roasting fish meats and making our well-known pizzas. We have a large grill for fish, chicken, lamb, and beef with another six-burner stove for sautéeing other main courses. We also have two french fryers to create various tempura dishes, fresh french fries, and vegetable chips.

"The front kitchen has places to accommodate pasta racks, storage, and undercounter front line refrigeration for *mise en place*. The back kitchen has two 10' by 12' walk-in refrigerators, a large pastry section, and bakery with convection ovens where we produce our fresh breads, rolls, and breadsticks daily. Our back kitchen at Eureka is a luxury—because of this space we are able to experiment greatly in the bakery and pastry department, and, additionally, it is the only restaurant with a separate charcuterie for the butchering and preparation of sausages and other meats. We also have an automatic smoker for smoking our meat, sausages, and fish. Many people believe that you need an extremely large kitchen to produce many covers every evening. Actually, the amount of dinners is more directly related to the composition and complexity of the dishes."[1]

COST OF OPERATIONS

Eureka currently serves approximately 500 covers daily to local and regional residents, film production workers, tourists and celebrities. The brewery and the restaurant continue to be a hot destination. Its cost of operations are as follows:

SEATING CAPACITY: dining, 170; counter, 10; bar, 20-34
AVERAGE WEEKLY COVERS: lunch, 170; dinner, 750
AVERAGE CHECK: lunch, $20; dinner, $32
BEER AND WINE SALES: 30%
FOOD COST: 32%
LABOR COST: 35%
TOTAL EMPLOYEES: 124
RENT: approximately $1.10 per sq. ft. (industrial space)
YEARLY SALES: $6 million

Eureka Restaurant and Brewery is a complex project that combines a state-of-the-art brewery and a modern-day version of a beer hall with a whimsical neoindustrial-themed restaurant.

Eureka's restaurant location in an industrial area made it possible to function as a brewery as well. The rental rate for industrial space contributes to lower operational costs for the restaurant. Additionally, its proximity to postproduction film studios provides a great deal of customers at lunch. The dinner crowd comes from nearby West Los Angeles, Santa Monica, and from Malibu, and indeed it is becoming a "happening" destination restaurant for individuals from all over the world who wish to experience this highly original setting.

Eureka's sparkling environment of innovative industrial materials. open kitchen, and brew tanks, combined with the large open dining room and dramatic bar area, create a public space that is great for people watching. It is a wonderful backdrop for drinking beer, munching on a wild boar bratwurst, or eating wok-charred duck. The biggest surprise is that all this delightful food coupled with the incredible environment is a great bargain. The average check is $20 for lunch and $32 for dinner, including beer and wine.

NOTES

1. © 1992 by Barbara Lazaroff.

G R A N I T A

OWNERS

Wolfgang Puck and Barbara Lazaroff

DESIGNER

Barbara Lazaroff, Imaginings Interior Design, Inc.

WOLFGANG PUCK AND BARBARA LAZAROFF. PHOTOGRAPH © PAUL HARRIS.

SOURCES

ARCHITECTURAL DESIGN, INTERIORS, AND OVERALL LIGHTING: Barbara Lazaroff, Imaginings Interior Design, Inc.
CONTRACTOR: Pacific Southwest Development
PROJECT SUPERINTENDENT: Bill Lazarony
ADDT'L RENDERING AND DETAILING: Deborah Forbes
SHELL ARCHITECT: Ben Burkhalter
PHOTOGRAPHY: Penny Wolin
TILES, MARBLE AND TERRAZZO: Mike Payne & Associates
TILE PAINTING AND GLAZING: Betty Busby, Rachel Clawson, and Judith Pauli
HAND-BLOWN GLASS LIGHT FIXTURES AND NICHE SCULPTURES: Pam Morris, Exciting Lighting
GENERAL AND TASK LIGHTING: CSL
RECESSED LIGHTING IN KITCHEN AND SOFFIT AREAS: Lightolier
WALL WASHERS AND EYEBALLS: Prescolite
LANDSCAPE LIGHTING: Luminere
LYTEMODE COMPUTER CONTROL PANEL: Lightolier
SPECIAL EFFECT PROJECTORS: Art Environments
NEON LIGHTING: Archigraphics
METAL WORK FABRICATION: Metalmorphosis
FUSED/SLUMPED GLASS PANELS: Duane Dahl
ETCHED GLASS: Polly Gessel
PATIO GLASS/ART GLASS: Venice Glass and Gardens in Glass
CORAL REEF AQUARIUMS: Aquatic Art, Richard Bilow
INTERIOR PAINT SURFACES: Tim Harris
FAUX FINISH PAINT: Shulman & Ortiz
INTERIOR CHAIRS: Bob Josten

EXTERIOR CHAIRS: Fong Bros.
KOI POND: Mr. Fish, Bob Morris, design by Barbara Lazaroff
LANDSCAPING: Jackie Tone and Rob Takiguchi with Barbara Lazaroff
TREES: Mission Tree
ENTRANCE PORTAL: Brian Tedrick
CAST GLASS SCULPTURE: David Ruth, Gomeisa
LOGO WATERCOLOR: Tom Pomatti with Barbara Lazaroff
ARTWORK: Eugene Jardin, Paul Lindhard, Marie Laurie Ilie, Jim DeFrance, Sharleen Collicut, Karoy Kovach, Glenda Schwartzman, Tina Hulett, Kakine, Muramasa Kudo, Malcolm Morley, Richard Clopton, D. H. Roettinger, Anna Silver
SOUND SYSTEM: TAB Technical Services
PIANO: Yamaha Disklavier, David Abell
WINE RACK: T & R Carpentry, design by Barbara Lazaroff
RECEPTION DESK: Performance Woodwork, design by Barbara Lazaroff
ARMOIRE/BAR WOODWORK: The Gentrywoods, Bob Gentry, design by Barbara Lazaroff
LOUNGE TABLES: Barry Weiss
WAITER UNIFORM FABRIC: Sandra Wright
PATIO UMBRELLAS: Santa Barbara Umbrellas
BOOTH AND LOUNGE SEATING: West Coast Industries
FABRIC FOR BOOTHS: Grey Watkin
FABRIC FOR LOUNGE: Majilite, "Nova Suede"
CUSTOM AWNINGS: Van Nuys Awning

Granita is a 6,500 sq. ft. (with an additional outdoor dining area of 1,500 sq. ft.) full-service restaurant that seats 160 people and is located in the Malibu Colony Plaza shopping area in Malibu, California. It opened in August 1991, and its menu includes favorites from Wolfgang Puck's other kitchens and a wonderful selection of fresh fish and seafood.

Inspired by the "visceral and emotional elements of the sea," Barbara Lazaroff has created in Granita an incredible abstract fantasy for all of us to share. She proudly states, "It's a celebration of the cooperative efforts of one hundred of America's most talented artisans."

Granita developed as a concept because there were very few fine dining establishments in Malibu. Wolfgang Puck states, "Many of our customers at Spago, Chinois, and Eureka live and vacation in Malibu and asked us when we were going to open a restaurant in their community.

The strategic location is adjacent to the affluent Malibu Colony residential compound. The restaurant's location on Pacific Coast Highway, and near the Las Virgenes Pass, is easily accessible from Malibu, Pacific Palisades, Brentwood, and other Los Angeles residents, as well as the San Fernando Valley.

Barbara Lazaroff states, "I wanted to create a beautiful restaurant that embodied all of my feelings about space, form, texture, light, and color. Since it was probably going to be the last restaurant I would personally design for myself and Wolf, I wanted to create an environment that was visually dazzling."

MENU DEVELOPMENT

Wolfgang Puck states, "The food at Granita needed to be simple to appeal to customers who wanted to dine there frequently. People in Malibu are relaxed and dress casually, and they don't want overly complex food. They want simply prepared fish and a variety of their favorite items from our other kitchens."

Granita's cuisine features the collaborative efforts of Puck and chefs Joseph Manzare and Kevin Ripley. Ripley came to Granita after eight years of training with Puck at Spago, where he worked in the pastry, prep, and line departments. He was also the opening sous chef at Eureka, and remained there for over a year. Manzare began his association with Puck as a Spago line cook in 1986 and worked there for two years. He helped open Postrio and was the sous chef for a year, and he was the executive chef at the Royalton Hotel in New York before settling at Granita.

Granita's dinner, lunch, and dessert menus change seasonally. Fresh fish and seafood are emphasized in such signature dishes as Mediterranean fish soup with a half lobster and

WHIMSICAL NEOCLASSICAL COLUMNS AND BIOMORPHICALLY SHAPED TILES ADORN THE ENTRANCE. PHOTOGRAPH © PENNY WOLIN.

couscous; fritto misto with shrimp, calamari and scorpion fish with lemon aioli; steamed Chatham mussels and clams with Chinese black bean sauce; and roasted whole black bass with fennel salad and white truffle vinaigrette. Puck classics appearing on the menu include chopped vegetable salad with grated parmesan; lamb sausage pizza with eggplant, sweet peppers, and red onions; and Chinese-style duck with plum chutney and summer greens. Weekend brunch offers such wonderful dishes as sour cherry and cinnamon French toast with warm strawberry compote, and sunny-side-up pizza with smoked ham and fontina cheese. Sourdough breads, grissini, rolls, and cracker bread are homemade daily.

Pastry chef Rochelle Huppin prepares the restaurant's trademark granitas (an Italian shaved ice dessert) in such tempting flavors as pomegranate with lemon gelato in an almond tuile. Equally

CHEFS KEVIN RIPLEY AND JOSEPH MANZARE

APPETIZERS

Sauteed Gulf shrimp with Thai cucumber salad $11.00

Cold asparagus with whole grain mustard vinaigrette $8.50

Steamed Chatham mussels and clams with Chinese black bean sauce $10.00

Mandarin quail with julienne of ginger and spicy greens $12.50

Grilled sea scallops with green and yellow bean salad and nicoise olive vinaigrette . . . $10.50

Chopped vegetable salad with grated Parmesan $9.50

Scallopini of salmon with crisp potatoes and warm sherry vinaigrette $11.50

Caesar salad with oven baked bruschetta $8.50

Bluefin tuna carpaccio with ginger rice and soy vinaigrette $12.00

PASTAS

Black and gold tagliatelli with saffron and seared scallops $12.00

Ricotta and goat cheese ravioli with wild mushrooms $14.00

Spagettini with sweet mussels, rapini and botarga $11.00

Pappardelle with grilled lobster and tomato basil fondue $16.00

FROM OUR WOOD-BURNING OVEN

Crisp potato galette with gravlax, dill cream and fresh salmon caviar $14.00

Pizza with grilled vegetables, caramelized garlic and goat cheese $11.00

Spicy shrimp pizza with basil, sun dried tomatoes and mozzarella $13.00

Lamb sausage pizza with eggplant, sweet peppers, cilantro and red onions $11.00

MAIN COURSES

Seared Maine scallops with rosti potatoes and spicy parsley sauce $18.00

Sauteed monkfish with wild mushrooms and haricots verts $21.00

Grilled New York steak on a bed of watercress and caramelized onions $22.00

Mediterranean fish soup with a half lobster and couscous $24.00

Grilled chicken with potato puree and sizzling lime butter $19.00

Alaskan salmon grilled with Tuscan bean salad and fresh basil sauce $21.00

Chinese style duck with plum chutney and summer greens $19.00

Atlantic black bass grilled whole with fennel salad and white truffle oil vinaigrette . . . $22.00

Whole scorpion fish en papillote with shiitake mushrooms $21.00

Roasted Sonoma lamb with artichoke mousse and garlic sage sauce $24.00

Split $2.00

GRANITA IS NOW OPEN FOR LUNCH WEDNESDAY THROUGH SUNDAY!

GRANITA DINNER MENU. PHOTOGRAPH © WOLFGANG PUCK/BARBARA LAZAROFF.

popular desserts are apple fennel tart with creme fraiche ice cream, and Barbara Lazaroff's favorite, pot de creme au chocolat caramelis. All pastries, ice creams, and cookies are homemade.

Granita's wine list includes the best selections from California as well as from the Rhône, Bandol, and other Mediterranean regions. Wines from Bordeaux, Burgundy, and Tuscany are also featured.

Granita serves lunch from Wednesday through Saturday with a great brunch on Sunday.

BUDGET

The budget for Granita was approximately $3.2 million. Originally, the budget was $1.2 million, but it was increased to $1.8 million with additional funds coming from the initial landlord who agreed to contribute to the shell construction. Lazaroff felt it would be very difficult to create a building from the ground up and create a distinctive interior for $1.8 million.

Barbara Lazaroff states, "I wanted to create a separate building six feet away from the existing shopping center and utilize materials, colors, and forms dissimilar from those used for the other existing structures, knowing that this would set the restaurant apart from the shopping center environment. I wanted to create a uniquely beautiful space that showcased my work along with commissioning and integrating the talents of some of the best artisans in the United States. I assured Wolfgang and the accountants that the environment that we created would be a visual landmark that people would be drawn to. A lot of what happened at Granita without question was personal self-gratification and sheer stubborn determination.

"The shell construction was $240,000, which was relatively inexpensive, allowing for the greater portion of the monies to be directed toward the tenant improvement work and other specialties. But part-way into the building phase, additional funds had to be spent on heating the patio area because I was unfamiliar with the climate in Malibu. After having experienced many cold nights on the jobsite, I was surprised by the temperature conditions and surmised that we would need heating even on summer nights, when the demand for seating would be the greatest and the patio would be essential. Another $350,000 was spent on the kitchen, and $250,000 was spent on lighting. Another $350,000 went toward the marble and terrazzo flooring and counter tops, the fabrication and installation of custom tile, stucco, and shell inlaid patio walls, the custom plastered and 'bejewelled' fireplace surface, the elaborate interior and exterior columns, and a myriad of other stone and ceramic details. An additional $200,000 was spent on a variety of other design entities, such as fine art, although as with all of the restaurants, most of these pieces are on consignment."

Lazaroff speculates, "Would the restaurant be as successful if I hadn't spent as much money? Perhaps the answer is yes. I could have spent less on the lighting, tile work, and the other finishes, and the restaurant certainly would be successful. However, I think this is one time where I feel the design attracts customers as much as the food. Many people tell me that they come here just to see the overall environment, lighting fixtures, and tile work. Johnny Carson, who lives in Malibu and is our single largest investor, came to see the restaurant every other day during construction, and he was so taken by it that he gave me greatly appreciated emotional support and decided to invest much-needed additional funds."

DESIGN CONCEPT

Barbara Lazaroff has designed an incredibly beautiful restaurant that combines soft, diffused lighting, undulating curves, textured glass, and custom-fabricated and glazed tiles to create, as Lazaroff describes it, "an abstract interpretation of the visceral and emotional elements of the sea with its changing sense of movement and light."

Lazaroff maintains that "Granita's distinctive feeling is one of a three-dimensional watercolor—I assembled a team of the finest American artisans, including ceramicists, hand-blown glass formulators, stone masons, glass etchers, metal craftspeople, and woodworkers, as well as commissioning fine art. My vision was one of 'life upon life' as in the coral reefs. I wanted to translate that concept into the ceramic tile and stone work that would cover a vast variety of surfaces. This effect was realized with watercolor, crackled, halo, and other special-effect glazes and a myriad of multicolored and patterned marble and onyx. The team of ceramic artists, headed up by Mike Payne of Mike Payne Architectural Ceramics, along with students I commissioned from Otis/Parsons, created these biomorphic shapes that adorn the open kitchen, rest rooms, and elegant neoclassical columns that surround the exterior structure and provide internal support.

"This macro and micro version of life forms and their textures was extrapolated to the design of the custom lighting as well. I commissioned Pam Morris to create the exquisite hand-blown light sculptures inspired by the colors and forms of the sea, as well as the singular glass sculptural forms that adorn the illuminated architectural display niches. These lit art sculptures are one of the most emotionally provocative elements in the restaurant.

"The interior panels of dramatically etched glass produced by artist Polly Gessel investigate a fantasy world of abstract and whimsical underwater creatures and patterns, and serve to create private dining spaces, while regular service continues in the main dining areas.

"Elaborate 2' by 3' double-sided salt water coral reef tanks border each side of the private dining rooms. Instead of the oversized flower displays I've showcased at Spago and Chinois, I commissioned Richard Bilow of Aquatic Art to create a watery fantasy world of exotic corals that resemble underwater flowers.

"Granita's exterior includes custom tile, dramatic lush landscaping, and a koi fish pond and etched rock garden filled with olive trees, bromeliads, and other exotica near the entrance. Guests enter the restaurant through Brian Tedrick's 12' by 12' iron and redwood portal. Sculptor David Ruth's 7'-high 'frozen wave' of cast glass, entitled Gomeisa, adorns the koi pond and front patio. The primary hues are pastels—sea-foam green, cream, antique rose, soft gray, muted copper, amber, and apricot tones—which serve as a subtle backdrop for the fine art, glass work, custom tile, and metal works used throughout the restaurant. Hand-wrought copper edging, produced in collaboration with metal artists at Metalmorphosis, with petroglyph cutouts, allows gold neon light to drip through the openings. This lit decorative detail is echoed throughout the restaurant's surfaces, from the bar and exposed kitchen counter edge to the patio beams.

"I expanded the outdoor feeling of Granita by designing extensive panels of elegant doors that frame the front and side patios, which when opened provide a view of the lovely landscaping, the 12' by 8' water cascade, and the koi fish pond. I worked with New Mexico artist Duane Dahl to produce the exterior and interior partition doors, which are inset with an interplay of slumped and hand-blown glass, copper wire, and free-form color glass rods.

"The open kitchen and wood-burning oven are highlighted by an intricately tiled mosaic wall and kitchen hood and an asymmetrical soffit above the kitchen adorned with ceramic sea grass. Artist Anna Silver's grandly oversized platters are displayed on the vertical of the kitchen soffit.

GRANITA COMBINES SOFT DIFFUSED LIGHTING, UNDULATING CURVES, TEXTURED GLASS, AND CUSTOM FABRICATED GLAZED TILES. PHOTOGRAPH © PENNY WOLIN.

THE HANDCRAFTED FIREPLACE IS INSET WITH INTRICATELY PAINTED, BIOMORPHICALLY SHAPED TILES AND VARIOUS STONES AND GEODES. CURVING PLUSH BANQUETTES APPEAR TO ENVELOPE THE FIREPLACE SEDUCTIVELY. PHOTOGRAPH © PENNY WOLIN.

"The elevated bar area showcases an unusual bar top of various marble and onyx in an interplay of multicolored terrazzo inlaid with precious and semi-precious stones. The handcrafted fireplace is inset with intricately painted biomorphically shaped tiles and various stones and geodes. Areas of curving plush banquettes, in sea-foam green suede, appear to seductively envelope the fireplace.

"Granita is a design statement of the counterpoint of man and nature. The rectilinear architecture, the organic soffits, and other structure and applied forms are played against one another to infuse the viewer's eye and the individual spirit with both dynamic and static points of reference."

The intricate array of lighting fixtures at Granita is controlled by a 117-channel Lytemode system that Barbara Lazaroff programmed to adjust for any number of variables from day to night. The lighting scheme includes custom-engineered projectors by Art Environments that produce a soft, undulating effect of dappling water.

Lazaroff states, "My vision for Granita was to produce the variation and complexity of light that exists underwater. I knew a great part of this dream would be realized by creating beautiful hand-blown glass elements that would create a mysterious yet translucent glow. Pam Morris of Exciting Lighting turned fantasy into reality with her exquisite hand-blown glass sculptures, which are abstract interpretations of the magical creatures that inhabit the sea.

"The exterior and interior columns are capped with *bubble collars* by Pam Morris, encased with verdigris copper forms that resemble sea kelp.

"Besides the custom-blown glass fixtures, which seem to drip luxuriously, there are over eighty recessed Prescolite wall washers and adjustable eyeballs to illuminate various artworks and architectural elements, such as curving soffits, the reception desk, and the stone design on the face of our wood-burning oven. I prefer halogen light for art; it imparts a whiter light to the paintings, thus providing a truer color rendition. One negative is the possibility of the fading of paint pigment over time.

"Large recessed Lightolier fixtures were utilized in the vaulted areas to illuminate the 2' by 2' Leucos glass panels that provide beauty and interest to the exterior as well as the interior of the building. Similar fixtures were used for general lighting in the kitchen with cooler lamps.

THE OPEN KITCHEN IS HIGHLIGHTED BY AN INTRICATELY TILED MOSAIC WALL AND KITCHEN HOOD. PHOTOGRAPH *of* PENNY WOLIN.

Additional wall washers were added in the kitchen to highlight the mosaic-tiled ventilation hood.

"Custom CSL low-voltage Jewel Lights, which create star-like patterns of light across the ceiling have been placed in the lounge and bar areas as well as in the private dining areas. The skylight soffits house a special effects projector that produces an illusion of dappling water. The hand-poured and fused Leucos panels in the skylight are backlit with cold cathode light. The numerous art niches that house glass sculptures are underlit by cathode and toplit with low-voltage CSL spots.

"I spent close to a year designing and refining the lighting schedule for Granita. It is certainly one of the most complex and elaborate designs short of a discotheque. However, I knew that so much of the magic and drama I was trying to create would rely upon the creative use of lighting. The Lytemode computer I incorporated was a costly but necessary addition; without it the balancing of lights would be a technical nightmare for the staff. It was also fabulous on New Year's Eve, when the lights dimmed suddenly at the stroke of midnight and slowly rose up!"

SPACE PLANNING

Lazaroff states, "One of the first things I did was to move the proposed new structure as far away from the existing store front on the right as I could without severely diminishing the space allotted to Granita (a wide unalterable access street borders the left side of the building). Six

feet was the maximum space I could provide, but this adjustment helped create Granita's separate, distinct image.

"I then set back the entrance to the building so that I could create a landscaped area that would serve as a visual buffer between Granita and the adjacent building and also created a grand approach walkway to the front doors. We also knew that because this is a people-watching space, we needed outdoor seating in the front of the building. This outdoor seating also wraps around the left side of the building. We planted a lot of mature trees to create a sense of enclosure.

"The footprint of the building and the dimensions of the setback for the outdoor seating had to be carefully planned to insure that we had enough seating capacity indoors, since people couldn't sit outdoors during the winter, even in Malibu. During the spring and summer, we have 60 people seated outdoors, and 110 inside. During the winter (when it would be too cold to seat outdoors, even with the comprehensive heating system we installed), we have enough space to move about 30 people indoors.

"The reception area was located prominently at the entrance. The bar and lounge areas are located to the right of the reception area, and are slightly elevated, providing waiting patrons an exciting and entertaining overview of the dining room. All areas of the restaurant, as in all of our restaurants, are accessible to the physically challenged.

"We have a large open dining room with private dining areas that can be partitioned into spaces for 25 or 50 people. I have a lot of flexibility and can open either the entire private dining area to the outdoor patio, or only a portion of it, creating areas for 75 or 100 patrons by utilizing various adjacent combinations of indoor and outdoor spaces." The 6,500 sq. ft. of Granita breaks down as follows:

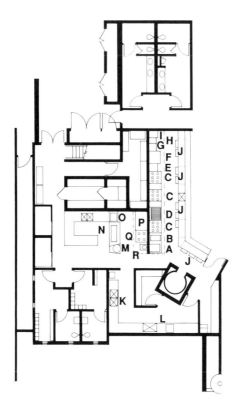

GRANITA FLOOR PLAN. COURTESY OF IMAGININGS INTERIOR DESIGN, INC. REDRAWN BY IVONNE DORF.
REFERENCE TABLE: 1. ENTRY; 2. COAT AND STORAGE; 3. RECEPTION DESK; 4. LOUNGE; 5. BAR; 6. GLASS SCULPTURE; 7. POND; 8. AQUARIUM; 9. UMBRELLA STORAGE; 10. DINING; 11. PRIVATE DINING; 12. PATIO DINING; 13. PIZZA OVEN; 14. BEVERAGE STATION, COFFEE, EXPRESSO; 15. SCULLERY; 16. LINEN; 17. PREP KITCHEN; 18. FRONT KITCHEN EXHIBITION; 19. STORAGE; 20. REFRIGERATOR/FREEZER; 21. EMPLOYEE'S LOCKERS (WOMEN'S); 22. EMPLOYEE'S BATHROOM (WOMEN'S); 23. EMPLOYEE'S BATHROOM (MEN'S); 24. EMPLOYEE'S LOCKERS (MEN'S); 25. TELEPHONE CLOSET; 26. STORAGE; 27. WOMEN'S ROOM; 28. MEN'S ROOM; 29. PUBLIC PHONES; 30. BUS STATION; 31. CASHIER; 32. BAR STORAGE; 33. WAIT STAFF PICK-UP

GRANITA KITCHEN PLAN. COURTESY OF IMAGININGS INTERIOR DESIGN, INC. REDRAWN BY IVONNE DORF
REFERENCE TABLE:
A. STEAMER; B. FRYER; C. OPEN 6-BURNER OVEN; D. CHARCOAL BROILER; E. BAKER'S RACK; F. CONVECTION OVEN; G. 20 QT. MIXER; H. ICE CREAM MACHINE; I. GRANITA MACHINE; J. UNDERCOUNTER REFRIGERATION; K. POT WASHING; L. DISHWASHING; M. 60 QT. MIXER; N. DOUGH MACHINE; O. BREAD RACK; P. PIZZA OVEN; Q. OPEN 4-BURNER W/OVEN; R. STOCK POT

ENTRY/RECEPTION: 200 sq. ft.
DINING AREAS: indoor, 2,200 sq. ft.; outdoor, 1,500 sq. ft.
BAR LOUNGE: 1,150 sq. ft.
PUBLIC BATHROOMS: 440 sq. ft.
EXHIBITION KITCHEN: 500 sq. ft.
COFFEE STATION: 60 sq. ft.
SCULLERY: 250 sq. ft.
EMPLOYEE'S BATHROOMS/LOCKERS: 400 sq. ft.
PREP KITCHEN/STORAGE: 1,100 sq. ft.
MISCELLANEOUS STORAGE: 250 sq. ft.

KITCHEN DESIGN

Barbara Lazaroff states, "Once again the initial consideration was to place the exhibition kitchen in a position where it would be in view for the greatest number of diners. The wood-burning oven was placed catty-corner to allow viewing from the bar and lounge areas as well as the dining room, and also put it in a position where it was directly in line with the front entrance. The kitchen line, with its undulating soffit bordered by 'swaying ceramic sea grass tiles,' is the central grotto in this underwater world of food and wine. The activity of the chefs within the kitchen provides a sense of excitement and even a bit of casual play to this rather elegant space."

Wolfgang Puck states, "I dreamed about roasting whole fish and other meats, such as crispy Chinese ducks, in our wood-burning ovens. This accounts for the particularly large dimensions of the oven. Our appetizer station has a small grill, french fryer, and a six-burner stove for hot and cold appetizers. Next to the grill, we have two six-burner stoves: one has a griddle top used to make pancakes and French toast for Sunday brunch and acts as a heating plate for *bain maries*, which keep our sauces warm. Next on the line is the pasta cooker with a six-burner stove where we make our risottos and fresh pastas. Directly across from the pasta station is a speed rack where we store a portion of the *mise en place* that does not need to be refrigerated. The next area on the line has a convection oven to bake our pastries and a small hand sink, a mixer, and a granita maker. Owing to space restrictions in the back kitchen, this is the only restaurant where the baking area is out on the front line.

"Granita has a full service station with an espresso and coffee machine, ice tea machine, ice machine, and full storage for cups, pots, and silverware. This positioning allows the busboys to bring used dishes to the back kitchen while allowing them to pick up coffee on their way back to the dining room. We tried a new idea of not building a so-called store room. All of our store room facilities are in lockable wire shelving and have inspired the staff to be clean and neat because they are always visible. We do have a large enclosed locked area for our china and linen and a 58° temperature-controlled store room for our wine and liquor inventory.

"Our walk-in refrigeration is relatively small for the size of our restaurant, but by buying fresh ingredients every day, we can make the best food and keep inventory low. It is unfortunate to see produce and other products going to waste. My dream is to start every day with a vacant, spotless cooler and have to replenish it every morning! I have yet to come up with the ultimate kitchen design; perfection is never truly achieved because of space limitations and constant menu changes."[1]

COST OF OPERATIONS

Granita opened in 1991 to rave reviews. It is a visually dazzling space that serves approximately 400 covers daily to local and regional residents, businesspeople, tourists, and celebrities. Its cost of operations are as follows:

SEATING CAPACITY: 160
AVERAGE COVERS: lunch, 150 (Wednesday-Saturday; Sunday brunch); dinner, 320 (summer), 280 (winter)
AVERAGE CHECK: lunch, $23; dinner, $42
LIQUOR AND WINE SALES: 35%
FOOD COST: 32%
LABOR COST: 30%
TOTAL EMPLOYEES: 125
RENT: 5.5% of net sales
YEARLY PROJECTED SALES: $5 million

Granita is a fantasy come true for Barbara Lazaroff and Wolfgang Puck. Lazaroff assembled a team of the finest artisans and craftspeople in the United States to produce a highly personalized and sensually vivid environment. The architecture, tile, and stone work, lighting, glass work, and other fine art combine to create a surreal interpretation of "the visceral and emotional elements of the sea, with its changing sense of movement and light."

Barbara Lazaroff states, "People come to Granita to experience the combination of great food that both enlivens and satiates both the soul and the stomach, served in an environment that stimulates them emotionally and possibly intellectually."

The fresh fish, seafood, and other signature menu items rise to new heights in this magnificent space. Granita is the vehicle through which Barbara Lazaroff and Wolfgang Puck share the passion, love, and commitment to excellence that they wish to share with the rest of the world.

NOTES

1. © 1992 by Barbara Lazaroff.

C H O P S

OWNER

Chops is one of six restaurants owned and operated by the Buckhead Life Restaurant Group, whose president is Pano Karatassos. Originally from Savannah, Georgia, Karatossos is one of America's premier restaurateurs. In addition to overseeing the day-to-day operations and regulating the food, personnel, and decor-quality standards of his restaurants, he serves on the boards of the Georgia Hospitality and Travel Association and other industry organizations and is an alumnus ambassador of the Culinary Institute of America. Karatossos has also received many professional awards.

DESIGNER

Chops was designed by Pat Kuleto of Pat Kuleto Consulting & Design. Kuleto has designed many successful restaurants, including Fog City Diner, Lascaux, Corona Bar & Grill, his namesake restaurant, Kuleto's, Postrio, the signature restaurant of chef Wolfgang Puck, and the new smash restaurant Splendido's. One of his more recent projects, the Buckhead Diner in Atlanta, Georgia, was selected as the best designed restaurant on two continents in an international competition. In all, the Sausalito, California-based architect/designer has created some 140 restaurants around the world. He is also owner of McCormick & Kuleto's Seafood Restaurant in San Francisco at Ghirardelli Square.

SOURCES

ARCHITECT: Pat Kuleto Consulting & Design
GENERAL CONTRACTOR: W. P. Tatum Company, Decatur, Georgia
MILLWORK CONTRACTOR: Contract Fabricators, Montgomery, Alabama
CUSTOM LIGHTING: Pam Morris Designs Exciting Lighting, Larkspur, California
GLASS SCREEN: Farallon Studios, Sausalito, California
CHAIRS: Shelby Williams, CCF, Loewenstein
FABRICS: Glant, Shelby Williams, Boussac of France, Grey Watkins, Design Tex
BOOTH FABRICS: Randolph & Hein, Inc., Sloan Miyasato, Momentum Textiles
CARPET: Patton Industries
PHOTOGRAPHER: E. Alan McGee

PANO KARATASSOS.
PHOTOGRAPH © LARRY SKAGGS.

PAT KULETO. PHOTOGRAPH
© BY JOE BURULL.

hops is an 8,200 sq. ft. steak house that seats 180 people and is located on 70 West Paces Ferry Road in the Buckhead section of Atlanta. It was opened in 1989 and is considered one of Atlanta's finest restaurants.

Pano Karatossos states that "Atlanta needed a great steak house. We felt, however, that in order to be successful, we needed to be head and shoulders above the rest. We had to prepare, execute, and serve the finest meats and fish in Atlanta. The number of red meat eaters was shrinking. In order to capture this shrinking market, you also must offer a wide selection of other entrées, including fish, without detracting

from a steak house concept. The chances of a party of six all craving a 20-ounce sirloin are slim.

"The name *Chops* was chosen because it sounded exactly like the kind of restaurant we were trying to create; a friendly, warm gathering place that was macho yet appealing to women as well.

"Chops' location was chosen because of its proximity to the other restaurants that we own in Buckhead. It is conveniently located for our regular customers, visitors, and conventioneers, and it is in an office complex where we can draw from the working force. It also was attractive because there was ample parking.

"I would never have chosen this particular location unless the landlord had made a substantial contribution to the construction costs."

STAFF

"We have approximately 75 people at Chops," says Karatossos. "We have a general manager, Daniel Zillweger, two assistant managers, and an executive chef, Tenney Flynn. The people who work for me believe in trying to be the best. [The Buckhead Life Restaurant Group has] over 550 employees, and we promote and train employees from within our organization.

"Management prepares a questionnaire to determine how much each candidate knows. We also rate them visually and score them from one to ten. We're looking for the particular personality traits and personal grooming.

"We have medical insurance, vacation, and other benefits for all of our staff, and we also provide them with the opportunity to work in the busiest and most successful restaurants in town. Because of our commitment to quality, we've developed a great reputation. The best people in the city want to work in our restaurants.

"Customers return to our restaurants because we provide personalized, attentive service. Our staff is committed to being the best. Running a restaurant is no big thing; it's a thousand little things. We've compiled a list of hundreds of service-related items we try to execute—everything from properly removing ashtrays to knowing if a guest is celebrating a birthday."

Managers have frequent meetings with the staff on a variety of subjects, including wine, desserts, service points, and specials. Exams are given, and Pano Karatossos often drops in unexpectedly.

Execution and quality are the most important aspects of service in Chops and in all of Pano Karatossos' restaurants. In order to establish customer trust, many items are prepared tableside. "Our oysters are shucked to order, and are not preopened," says Karatossos. "Our famous steak

THE MOST CRUCIAL ELEMENT IN THE DESIGN IS THE TREMENDOUS SENSE OF ARRIVAL. PHOTOGRAPH © 1990 E. ALAN MCGEE.

tartare is prepared at the table freshly cut, bright bloomed, and delicious. Our smoked salmon is also freshly 'cut-to-order' tableside."

He continues, "We don't use heat lamps to keep food hot. Our raw steaks are kept at room temperature prior to cooking so that a rare steak order is not cold in the center. Everything is timing! The wait staff are trained to ring in their entrées immediately after serving the previous course. The steaks are fired at that moment; the firing of the fish is coordinated by the broiler chef. Steaks and fish come off the broiler and get served immediately to the guest. This insures that food is served piping hot and at its peak of doneness. We use 1800° cooking equipment that carmelizes and puffs up the steaks and chops, making them look and taste wonderful."

MENU DEVELOPMENT

According to Pano Karatossos, "The person that is coming to overdose on a 20-ounce sirloin wants it to be the best steak he ever had. He doesn't care if he's spending $28, since he probably is having steak only once a month. Understanding this, we purchase our steaks from the finest purveyors in the country. When the steaks are delivered and they don't meet our standards, we send them back. Our steaks are USDA Prime Grade beef straight from the rich Corn Belt. We usually purchase from cattle farmers in places like Joplin, Illinois, where raising cattle is still an art form. We own our own fish market, and I'm the head buyer. We select the freshest seasonal varieties of fish that meet our strict quality standards. If we didn't offer this wonderful variety of fish, I don't think we would be as successful.

"In addition to our meat and fish entrées, we offer a great variety of appetizers and wonderful desserts made at Chops that top off the meal. They are compatible with entrées and unique enough to be memorable.

"Years ago, it was okay to serve soft, yeast-based bread at the table. Those days are over, because our well-traveled customers have tasted a great variety of wonderful breads all over the world. They come back to Atlanta and ask, 'why don't we have great breads here?' In order to continue to be the best, we've just built a half-million-dollar state-of-the-art bakery at Pricci that prepares freshly baked, hand-crafted, crusty,

sourdough breads for all of our restaurants. We use natural starters, organic flours, and bake in stone-hearthed European ovens.

"Early on, I personally developed 75 to 80 percent of the menus at our restaurants. Now, if I continue to do that, it would be like using the same designer at all of our restaurants. I now play off the executive chefs and managing partners. It's

---

APPETIZERS & SOUPS

PREPARED TABLESIDE

NORWEGIAN SMOKED SALMON 7.95	FILET MIGNON STEAK TARTAR 8.75

FRESH SHUCKED OYSTERS AND CLAMS
with a horseradish chili sauce and a peppery mignonette

LONG ISLAND BLUE POINT OYSTERS	7.50	CHESAPEAKE TOP NECK CLAMS
JUMBO WEST LOUISIANA OYSTERS	6.75	ASSORTMENT OF OYSTERS AND CLAMS
ICED JUMBO LUMP CRAB MEAT	7.95	ICED JUMBO GULF SHRIMP
with Creole and horseradish chili sauce		with 2 sauces
CRISPED MARYLAND SOFT SHELL CRAB	7.75	DEVILED CRAB CAKES, SAVANNAH
spicy lemon mustard and red pepper sauce		with tartar sauce
SAN DANIELE PROSCIUTTO ON FRESH MELON WITH CHEESE CROUTON	6.75	CRISPED THICK CUT ONION RINGS
		with "Chops" steak sauce
SPANISH BLACK BEAN SOUP	3.75	ESCARGOTS IN MUSHROOMS CAPS
with salsa, sour cream & Sherry		garlic, white wine, butter, & parsley

SOUP OF THE DAY

SALADS

"CHOPS" CHOPPED SALAD   4.50
with lettuces, hearts of palm, sliced egg, tomatoes, blue cheese, etc.

BEEFSTEAK TOMATOES AND VIDALIA ONIONS, VINAIGRETTE   4.25

CAESAR SALAD   4.50
with fresh grated Parmesan cheese

SPINACH SALAD WITH BUTTON MUSHROOMS   4.50
Roasted Pecans and a warm bacon dressing

TOSSED SALAD GREENS   3.95
with anchovy filets, Chopped Eggs & "Chops" Creamy Dressing

PRIME SEAFOOD

Our fresh fish is U.S.D.C. inspected and is based on daily availability only.
Prepared with 100% cholesterol free oils

LARGE LIVE MAINE LOBSTERS

sizes from 2 to 5 lbs.   MARKET

BONELESS WHOLE RAINBOW TROUT (over 1 lb.)   14.75
sauteed with diced lemon croutons, capers, mushrooms and peppers

GULF RED SNAPPER   19.75
fresh tomatoe fondue, olives, mushrooms and steamed potatoes

SWORDFISH STEAK, CRACKED PEPPER AND ALMOND CRUST   19.50
on mashed potatoes, white wine veal jus

GRILLED SALMON FILLET, THICK CUT, BEARNAISE   18.95
with fresh tomatoes, thin green beans, and capers

GRILLED FLORIDA YELLOW TAIL GROUPER   17.95
with a red pepper coulis and jumbo asparagus hollandaise

LIVE MARYLAND SOFT SHELL CRABS LIGHTLY CRISPED   17.95
with a spicy tartar sauce and shoestring potatoes

JUMBO GULF SHRIMP AND GIANT SEA SCALLOPS, SCAMPI STYLE   17.95
with fresh spinach linguini

FLORIDA POMPANO   18.95
with three citrus fruits, roasted almonds and steamed potatoes

much more fun. I get much more enthusiasm and loyalty now that these young creative chefs have more control over the menu development. We have very tight centralized purchasing techniques, all computer-controlled. This allows us to control food costs. We find the best purveyors in the country, and because we own six restaurants, our purchasing power is substantial, allowing us to obtain better quality at the best possible cost. We pass that value straight to our customer. The chef at Chops does not order on his own; he must order through our centralized purchasing system.

"The food cost at Chops is 41 percent. The only way to make money in a steak house is to keep labor costs to a minimum. You don't need as

CHOPS MENU.

STEAKS AND CHOPS

"CHOPS" steaks are specially aged and selected corn-fed beef.
We serve only the finest quality U.S.D.A. "PRIME GRADE" available in the U.S.

"CHOPS" PORTERHOUSE FOR TWO (3 lbs.)
28.50 Per Person

"CHOPS" NEW YORK STRIP 20 oz.	29.50	PORTERHOUSE 24 oz.	28.50
NEW YORK STRIP 12 oz.	22.50	RIBEYE 16 oz.	21.50
"CHOPS" DOUBLE FILET FOR ONE	24.95	LAMB LOIN CHOPS TRIPLE CUT	24.50
PETITE FILET 8 oz.	18.50	VEAL RIB CHOP EXTRA THICK CUT	24.95

BOSTON CLUB SIRLOIN STEAK, BEARNAISE 19.50

ROAST PRIME RIB OF BEEF "DOUBLE CUT" AU JUS 24.50
"creamy horseradish sauce"

VEAL RIBEYE STEAK, 18.95
Parmesan crust on fresh sauteed spinach and mushrooms

SICILIAN VEAL CHOP 24.50
golden crumbs, crushed tomatoes, fontina cheese & penne pasta

GRILLED SMOKED PORK CHOPS, MUSTARD SAUCE 14.75
pesto mashed potatoes, thin beans and mushrooms

DINO'S PAN ROASTED CHICKEN VESUVIO 14.75
smothered with vidalia onions and beans on Parmesan potatoes

POTATOES AND SIDES

Cottage Fried Potatoes	2.95	Sauteed Spinach and Mushrooms	3.95
Hashed Brown Potatoes	2.95	Creamed Spinach	3.95
Big Baked Potato, Sour Cream, Chives	3.50	Jumbo Asparagus Hollandaise	4.75
Crisped Thick Cut Onion Rings	3.95	Skillet Steak Mushroom Caps	3.95
Penne Pasta Marinara	2.75	A Saute of Fresh Vegetables	3.50

Hollandaise or Bearnaise (serves two) 2.00

"CHOPS BAKERY"

CHOCOLATE CHIP BUTTERSCOTCH PIE	4.00	DARK CHOCOLATE "MELT" CAKE
with coffee bean sauce	4.00
CREAMY BLACK BOTTOM PIE	4.00	FRESH RASPBERRY TART
with Chambord cream	4.75
CHICAGO STYLE CHEESECAKE	4.50	FROZEN CHOCOLATE PEANUT
BRITTLE PIE	4.00

FRESH BERRIES with real whipped cream 3.75

"CHOPS" HOMEMADE ICE CREAMS

FRUIT SORBET CHANGES DAILY	3.00	CHUNKY OREO COOKIE ICE CREAM	3.75
ROASTED COFFEE CARAMEL SWIRL	3.75	BANANA WHITE CHOCOLATE FUDGE	3.75

CONSISTENT WITH OUR HIGH STANDARDS,
WE SERVE ONLY PURE FILTERED WATER AND ICE

Your Safety Is Important To Us.
We Encourage You to Not Mix Drinking and Driving.
Please Consult Hostess Desk to Arrange Transportation.

We gladly accept American Express and other Major Credit Cards

910403

many employees, and the salaries for kitchen staff are not as expensive as for other fussier, more complex restaurant menus."

BUDGET

Karatossos states, "Our commitment to quality is reflected in the finishes, lighting, and furniture that we selected for Chops. We very rarely compromise on the look of our restaurants because our customers are expecting the best, and we give it to them.

"The budget for Chops was $300 a square foot for a total of approximately $2 million. This included general construction, kitchen equipment, preopening expenses, and inventory. I usually don't have a fixed budget. If I like a higher level of finishes suggested by the designer, and I can afford them, I usually approve them. I trust the designers I work with, and I only want to work with the best. Their experience and creativity are going to help make me more successful.

"It is difficult to make money carrying that much debt service on the construction loan.

However, I was committed to providing the best high-end quality steak house I could. It had to be a slam-dunk. I negotiated over a year with the landlord, and walked out of their offices three or four times, until I got a $150 per square foot construction allowance and a straight 6 percent rent deal. Without that contribution from the landlord, I couldn't build the restaurant.

"Everybody comes out a winner—the city of Atlanta gets a great steak house, we get a profitable restaurant, and the landlord gets a fair return on his investment, plus he entices quality tenants to lease his office building. Several tenants leased space because Chops was located there."

Pat Kuleto states emphatically that there must be two approaches to budget planning. One is the economic reality and the other is the market reality. The economic reality is, how much can the restaurant cost when measured against the debt service, projected gross income, average check, and seating capacity? Will there be a fair return on the investment? The market reality becomes important when one is developing a high-end casual restaurant. Customers will

THE FINISHES, SUCH AS MARBLE FLOORS, MAHOGANY WOODWORK, ETCHED GLASS, AND THE LIGHTING FIXTURES, ARE MADE OF "REAL" ORGANIC MATERIALS. PHOTOGRAPH © 1990 E. ALAN MCGEE.

demand a high level of design and visual imagery. If the restaurant is expecting to gross $5 million a year, and last ten years or more, it must make a substantial investment in the design.

The economic reality exercise may have a projected gross income of $3.5 million a year and can only afford $200 per square foot for construction. A better, richer design that may cost $250 to $300 per square foot may provide an income of $5 to $6 million a year. If the better design perfectly fits the market niche and satisfies the customer demand, it can be a superstar restaurant. The $200 per square foot project may never provide the environment that will make it a hit.

The difference between a $200 per square foot space and a $300 per square foot budget is in the millwork, lighting, and special details. Chops is an example of a project where the market reality proved correct. Without the millwork, custom lighting, and special details, it would have been rather ordinary. It would never have the visual richness and sense of quality that established customer trust.

Pat Kuleto states, "Chops was conceived as a quintessential macho steak house. It was designed to convey a men's club image, but had to be appealing to women as well. The finishes, such as marble floors, mahogany woodwork, and etched glass, and the lighting fixtures are all made of 'real' materials. I feel the materials used in a restaurant should be organic, not synthetic, because food is organic.

"The visually rich environment with its fine architectural detailing conveys a sense of quality to the customer and establishes a level of trust and heightens the perceived value of the whole experience. Customers are not only buying food and service, they're buying a sensory experience as well, and if the environment is visually rich, they will feel they're getting their money's worth.

"I get most of my inspiration from my travels, especially to Europe. I have a photographic memory for places, and I use my 'collective memory' to conjure up rich visual imagery for my designs. This imagery is what I feel is in most people's collective memory as well."

THE VISUALLY RICH ENVIRONMENT WITH ITS FINE ARCHITECTURAL DETAILING CONVEYS A SENSE OF QUALITY TO THE CUSTOMER. PHOTOGRAPH © 1990 E. ALAN MCGEE.

"The lighting in Chops is the key element in the design. It sets the mood and makes everyone look great, and it focuses attention and adds a sense of drama to the cooking line and the bar area. I wanted the lighting to be reminiscent of the mission style, so I commissioned lighting designer Pam Morris, a California craftsperson, to design the lighting. There is no one, in my opinion, who is better at conveying a mood through light than Pam Morris."

SPACE PLANNING

Pat Kuleto states that "the most crucial element in the design of Chops or any of Pano Karatossos' restaurants is the tremendous sense of arrival. Upon entering the space, I want people to be able to see and feel the excitement and drama of the entire space. At Chops, as soon as you enter, you can see the bustling cooking line, the bar, and a good portion of the dining room. It dazzles the senses and heightens expectations. The maitre d' station is positioned in order to usher people to the bar or the dining room."

The space planning for Chops followed a logical progression. The kitchen is located adjacent to the service elevator, accessible to the loading dock in the basement, and bathrooms were placed near the bar. The dining rooms are placed on several levels to create a sense of place and to view the cooking line and the bar.

In order to maximize seating capacity, the cooking line, prep area, and dishwashing functions were kept to a minimum, occupying less than 20 percent of the 6,700 sq. ft. on the main level. An additional 1,500 sq. ft. were obtained from the landlord in the basement for more storage, receiving, and prep areas.

Overstuffed big booths were designed, along with big armchairs and tables to create a club atmosphere for business people. Generally, Kuleto states, "I use a rule of thumb of 27 to 32 sq. ft. per person to determine seating capacity for high-end casual restaurants. This rule of thumb proves useful when determining if a particular restaurant concept is feasible.

"Banquettes are the most space-efficient type of seating, but are the least private and desirable for a businessperson's meeting. I didn't provide any banquettes, and probably didn't squeeze in as many seats as I could have. I opted for comfort."

The 8,200 sq. ft. of Chops occupies two floors and is organized as follows:

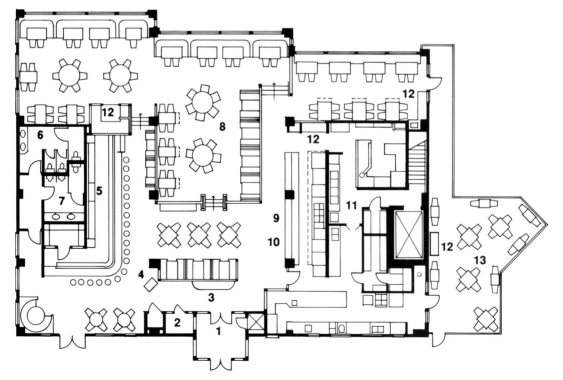

CHOPS FLOOR PLAN. PLANS ABOVE AND OPPOSITE COURTESY OF PAT KULETO. REDRAWN BY LORRAINE KNAPP.
REFERENCE TABLE: 1. ENTRY; 2. WINE DISPLAY; 3. FOOD DISPLAY; 4. MAITRE D'; 5. BAR; 6. WOMEN'S BATHROOM; 7. MEN'S BATHROOM;
8. DINING; 9. WAITER'S PICK-UP AREA; 10. EXPEDITOR; 11. KITCHEN; 12. WAITER'S STATIONS; 13. EXTERIOR TERRACE DINING

ENTRY AND RECEPTION: 250 sq. ft.
BAR/LOUNGE: 1,150 sq. ft.
DINING AREAS, INTERIOR: 3,000 sq. ft.
OUTDOOR DINING: 700 sq. ft.
FINISHING KITCHEN/PREP: 1,500 sq. ft.
BASEMENT LEVEL STORAGE, PREP, OFFICES,
    LOCKERS: 1,500 sq. ft.

KITCHEN DESIGN

Pano Karatossos states, "The kitchen design at Chops was done by me, with the assistance of a local kitchen designer in Atlanta. The kitchen square footage was kept to a minimum on the ground level in order to maximize seating. With steak food cost at 60 percent, and an overall food cost at 41 percent, you have to sell a lot of seafood to increase profits.

"The simple menu doesn't require a lot of storage space. We have one small cut meat and seafood cooler kept at 30°, and a small dry storage area on the main level, plus a dry aging cooler for short loins and prime ribs located in the dining room."

Daniel Zillweger, the general manager of Chops states, "much less storage is needed because our purveyors make frequent deliveries. We take inventory on steaks twice a day for controls. We inspect each delivery to determine if the quality meets our standards before we accept delivery."

Zillweger says that Chops uses "every square inch of wall and ceiling space to store pots and pans, dish and dry goods, and we keep the kitchen spotless to boost morale and efficiency. We have four chefs on the cooking line, with the executive chef, Tenney Flynn, expediting on the guest side of the line. The cooking line is visible from the dining room, and the chef and the line cooks like this, because they're on stage. We also have two people shucking clams and oysters and preparing appetizers and desserts."

COST OF OPERATIONS

Chops serves lunch and dinner daily to businesspeople, local residents, celebrities, and tourists. It continues to be rated the best steak house in Atlanta, and it is always packed. Its cost of operations are as follows:

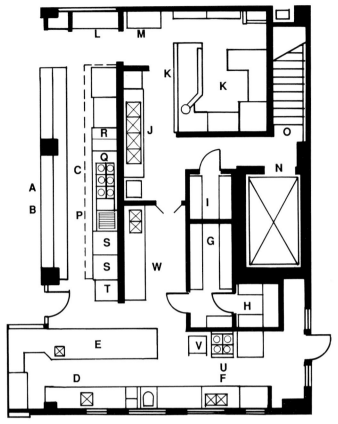

CHOPS KITCHEN PLAN. REDRAWN BY LORRAINE KNAPP.
REFERENCE TABLE: A. WAITERS PICK-UP AREA; B. EXPEDITOR; C. HOT LINE; D. GARDE MANGER; E. OYSTERS, CLAMS, SHRIMP, AND FISH DISPLAY; F. HOT PREP; G. WALK-IN COOLER; H. FREEZERS; I. STEAK FREEZER; J. POT WASHING; K. DISHWASHING; L. WAITER'S STATION; M. ICE; N. ELEVATOR TO DOWNSTAIRS LOADING DOCK; O. STAIRWAY TO OFFICES AND STORAGE AREA.; P. GRILL; Q. 6-BURNER STOVE; R. FRYERS; S. CONVECTION OVENS; T. REFRIGERATOR; U. 4-BURNER STOVE; V. KETTLE; W. PREP

SEATING CAPACITY: dining room, 175; bar, 30
AVERAGE COVERS: lunch, 140; dinner, 260
AVERAGE CHECK: lunch, $18; dinner, $46
LIQUOR AND WINE SALES: 22%
FOOD COST: 41%
LABOR COST: 18%
TOTAL EMPLOYEES: 75
YEARLY SALES: $4 million

Pano Karatossos clearly states that his passion and commitment to quality have made his restaurants successful. He knew early on that because of his own training in high-end establishments that he would only feel comfortable creating and operating high-end restaurants. He chose the affluent Buckhead section, the "Beverly Hills of Atlanta," and created six restaurants that meet customer demand and expectations. His standards for the best quality and execution in food service and design have created a loyal, trusting customer base.

SMITH & WOLLENSKY

OWNERS

Smith & Wollensky is owned by the New York Restaurant Group, whose president is Alan Stillman.

DESIGNER

Arnold Syrop Associates of New York City is the architect and interior designer for all four phases of Smith & Wollensky. This company also designed The Post House, The Manhattan Ocean Club, and La Cité for the New York Restaurant Group.

ALAN STILLMAN. PHOTOGRAPH
© LOU MANNA STUDIO INC.

ARNOLD SYROP. PHOTOGRAPH
© JOANNE SYROP.

SOURCES

ARCHITECT: Arnold Syrop Associates
GRAPHIC DESIGNER: Linda Rossin
KITCHEN CONSULTANT: H. Friedman & Sons, Inc.
CONSTRUCTION MANAGER: Jerry Devine
STRUCTURAL ENGINEER: Eipel Engineering, PC
MECHANICAL ENGINEER: Piccirillo & Brown
PHOTOGRAPHERS: Mark Ross, Peter Paige
MIRRORS AND GLAZING: Schuldiner
TIN WALL-FACING: Shanker Steel
GLASSWARE: first floor, H. Friedman & Sons, Inc.; second floor, Libby
LITHOGRAPHS: Argosy Gallery
MARBLE: Foro Marble
LADDER-BACK CHAIRS: Empire Chair
BOOTH FABRICATION: Jerry Devine
ALABASTER CHANDELIER, ANTIQUE TABLE, AND VASE: Artisan Antiques
BAR CHANDELIER AND COPPER-CLAD EAGLE: Four Seasons
OTHER CHANDELIERS: Louis Mattia Antiques
CABINET RESTORATION (BAR): David Aprea
BACK BAR: Howard Kaplan
BRONZE SCULPTURE: Charles Cheriff
CHAIRS: Empire State Chair
LIGHTING: Lightolier
ANTIQUE LIGHT FIXTURES: Ann Morris Antiques
LINENS: Roamer
TABLECLOTHS: Standard White (supplied by laundry)
TABLEWARE: Minners
CHINA: Oneida
STAINLESS STEEL: Reed & Barton

Smith & Wollensky is a 16,200 sq. ft. restaurant with a seating capacity of 575 people consisting of a ground floor dining area, Wollensky's Grill, and a second floor dining/banquet area. The restaurant is located in a freestanding two-story building on Third Avenue and Forty-ninth Street in Manhattan. It was constructed in four phases between 1977 and 1989, concluding with the total renovation of the cellar food preparation and operations area. The thriving Smith & Wollensky is both a New York landmark and a destination restaurant.

Alan Stillman states, "When Smith & Wollensky was built in 1977, I had fifteen successful restaurants under my belt, and this experience allowed us [the New York Restaurant Group] to make decisions about location, concept, menu, and decor that influenced the success of this establishment. Successful restaurants fit a particular market niche. When we built Smith & Wollensky, we felt a great new steak house concept had not been developed in the past thirty years. We looked at our competition, including The Assembly, The Palm, and Christ Cella, and decided that there was sufficient market demand for a great steak house in New York. We would use the best quality steaks, create a fine wine list, and serve the best desserts in town. Our concept was to provide the finest quality steak house in order to attract our share of the market.

"We selected Forty-ninth Street and Third Avenue for Smith & Wollensky because it was formerly Manny Wolf's and was right smack in the middle of steak house row. It had been damaged by fire, and this corner had become available at a time when land and buildings were inexpensive. We didn't need an extensive demographic analysis to determine if this was a great location for this concept. Just go out there and look at the street traffic and office and residential buildings. We knew this area extremely well because we had extensive experience in midtown Manhattan.

"We instructed our architect, Arnold Syrop, to look at all the steak houses in New York to determine what decorative elements were appropriate for this concept. They all had wood floors, wainscoting, antiques, and paintings, and we decided not to depart from this basic theme. However, we felt it was necessary to choose the finest antiques and paintings that were available, and develop a design that would establish this as the best steak house in New York. It was also important that it should look like a mom-and-pop operation that had always been there."

MENU DEVELOPMENT

Alan Stillman states, "All menu selections are formulated in the home office. The general manager, the director of operations, the two assistant managers, the chef, the sous chef, the purchasing agent, and I meet to prepare the menu, and the chef prepares alternative recipes and invites the team for a tasting. The menu is refined and food costs are determined.

SECOND FLOOR BANQUET/DINING SPACE. THE DESIGN INCORPORATES IN A UNIQUE WAY ALL OF THE DESIGN IDIOMS OF A CLASSIC NEW YORK STEAKHOUSE. PHOTOGRAPH © PETER PAIGE.

"I feel that you should develop the best-tasting food available, then worry about the food cost, not the other way around. This commitment to quality and value is perceived and appreciated by the customer. Smith & Wollensky has over a $1 million wine inventory. We have over $2 million invested in wine among all our restaurants. We use the best steaks and age them on premises, and our desserts are also known for their quality and taste."

BUDGET

Alan Stillman explains that the "budget for Smith & Wollensky was not predetermined. Money was raised through a limited partnership with several partners contributing. A design concept was developed and a model built of the space by Arnold Syrop. We went right into construction on a fast-track basis. We knew we had to build a kitchen and other necessities and were modest in our approach toward finishes. A great deal of money was spent on artwork and decoration. Smith & Wollensky's ground floor space took two months to build and cost $1 million. In fact, the restaurant was open for business sixty days after Arnold Syrop started designing.

"Wollensky's Grill had a three-month construction period, the second floor dining/banquet facility took six months, and the cellar food preparation/operations area, which was constructed without interrupting the operation of the three dining areas in the building or its own functioning, required one year to build at a cost of $1.55 million. Following the construction of the first space, a construction manager, Jerry Devine, joined the staff of the New York Restaurant Group. He has been responsible for all subsequent construction and has helped tremendously to maintain difficult schedules."

DESIGN CONCEPT

Alan Stillman states, "I have traveled extensively, collecting artwork and sculpture, and many of these pieces are in Smith & Wollensky, as well as the other restaurants. This personal passion for creating visual richness is a trademark of the New York Restaurant Group, and our architects, Arnold Syrop Associates. Syrop's personal attention to the details and my involvement in selecting the decorative elements allows us to create environments that reflect our image of a

space. This is critical to each restaurant's success."

Arnold Syrop states, "We were asked to create a steak house that looked as though it had been there since the turn of the century. The interior was to have the feeling of a restoration and seem perfectly plausible to patrons familiar with the funky green and white facade of this landmark midtown Manhattan building.

"The space was to have a distinctly masculine ambience, but also appeal to women more than any existing New York steak house. The interior was to be relaxed and not appear as though it had been designed by an architect, but rather give the sense that it had evolved over many years as might a family run restaurant.

"The design solution would incorporate, in a unique way, all of the design idioms associated with a classic New York steak house: beaded wood wainscoting, pendant lighting fixtures, hardwood flooring, blackboards featuring the day's special, and pressed tin.

"The copper-topped bar would provide a large holding area as well as an upscale gathering place. Antique vitrines flanked by vertical wood wine-storage cabinets would form a unique, eclectic back bar. The use of architectural found objects, such as the vitrines, in the design of restaurant spaces has been a trademark of our work with the New York Restaurant Group. Found objects lend authenticity, personality, a touch of wit, and, most of all, uniqueness to all of their projects.

"The ground floor dining space was divided into a variety of intimate areas, each of which has its own identity, but all of which interact with one another. See-through niches in the walls filled with folk art, a signature feature of the restaurant, allow visual access between all areas, giving the patrons a feeling of privacy while making them a part of the vibrant action of all the surrounding spaces.

"The tremendous success of Smith & Wollensky prompted Alan Stillman to forge forward with the design of Wollensky's Grill. This robustly detailed mahogany, green marble, and bronze 75-seat restaurant followed the ground floor dining space by several years. The focal point of Wollensky's Grill is a towering marble and bronze back bar, its niches filled with antique toys. In its former life, this unit, which I discovered and reconstructed, had been the service wall of a turn-of-the-century barber shop in lower Manhattan. Overscaled antique bronze lanterns are suspended over the mahogany and marble bar. A raised dining platform fronts on the active bar, providing a tremendous concentration of energy. Wollensky's Grill has such a casual and tumultuous atmosphere that you are likely to find at any given time a patron's overcoat draped over one of the antique bronze eagles that flank the dining platform. The place, with good reason, is always packed and is in its own right one of the most successful small restaurants in the United States.

"When Alan Stillman decided to open the second floor of the building, he wanted total flexibility for normal dining, banquets for up to 300 people in a single space, or smaller, multiple private parties, or a combination of any of the three. This vast wooden loft was opened to the

SMITH & WOLLENSKY

Prosciutto with Melon	$ 8.50
Shrimp Cocktail	12.75
Fresh Lump Crabmeat	12.75
Lobster Cocktail	13.50
Stone Crabs (In Season)	- -
Soup du Jour	4.75
Artichoke	5.50
S&W Famous Pea Soup	4.50
Asparagus	7.50

****

THE S & W CLASSICS

Sliced Steak Wollensky	29.75
Sirloin	
Filet Mignon	
Filet au Poivre	
Prime Ribs of Beef	
Triple Lamb Chops	
Veal Chop	

****

Veal Dishes	19.50
Chopped Steak	15.50
Calf's Liver	17.50
Sole	19.50
Scallops	- -
Fish	23.50 to 28.50
Stone Crabs	- -
Lobster 4 to 13 lbs	- -
Lemon Pepper Chicken	19.50
Double Sirloin or	
Chateau Briand (for two)	30.00
	per person

****

Salads	6.75
Vegetables	6.75
Potatoes	3.75
Cottage Fries, Onion Rings, Hashed Browns or Fried Zucchini	6.75

SMITH & WOLLENSKY
Steak & Chop House

KITCHEN WITHIN A KITCHEN	
This new menu features unique recipes from our talented chef VICTOR CHAVEZ	
Pan Roasted Fish Steak	24.25
Grilled Chicken Breast	19.50
Cajun Spiced Filet Mignon	22.50
Shrimp Natchez	23.50
Served at Lunch Only	

LUNCH ONLY

Sliced Steak Wollensky	$ 25.75
Sirloin	" "
Filet Mignon	
Filet au Poivre	" "
Prime Ribs of Beef	" "
Triple Lamb Chops	" "
Veal Chop	26.50
Veal Dishes	19.50
Chopped Steak	13.50
Calf's Liver	15.50
Sole	18.50
Scallops	- -
Fish	19.50 to 25.50
Lemon Pepper Chicken	15.50

****

DESSERTS

Cheese Cake	$ 6.50	Mixed Fruit	$ 7.50
Ice Cream/Sherbet	5.50	Melon	5.50
Chocolate Cake	7.50	Hot Deep Dish Apple Pie	
Homemade Fresh Fruit Tart	7.50	with vanilla sauce	6.75
Napoleon	7.25	Wollensky's Basket	7.50
Homemade Austrian Strudel	7.50	Pecan Pie	6.75

****

...OUR GRILL, ENTRANCE ON 49TH STREET, IS OPEN EVERY DAY FROM 11:30 A.M.
      TO 2A.M.
...OUR CLASSIC SMITH & WOLLENSKY STEAK KNIFE IS AVAILABLE FOR PURCHASE

797 Third Ave., N.Y. 10022, Telephone: PL3-1530.

SMITH & WOLLENSKY MENU.

THE COPPER TOPPED BAR AND THE ANTIQUE VITRINES FLANKED BY VERTICLE WOOD WINE STORAGE CABINETS COMBINE TO CREATE AN ECLECTIC GATHERING PLACE. PHOTOGRAPH © MARK ROSS 1991. ALL RIGHTS RESERVED.

THE GROUND FLOOR DINING SPACE WAS DIVIDED INTO A VARIETY OF INTIMATE AREAS, EACH HAVING THEIR OWN IDENTITY. PHOTOGRAPH © MARK ROSS 1991. ALL RIGHTS RESERVED.

sky in three places, and industrial skylights with retractable awnings were installed, thus creating one of the unique skylit dining spaces in midtown Manhattan. Intimate scale was created via the addition of deep and generous coffering trimmed with deep green tile and dark wood, with antique lanterns from the Brighton, England, boardwalk suspended within the coffers. An imaginative system of sliding panels, detailed to match the rich wall wainscoting, enable portions of the room to be partially or completely closed off according to the restaurant's needs. It is probably the only banquet facility in the country that has sufficient warmth and character to function as prime dining space 90 percent of the time without the patrons knowing that it is a banquet room.

The tabletop design at Smith & Wollensky is an extension of the masculine, classic New York steak house image, which is created by the architecture and the foodservice approach.

The white dinner plates are banded with a heavy hunter green edge overlaid with a white logo showing the Smith & Wollensky building.

White tablecloths are used throughout the space. The graphic theme of the china is repeated in the napkins manufactured by Frette, the high-end Italian linen manufacturer. A heavy border of green on the white napkins again incorporates the restaurant logo. The small menu is presented under glass, framed in stained pine. Silverware is simple and robust.

Virtually all of the lighting at Smith & Wollensky is authentic, antique, or invisible. Period lanterns, often overscaled for effect, punctuate the second floor dining/banquet space as well as Wollensky's Grill. Commercial fixtures purchased from catalogs were avoided. The intent of our lighting is to create a warm glow that is complimentary to the patrons. Selected found objects, antique terra-cotta plaques, sculptures, and flower vases are subtly highlighted to provide a variety of light levels within the spaces.

SPACE PLANNING

Architect Arnold Syrop states, "The ground floor dining space is loosely organized into a series of interconnected but varied spaces, each of which is cozy and self-contained, flowing spatially into contiguous spaces through openings in the dividing walls, allowing customers to participate in the action of the entire restaurant. The dining room culminates in the immensely popular "kitchen table," a small, semi-enclosed space adjoining the kitchen and separated from it by a floor-to-ceiling pane of glass.

"Wollensky's Grill shares the ground floor kitchen with the ground floor dining space of Smith & Wollensky. The 25-foot wide grill is laterally divided into a bar area and a platformed dining area that overlooks it. The simplicity of the space plan serves as a foil to the layers of detailing and found objects that define the space.

"The second floor dining/banquet area is a long rectangular space with the potential to be subdivided into four individual dining spaces by means of its sliding panel system. Each of the first three dining/party spaces is individually skylit.

"Running the length of the dining/banquet space and adjoining it is a generous corridor servicing the long rectangular second floor kitchen and continuously accessing the dining/banquet area through a series of entry points. This corridor also links a service bar at the second floor entrance space and a second smaller service bar at the opposite end of the corridor and permits patron access to the rest rooms.

Smith & Wollensky's 16,200 sq. ft. is spread out over three floors. The space for Smith & Wollensky's is divided up as follows:

GROUND LEVEL: 4,230 sq. ft.
ENTRANCE AREA: 120 sq. ft.
COAT ROOM: 60 sq. ft.
BAR AREA: 715 sq. ft.
DINING ROOM: 1,400 sq. ft.
RAISED DINING AREAS: 340 sq. ft.
SERVICE STATIONS: 70 sq. ft.
KITCHEN: 1,480 sq. ft.
BATHROOMS: 220 sq. ft.

The space for Wollensky's Grill is divided up as follows:

GROUND LEVEL: 1,150 sq. ft.
ENTRANCE AREA: 60 sq. ft.
COAT ROOM: none
BAR AREA: 375 sq. ft.
DINING ROOM: 180 sq. ft.
RAISED DINING AREAS: 500 sq. ft.
SERVICE STATIONS: none
KITCHEN: shared with dining area
BATHROOMS: shared with dining area

The space for the dining/banquet facility is divided up as follows:

SECOND FLOOR: 5,380 sq. ft.
ENTRANCE AREA: 225 sq. ft.
COAT ROOM: 80 sq. ft.
BAR AREA: 375 sq. ft.
DINING ROOMS: 2,260 sq. ft.
RAISED DINING AREAS: none
SERVICE STATIONS: 100 sq. ft.
KITCHEN: 1,020 sq. ft.
BATHROOMS: 375 sq. ft.
OFFICE: 300 sq. ft.

The basement space is divided up as follows:

CELLAR: 5,380 sq. ft.
STORAGE AREAS: dry, 1,400 sq. ft.; wet, 1,300 sq. ft.
WINE CELLAR: 660 sq. ft.
BAKERY: 225 sq. ft.
OFFICE: 100 sq. ft.
LOCKERS, EMPLOYEE BATHROOMS: 475 sq. ft.
FOOD PREPARATION: 420 sq. ft.

Alan Stillman explains, "We work with a kitchen designer along with the chef to develop the kitchen design after the menu is developed. If another chef takes over in a few years, if necessary, we will change the kitchen design to suit that chef."

The finishing kitchens, according to Marty Friedman of M. Tucker Co., Inc., are efficient, straightforward spaces for the high-volume production of quality food. The 9,000 sq. ft. prep and storage area in the basement is a "food factory" that includes a pastry bakery, a 2,500 sq. ft. steak aging facility, a butcher shop, a 2,000 sq. ft. wine cellar, refrigerated and dry storage, employee's bathrooms, and lockers, in addition to a repair room, compressor rooms, and a beer and soda room.

The finishing kitchen on the ground level features a 25" hot line that is visible from the dining room through an 8' by 8' window. A 12' *garde manger* station is located at right angles to the hot line, with the expeditor stationed in the middle of the hot line on the pick-up side. Each station is self-contained and has sufficient par stock space to meet heavy demands. The broiler station has a Traulsen upright refrigerator with tray compartments in addition to under-counter

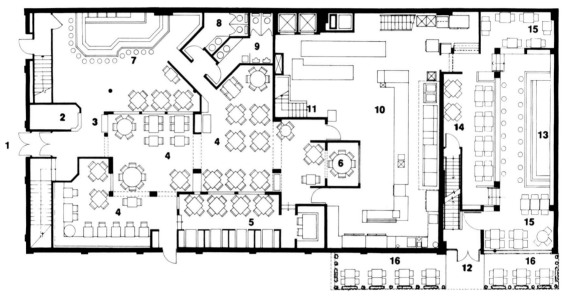

SMITH & WOLLENSKY AND WOLLENSKY'S GRILL GROUND LEVEL FLOOR PLAN. COURTESY OF ARNOLD SYROP.
REFERENCE TABLE: 1. ENTRY; 2. COAT CHECK; 3. MAITRE D' STATION; 4. DINING AREA; 5. RAISED DINING PLATFORM; 6. "KITCHEN TABLE"; 7. BAR/LOUNGE; 8. WOMEN'S RESTROOM; 9. MEN'S RESTROOM; 10. KITCHEN; 11. STAIR TO UPPER AND LOWER LEVELS; 12. WOLLENSKY'S GRILL ENTRY; 13. WOLLENSKY'S GRILL BAR; 14. WOLLENSKY'S GRILL RAISED DINING PLATFORM; 15. WOLLENSKY'S GRILL DINING AREA; 16. WOLLENSKY'S GRILL OUTDOOR DINING

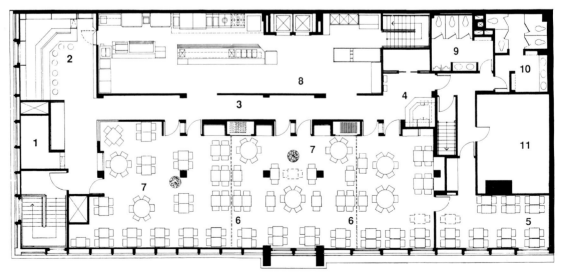

SMITH & WOLLENSKY DINING/BANQUET FACILITY SECOND LEVEL FLOOR PLAN. COURTESY OF ARNOLD SYROP. REDRAWN BY IVONNE DORF.
REFERENCE TABLE: 1. COAT CHECK; 2. BAR; 3. SERVICE HALL; 4. SERVICE BAR; 5. PARTY ROOM; 6. DIVIDER WALLS; 7. DINING/BANQUET ROOMS; 8. KITCHEN; 9. MEN'S RESTROOM; 10. WOMEN'S RESTROOM; 11. OFFICE

refrigerated drawers located in the pick-up counter. These refrigerated drawers have two 12" hotel pans that create several compartments for chicken and fish. The frying section has undercounter refrigeration as well, for onions and other items. All of the items to be cooked are butchered and placed in a refrigerated portion box on trays in the basement and are then brought upstairs and placed in the upright and undercounter refrigerated units. This portion control and storage reduces waste and improves efficiency.

In addition to the ground level kitchen, there is an identical finishing kitchen upstairs that serves the second floor dining room (plan not shown). A dumbwaiter supplies raw ingredients and preprepped food to this second floor kitchen from the basement prep area, while the ground level kitchen is accessed by a stairway. Wollensky's Grill is served from the ground floor kitchen through a pass-through window. This self-contained hot and cold line has a broiler, fryolators, and a small range.

There are eight runners in each of the first and second-floor kitchens that pick up food and place it on a rolling cart or Gueridon that is wheeled out to the dining area. The high level of service offered at Smith & Wollensky requires more flatware and dinnerware than at other restaurants. This puts a great deal of demand on the dishwasher in this high-volume establishment and required the installation of flight-type equipment. This dishwasher doesn't require racks for dinnerware and has a continuous conveyor mechanism, thus improving efficiency and reducing labor costs. No one has to continually load and unload racks of dishes. The dishwasher on the second floor is smaller owing to spatial constraints.

COST OF OPERATIONS

Smith & Wollensky serves local businesspeople and residents of midtown Manhattan, and it has become a destination restaurant for visitors from around the country. Cost of operations are as follows:

SEATING CAPACITY: 340
AVERAGE MONTHLY COVERS: lunch, 4,920; dinner, 17,339
AVERAGE CHECK: lunch, $45; dinner, $60
LIQUOR, WINE, AND BEER SALES: 25%
FOOD COST: 27% to 31%.
TOTAL EMPLOYEES: 199
YEARLY SALES: $14.6 million

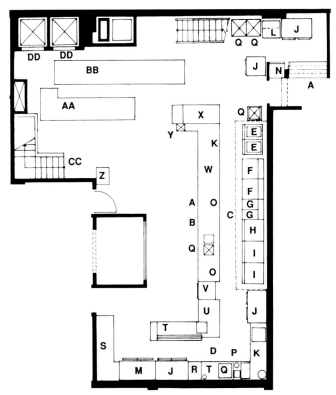

SMITH & WOLLENSKY AND WOLLENSKY'S GRILL KITCHEN PLAN. COURTESY OF ARNOLD SYROP.
REFERENCE TABLE: A. WAITER'S PICK-UP AREA; B. EXPEDITOR; C. HOT LINE; D. GARDE MANGER; E. CONVECTION STEAMER; F. 4-BURNER STOVE; G. FRYER; H. FISH BROILER; I. HI-SPEED BROILER; J. REFRIGERATOR; K. UNDERCOUNTER REFRIGERATOR; L. UNDERCOUNTER FREEZER; M. DISPLAY REFRIGERATOR; N. PASS-THROUGH REFRIGERATOR; O. REFRIGERATED DRAWER; P. OYSTER BAR; Q. SINK; R. ICE CREAM CABINET; S. ESPRESSO/COFFEE STATION; T. WORK TABLE; U. SALAD PREP; V. SALAD PLATE FREEZER; W. STEAM TABLE; X. LOBSTER TABLE; Y. ICE CHEST; Z. BREAD COUNTER; AA. DISH TABLE; BB. DISHWASHING; CC. STAIR TO BASEMENT; DD. DUMBWAITER

Smith & Wollensky's success is owed in a large degree to Alan Stillman's ability to understand the needs of his customer and deliver the best in quality, food, and service. The New York Restaurant Group's experience allowed them to choose a concept and a location that fit a particular market niche without the benefit of in-depth demographic analysis.

Arnold Syrop translated the client's desire into uniquely informal dining spaces that, though strongly related to one another, have tremendous variety, a distinctly eclectic architectural quality, enormous personality and warmth, and feel as though they have been there forever.

From the outset, Alan Stillman strove to create the quintessential New York steak house. This commitment to quality extends from the robust portions of food served in the restaurant to the quest for a visually dynamic environment combined with the most casual and welcoming ambience. It is this distinct personality that has made Smith & Wollensky a destination restaurant for both New Yorkers and visitors to the city.

G O T H A M

OWNERS

Gotham is owned by Jerome Kretchmer and Jeff Bliss, the president and vice president respectively of K B Companies, along with partners Robert and Rick Rathe and chef Alfred Portale.

DESIGNER

Gotham was designed by Paul Segal Associates, Architects. Paul Segal, FAIA, was the partner in charge, and James R. Biber, AIA, was the project architect.

SOURCES

ARCHITECT: Paul Segal Associates, Architects
LIGHTING CONSULTANTS: Jules Fisher-Paul Marantz Design, Jerry Kugler Associates
GRAPHIC DESIGN: Donovan and Green
FOODSERVICE CONSULTANT: Barbara Kafka Associates
BAR: Rathe Productions
CAST STONE ORNAMENTS: Cusano Brothers
SHEET RUBBER FLOORING: American Flooring Products
TRACK LIGHTING: Lightolier
UPHOLSTERY MATERIALS: Naco Fabrics
CHAIRS: Shelby Williams
GLASSWARE: Cardinal International, Schott Zweisel
FLATWARE: DJ Industries, Alfredo Zanger
CHINA: Hall China, Villeroy and Bosch
PHOTOGRAPHER: Norman McGrath

ALFRED PORTALE. PHOTOGRAPH © PRIMOSZ.

PAUL SEGAL. PHOTOGRAPH © PAUL SEGAL ASSOCIATES.

otham, which opened in 1984, is a 7,500 sq. ft. full-service restaurant that seats 165 people and is located on East Twelfth Street in Manhattan. It is one of the top five restaurants in New York, according to Zagat's *Restaurant Survey*, and has earned three stars from Bryan Miller, writing for the *New York Times*.

Jerry Kretchmer was the head of the environmental protection administration in New York City when John Lindsay was mayor. After leaving city government, he and Jeff Bliss, his partner, became successful real estate developers and builders who were always interested in projects that would challenge them creatively, so they decided to open a restaurant.

Jerry Kretchmer states, "I was always interested in the restaurant business and felt I understood what made it work. I spent a lot of time eating out and particularly liked large, wide-open spaces

where there was a lot of energy and people could see and be seen. I felt I knew how to attract and satisfy a young, hip, active crowd of professionals and artists who were relocating their businesses and studios to this part of town. I liked the size and feeling of Café Seyoken and Joanna's and used them as models for the kind of style and scale of restaurant I wanted to develop.

Knowing who my potential customer was and the size and style of the restaurant, it took me three days to find the location on Twelfth Street between University Place and Fifth Avenue. It was a large space with high ceilings and large windows, which perfectly matched my vision for a theatrical, energized restaurant concept.

Creating a successful restaurant is a lot like politics. You have to understand what people want and give it to them. Restaurants are about people and service, and I felt I had a knack for making people feel comfortable and happy. Like any good politician, I also knew I couldn't develop a restaurant without assembling a great team. We hired Barbara Kafka after interviewing several restaurant consultants. Barbara was instrumental in assisting us with the development of the food and the style of the restaurant. She also helped us with the economics of the project by determining the amount of seats, the average check, labor, and food costs, and the overall layout of the dining room and kitchen.

We hired Paul Segal Associates, Architects, after commissioning several architects to submit conceptual designs. Paul Segal and James Biber, the project architect, Barbara Kafka, and the four partners worked together on the foodservice style and design of the place. I wanted an energized, simple, grand space that was a bit noisy, where there was a lot of movement and action.

Ultimately what developed was a grand space that was more subdued and classical than I had originally wanted, but it captured the energy and scale that I felt was necessary. The restaurant opened to great reviews and was doing great business for the first four months and then disaster struck. We got a bad review and I had some problems with the chef. Over the next six months it went from bad to worse. We went through several chefs and started to lose a substantial amount of money. I'm not a quitter, and approximately a year after we opened, I was introduced to Alfred Portale, an extremely talented chef, who turned the restaurant completely around and developed it into one of the top five restaurants in New York City.

It is now a three-star restaurant and Alfred Portale is considered by many as one of the top three chefs in the country. Even more important, however, is the fact that Gotham is a great value. Our average check is $30 less than the other top restaurants in New York because we are committed to offering quality food and service that is also affordable.

MENU DEVELOPMENT

Alfred Portale had not held a position as head chef before he came to Gotham, but he had gained a great deal of experience working with some of the best chefs in the world. The initial concept for the food was the product of those years of experience and was influenced by the design of the space. Portale states, "The grand, dramatic

THE GREENHOUSE ENTRANCE, WITH ITS PANES OF GLASS TRIMMED IN SLATE BLUE LATTICEWORK ATTACHED TO CEMENT COLUMNS AND TOPPED WITH A LIGHTED PYRAMID, ESTABLISHES A POINT OF ARRIVAL. PHOTOGRAPH © NORMAN MCGRATH.

space inspired me to create food that was equally dramatic and energetic in its presentation.

"The food now at Gotham is much different than it was seven years ago when I started. I had a strong style then, but I have a much, much stronger style now. I developed my style here and I began to rely less and less on my prior experience and started creating the food just for Gotham.

"My philosophy has always been to provide the best quality food at affordable prices. I believe that customers are aware of the great value at Gotham. We are highly efficient in the kitchen, and I have highly trained culinary school graduates that know how to handle the products, thus avoiding waste. The sous chef does the ordering for the restaurant and is very conscious of food cost.

"We have a good relationship with all of our purveyors, and we are continually looking for the best possible products at reasonable prices. In addition, we purchase some of our fresh produce at the green market at nearby Union Square, where I usually stop by twice a week to get inspired by the fresh seasonal produce.

"We are obsessed at Gotham with quality and performance of both the food and the service. I'm scared to death to do anything that isn't the best.

"I can't design a menu for myself because this is a high-volume three-star restaurant, and the line cooks must be capable of executing the food by themselves. The challenge is to consistently prepare the food the same way; there is no room for deviation. The food is labor-intensive and requires highly skilled staff to produce it."

STAFF

Jeff Bliss states, "Gotham is run like a corporation. Partners Jerry Kretchmer and Rick Rathe act as a kind of board of directors and guide the entire operation by meeting with the management team to discuss food, service, and financial matters. Chef/partner Alfred Portale, Scott Carney, the general manager, and Laurie Tomasino, director of services, together form the management team and interact constantly to coordinate front- and back-of-the-house issues. Portale is primarily responsible for the kitchen staff and the menu, while Carney runs the financial components of the business, and Tomasino handles all front-of-the-house staff and service functions.

Jerry Kretchmer states, "My director of services, Laurie Tomasino, has been with me since the night we opened. Many of the wait and kitchen staff have also been with us for many years, because it is a great place to work. We pay well and have good medical benefits and provide paid vacations for our staff."

Laurie Tomasino explains the staff selection and training procedures: "Fifty percent of our wait staff have worked for us for over three years. We involve our employees in decisions that affect them, treat them fairly and with respect, and offer rewards for suggestions on how to cut costs and improve service. When a position becomes available, we carefully interview several candidates to make sure they fit our profile. We do not necessarily look for waiters who have a great deal of experience in four-star restaurants; our service is not that scientific. Our service is friendly, enthusiastic, knowledgeable, and correct. It is important that

we find a candidate who has a guest-first mentality, shares an enthusiasm for great food and wine, and can share that enthusiasm with our guests. The best training program in the world cannot make fundamental changes in a person.

"Once a candidate has been selected, they receive a detailed training and house manual. The candidate is then paired with a trainer (an employee trained by the house to train new employees), and the orientation begins. Our orientation/training program lasts three days, and is divided into four parts:

1. House policies: payroll, declaration, schedule, absence, vacations, grooming, uniforms, etc.
2. Service procedures: job descriptions, sidework, task analysis, how to's, handling complaints, etc.

First Course

SELECT OYSTERS AND CLAMS
Served Chilled with Cocktail Sauce and Champagne Mignonette   Priced Daily

FOIE GRAS AND PHEASANT TERRINE
Haricots Verts, Green Lentils, Lettuces and Walnut Oil $13.50

WINTER WILD MUSHROOM RAVIOLIS
In Mushroom Broth, with Chervil and White Truffle Oil $10.50

SMOKED DUCK BREAST
Basmati Rice Salad and Apricot-Pear Chutney $11.00

GOTHAM GARDEN SALAD
Mixed Lettuces, Sherry Vinaigrette and Extra Virgin Olive Oil $8.75

AUTUMN SALAD
Mixed Bitter Greens, Bosc Pear and Sweet Gorgonzola with Walnut Oil Vinaigrette $9

ROAST SQUAB
Cous-Cous, Curry and Apple-Cherry Chutney $12.50

COLD SMOKED SALMON WITH WARM POTATO GALETTE
Crème Fraiche, Salmon Roe, Chives and Chervil $13.00

GOTHAM PASTA
Composed Daily

SEAFOOD SALAD
Squid, Scallops, Japanese Octopus and Lobster,
dressed in Lemon and Extra Virgin Olive Oil $12.50

GOAT CHEESE SALAD
Beets, Grilled Leeks, Marinated Peppers and Grilled Bread $11.25

ROAST QUAIL
Carnaroli Risotto, Chanterelles, Chard and Deep Fried Sage $12.00

Chef de Cuisine: Alfred Po

3. Remanco computer training: payment methods, correcting errors, crash procedures, etc.
4. Food and wine: food and wine descriptions, appropriate flatware, wine service.

"We emphasize to our trainers the importance of teaching one task at a time, demonstration, and explanation. Once the training has been completed, the trainee is required to take a written quiz based on information covered in the training.

"Each of our employees is evaluated twice a year. The evaluations allow us an opportunity to meet with employees one on one, discuss strengths and weaknesses, reinforce service goals, and remind them that the act of giving in service makes all the difference.

"The floor staff at Gotham is divided into three departments, each with a very clear job description. We emphasize teamwork and lead by example. Thus, the tips are pooled and the work load shared equally. The dining room floor is staffed with 10 waiters, 4 runners, 6 bussers, 2 bartenders, and 2 managers nightly.

"Our reservation book is designed to accommodate up to thirty-four guests a half-hour. Each half-hour has space for 1 to 2 large parties, 4 four-tops, and 4 deuces. Each guest receives a reservation number and is asked to call and confirm on the day of their reservation. We do remind each guest that if we do not receive a confirmation, we cannot guarantee a table. We allow three hours for large parties and two and a half hours for deuces and four-tops."

GOTHAM BAR & GRILL
DINNER MENU.

Second Course

SEARED SEA SCALLOPS
On Linguine, with Spinach, Tarragon, Chervil and Scallop Butter $26.50

RED SNAPPER
Roasted with Potatoes, Whole Garlic, Olive Oil and Rosemary $27.50

GOTHAM FISH SPECIAL
Composed and Priced Nightly

SHELLFISH BOUILLABAISSE
Mussels, Scallops and Prawns and Lobster in a Saffron-Shellfish Stock $28.50

STEAMED ATLANTIC SALMON
Boiled Potatoes, Savoy Cabbage, Smoked Onions and Sauce Verjus $28.50

ROAST PHEASANT
Braised Salsify, Brussel Sprouts, Juniper and a Pumpkin Squash Purée $28.50

DUCK 'CHOUCROUTE'
Muscovy Duck Breast, Sauerkraut, Crab Apple and Potato Purée $28.00

SADDLE OF RABBIT
Grilled, with Spinach, White Beans and Baby Fennel $27.50

GRILLED SQUAB
Roasted Garlic, Pancetta, Cremini and Sage $27.50

VENISON
Roasted Winter Vegetables, Onion Marmelade, and Red Wine Vinegar Sauce $30.00

RACK OF LAMB
Dijon Mustard and Sweet Garlic Custard $29.50

ROAST FREE RANGE CHICKEN
Served with Vegetables, Shoestring Potatoes and Rosemary $26.00

GRILLED NEW YORK STEAK
Crushed White Peppercorns, a Marrow Mustard Custard and Deep Fried Shallots $29.50

** Subject to Availability.
Water served upon request.
Please, no pipe or cigar smoking.

Scott Carney has been instrumental in improving operations and speed of service issues during the growth of the business over the past six years. He states, "Operational areas that once satisfied a far smaller business volume had to be redesigned to speed the diner through various phases of his or her visit to the restaurant. For example, I worked with James Biber to add a second tier of coat racks to the coatcheck area, where speed of service and adequate capacity are crucial. Improvements to speed of service included consolidation of the Busser charge card processing station and provision of a well-lit, well-appointed voucher station with the most advanced data processing equipment.

"Front of the house design was also modified to meet our growing demand, including the evolution of our bar tables into regularly set and staffed dining tables, increasing our capacity by some thirty seats.

"Communication between restaurant and customer, front and back of house, day and night shift, department to department, often determines the quality of dining experience received by our customers. The management group meets twice a month to address current issues and continue thinking ahead. Our primary communication vehicle, however, is our log book, through which the crucial connections between night and day are made. Management and the bartending staff meet monthly to make procedural improvements and discuss the previous month's profitability. The bread and butter of the communication scheme, however, are the nightly briefings between management/kitchen and wait staff—a sort of evening news update that brings everyone current with the changes and special concerns of the evening. This takes place for 15 to 20 minutes before service every day."

In addition to accounting, payroll, and other operational functions, Carney is a master sommelier and is responsible for the wine program at Gotham. There are only approximately twenty other people who have earned that title in America, and Carney believes that since the sommelier is a dying breed on the dining room floor, there is a need for wine-knowledgeable wait staff.

Carney states, "We sponsor an in-house education through a year-long series of wine seminars, which includes blind tastings, lectures, wine quizzes, wine and food matching, and guest speakers. The sum total of the experience brings a more knowledgeable, more enthused waiter to the customer, and we support their learning with a small reference library in house. In the final analysis, the wait staff is a sales staff, and their success can only come from knowing their products."

BUDGET

Jerry Kretchmer and Jeff Bliss had a great deal of experience developing and building projects in New York City and were able, with the assistance of their construction team, to establish a realistic budget for this project. They allocated $650,000 for construction, with an FFE (furnishings, fixtures, and equipment) budget of $100,000 and $100,000 for consultants and architects. The project was built without any major surprises and was on time and on budget.

The design took three to four months to complete and was in process while general construction was underway. Paul Segal Associates prepared many alternative schematic drawings for pricing that were scrutinized, revised, and eventually accepted. Acting as their own general contractors, the partners built the restaurant in four months.

The design is a combination of many low-cost elements, including prefabricated, precast, sandblasted stone, concrete block and stucco, stained existing wood floors, golf-club rubber mat floors, paint, and stock molding. The total square footage is approximately 7,500 sq. ft., with a total budget of $650,000. This design was accomplished for under $100 per square foot, including the kitchen.

DESIGN CONCEPT

This space was originally conceived by Jerry Kretchmer as a stark, white, hard-edged theatrical space and evolved into a visually rich, fun, metaphorically classical juxtaposition of an urban garden within an urban space.

Says Kretchmer, "Through the use of space manipulation, metaphorical materials and lighting, Paul Segal, James Biber, and lighting designer Jerry Kugler were able to dazzle the senses, yet create an environment that was soothing as well." To attract the eye from the outside, large billowy parachutes, or cloudlike fabric lighting fixtures were utilized. Paul Segal feels that "these fixtures are the single most important feature in the design, because they attract attention and evoke a sense of romance and fantasy."

James Biber and Paul Segal feel that "the tension created by the juxtaposition of hard, massive, solid objects against willowy, soft, delicate ones created vitality and energy in the space. Bringing things inside that ordinarily one associates with the outdoors, like the garden ornaments, creates a kind of contextual surprise.

"The greenhouse entrance, with its panes of glass trimmed in slate-blue latticework attached to cement columns and topped with a lighted pyramid, establishes a point of arrival and creates a visual surprise to passersby on the street. Inside, a vertical progression of textures, from real to illusory, is capped by a green moulding, allowing the upper half of the space to dissolve in a pattern of pipes, exposed lights, and other unwelcome items.

"The columns in the space are massive urban shapes. The silver pyramidal studs on these columns contribute to a masculine texture that contrasts dramatically with the billowy, delicate, feminine lighting fixtures and draperies. The main dining room is slanted off the main axis of the space, created by the massive columns. This tilting of the axis created intimately scaled raised dining areas that allowed diners to view the processional march below."

The large bar area, positioned perfectly, commands a view of the entire show.

The rich palette of color, texture, form, and light in this space is a visual treat for all the senses. It is a design that is both energized and romantic at the same time. It can be perceived as formal or funky, depending on your mood or expectations. It is spatially organized to be viewed as a grand café or an intimate dining experience. Above all, this design has endured and matured along with the clientele and the food.

Jerry Kugler, the lighting designer states, "The soft, billowy parachutes or cloud light fixtures provide a soft warm light that is flattering to facial skin tones. They are made of flame-retardant fabric that is draped over steel tubing and hung on steel cable from the ceiling and are lit with simple track fixtures. These fixtures were relatively inexpensive to produce when compared to custom UL-approved glass fixtures."

The rest of the space is lit with low-voltage track fixtures that illuminate the tables and food, while framing projectors illuminate paintings, architectural elements, and flowers.

THE TENSION CREATED BY THE JUXTAPOSITION OF HARD, MASSIVE OBJECTS AGAINST WILLOWY, SOFT, DELICATE ONES PRODUCES VITALITY AND ENERGY IN THE SPACE. PHOTOGRAPH © NORMAN MCGRATH.

THE BAR COULD NOT HAVE BEEN IN A BETTER LOCATION. IT'S A GREAT GATHERING PLACE WHERE YOU CAN VIEW THE ENERGY OF THE SPACE. PHOTOGRAPH © NORMAN MCGRATH.

Jerry Kretchmer asserts that "the bar at Gotham could not have been in a better location. It is a comfortable distance from the entrance, and you pass some action on the way to the bar while having a great view of the dining area."

James Biber states, "The original space plan was based on a Basilica plan with the entrance as the Campanile, the bar as the Baptistry, and the dining room as the Nave and Transcept. This idea evolved into the entry as greenhouse or gazebo, the dining room as urban garden and the bar as built urban environment. The original plan attempted to maximize seating by constructing a mezzanine with the kitchen tucked underneath. It was thought that this kitchen was too small and, reluctantly, the design team placed the kitchen downstairs, eliminating the need for the mezzanine. The bathrooms are also downstairs. The large bar was deliberately placed on a platform near the entrance to enable customers to view all the action below."

Paul Segal and James Biber designed the space plan to accomplish the sense of theater that Jerry Kretchmer wanted, and at the same time they created intimately scaled, distinct areas that provide privacy within the larger space. This allows regular customers to try out different areas of this space each time they dine. Gotham's 7,500 square feet is spread out over two floors as follows:

GROUND LEVEL: 4,200 sq. ft.

ENTRANCE AREA: 250 sq. ft.

COAT ROOM: 100 sq. ft.

BAR AREA: 900 sq. ft.

LOWER DINING AREA: 2,000 sq. ft.

GOTHAM BAR & GRILL FIRST FLOOR PLAN. COURTESY OF PAUL SEGAL ASSOCIATES. REFERENCE TABLE: 1. ENTRY; 2. COAT CHECK; 3. MAITRE D'; 4. BAR; 5. DINING AREA; 6. DOWNSTAIRS TO BATHROOMS; 7. DOWNSTAIRS TO KITCHEN; 8. BEVERAGE STATION; 9. BAR PICK-UP AREA; 10. REAR EXIT

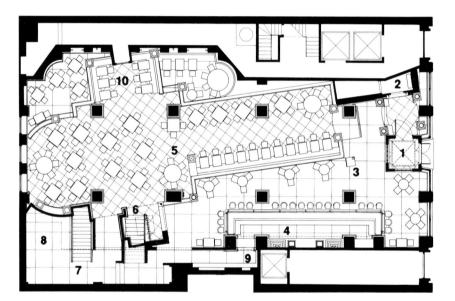

GOTHAM BAR & GRILL BASEMENT LEVEL KITCHEN PLAN. COURTESY OF PAUL SEGAL ASSOCIATES. REDRAWN BY LORRAINE KNAPP. REFERENCE TABLE: A. PICK-UP COUNTER; B. HOT LINE; C. GARDE MANGER; D. PASTRY PREP; E. REACH-IN REFRIGERATORS; F. PREP AREA; G. WALK-IN REFRIGERATOR; H. WALK-IN FREEZER; I. WINE AND BEER STORAGE; J. TRASH ROOM; K. DRY STORAGE; L. MANAGER'S OFFICE; M. CHEF'S OFFICE; N. EMPLOYEE'S BATHROOMS; O. EMPLOYEE'S LOCKERS; P. MEN'S BATHROOMS; Q. WOMEN'S BATHROOMS; R. FRYOLATORS; S. GRILL; T. STOVE

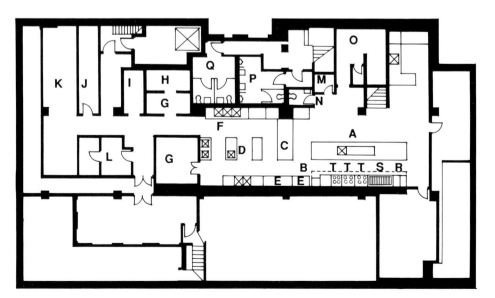

RAISED DINING AREAS: 350 sq. ft.
SERVICE AREAS: 600 sq. ft.
BASEMENT: 3,300 sq. ft.
KITCHEN: 1,450 sq. ft.
BATHROOMS: 400 sq. ft.
STORAGE AREAS: dry, 800 sq. ft.; wet, 400 sq. ft.
OFFICE: 250 sq. ft.

KITCHEN DESIGN

The entire kitchen is located in the basement, with the exception of the beverage area and waiter's station, which is upstairs near the dining room. Alfred Portale says, "There is no great disadvantage to having the kitchen in the basement, other than having to have runners with strong legs."

Alfred continues, "The kitchen is arranged in a straight line with the *garde manger* at right angles to the hot line. I expedite on the cooking side of the line because I can have more contact with the food and the other cooks can learn by my example. The food at Gotham is complex, and I feel I can teach technique constantly if I'm behind the line. My job is to motivate the staff by bringing them excerpts from cookbooks and clippings from food magazines, in addition to bringing them new, fresh ingredients from my trips to the produce markets.

"Most of my highly trained staff have been with me for many years, because they are challenged creatively and they respect the commitment to quality and excellence at Gotham. I need this staff to stay together in order to maintain consistency and I tell each new cook that they must stay at least one year. These line cooks and all the kitchen staff are under tremendous pressure and work very long hours. As an employer, I must earn their respect or they are not going to stay. Gotham could not succeed with a tense atmosphere and without teamwork.

"One difficulty in operating a restaurant where complex food is prepared by very skilled cooks is the payroll. We need their commitment, but the longer they stay, the more money it costs. This increased payroll cuts into profits, but because we are here for the long haul, we feel the level of quality and consistency far outweighs increased costs. Unfortunately, the growth of the payroll doesn't match the growth of the dining room. It isn't getting any bigger, and in a recessionary economy, it is difficult to raise prices, which leaves control of food costs as the only way to reduce operating expenses. Fortunately, skilled staff and

an efficient kitchen with enough storage capacity can reduce waste, thus reducing food costs.

"We have an abundant amount of space behind the line, which helps during peak periods. We have six cooks on the line, including myself and four at the *garde manger*, and three at the pastry station, in addition to four runners. We use plate covers and we have heat lamps, but I don't use them because our food would break down if it were not timed properly and left under heat lamps."

COST OF OPERATIONS

Gotham is a three-star destination restaurant and serves wonderfully prepared food to customers from all over the world in a dramatic setting. It is one of the best values for a high-end restaurant in New York City, with an average check of $55 for dinner. It is also rated fifth among New York's top fifty restaurants by Zagat's *Restaurant Survey*. Cost of operations are as follows:

SEATING CAPACITY: dining room, 140; bar dining, 25; bar stools, 20
TOTAL WEEKLY COVERS: lunch, 80-120; dinner, 230-340
AVERAGE CHECK: dinner, $55; lunch, $22
LIQUOR AND WINE SALES: 30%
FOOD COST: 33%
TOTAL EMPLOYEES: 68
TOTAL YEARLY SALES: $6 million

Gotham is truly a restaurant whose success has depended on a commitment to quality and value. It has also endured because Jerry Kretchmer and his partners didn't give up when the restaurant struggled in the first year of operation. They found Alfred Portale, who is now considered one of the best chefs in the country, and their management style has kept their staff virtually intact since the day they opened. Alfred Portale, Scott Carney, and Laurie Tomasino motivate their staff and run the operation in a corporate manner with everyone's responsibilities clearly defined. Costs are carefully controlled, and these cost savings are passed on to the customer.

Alfred Portale's food is masterfully prepared and plated by his highly trained staff and is served by an enthusiastic and caring service staff. Paul Segal and James Biber's dynamic metaphorical design is a timeless environment that is still captivating customers.

MESA GRILL

OWNERS

Mesa Grill is owned by Jerome and Laurence Kretchmer and Jeff Bliss, of K B Companies, a restaurant and real estate development organization in New York City.

DESIGNER

Mesa Grill was designed by James Biber of Pentagram Architectural Services. James Biber graduated with honors from Cornell University College of Architecture, Art, and Planning. He worked as a senior associate with Paul Segal Associates before opening his own office, James Biber Architect, in 1984. He joined Pentagram Design as a partner in New York and established Pentagram Architectural Services in November 1991.

SOURCES

ARCHITECT: James Biber, Pentagram Architectural Services
CONSTRUCTION MANAGER: Laurence Kretchmer
BAR TOP: Domestic Marble & Stone
CUSTOM PENDANT, SCONCE, AND METAL RAILING: Giza and Sons
LIGHT FIXTURES: Halo, C.J. Lighting Co.
BLACK-AND-WHITE PHOTOGRAPHS: Ewing-Galloway, printing by Giant Photo, frames by Frames New York Inc.
CABINETRY MATERIALS: hardware by Knape & Voigt, plastic laminate by Color Core by Formica
CABINETRY: MLMA Inc.
KITCHEN DOORS: Eliason Restaurant Doors
PAINT: Benjamin Moore
GRAPHIC DESIGN: Alexander Isley Design
ACOUSTICAL CEILING PANELS: Efros and Assoc.
AWNING: Patio Awning Co.
BANQUETTES: All State Upholstery
FLOOR REFINISHING: M Floors, Inc.
CEILING FANS: Leading Edge
WOOD AND GLASS PARTITION: Bronx Builders
FABRIC: Full Swing Textile Collection
CHAIR REFINISHING: Leathercraft
PHOTOGRAPHER: Peter Mauss/Esto

JEROME KRETCHMER, BOBBY FLAY, JEFF BLISS. PHOTOGRAPH © MICHAEL MCLAUGHLIN.

JAMES BIBER. PHOTOGRAPH © MARK BABUSHKIN.

Mesa Grill is a 6,400 sq. ft. southwestern-style restaurant that seats 150 people and is located on Fifth Avenue between Fifteenth and Sixteenth streets in Manhattan. It was completed in January 1991 and has become one of New York's hottest restaurants.

Co-owner Jeff Bliss states, "Many people thought we were absolutely crazy to open a restaurant in the teeth of the recession in 1991. Restaurants were failing all over town, and the industry as a whole had experienced a substantial drop in sales. However, Jerry Kretchmer and I both felt that the reason that so many restaurants had failed recently was that they were unable to change their menu, price structure, and overall concepts to adapt to changing economic conditions. Many people felt that the restaurant industry was dead in New York and that there was no opportunity for new restaurant concepts. Jerry and I still believed, however, in the vitality of New York, and were committed to developing a concept that would work despite the gloomy economic conditions.

"One friend remarked, 'I've attended the funeral for New York City several times, but the body never shows up.' We felt we could succeed if we could develop a restaurant where there was great food and service combined with a low average check in an energized, fun environment. The trick was that we needed to spend as little money as possible on the renovation and try to negotiate the best possible deal in order for this concept to work.

"We felt the lower Fifth Avenue area of Manhattan was still a vital one, because many new retail clothing companies, including Georgio Armani, Kenneth Cole, Cignal, The Gap, and Banana Republic had located their stores between Fourteenth and Twenty-first streets. In addition, many young professionals, architects, graphic designers, photographers, and advertising agencies had located their businesses in this area and didn't have an affordable place where they could hang out and have great food.

"We found a space between Fifteenth and Sixteenth streets on Fifth Avenue that had been occupied by two previous restaurants. The space was large in scale, with high ceilings, large columns, a mezzanine, and large front windows, and it suited our concept perfectly, since we could transform it without a major investment."

Jerry Kretchmer states, "This space fit my idea for an exuberant southwestern restaurant that crystalized after many trips to Arizona and New Mexico. Southwestern food is flavorful, colorful, exciting, and healthy and would suit the taste

THE COLOR PALETTE OF THE RESTAURANT WAS INFLUENCED BY THE EXUBERANCE AND COLOR OF THE FOOD. PHOTOGRAPH © PETER MAUSYS/ESTO.

buds of a young, hip crowd. This style of cooking worked with the concept of a high-volume, high-quality, low-average-check restaurant."

MENU DEVELOPMENT

Jerry Kretchmer states, "We were committed to hiring a great chef who could produce innovative southwestern-style food at reasonable prices that would encourage people to come back several times a week. We selected Bobby Flay as the chef for Mesa Grill because of his enthusiasm and knowledge of southwestern cooking and city folk. He is extremely creative and commands a great deal of respect from his staff. Bobby creates a draft menu and we taste items to determine if they have popular appeal. The menu is changed four times a year with minor modifications between each change."

Bobby Flay is twenty-six-years old and has already had several years of experience in New York kitchens. He was educated at French Culinary Institute and was a chef at the age of nineteen in a grill restaurant on the Upper East Side. He worked for several years as the chef at the Miracle Grill, and he worked for Jonathan Waxman at Jam's in New York City. He's developed a keen understanding of the kind of food New Yorkers crave and has tailored the southwestern menu at Mesa Grill to suit the tastes of this area.

This restaurant received a lot of advance publicity and was much anticipated. Bobby Flay had built a reputation as an innovator, and he was determined to create a menu that met everyone's expectations. The menu draws its influence from the American southwest, and the food is colorful, fun, and energized, delighting the palate as well as the eye.

Bobby Flay believes that you can't be all things to all people, and if you can't describe the food and decor in a few words, it is probably overcomplicated. He describes his food as "healthful, colorful, and extremely flavorful." He feels also that the design of the restaurant, with its bold colors, big scale, and funky southwest lighting fixtures is a wonderful stage set for his food. "This food probably wouldn't work as well in a small space with low ceilings," says Bobby Flay.

STAFF

Don Sisemore, Mesa's general manager, states that "Mesa Grill is a casual, fun, upbeat space where the service style can be less structured than at a fine dining restaurant. When I'm interviewing a potential wait staff candidate, I look for a combination of enthusiasm, attitude, and experience. I look for a person who is well schooled in the art of service, because I feel it is harder to train staff people in a high-energy, casual dining environment. I ask them why they want to work at Mesa, why they left their last position, and what they feel are ideal working conditions. Often, I rely on personal recommendations from connections I have in the industry rather than newspaper advertisements to screen potential employees.

"This is a great place to work because wait staff can make a lot of money in salary and tips in this high-volume, energy-packed environment. We have 60 employees who, for the most part, work a single shift, with 44 staff members in the front of the house and 16 in the kitchen. Including myself, we have a dining room manager, two assistant dining room managers, a bookkeeper, and a steward, in addition to the chef and a sous chef. The dining room manager is responsible for all the service staff, the flow of the room, printing and updating the menu, and making sure customers are happy. We don't overbook the room because we have a lot of walk-in traffic with people waiting for tables. They don't seem to mind because the bar is packed with people and there's a lot of opportunity to enjoy the space and people-watch.

Jerry Kretchmer and Jeff Bliss spend a great deal of time in the restaurant, and attend to the smallest detail. Their presence is very important and contributes to the success of the restaurant.

BUDGET

Jeff Bliss states, "In order for this high-quality, low-average-check concept to work, we had to apply tremendous constraints on the budget." Mesa Grill was a renovation of an existing restaurant where the storefront and most of the architectural features were left untouched. A new kitchen that utilized much of the existing kitchen equipment was

GRILL

Chef: BOBBY FLAY

CORN + ZUCCHINI QUESADILLA
filled with
Two Cheeses +
served with Avocado
Relish + Smoked
Tomato Salsa
$9.25

SWEET POTATO SOUP
with Smoked
Chilies + *garnished*
with Yellow + Blue
Corn Tortillas
$5.75

SPICY SALMON TARTAR
with Plantain
Croutons +
Cilantro Oil
$8.75

SHRIMP + ROASTED GARLIC CORN TAMALE
$9.50

CORNMEAL COATED CHILE RELLENO
filled with Goat
Cheese + *served with*
Black Bean Sauce
$8.50

ROMAINE SALAD
with Spicy Caesar
Dressing,
Anchovies + Red
Chile Croutons
$5.75

FRISEE SALAD
with Chorizo,
Asiago Cheese,
Tomatoes +
Roasted Garlic
Vinaigrette
$6.00

GRILLED TUNA TOSTADA
with Black Bean-
Mango Salsa +
Avocado Vinaigrette
$9.50

POMEGRANATE GLAZED QUAIL SALAD
with Walnut Oil
Dressing + Hominy
Croutons
$9.50

DUCK + ROASTED CORN TACO
with Smoked Red
Pepper Sauce
$8.75

PAN SEARED WILD MUSHROOMS
on Chipotle Brioche
$6.50

RED CHILE CRUSTED SEA SCALLOPS
with Mango +
Tortilla Salad +
Orange Vinaigrette
$8.50

GRILLED LOIN OF LAMB CHOPS
with Jalapeno Preserves + Spinach + Sweet Potato Gratin
$19.00

PAN FRIED GROUPER
in a Roasted Vegetable + Green Chili Broth
with Sage Pesto + Fall Herbs
$18.75

GRILLED + MARINATED VEGETABLE SALAD
with Tender Greens, Goat Cheese Croutons + Balsamic Vinaigrette
$15.50

ROASTED CHICKEN WITH RED CHILE OIL, FRESH SAGE + GARLIC
served with Mashed Potatoes + Acorn Squash
$17.75

GRILLED YUCATAN STYLE SHRIMP,
with Roasted Poblano Sauce, White Bean Salad +
Buttermilk Onion Rings
$19.75

GRILLED SALMON
with Ancho Chili-Honey Glaze
served with Spaghetti Squash + a Zucchini Taco
$20.00

GRILLED HALIBUT
in a Curried Corn Sauce *served with* Zucchini Noodles + Roasted Beets
$20.00

GRILLED PORK TENDERLOIN
with Spicy Apple Chutney + Pumpkin Tamale
$18.00

GRILLED SWORDFISH
with Smoked Yellow Pepper Sauce, Cilantro Pesto Potatoes +
Sauteed Brussel Sprouts
$19.75

CORNMEAL COATED RABBIT
with Wild Mushroom-Ancho Chile Sauce + a Black Bean Torta
$21.50

GRILLED NY STEAK
with Red Chile Mustard, Thyme-Marinated Tomatoes +
Southwestern Fries
$21.00

Pumpkin Tamale	Zucchini Taco
Black Bean Torta	Southwestern Fries
Mashed Potatoes	Acorn Squash
Cilantro Pesto Potatoes	Sweet Potato Gratin

$4.00

designed for under $30,000, and a new glass wall separating the kitchen and dining areas was added, along with new lighting, paint, and other decorative elements for a total budget of under $300,000.

James Biber explains, "The budget for the front of the house was $150,000, and we divided up the money among the major design features in the space to maximize their appeal. Tight budgets are the mother of invention, and this process lead to many interesting design elements, including the inexpensive stock photos on the walls and the lighting fixtures. We controlled the budget by providing alternative design sketches of various elements to the construction manager for pricing. Certain elements were approved, while other elements were redesigned and presented to meet the budget. Many alternatives were explored before the final budget was approved, and we drew several sketches of the glass wall and

lighting fixtures for pricing purposes, then picked the ones that fit the budget.

"All of this was going on while demolition and construction were underway. This was a *fast-track* project that took a total of three months to design and build. During this time of trial and error, it was essential that we had the complete faith of the owner. Some of the elements I suggested were way over budget, but there was no screaming or yelling, I just went back to the drawing board. There were certain elements, however, that I thought were essential to the concept, and the owners had faith in my ability to understand the needs of the concept and that I was not just allowing my ego to control the project.

"Several compromises were made that affected the budget. The chairs from the previous restaurant were painted, although I would have preferred a different chair. Some of the banquettes in the

WALL SCONCES AND BLACK-AND-WHITE PHOTOGRAPHS ATTRACT THE EYE AND CREATE VISUAL EXCITMENT. PHOTOGRAPH © PETER MAUSS.

THE FRONT AREA WAS FORMERLY A WAITING AREA AND IS NOW A WONDERFUL DINING AREA WHERE PEOPLE CAN LOOK IN AND VIEW THE ACTION.
PHOTOGRAPH © PETER MAUSS.

front of the restaurant were existing, and they were modified, regrouped, and recovered."

DESIGN CONCEPT

The color of the restaurant was influenced by the exuberance and color of the food. It has a very "cranked-up" palette, with vibrant colors that are alive with energy.

James Biber states, "I met the chef, Bobby Flay, before I started the design and was impressed with his self-assurance, enthusiasm, and style. The color and textures of his food influenced my use of strong saturated colors, large graphics, and large, funky, southwestern-styled lighting fixtures. I wanted to create an exuberant Grand Café that would match Bobby Flay's exuberant style of cooking.

"I have not designed hundreds of restaurants, so I bring a certain fresh naiveté to these projects. I don't rely on preset formulas about restaurant

design, because I don't know what they are. This design specifically suited this client, this space, and this menu. I'm sure the next restaurant I do will look quite different.

"The existing wood floor was stained black and polyurethaned in order to allow the vibrant colors to read. The finish is a new water-based product that wears quite well, and doesn't create dangerous odors when it is applied. The most important design issue was that Mesa had to be a complete transformation from the previous restaurant. People had to say, 'I can't believe this is the same space.'

"Originally, we designed a quilted acoustical wall-treatment because we thought the noise levels were dangerously high, even for this exuberant space. This item was priced at about $40,000 and was eliminated owing to budget constraints. Eventually, after the opening, we installed sound-soak panels on the ceiling to reduce sound levels."

James Biber states, "There were too few lighting circuits in the space, and the existing space was too dark. To solve this problem, we used a new GE HIR halogen PAR lamp, which gave us the brightness we needed and utilized much less energy. The track lights bounce light off the walls in order to maximize the illusion of brightness.

"We also felt it was important to introduce more 'stuff' into the space—hanging fixtures and wall sconces that attracted the eye and created excitement. The decorative lighting fixtures are the key element in the space. They are its personality. The space itself is large, hard-edged, and made of solid materials. The lighting fixtures, in contrast, are light and delicate, providing the needed tension in the space that makes it an event. More time was probably spent on the custom lighting fixtures than any other single element in the space, and full-size mock-ups were made so that we could see if they met our expectations."

SPACE PLANNING

Jerry Kretchmer says, "The bar at Mesa, like Gotham, couldn't be in a better location. You walk past an energized front area to this great hangout bar where you can view the entire space. The energy is incredible! The bathrooms are located in the rear, allowing customers to see and be seen on their way there. The kitchen is in the rear as well, visible through a glass wall, allowing customers to peek in, adding to the energy and excitement at Mesa. I wish I had 180 seats, because we have a lot of capacity in the kitchen, and there are times when Bobby could produce more food."

James Biber asserts, "Part of the concept for this space was that everyone has a view of either the front window or the new, rear kitchen window. People like to see everyone coming and going, and I had to redefine the areas with seating, since we wanted to create a variety of seating experiences. The front area was formerly a waiting area, and now it is a wonderful dining area where people can look in and view the action. There is so much street traffic that we had to dress the window to attract the crowd. Once inside, the front area is a wonderful place to watch the action on the street."

Mesa Grill's 6,400 sq. ft. are divided up into a ground floor, a mezzanine, and a basement. The space planning breakdown is as follows:

ENTRY: 400 sq. ft.
FRONT BANQUETTE DINING: 280 sq. ft.
MAIN DINING AREA: 1,050 sq. ft. (includes 2 service stations)
BAR: 400 sq. ft.
COAT ROOM: 60 sq. ft.
BATHROOMS: 300 sq. ft.
KITCHEN: 1,150 sq. ft.
MEZZANINE DINING AREA: 600 sq. ft. (includes 1 service station)

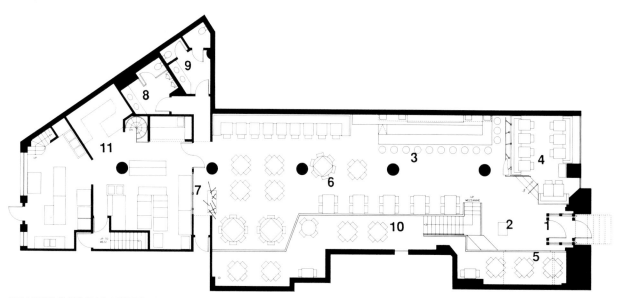

MESA GRILL FLOOR PLAN. COURTESY OF JAMES BIBER.
REFERENCE TABLE: 1. ENTRY; 2. MAITRE D'; 3. BAR; 4. RAISED DINING AREA; 5. COAT ROOM; 6. DINING AREA; 7. WAITER'S STATION; 8. MEN'S BATHROOM; 9. LADIES' BATHROOM; 10. MEZZANINE DINING; 11. KITCHEN

MEZZANINE OFFICES: 600 sq. ft.
BASEMENT STORAGE/PREP: 1,500 sq. ft.
BASEMENT OFFICE FOR STEWARD: 100 sq. ft.

KITCHEN DESIGN

Mesa Grill's kitchen was inherited from the restaurant that had previously occupied this space. The island layout of this kitchen is based on the typical French method of cooking. At first, chef Bobby Flay was concerned that this layout would not be efficient for the style of food and the amount of meals that had to be served. This layout is not well-suited for high volume, since plates are handled by several people. Coordination becomes difficult during peak periods, since there isn't a lot of room for plating and expediting. Bobby Flay found that if he kept all appetizers on one side of the island and entrées on the other, he had more visual control and could minimize confusion. All dishes are passed forward to a central plating table, which Flay added so that he could see all plates before they are passed to the waiter.

Bobby Flay feels that he has much more visual control with this layout than with a long, straight cooking line, and it's much easier to see what everyone is doing. The only drawback is that the dessert prep area could not be located anywhere near the line. This prevents him from having as much control as he would like.

Since there are a lot of hot appetizers, a small 24" grill, two fryolators, a six-burner stove, and a convection oven were added to the *garde manger* section to allow this area to be totally self-contained.

COST OF OPERATIONS

Mesa Grill serves a young crowd and is a neighborhood hangout and a destination location. The average check is low, and it is one of the New York's hottest new restaurants. Their cost of operations are as follows:

SEATING CAPACITY: first floor, 100; bar, 20; mezzanine, 38
AVERAGE COVERS: lunch, 125; dinner, 220-350
AVERAGE CHECK: lunch, $21; dinner, $37
    (includes liquor and wine)
FOOD COST: 30%
LABOR COST: 30%

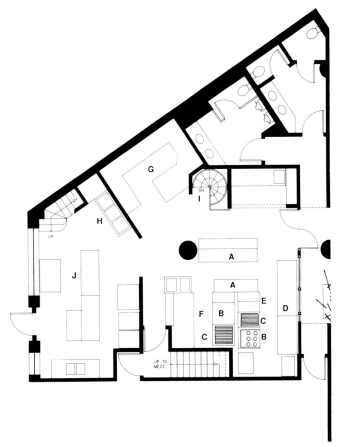

MESA GRILL KITCHEN FLOOR PLAN. COURTESY OF JAMES BIBER. REFERENCE TABLE: A. PLATING AND EXPEDITING; B. SAUTÉE; C. GRILL; D. GARDE MANGER; E. APPETIZERS; F. ENTRÉES; G. DISHWASHING; H. POT WASHING; I. DOWN TO STORAGE AND PREP; J. PASTRY AND DESSERT

TOTAL EMPLOYEES: 60
TOTAL YEARLY SALES: $4 million

Jerry Kretchmer and Jeff Bliss determined that the restaurant industry in New York was not dead, and they decided that the time was right to develop a low-budget, low-average-check concept that combined great food and service in an exuberant, fun environment. They found a space that was grand in scale, and because they are experienced restaurant owners and real estate developers, they were able to control costs yet produce an innovative design that completely transformed the space.

Mesa Grill is a restaurant that truly blends the foodservice style and the design in a location where high-quality affordable food meets the needs of a young, hip professional crowd. Bobby Flay's inventive, flavorful, and healthful food is a great value and is suited for this high-energy, high-volume restaurant. James Biber's design explodes with equal intensity and was accomplished on a very tight budget.

B   I   C   E

Bice is a 7,000 sq. ft. northern Italian restaurant that seats 180 people and is located on East Fifty-fourth Street between Park and Madison avenues in Manhattan. It was opened in 1987 and is one of New York's favorite Italian restaurants.

Adam Tihany states that Bice has been an institution in Milan since 1926. Bice Milan is a "happening," and it is the prime hangout for people in fashion and the arts. It has been a family operation and is run by the current owner Roberto Ruggeri's mother. It is a traditional trattoria and has built its reputation on personalized, friendly service where everyone feels special. The food and service are good, but not pretentious. Bice wants to provide a complete, good-quality package and does not want to be an exclusive three-star restaurant.

When Roberto Ruggeri approached Tihany to design the first new Bice in New York, it presented a tremendous challenge. How do you take a landmark institution that has lasted for sixty years in Italy and recast it in New York? It was a big responsibility and took a lot of courage on the part of the owner.

The original Bice in Milan wasn't designed by anyone. It is eclectic and has just happened, and it doesn't have a "look"; it has a distinctive cachet; people go there to socialize as well as eat. The new generation of Bice owners and Adam Tihany had to create an environment that captured this social spirit, and they had to package it in a design that met the expectations of a fashion-conscious international clientele. They had to find the kind of interior that would make this socially conscious international crowd comfortable and at home. The symbols they found to represent the image of Italian culture today are Armani, Ferrari, Versace, and so forth. They're definitely not checkered tablecloths and Chianti bottles.

Tihany says, "We certainly didn't want to create a bad imitation of Mama Leone's. It needed to be contemporary and stylish. The next step, after defining our market and overall design theme, was finding a location that could support this concept. It had to be in midtown Manhattan, close to shopping streets, hotels, offices, and residences. It had to be convenient to the international crowd we were trying to attract. It was critical to the success. We wanted customers to treat it as their home away from home."

Paul Guzzardo, vice president of operations of Bice USA, states that "you can get a table for eight and laugh, sing, cheer, eat, drink, and have a wonderful time. We do what every other restaurateur dislikes doing: we cater to our customers' whims. We treat them like one of the family and make dishes to order and change the menu daily."

According to Paul Guzzardo, Bice USA looks for an area that has a mixture of businesspeople and local residents. Rather than depend on in-depth demographic analysis, the site selection team evaluates each location by personally observing pedestrian traffic on the sidewalk and in and out of office buildings and shops. They observe how people are dressed and where they're going for lunch and dinner. They also observe other similar restaurants in the area to see how busy they are at lunch and dinner.

"It is very important to have a strong lunch crowd in order to build up our clientele," says Guzzardo. "This lunch crowd word of mouth helps build our dinner business. We are a destination restaurant and don't mind being a little out of the way. We build a strong friendship and relationship with other restaurateurs in the neighborhood. We do not compete with them and feel that more choices of restaurants in a given area benefits everyone. We get opinions from them and learn from their mistakes.

THE ENERGY IN THIS ELEGANT BAR AREA ENTICES PASSERSBY TO WALK IN. PHOTOGRAPH © KARL FRANCETIC.

"We do not depend on location alone. A good restaurant recently closed across the street. We depend on international clientele. Many Italian businesspeople would find us no matter where we were, because it's their home away from home. We picked this location, however, because it was conveniently located near shopping, hotels, office buildings, and residences. This location attracted the clientele we identified in our market analysis."

MENU DEVELOPMENT

Paul Guzzardo states, "The menu at Bice is authentic Italian cuisine. We let our customers order whatever they want or from our menu that changes daily. Although we were a hit from the start, our menu has changed drastically from when we first opened. We had problems that stemmed from the differences in dining patterns between the Italian market and the U.S. market. In Italy, you have antipasti, then a first course, and then a second course. In America, people want pasta as an entreé, whereas in Italy it is usually an appetizer or first course. In Italy, people take two hours for lunch, while in the U.S., people want to get in and out in 45 minutes. Our menu direction had to change to enable us to offer food that can be prepared for a 45-minute lunch.

"The original menu's style and portion size was based on the restaurant in Milan. In Italy, the waiter, once he gets to know you, does the ordering. Here, everything is computerized. Cooking equipment and systems are much more sophisticated in the United States. We hired an American-trained Italian chef to train the staff from Italy. We were humble enough to realize we had to learn how to satisfy American palates.

"People in the United States are more health-conscious, and the heavy flour-based sauces popular in trattorias in Italy were not well-received here. We adapted to dietary habits here in America. Food served in Milan is simple and more subtle and not made with a lot of garlic. Americans want food to explode on their palate. This process of change at Bice evolved over eight months to a year and improved its market appeal.

"The food cost is 24 percent in New York, and the labor cost is 23 percent. This is owed to the fact that we offer a wonderful variety of pasta. Our check average is higher in New York than in Atlanta, where the food cost is 31 percent. Our volume of 700 covers a day also reduces food cost percentages.

"We constantly monitor what is selling and not selling, so that we can change the menu to maximize appeal.

"Roberto sets the theme and discusses it with chefs, who then use their own creativity and experience to refine the menu. We use the highest quality ingredients to produce our food. We don't skimp on portions because we don't feel that's where you save on food costs. Our commitment to control over spoilage and waste is passed along to our customer in bigger portions.

"Pasta is made in-house to our standards, further reducing food costs. Our chefs receive weekly and sometimes daily computer updates on the price of many food items. If a chef sees that raspberries are $82 a flat, he will pick an alternative, like kiwis at $22 a flat, to make a tart.

PRIMI PIATTI

*TAGLIOLINI CON SCAMPI, LENTICCHIE E POMODORO
Tagliolini with shrimp and lentils in fresh tomato sa
*MALTAGLIATI CON RAGU' DI SELVAGGINA E CARCIOFINI
Square pasta with game sauce and baby artichokes
LINGUINE ALLE VONGOLE DEL GOLFO
Linguine with baby clams
*TORTELLONI DI ZUCCA AL BURRO E TIMO
Pumpkin ravioli in butter and thyme sauce
*PAGLIA E FIENO CON PISELLI E PROSCIUTTO
Green and white noodles with peas and prosciutto
*RAVIOLI DI BRANZINO IN SALSA D'ARAGOSTA
Sea-bass ravioli in lobster sauce
*SPAGHETTI ALLA CHITARRA CON RAGU' DI CARNE ALLA BOLOGNE
Spaghetti with meat sauce
*AGNOLOTTI DI CARNE ALLA TOSCANA
Veal ravioli with meat sauce Tuscan style
*FETTUCCINE CON FUNGHI
Fettuccine with mushrooms
*PAPPARDELLE FRESCHE AL TELEFONO
Large noodles in tomato sauce with mozzarella and bas
PENNE ALL'ARRABIATA
Penne in a spicy tomato sauce
RIGATONI AL POMODORO, MELANZANE E MOZZARELLA
Rigatoni with tomatoes, eggplant and mozzarella

RISOTTO CON VONGOLE E COZZE DEL MEDITERRANEO
Risotto with baby clams and mussels
RISOTTO AI FUNGHI PRATAIOLI
Risotto with prataioli mushrooms
ZUPPA DI CARCIOFI E PATATE
Artichoke and potato soup
GATZPACHO ALLA CATALANA
Cold gatzpacho soup

We make our fresh pastas daily.

"We constantly rotate the staff so that no one of the line cooks or chefs gets bored or burned out. The chef or sous chef in Atlanta may rotate with the chef in Chicago, each bringing fresh ideas.

"We try and stay with an authentic Italian menu and steer clear of trying to be on the cover of food magazines. We are a two-star restaurant and feel that a three-star identification would alter how people would perceive us. A three-star rating wouldn't allow us to have some of the unfashionable 'favorite foods' on our menu that our Italian clientele demands."

STAFF

Bice pays above-market salaries to attract the best possible employees, according to Paul Guzzardo.

"We find that well-paid employees are more productive and stay longer, improving consistency," he says. "We have a strong reputation for promotion within our organization. Waiters have become managers, busboys have become general managers, and salad men have become sous chefs. These career opportunities encourage people to stay within our organization for a long time. Since we have several restaurants in different locations, employees have the opportunity to be promoted and shifted to other locations as well. This boosts morale, which has a direct bearing on Bice's quality and consistency. Sixty percent of our staff has been with us since 1987.

"We have five key people in each restaurant, including a chef, a back-of-the-house manager, a general manager, a dining room director and a

BICE MENU.

PIATTI DEL GIORNO

PICCIONE ARROSTITO CON VERDURE AL VAPORE
Roasted squab with steamed vegetables — 24.--
FILETTO DI MANZO IN PADELLA CON ERBE AROMATICHE E PATATE CROCCANTI
Filet mignon with aromatic herbs and crispy potatoes — 28.--
FILETTO D'AGNELLO CON CREMA D'ASPARAGI
Filet of lamb with asparagus cream sauce — 28.--
SALTIMBOCCA ALLA ROMANA CON SPINACI
Veal scaloppine with prosciutto, sage and spinach — 24.--
OSSOBUCO CON POLENTA SOFFICE
Veal ossobuco with polenta — 24.--
CARRE' DI VITELLO ARROSTO CON ERBE DI MONTAGNA
Roasted rack of veal with aromatic herbs — 25.--
ENTRECOTE ALLA ROBESPIERRE
Sliced steak with arrugola — 25.--
COSTOLETTA DI VITELLO ALLA MILANESE
Classic breaded veal cutlet, Milanese style — 25.--
PAILLARD DI POLLO ALLA GRIGLIA CON BURRO ALLE ERBE
Grilled paillard of chicken with herb butter — 20.--
NODINO DI VITELLO ALLA GRIGLIA
Grilled veal t-bone — 28.--
GALLETTINO SCHIACCIATO ALLA GRIGLIA CON ERBE
Grilled baby chicken with herbs — 20.--
FEGATO DI VITELLO ALLA VENEZIANA
Calf's liver with onions and balsamic vinegar — 22.--

PESCI

SALMONE CON SALSA D'ARAGOSTA E ZUCCHINE NANE
Salmon with lobster sauce and baby zucchini — 24.--
PAGELLO ARROSTITO CON SPEZIE E DADOLATA DI POMODORI
Roasted red snapper with herbs and tomatoes — 25.--
TRANCIO DI PESCE SPADA LEGGERMENTE IMPANATO
Swordfish lightly breaded with oil and lemon — 25.--
ROMBO CON CREMA DI PEPERONI DOLCI
Turbot with sweet pepper sauce — 26.--

maitre d'. Each person has a responsibility to oversee the other four. This team is ultimately responsible for hiring, training, food and labor cost control, menu changes, and all other operational and management issues.

"The chef and the back-of-the-house manager spend three hours a day checking inventory on every item in the restaurant. They check to see what's moving and what's not moving. Ninety-two percent of our food items is perishable. All food must be rotated to insure that we are serving the freshest food to our customer. If we order twenty lobsters and our point-of-sale report indicates nine sold the next day, we know there must be eleven left. This daily inventory system reduces the incidence of theft and prevents overbuying and spoilage, thus improving food costs. This inventory system also tells us if an item, let's say swordfish, is not moving, so to avoid spoilage we use it and create a wonderful pasta dish. We try very hard not to waste any food. Our staff understands this because we are serious about inventory control.

"Other items such as linens, flatware, and china are also subject to strict inventory control. Our linen bill in New York is $12,000 a month, and it used to be higher. We were working with the assumption that each customer used 1.4 napkins, until we heard that our Chicago operation used 1.2 napkins. This may sound insignificant, but over a year in several locations, this can add up to thousands of dollars. We have instituted a policy where staff signs in and out for uniforms. We also count flatware on a weekly basis and record how many are missing for reordering purposes. Again, this inventory atmosphere reduces the temptation for theft."

Roberto Ruggeri believes in reinvesting in each restaurant before he will open a new one. He believes in raising salaries and seeking out new top-of-the-line employees to reinforce his current successful operations. New staff are selected and trained for each new restaurant three to four weeks prior to opening.

Each staff member is trained to cater to customer needs. They are trained never to say no to a special order. If someone complains about an order, it is immediately taken off the check or replaced. Wait staff are also trained to be friendly, not snobby or pretentious. People should be treated as though this were their personal dining room. In addition, all staff members have bonus programs, medical benefits, vacation, and sick-leave pay.

BUDGET

The project cost of Bice in New York was $1.9 million and took six months to build, according to Paul Guzzardo. Adam Tihany completed the design and construction documents in two months. "We now can build Bices in four months," he says.

Paul Guzzardo feels that the project could have been built for much less, now that he has acquired a lot of construction experience building several other Bices. The air conditioning, for example, was undersized, and had to be changed after it was installed, causing substantial overtime and expense. In addition, there was a two-month delay waiting for Con Edison to turn on the gas to the building, as it had been shut off by a previous tenant that had no need for gas.

"We used curly sycamore in many of our restaurants," Guzzardo says, "including New York. Sometimes the long lead time for this material requires us to substitute another similar wood species. We don't control the budget by substituting less expensive materials. We are committed to quality, and feel substitutions may alter the perceived value of our restaurants. People are purchasing the ambience as well as food and service. However, without changing the overall appearance, Adam Tihany has managed to reduce the budget from the original $250 per square foot in New York to $200 per square foot in other locations."

DESIGN CONCEPT

Adam Tihany's Bice in New York is his masterpiece, according to Paul Guzzardo. The richly detailed woods, sparkling glass, warm skin-flattering lighting, and the bright acoustics create a bustling, energized dining room. The doors spring open in the front of the restaurant in spring and summer to unveil an intimate bar area with casual seating. People can have desserts, cappuccino, or a complete meal. The energy in this front area and its close relationship to the sidewalk create a wonderful gathering place that is a great billboard enticing people to come in and experience it.

Adam Tihany confesses that it was a terrific challenge to recreate the cachet of the original Bice and design an environment that symbolized modern Italy. "The client is not a designer," he says, "but has strong feelings about the personality of the space. We developed a sense of mutual trust because Roberto knew that I understood our potential customers and how to satisfy their expectations.

"I derived inspiration from a series of abstract constructivist prints from a French artist named Sergai Gladsky. The color in these prints combined with references from the Tuscan landscape provided the color palette. Bice was opened in Milan in 1926. Art deco design was a prominent force at that time, so we borrowed references from Italian and American deco style. Much of the woodwork and detailing is deco. The detailed woodwork, color palette, sparkle, and dramatic lighting create a fashionable experience that encourages socializing and people-watching. The plaid carpet is the only material similar to the one used in Bice Milan.

"Our aim was to design a contemporary Italian trattoria where the spirit of hospitality was the most important element. Customers are buying the experience of dining as much as they are going to eat. The experience must have quality, substance, and style."

Adam Tihany describes the lighting at Bice as bright and warm. It makes everyone look great and creates a lively, energized feeling. It is dramatic and puts a glow on everyone's face. When you look good in a restaurant, you want to come back.

The ceiling's four quadrants each have an uplight cove that provides a bright ambient light. The colorful wall sconces provide the warm tones on customers' faces. The dramatic, bright, warm lighting makes everyone feel they've walked onto a stage. It makes the grand entrance even grander.

SPACE PLANNING

Paul Guzzardo states, "The space as planned in New York is very easy to work operationally. The placement of the kitchen, waiter's stations, and the square shape of the dining room contribute to minimizing walking by wait staff. The close proximity of the kitchen to every seat in the house keeps food hot on the way to the tables. The placement of the bar and cafe in the front of the restaurant makes the whole space feel full, even on a Sunday night, when the dining room, hidden by the bar, is empty."

Adam Tihany says that "the shape of the dining room had a lot to do with the concept of Bice. It is a hangout and a space where fashionable people go to socialize. The room was designed so that there is not a bad seat in the house. The entrance to the dining room was placed so that everyone could see who is entering and everyone who is

THE RICHLY DETAILED WOODS, SPARKLING GLASS, WARM SKIN-FLATTERING LIGHTING, AND BRIGHT ACOUSTICS CREATE A BUSTLING, ENERGIZED "HAPPENING." PHOTOGRAPH © KARL FRANCETIC.

THE LARGE SQUARE ROOM IS DIVIDED INTO FOUR INTIMATELY SCALED SPACES BY THE FORMS IN THE CEILING AND THE PLACEMENT OF THE BANQUETTES. PHOTOGRAPH © KARL FRANCETIC.

entering could see everyone in the dining room. This is the hallmark of the Bice concept.

"The dining room is a large open square that is divided into four quadrants. The ceiling, also divided in four quadrants, creates an intimate scale and creates the illusion that the dining room is much smaller. The first guests don't feel like they're being seated in a big empty room.

"One of the problems in space planning this restaurant was adapting a successful Milanese restaurant to the New York market. In Europe, the bar is not prominent, and you are seated there like bad Russians were sent to Siberia. Here in New York, the bar is very much a part of the social scene, and its placement was crucial to the energy needed at the entrance. It has become a hangout and is very visible from the sidewalk."

The finishing kitchen was kept to a minimum of 1,000 square feet on street level to maximize seating capacity. Bathrooms, storage, and the prep kitchen are downstairs. Bice's 7,500 sq. ft. are located on two levels as follows:

DINING ROOM (SEATING 180): 3,500 sq. ft.
BAR AREA (SEATING 20) AND COATROOM: 500 sq. ft.
KITCHEN COOKING LINE: 1,000 sq. ft.
PREP KITCHEN, STORAGE, AND OFFICES (BASEMENT): 2,000 sq. ft.
BATHROOMS (BASEMENT): 400 sq. ft.

KITCHEN DESIGN

The cooking line and waiter's and beverage station are on street level and occupy 1,000 sq. ft. of space. The prep kitchen, storage, and receiving are located in the basement and occupy 2,000 sq. ft. (plan not shown). Gelato and all other desserts are prepared and picked up downstairs. According to Vic Kasner of Colonel Food Service Equipment Company, who worked with Tihany and Ruggeri on the design of the kitchen, an early compromise was made on the size of the kitchen upstairs. Obviously, it would have been better to have more space upstairs to avoid crowding, but that would have meant sixteen fewer seats. Kasner explains, "We knew there would be a struggle in the kitchen, but the proportions of the raised dining area are a very important element in this customer-oriented restaurant. Since espresso, cappuccino and mineral water are profitable items, space was allocated for them upstairs, eliminating some space for circulation."

According to Vito Gnazzo, the current head chef at Bice, lunch is a war zone. "We have to prepare 250 covers between 12:30 and 2:00 and have eight line cooks, two people at the *garde manger*, and five other support staff, with the sous chef and myself as expeditors. Although we do 300 to 450 covers at dinner, it is spread out over six hours, which makes it a little easier on the kitchen.

"Nothing on the menu is prepared in advance, because every item is made to order. The menu changes every day, and we make anything

BICE FIRST FLOOR PLAN.
COURTESY OF ADAM TIHANY INTERNATIONAL LTD.
REFERENCE TABLE: 1. ENTRY; 2. COAT ROOM; 3. MAITRE'D;
4. BAR/WINE DISPLAY; 5. LOUNGE/WAITING AREA; 6. DINING
ROOMS; 7. WAITER'S STATION; 8. DISHWASHING; 9. BEVERAGE
STATION, WATER STATION; 10. KITCHEN; 11. STAITWAY TO
BASEMENT, PREP, STORAGE, AND OFFICE; 12. STAIRWAY TO
BATHROOMS IN BASEMENT

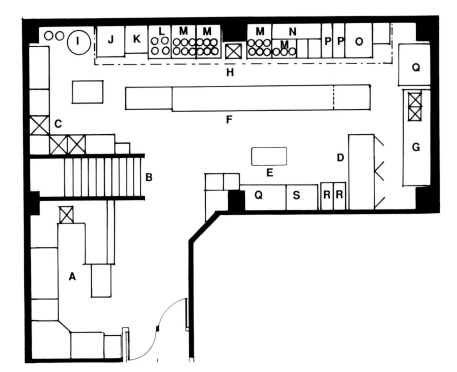

customers want, within reason. Ninety percent of our food is prepared within four minutes, since many of our pasta dishes are sautéed. The pasta cooker we have is imported from Italy and produces our freshly prepared pasta quickly.

"Because this is such a high-volume production restaurant, we have a double shift where everyone is under constant pressure. My role here is to keep the staff involved, motivated, and happy. I must earn the respect of every one of my employees in order to maintain quality and consistency. I must constantly inspire them with new ideas."

COST OF OPERATIONS

Bice currently serves approximately 650 to 750 covers daily to business people, local and regional residents, tourists, and celebrities. It continues to be a hot attraction and is one of New York's favorite Italian restaurants and hangouts. Its cost of operations are as follows:

SEATING CAPACITY: 190
AVERAGE COVERS: lunch, 300; dinner, 400
AVERAGE CHECK: lunch, $45; dinner, $62
LIQUOR AND WINE SALES: 25%
FOOD COST: 24%
LABOR COST: 23%
TOTAL EMPLOYEES: 90
RENT: 4%

YEARLY SALES: $10.5 million
NET PROFIT: 20%

What sets Bice apart from other restaurants and why the Bices are so successful is best explained by Paul Guzzardo: "Roberto grew up in Bice in Milan, owned and operated by his family. The concept of an intimate, friendly, energized 'happening' is in his blood. Everything from the food served, the service style, and the style of the design is of the highest quality and is directed by Roberto.

"All of the Bices in the United States and Europe are operated as a family run business. Customers are made to feel welcome. The maitre d' will usher them to the bar and buy them a drink and treat them like family. The wait staff and the maitre d' will take requests for food made to order and cater to each individual's needs. The ambience, food, and service combine to create a mood where people feel comfortable, laughing, singing, and engaging in spirited conversation. This club atmosphere makes it a home away from home for many international travelers as well as businesspeople and residents."

This intimate, friendly, personalized and energized atmosphere where unpretentious food is served by a staff who caters to each individual is the goal of each Bice. This concept combined with disciplined corporate controls is what makes Bice successful.

R E M I

OWNERS

Remi is owned by chef Francesco Antonucci and designer Adam Tihany.

Venetian-born Francesco Antonucci brings sixteen years of professional experience to Remi New York. Educated at the cooking school ANEL in Venice, Italy, he began his illustrious career with El Toula, the internationally renowned, elegant Italian restaurant chain, starting as assistant cook and working his way up to chef. In the process, he became protegé to the chain's founder, the legendary Alfredo Beltrame. In 1980, Antonucci left Italy to become the executive chef at La Romana, the signature Italian restaurant at the luxury resort, Casa di Campo, in Santo Domingo. His career in America started at the acclaimed Valentino restaurant in Santa Monica, California, where he worked as sous chef until joining forces with Dino De Laurentiis at DDL Foodshow in New York and DDL Bistro in Trump Tower. After he helped open and run the kitchen in the two locations, he spent two years as executive chef at Alo Alo restaurant in New York, which is owned by De Laurentiis.

DESIGNER

Adam Tihany is principal of Adam Tihany International Ltd. Tihany is considered one of the foremost restaurant designers in America today (see p. 152).

SOURCES

ARCHITECT: Adam Tihany International Ltd.
PROJECT DIRECTOR: Andrea Riecken
BANQUETTES, TABLETOPS, TABLES: Trocadero
CHAIRS, BARSTOOLS: Trocadero, designed by Adam D. Tihany
BLUE-AND-WHITE STRIPED FABRIC: Trocadero
WOOD FLOOR: Hardwood Flooring Inc.
CONSTRUCTION MANAGER: Mariano Construction Corp.
CABINET WORK: Capitol Cabinet
WALL SCONCES: Foscarini, designed by Adam D. Tihany
CHANDELIERS: Fondamenta Manin 3, designed by Adam D. Tihany
MURAL LIGHT: Rambusch Lighting
MURAL PAINTING: Paulin Paris
DRAPERY, FABRIC, TRIM: DFB Sales, Inc., Dravet Fabrics, Clarence House
CHINA: Rosenthal Commercial China
SILVER: Sambonet
COMPUTER: Squirrel
PHOTOGRAPHER: Peter Paige

FRANCESCO ANTONUCCI/ADAM TIHANY. PHOTOGRAPH © ANTONIO SFERLAZZO.

Remi is an 8,500 sq. ft. restaurant located on West Fifty-third Street between Sixth and Seventh avenues in Manhattan. It was completed in 1990 and serves delicious northern Italian (Venetian) food in an upbeat, exuberant space. It is now one of New York's top restaurants and has earned two stars in the *New York Times*.

Adam Tihany states, "When Remi opened in May 1990, it was not the happiest time for restaurateurs. Consumer spending was down, especially for big budget restaurants with high average checks. Francesco and I decided that Remi had to be a restaurant where customers perceived value, and left thinking that they received much more than they paid for. The average check had to be kept down so that people left feeling that they had received a bargain, but the presentation of the food had to look, smell, and taste like something selling at a much higher price. In addition, the design of the space had to be visually impressive so that customers felt they had experienced something special.

"The first Remi opened in 1987 and was located on East Seventy-ninth Street. It was a successful 2,000 sq. ft. restaurant that seated 75 people. Its location did a respectable dinner business, but did not have a lunch crowd. We both felt that we needed to cultivate stronger lunch business in order to be successful, and we began to explore relocating Remi to a midtown location. After spending some time looking at several spaces, we chose Fifty-third Street for several reasons. The landlord wanted us in his building and offered us a substantial amount of

UPON ENTERING THE SPACE, CUSTOMERS FEEL A GREAT SENSE OF ARRIVAL AND ANTICIPATION AS THEY PERCEIVE THE MIXTURE OF ELEGANT STYLE, LARGE SCALE, AND BRIGHT COLORS. PHOTOGRAPH © KARL FRANCETIC.

DINNER

ANTIPASTI

INSALATA MISTA
Assorted Greens with Vinaigrette
$7.50

RUCOLA CON SCALOGNO
Arugola with Sweet and Sour Shallots
and Parmiggiano Slices with
a Walnut-Olive Dressing
$8.50

ENDIVA IN SALSA DI MOSTARDA
Sliced Endive in a Mustard Dressing
with Marinated Silversides
$7.50

POMODORI CON CIPOLLE MARINATE
Sliced Tomato and Marinated Onions with
Sundried Tomatoes, Black Olives
and Basil Dressing
$6.50

GRIGLIATA DI VERDURA
Grilled Fresh Vegetables with
Garlic Scented Olive Oil
$9.50

SARDINE CON PATATE
Marinated and Grilled Fresh Sardines
Served with Sour Potatoes
$9.50

CAPESANTE CON INSALATA DI FAGIOLI
Sauteed Sea Scallops with an
Onion Prosecco Vinaigrette Served with
Canellini Beans and Rosemary
$11.50

SALMONE CON ASPARAGI
Homemade Cured Salmon with Steamed
Asparagus in a Lemon Dressing
$10.50

PROSCIUTTO D'OCA
Smoked Goose Prosciutto with Fresh Greens
and Truffle Olive Oil
$10.00

QUAGLIE CON LENTICCHIE
Sauteed Quail Wrapped in Bacon
with Baby Green Lentils in a
Balsamic Dressing
$11.50

CARPACCIO DI VITELLO AL PEPE NERO
Veal Carpaccio with Cracked Black Pepper
in a Tarragon Mayonnaise Sauce
$10.00

PESCI

SALMONE ALLA GRIGLIA
Grilled Salmon with Baby Lettuce and
Spring Vegetables in a Horseradish Dressing
$23.00

TONNO AI SAPORI DEL MEDITERRANEO
Seared Medium Rare Tuna with Oven Dried
Tomatoes, Black Olives and Herbs
$22.00

DENTICE IN SAOR
Roasted Red Snapper with Red Glazed Onions,
Orange Vinegar, Pignolias and Raisins
$23.00

BRANZINO DOMESTICO AL CARTOCCIO
Black Sea Bass Baked in Parchment
in its Own Juice
$24.00

REMI DINNER MENU.

money to construct the restaurant. In addition, this location had 10,000 hotel rooms within a mile radius, was two blocks from the theater district, and a few blocks from Radio City and the Museum of Modern Art. It was also right in the middle of the densest office population in the world. It was overwhelming and was three steps ahead of what we were looking for, but the deal was right, and the location was incredible.

"We felt we could do one turn at lunch and 1.25 turns at dinner, drawing our customers from several markets, including local businesspeople in advertising, film, and the publishing industry, along with local and regional residents and tourists. We also were counting on some pre-theater business."

Antonucci states, "The location of Remi contributes greatly to the financial success of the restaurant, because lunch business is consistent, and dinner is supported by the pre-theater crowd and the hotels. If we don't fill up tables at the second seating at dinner, we have a third after-theater seating that's been a pleasant surprise. On a good night, we can do 400 covers."

Remi on Seventy-ninth Street was closed, since part of the deal with the landlord dictated that there could only be one Remi in New York.

MENU DEVELOPMENT

Francesco Antonucci feels that his ability to adapt to American and, more specifically, New York eating habits contributed to his success. He states, "I am willing to wager that the most experienced chefs in Italy would fail in the United States if they couldn't adapt to the American palate. My style of cooking is Venetian-New York, and I adapted this Venetian style of cooking by studying already established ways of preparing food in New York. For example, tuna prepared in Italy is dry because it is cooked longer. After studying how popular seared tuna is prepared in Japanese-influenced restaurants in New York, I adapted my recipes.

"I love cooking in New York. The talented chefs that surround me here and in America provide me with needed competition, which stimulates me to strive for improvement."

Remi's menu is changed seasonally, and it can change as frequently as every three to four weeks.

Francesco Antonucci explains, "Food costs are around 28 percent because there are many pasta dishes on the menu. However, we also have to serve a veal chop, whose food costs are much higher, or else people would be angry with us."

Antonucci strongly believes that all the food, vegetables, herbs, and other ingredients must be of the highest quality. He has his own extra-virgin olive oil produced and bottled in Italy, and his wine cellar is among the best in New York. His wine steward knows how to purchase the finest wines at the lowest cost, and these savings are passed along to the customer.

The restaurant opened for three days to invited guests, and this was all the staff and kitchen needed for training before opening. On the second day after the official opening, Bryan Miller included Remi in a favorable review in the *New York Times* and several weeks later awarded it two stars.

STAFF

Francesco Antonucci is in control of all aspects of the restaurant and states, "I am a perfectionist, and expect that everyone who works for me must try to be the best at what they do. I am in the kitchen seven days a week for 14 hours a day, and it is my home-away-from-home. The people who work for me are part of my family, and though I demand a lot from them, I am available to anyone who has a question or problem, and I try to solve it immediately. We have daily staff meetings, and also meet once a month, when everyone gets a chance to express themselves.

"We prefer not to hire professional waiters. Instead, we hire well-groomed, intelligent people that we can train ourselves. We have prepared a detailed training manual concerning service and the food and wine served at Remi. Staff are tested regularly on this manual.

"Since I am in the kitchen most of the time, I've hired managers and maitre d's who are responsible for recognizing frequent guests and making them feel welcome." Antonucci feels that "making the customer feel special is the single most important contributor to Remi's success. When Adam is in New York, he greets the customer at the door and floats around the dining room to make sure everyone is being attended to."

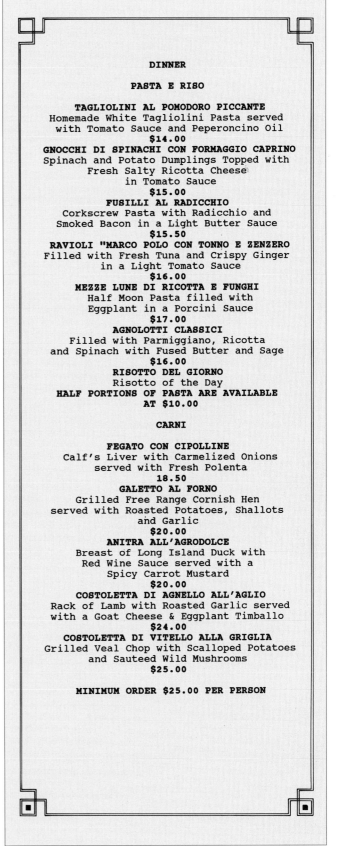

DINNER

PASTA E RISO

TAGLIOLINI AL POMODORO PICCANTE
Homemade White Tagliolini Pasta served
with Tomato Sauce and Peperoncino Oil
$14.00
GNOCCHI DI SPINACHI CON FORMAGGIO CAPRINO
Spinach and Potato Dumplings Topped with
Fresh Salty Ricotta Cheese
in Tomato Sauce
$15.00
FUSILLI AL RADICCHIO
Corkscrew Pasta with Radicchio and
Smoked Bacon in a Light Butter Sauce
$15.50
RAVIOLI "MARCO POLO CON TONNO E ZENZERO
Filled with Fresh Tuna and Crispy Ginger
in a Light Tomato Sauce
$16.00
MEZZE LUNE DI RICOTTA E FUNGHI
Half Moon Pasta filled with
Eggplant in a Porcini Sauce
$17.00
AGNOLOTTI CLASSICI
Filled with Parmiggiano, Ricotta
and Spinach with Fused Butter and Sage
$16.00
RISOTTO DEL GIORNO
Risotto of the Day
HALF PORTIONS OF PASTA ARE AVAILABLE
AT $10.00

CARNI

FEGATO CON CIPOLLINE
Calf's Liver with Carmelized Onions
served with Fresh Polenta
18.50
GALETTO AL FORNO
Grilled Free Range Cornish Hen
served with Roasted Potatoes, Shallots
and Garlic
$20.00
ANITRA ALL'AGRODOLCE
Breast of Long Island Duck with
Red Wine Sauce served with a
Spicy Carrot Mustard
$20.00
COSTOLETTA DI AGNELLO ALL'AGLIO
Rack of Lamb with Roasted Garlic served
with a Goat Cheese & Eggplant Timballo
$24.00
COSTOLETTA DI VITELLO ALLA GRIGLIA
Grilled Veal Chop with Scalloped Potatoes
and Sauteed Wild Mushrooms
$25.00

MINIMUM ORDER $25.00 PER PERSON

REMI DINNER MENU.

Adam Tihany states, "The total cost of this project was $2.4 million, including the take-out shop, which cost $250,000. The original estimate was $1.2 million, and after the bids came back, construction costs had escalated past the $2 million mark for the restaurant." Francesco Antonucci adds, "I was glad the estimate was $1.2 million, because if I had known that the restaurant would cost over $2 million, I would still be on Seventy-ninth Street."

"The space was long and narrow, with very high ceilings and large expanses of glass facing an atrium. We spent $500,000 on the heating and air conditioning in addition to the kitchen exhaust system. The 5,000 sq. ft. lower level was much larger than we needed, but couldn't be leased to another tenant, and this contributed to higher construction costs. The landlord, however, contributed funds for the project, and Francesco and I signed notes with the contractors guaranteeing payment after the project was open. We knew this was risky, but we felt confident that the restaurant would succeed."

Compromises were made to the design in order to reduce the budget. The mural on the wall was originally designed with several undulations and the column in the front of the restaurant was supposed to look like a giant umbrella. An elevator and dumbwaiter were planned, but they were abandoned as too expensive. The design process and construction drawings took four months, and the actual construction took an additional four months.

DESIGN CONCEPT

As Adam Tihany describes it, "Remi is a simple design based on the name, which means 'oars' in Italian." Since Francesco Antonucci comes from Venice and the food is primarily Venetian in style, Remi has many Venetian references, and the look is nautical. Gondoliers' oars hang over the entrance, and the bar has hand-blown Venetian glass decorating its shelves. A Venetian mural dominates the entire space, and the striped fabric selected for the banquettes was inspired by the striped shirt of the gondolier.

Upon entering the space, customers feel a great sense of arrival and anticipation, as they perceive the mixture of elegant style, energy, and excitement.

To the right there is a richly detailed mahogany bar with funky chandeliers, and to the left there is a coat room and bathrooms. Straight ahead, there is a maitre d' area and a richly detailed glass partition that allows a glimpse of the excitement yet to unfold. Moving from the entry area into the dining room is like discovering Saint Mark's Square after walking through narrow winding streets. The immensely large, colorful mural, striped fabric, and colorful wall sconces make entering this space a special event for first-time customers. Adam Tihany is a master at providing that sense of arrival at the entrance, and procession to the table, where one can see and be seen. The walk through this narrow dining room to your table is wonderful. For those who return again and again, the combination of warm wood floors, simple painted tongue-and-groove wainscoting, and flattering lighting feels comfortable.

Adam Tihany states, "The nautical Venetian theme for Remi inspired the selection of materials whose colors, shapes, and patterns metaphorically remind one of Venice. We used a dark-stained Brazilian cherry floor inlaid with maple, creating a striped pattern. We did quite a bit of research and found wood species and colors that were virtually maintenance-free. The off-white tongue-and-groove wainscoting behind the banquettes reaches a height of 7' and is a simple warm material that reinforces the nautical theme. Above the wainscoting, there is the immense mural of Venice that was painted by Paulin Paris.

"The ceilings are painted sheetrock and reach a height of 30', with flying buttresses supporting the muraled wall, so that you feel you are dining in a courtyard outside the walls of a church. Despite many hard surfaces, customers can have conversations in this space. This is owed to the unusually high ceilings, and the irregularly angled shape of the wall."

Adam Tihany feels that "you have to provide many different light sources throughout the restaurant. These different sources need to be controlled separately to create varying moods throughout the day and evening." Creating a feeling of intimacy is essential in a dining room, and this was accomplished at Remi with the colorful and playful wall sconces that radiate a warm light that is very flattering to skin color and food.

The light fixtures that light the mural were selected to provide ambient light throughout the space and not distort the subtle coloration in the mural. As Adam Tihany says, "Lighting is the key element in creating an appealing dining room."

SPACE PLANNING

Adam Tihany states, "The pro forma analysis dictated at least a 180-seat dining area, and since there was not enough room for the dining room and the kitchen upstairs, the kitchen was located in the basement. This meant, however, that wait staff and busboys had to walk up and down a long flight of stairs. To alleviate this problem, runners were used to bring hot food to wait staff upstairs. Francesco felt that an elevator would be a disaster, with wait staff standing on line to go up while the food was getting cold, and a dumbwaiter was ruled out for the same reason.

An elevator would have cost $150,000, while a dumbwaiter would have added $50,000 to the already mushrooming budget."

Remi's ground level is a long, narrow space with high ceilings and a large window wall facing an outdoor atrium. Banquette seating was installed to maximize capacity and encourage people watching, and there is a mixture of two- and four-tops. During the warmer months, there are an additional eighty seats outside in the atrium. Bathrooms were located up front near the entrance because Tihany believed that "women would want to freshen up before making their entrance into this grand space."

The lower level contains the kitchen, prep areas, wine cellar, offices, a cooking school, storage areas, and a private dining room that seats fourteen people. Francesco Antonucci states that

A VENETIAN MURAL PAINTED BY PAULIN PARIS DOMINATES THE SPACE, WHILE THE STRIPED MOTIF ON THE BANQUETTES, CHAIRS, AND FLOOR DRAWS ITS REFERENCE FROM THE GONDOLIER'S STRIPPED SHIRT. PHOTOGRAPH © PETER PAIGE.

the private dining room "is a special place where I can prepare family style feasts based on a prearranged price per person. Although this lower level was larger than needed, we felt it could be useful as a training center for future Remis."

Remi's ground level is 3,500 sq. ft. divided up as follows:

DINING ROOM: 2,050 sq. ft.
BAR AND ENTRY AREA: 400 sq. ft.
BATHROOMS: 200 sq. ft.
COAT ROOM: 50 sq. ft.
WAITERS STATION, BEVERAGE AREA, STAIRWAY:
    800 sq. ft.
ATRIUM AREA/OUTDOOR CAFE: 1,000 sq. ft.
TAKE-OUT SHOP: 1,000 sq. ft.

The lower level is 5,000 sq. ft. divided up as follows:

KITCHEN: 2,500 sq. ft.
WINE CELLAR: 300 sq. ft.
OFFICE: 200 sq. ft.
COOKING SCHOOL: 700 sq. ft.
TRAINING AREA: 500 sq. ft.
STORAGE: 500 sq. ft.
PRIVATE DINING AREA: 300 sq. ft.

KITCHEN DESIGN

Francesco Antonucci states, "I've worked in large and small kitchens throughout my career, and I feel a small, cramped kitchen can be made to work. If the restaurant is successful and the chef and staff are producing quality food, almost any space planning problem can be overcome. When things aren't going well, that's when the kitchen walls seem to be closing in on you." He also advises that "a qualified kitchen planner should be retained to design the kitchen, with some assistance from the chef, because if the chef customizes a kitchen for himself and leaves a year later, the next chef will want a complete overhaul, because they're accustomed to a different layout. The owner must have a kitchen that can produce the menu that the restaurant has built its reputation on."

"The hot cooking line is 25' long and consists of two fish grills, with three sauté stations, a pasta cooker, and stations for preparing meat and fish specials. Preprepped sliced vegetables and some pasta, like ravioli, are conveniently placed near the sauté areas to speed cooking time. There are six line cooks and two people at the 8' *garde manger*, which is at right angles to the hot line. An assistant and I have visual control over the entire operation and expedite from the pick-up side of the line."

The staircase has been conveniently placed so that the runners and busboys can go either to the line or the dishwashing area. The runners speed down the stairs and pick up the food from tray holders and never approach the line. The pre-theater dinner from 6:00 to 7:30 P.M. is very busy, and runners have to pick up food quickly in order for it not to get cold. Covers are placed on each plate when it is placed on the tray.

Another special feature of this kitchen is the bakery area, where Francesco Antonucci and his staff prepare a delectable variety of *dolci*.

COST OF OPERATIONS

Remi serves approximately 500 covers daily to a wide audience of businesspeople, tourists,

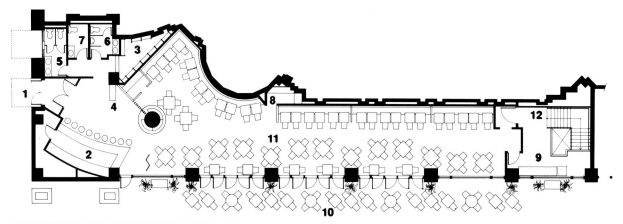

REMI FIRST FLOOR PLAN. COURTESY OF ADAM TIHANY INTERNATIONAL LTD.
REFERENCE TABLE: 1. ENTRY; 2. BAR; 3. COAT ROOM; 4. MAITRE D'; 5. WOMEN'S BATHROOM; 6. MEN'S BATHROOM; 7. HANDICAP BATHROOM;
8. WAITER'S STATION; 9. BEVERAGE AREA; 10. OUTDOOR DINING; 11. DINING; 12. STAIR DOWN TO KITCHEN

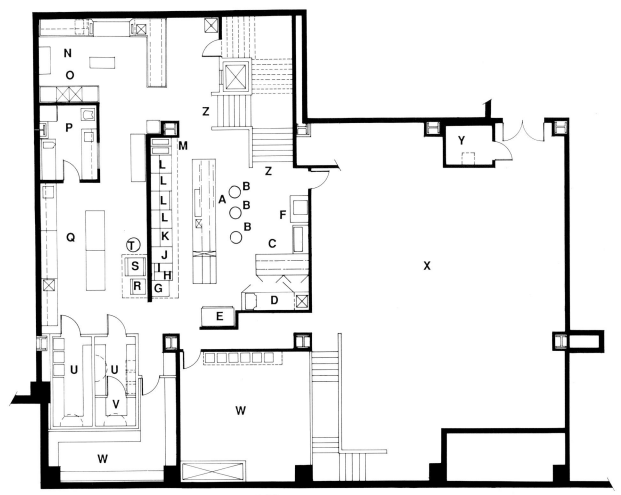

REMI CELLAR PLAN. COURTESY OF ADAM TIHANY INTERNATIONAL LTD.
REFERENCE TABLE: A. EXPEDITOR; B. TRAY HOLDERS; C. COLD PICK-UP; D. COLD PREP; E. REACH-IN REFRIGERATOR; F. ICE MACHINES; G. STEAMER;
H. FRYER; I. SPACER TABLE; J. CHAR GRILL; K. FRY TOP; L. 6-BURNER STOVE/OVEN; M. PASTA COOKER; N. DISHWASHING; O. POT WASHING;
P. PASTA/PASTRY PREP; Q. PREP AREA; R. CONVECTION OVEN; S. 4-BURNER STOVE; T. KETTLE; U. WALK-IN COOLER; V. FREEZER; W. DRY STORAGE;
X. OFFICES, SECRET DINING ROOM, EMPLOYEE'S LOCKERS/BATHROOMS; Y. GARBAGE WALK-IN; Z. STAIR UP TO RESTAURANT

theater-goers, and people who just want to go to a very special place. Remi's cost of operations are as follows:

SEATING CAPACITY: 170
AVERAGE COVERS: lunch, 180; dinner, 350-400
AVERAGE CHECK: lunch, $25; dinner, $42
LIQUOR AND WINE SALES: 23%
FOOD COST: 28%
LABOR COST: 29%
TOTAL EMPLOYEES: 102
RENT: 8%
YEARLY SALES: N.A.

Francesco Antonucci and Adam Tihany have created a very special place in Remi. Antonucci is an extraordinary chef and leader who motivates his staff and is in control of the entire operation. He has adapted his Venetian cooking style to fit the New York palate and strives continually to improve because he is committed to quality. The preparation and presentation of food is wonderful, and customers feel that they are receiving great value.

Adam Tihany has created a special environment that is theatrical and sophisticated, yet fun and comfortable, encouraging people to return. The nautical Venetian theme creates an unpretentious and exuberant atmosphere that makes people feel that they are celebrating an event. This, coupled with wonderful food at modest prices, is a powerful combination.

The success of the restaurant is owed in large part to the selection of the location. It draws from many markets, enabling Remi to maximize its lunch and dinner crowds. The staff is trained to provide excellent service, and the maitre d's special greeting at the door makes everyone feel welcome.

D O C K S

OWNERS

Arthur J. Cutler, Barry Corwin, and Howard Levine own two Docks restaurants in Manhattan. Artie Cutler, along with other partners, also owns two restaurants on Broadway: Carmine's, a hot new Italian trattoria; and Ollie's Noodle Shop, a popular Chinese restaurant. Each of these restaurants is very successful.

Artie Cutler grew up in Long Island and graduated from Columbia College in 1965. He also did graduate work in business at Columbia. He began his career in the fabric businesss and later spent some time as a social worker for the Jewish Board of Guardians.

When Cutler left social work, he decided to go into the food business. He took a job working as a counterman for a smoked fish store in Brooklyn's Brighton Beach. While working there he heard that Murray's Sturgeon Shop was for sale. He purchased the store in 1974. In 1978, he and a partner opened Reuben's Deli on Thirty-eighth Street and Madison Avenue. By 1984, he had sold his interest in Reuben's and opened Docks at Eighty-ninth Street and Broadway. Docks on Fortieth Street and Third Avenue opened in August 1988. Cutler has been married to his high school sweetheart for twenty-six years and has two daughters.

DESIGNER

Morris Nathanson Design of Pawtucket, Rhode Island, was the designer for Docks at both locations. Founded in 1967, Morris Nathanson Design is a comprehensive design firm, specializing in the food service and hospitality fields. Its solid reputation is based on years of award-winning designs. The firm's current work includes projects throughout the United States, the Caribbean, and Europe. The office has recently completed several projects, including Carmine's, New York, J.C. Hillary's, Massachusetts, and Legal Sea Foods in Boston and Natick, Massachusetts. Morris Nathanson Design's works in progress include nine "American-style" restaurants for the Euro Disney Retail Entertainment Center for the new Euro Disneyland just east of Paris.

SOURCES

ARCHITECT: Morris Nathanson Design, Inc.

FOODSERVICE CONSULTANT: Colonel Food Service Equipment Company

PHOTOGRAPHER: Warren Jagger Photography, Inc.

BARSTOOLS: Falcon Products, Inc.

UPHOLSTERED SIDE CHAIRS: Shelby Williams

BACKLESS BARSTOOLS: Empire State Chair

TABLES: L & B Products

CERAMIC FLOOR TILE, WALL TILE: American Olean

PAINT: Benjamin Moore

CUSTOM CHANDELIER: Coronet Chandeliers

UPHOLSTERED BANQUETTES: Alden Manufacturing

CUSTOM CANVAS WALLPAPER BORDER: Pia Peterson

MORRIS NATHANSON. PHOTOGRAPH © RON MANVILLE PHOTOGRAPHY.

Docks Oyster Bar and Seafood Grill, which opened in 1988, is an 8,900 sq. ft. full-service restaurant that seats 280 people and is located at 633 Third Avenue in New York City. It is also a seafood grill and oyster bar, and it is one of the most popular and successful restaurants in New York.

Artie Cutler states, "I had my eye on the location at Fortieth Street and Third Avenue for over ten years, even though many others felt it wasn't a great site." In fact, he had built Reuben's Deli several years earlier only because his first choice was unavailable at the time.

Cutler states, "I like sites that can service businesspeople during the day and have a strong residential clientele in the evening. Fortieth and Third is on the ground floor of a 1 million sq. ft. office building and is located in the Grand Central office district, one of the densest in the United States. Murray Hill, a vibrant residential neighborhood, is located to the south, with new high-rise residential construction springing up along First and Second avenues. The area has many hotels and has abundant parking facilities.

"We felt there wasn't a great place for businesspeople to have lunch in this area, other than the Oyster Bar at Grand Central, which had become touristy and expensive. The $100 lunch no longer could be justified and customers wanted a friendly establishment that offered a $25 white tablecloth lunch.

"There wasn't a grand seafood house in this neighborhood or in Manhattan, for that matter. Oscar's had closed and there wasn't a place where you could get great seafood at reasonable prices. We saw the opportunity to open a grand café for seafood at this location because it was a large space where we could seat 280 people. The low average check concept could only work with high volume.

THE FAMILIAR MATERIALS, SUCH AS BEADED WOOD, TILE, WOOD FLOORS, RICH MAHOGANY WOOD DETAILING, ALONG WITH COLORFUL ART DECO POSTERS AND BLACK BOARD MENUS, CREATE A WARM, FRIENDLY, NEIGHBORHOOD ATMOSPHERE. PHOTOGRAPH © WARREN JAGGER PHOTOGRAPHY, INC. R.I.

"We looked at the directories in surrounding office buildings and spoke to doormen concerning vacancies in both office and residential buildings. We also observed our potential customers' lunch and dinner habits in other restaurants in the area. The landlord made us a great offer because he realized that an experienced restaurateur and a wonderful environment would keep his tenants happy, thus reducing his vacancy rate.

"I did the pro forma for this restaurant on the back of a napkin by factoring in the average check, average covers, debt service, and so forth. I'm not suggesting that that's the way everyone should do it, but it worked for me on this project because I understood this location's and concept's potential. I travel around the world and love to eat. I have a passion for this business and feel I am in tune with what the customer expects, namely, value and service.

"We negotiated with the landlord for over two years and struck a $35 per square foot deal. Four percent of our total nut needed to be set aside for rent. This low rent made it possible to offer great value for our customer because we could afford to reduce our average check. Our food cost is 35 percent and labor is 32 percent because we feel that our commitment to quality keeps customers coming back. Because we do high-volume business and our bar is packed, we can afford to spend a little more on food and labor."

STAFF

Artie Cutler states, "I am the producer and orchestra leader for all my restaurants. I always take on two working partners for each restaurant. At Docks, Howard Levine and Barry Corwin are at the restaurant each day and are responsible for the daily operations. I am around during concept, design development, and construction, and I take a back seat once the restaurant is opened.

"We don't have a big corporate in-house staff. I walk the streets looking for sites and concept opportunities and pop into each of our restaurants, making sure that the place is clean, that the food looks good, and that everyone has a smile on his face."

MENU DEVELOPMENT

"Barry Corwin, Howard Levine and I selected the menu items for Docks," explains Artie Cutler. "We wanted a very simple back-to-basics New England seafood house with a lot less emphasis on fancy nouvelle cuisine. The recipe development emanated from my eating experiences all over the world.

"We were intent upon offering simply prepared broiled fish without heavy masking sauces. Until the first Docks was opened on the Upper West Side, there were very few places where one could eat a fresh, simple, broiled piece of tuna or swordfish.

"Our food cost is 35 percent, and we feel it could be higher, because we have a high-volume restaurant and a large bar crowd. We are committed to quality and don't want to compromise on food cost to make more profit."

BUDGET

Artie Cutler states that he and his partners "were astounded to learn how much this project would cost. Our original budget was $1.2 million, and the project ended up costing $2.8 million. When the bids came back, we were at $1.8 million, and we were hit with $1 million in extras. At that point, many restaurateurs would have just closed the doors and never opened. We just dug a little deeper into our pockets.

"Those were the two worst years of my life, but I learned a lot about building large restaurants in an urban location. We were babes in the woods and learned our lessons the hard way. However, I was not willing to compromise on the level of finishes and the overall concept for Docks. It had to be a comfortable space that looked like it had been there for years. We were trying to attract executives and businesspeople who couldn't afford the $100 lunch but still wanted an environment that was visually rich and handsome. The mahogany woodwork, mirrors, tile work, lighting, and artwork were necessary to create this image. We spent a fortune on the art deco posters, but felt they were needed to make the space feel real. We did not want to cash in on the finishes to meet an unrealistic budget because

DOCKS MENU.

DOCKS
OYSTER BAR & SEAFOOD GRILL

Starters

Soup of the Day	P/A
Docks Chowder	4.00
Steamers in Beer Broth	9.00
Mussels in Tomato and Garlic .	7.00
Fried Calamari	6.00
Maryland Crabcake	8.00
House Salad	4.00
Caesar Salad	6.00
Cold Marinated Seafood Salad .	8.00
Imported Malossol Caviar 1 oz. .	40.00

> **Caviar and Champagne Special:**
> Add 25.00 for the Caviar to the
> Price of Any Champagne. . . . .   P/A

The Shell Bar

Clams on the Half Shell	P/A
Oysters on the Half Shell	P/A
Shrimp in the Rough: 1/4 lb. . . .	6.50
1/2 lb. . . .	12.00
1 lb.	21.00
Lobster Cocktail	P/A

Chilled Entrees

Cold Poached Salmon Filet	18.50
Chilled Stuffed Lobster	P/A
Chefs Seafood Salad	16.50
Grilled Tuna Nicoise Salad	18.50

> **Pasta of the Day** . . . .   P/A
> Linguini with Red or
>   White Clam Sauce 10.00

Land Locked

Grilled N. Y. Shell Steak	20.00
Grilled Chicken	14.00
Docks Burger	8.50
with Bacon and/or Cheese	

*Above served with Docks Slaw
and choice of Potato or Rice*

> **Sunday and Monday Nights**
> **New England Clambake**
> Choice of Twin 1 lb. Lobsters . . .23.00
> or a 2 lb. Lobster . . .27.00
> Served with Salad - Mussels, Clams,
> New Potatoes, Corn on the Cob, Key
> Lime Pie or Ice Cream, Coffee or Tea

Grilled Seafood

Fresh Norwegian Salmon Steak	18.00
Fresh Swordfish	18.50
Fresh Tuna	17.50
Fresh Red Snapper	19.50
Barbequed Seafood Grill	16.50
Fresh Specials of the Day	P/A

*Above Served with Docks Slaw
and choice of Potato or Rice*

Lobsters

Steamed Lobsters: 1-9 LBS.	P/A
Larger sizes available upon request	
Two Lobster Special:	
two 1 lb. steamed Lobsters . . .	P/A
Three Lobster Special:	
three 1 lb. steamed Lobsters . .	P/A

Fried Seafood

Fried Sole (Broiled upon request)	16.00
Fried Scallops (Broiled upon request)	16.50
Fried Shrimp (Broiled upon request)	16.50
Fried Ipswich Clams	15.00
Fried Oysters	15.00
Fried Seafood Platter	17.00

*Above Served with Docks Slaw
and choice of Potato or Rice*

Side Orders

Fresh Vegetable of the Day	P/A
French Fried Potatoes	2.50
French Fried Yams	2.50
Steamed New Potatoes	2.50
Baked Potato	2.50
Brown Rice Pilaf	2.50
Docks Slaw	2.50

Desserts

Ice Creams and Sorbet	4.00
Fresh Fruit in Season	P/A
Hot Fudge Ice Cream Sundae . .	5.50
Chocolate Mud Cake	5.00
Docks Mud Fudge	6.50
Homemade Key Lime Pie	4.00
Coffee / Brewed Decaf	1.50
Assorted Teas	1.50
Espresso	2.00
Cappuccino	2.75

10.00 Food Minimum per Person
PLEASE REFRAIN FROM PIPE AND CIGAR SMOKING

we knew we needed to create an environment that met our potential customers' expectations.

"We're fortunate to have deep pockets and are not willing to compromise on the design if we feel it is appropriate for our potential customer. The project took six months longer to build than expected, and we suffered through it. It taught us, however, that if you want a project to be right, you have to be willing to let it take as much time as it needs."

DESIGN CONCEPT

Morris Nathanson states, "This is the second restaurant we have designed for the owners of Docks. Their first location on the Upper West Side is a very small space, and seats under 100 people. Its enormous success had encouraged the owners

THE BAR AND RAW BAR DISPLAY ACT AS A CENTRAL FOCUS AND DIVIDE THE SPACE INTO INTIMATELY SCALED DINING AREAS. PHOTOGRAPH © WARREN JAGGER PHOTOGRAPHY, INC. R.I.

to look for a second location, this time in midtown. What they settled on was an 8,000 sq. ft. space on the first floor of an office tower.

"Our job was to take this much larger 8,000 sq. ft. space and give it the character and feeling of their Upper West Side establishment. In other words, repeat the success by designing a midtown New York restaurant that would emphasize the good food, service, and exciting opportunities for people-watching that makes their smaller space so popular.

"The success of the bar in the uptown location made it clear that the bar would remain the focus of the space. It would provide a larger holding area during dinner hours as well as seating for the oyster bar. In a rush, on short lunch hours, business people could be accommodated quickly. In the evening, the bar would take on a life of its own, functioning as an exciting gathering place.

"It was also important to create interesting spaces for dining that would allow for a sense of closeness without blocking any views or hampering the ability to people-watch. To this end, the bar would be placed center stage to remain close to all the diners. To convey the feeling of establishment, the materials to be used would be decidedly down-scale. Glazed wall tiles, daily menu boards, and specials would all act to give that welcoming neighborhood feeling.

"Docks on Third Avenue is a big-city restaurant without a bad seat in the house. Its classic styling includes use of familiar materials such as beaded wood, painted walls, tile, wood floors, and rich mahogany stain on the wainscoting, chairs, and bar to create the look of an established restaurant, a place that has been around a while.

"The custom-designed chandeliers create a sense of uniqueness as well as bringing the massive space into a new scale. The coffered ceilings also help to break up the space and enhance the feeling of enclosure. Even the custom canvas border works to define the space and pull the room together. Multilevel dining provides the views that are so important in today's restaurants. As always, artwork is very important to create interest and excitement, and unique pieces have been selected for appropriate areas.

"These design elements, along with the excellent fresh seafood menu, oyster bars, and daily specials, provide Docks on Third Avenue with the same welcoming qualities—'the place you want to be in and seen in'—as Docks on the Upper West Side."

Artie Cutler states, "We spent an enormous amount of time on the design concept for Docks and all of our restaurants. We looked at alternative finishes, artwork, and lighting to determine if the design concept matched our notion of market demand. My job is to feel the pulse of the neighborhood and deliver what it needs."

On lighting design, Morris Nathanson states, "My background is in stage set design, and with my staff, I understand the importance of lighting in a restaurant. I don't like high-intensity pin spots that shoot across a room and light the flowers on your table. We don't design trendy restaurants and we don't select trendy lighting fixtures. We design restaurants, not discos. The first time a client has to change a $30 light bulb, they're going to get you on the phone and scream. There are inexpensive lamps and fixtures that aren't on the cutting edge that are efficient and dramatic.

"We try to stay away from fixtures that we can select from a catalog and design custom fixtures that fit each project and cost about the same as those from a catalog. The lighting at Docks creates a sense of grand scale and provides a warm glow. The large fixtures in the ceiling were custom-made in Canada and match the color of the wall sconces. Monopoint low voltage track fixtures highlight the columns, food displays, and menu boards, while picture lights mounted to each frame illuminate the artwork."

THE DINING ROOM AT DOCKS IS COMPOSED OF FRIENDLY, WARM MATERIALS AND HUMAN-SCALE DECORATIVE ELEMENTS. PHOTOGRAPH © WARREN JAGGER PHOTOGRAPHY, INC. R.I.

SPACE PLANNING

Morris Nathanson states, "The large square configuration of the site presented the biggest challenge. We wanted to create a grand café fashioned after place like La Coupoule in Paris, but needed to create a variety of intimate spaces within this large shell. Placing the bar in the center of the space divided up the space into quadrants and placed everyone near this activity center. Raised platform areas created intimately scaled dining areas within this grand space that is great for people watching. There's not a bad seat in the house, and there are very few floating tables. Everyone is anchored to a wall or a railing.

There is a variety of seating throughout the space for singles who can sit at the bar or at the drink rails. In addition, there are tables for two, four, or five. The bar functions as a gathering space and raw bar rather than the kind of bar you would find at a saloon. We wanted to create an urbane cosmopolitan atmosphere throughout the space and didn't want the bar to hide behind glass dividers. It creates energy at the door and sets the mood for the remainder of the evening.

Docks's 8,900 sq. ft. is located on three floors as follows:

ENTRY AREAS: 200 sq. ft.
BAR AREA: 950 sq. ft.
COAT ROOM: 70 sq. ft.
MAITRE D' AND WAITING AREAS: 260 sq. ft.
DINING AREAS: 4,000 sq. ft.
FINISHING KITCHEN AND PREP: 2,500 sq. ft.
SECOND LEVEL BATHROOMS: 350 sq. ft.
BASEMENT STORAGE: 550 sq. ft.

KITCHEN DESIGN

Artie Cutler states, "We work backward in planning our restaurants. We design our kitchens first to determine how much space we need to prepare and serve our high-quality food. When you have a lunch where every one is seated at the same time, and you're doing 400 covers within a two-hour period, you need a big kitchen, prep, and storage area.

Vic Kasner of Colonel Food Service Equipment Company designed in a counterclockwise fashion to insure efficiency. Kasner states, "There are short loops, long loops, and invisible loops in designing a kitchen. The short loop is almost always the dishwashing area. At Docks, it is immediately to the right of the entrance to the kitchen. Busboys enter and leave immediately. The longer loop is made by runners and wait staff entering the kitchen and proceeding to the pick-up area. The invisible loop is made when clean dishes are brought back to the line. This invisible loop should avoid conflicts with the short and long loops.

"Docks' menu is extremely clever. Fifty percent of all hot food is prepared at the broiling station because Docks is one of the first restaurants to offer fresh charcoal-broiled fish. The rest of the menu is simple as well, so that highly skilled labor is not required, reducing labor costs. Early on in the design process, because so much fish was offered, I placed four refrigerated drawers with two hotel pans as dividers, providing eight compartments for the storage of several varieties of fresh fish.

"This storage space and additional refrigerated storage nearby under the pick-up counter is essential for holding *par stock* in order to meet the demands of this high-volume restaurant. If a table of six orders different entrées and four are ready while the other two have to wait until someone goes downstairs to get the lobster, service will suffer. Most restaurants fail because not enough refrigerated par stock storage is planned for near the cooking line.

"At Docks, we have an upright refrigerator holding lobsters right next to the steamers as well as undercounter refrigerators with tray slides holding additional par stock. Steaming takes longer than charbroiling, so there must be enough par stock nearby to expedite the steamed items.

"When we started the design of Docks, approximately twelve seats had to be sacrificed to create enough space on the line and back-up par stock refrigeration. There must be a balance between the amount of space, equipment, menu, and seating capacity. It makes no sense to have 250 seats if the kitchen can't deliver the food. Sometimes three additional feet in the kitchen can determine whether a restaurant will succeed.

"All of the essential prep areas, refrigerated storage, the hot and cold lines, desserts, and dish and pot washing are located on the ground level, because this is a high-volume establishment. Six

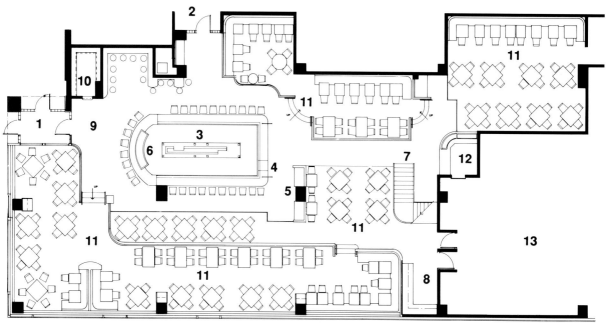

DOCKS FLOOR PLAN. COURTESY OF MORRIS NATHANSON.
REFERENCE TABLE: 1. ENTRY FROM STREET; 2. ENTRY FROM OFFICE BUILDING; 3. BAR; 4. SERVICE BAR; 5. SERVICE STATIONS; 6. RAW BAR DISPLAY; 7. UPSTAIRS TO BATHROOMS; 8. WAITER'S BEVERAGE AREA; 9. MAITRE D' STATION; 10. COAT ROOM; 11. DINING; 12. OYSTER BAR; 13. KITCHEN

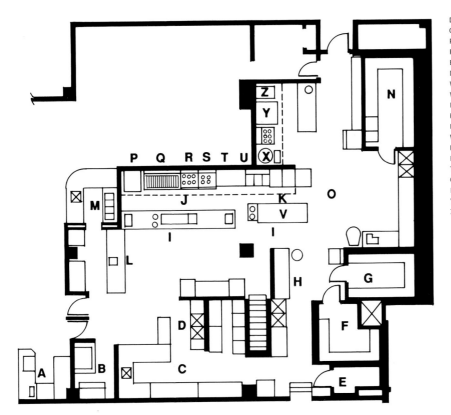

hundred square feet is allocated in the basement for beer and produce refrigerators and an extra freezer."

COST OF OPERATIONS

Docks Oyster Bar and Seafood Grill is one of the most popular and successful restaurants in New York. It continues to be a favorite hangout for office workers, executives, and local residents. Its cost of operations are as follows:

SEATING CAPACITY: dining room, 250; bar, 30
AVERAGE COVERS: lunch, 375; dinner, 500
AVERAGE CHECK: lunch, $27; dinner, $32
LIQUOR AND WINE SALES: 22%
FOOD COST: 35%
LABOR COST: 32%
RENT: 4%
YEARLY SALES: $9 million
NET PROFIT: 10.12%

Docks's success in large part is owed to Artie Cutler's ability to "feel the pulse of the neighborhood and deliver what is needed." He had been interested in the site on Fortieth Street and Third Avenue for ten years and knew what the potential customer in this commercial and residential area expected. He realized that there wasn't an inexpensive quality seafood house where local businesspeople and residents could go for lunch and dinner.

Artie Cutler was able to cut a good deal with the landlord and pass these savings on to customers with high-quality food at reasonable prices. His commitment to a comfortable, visually rich, casual environment led him to raise the funds required for this project so that major design compromises did not have to be made.

A seating capacity of 280 and a simple value-oriented menu enables Docks to do 375 covers at lunch and 500 at dinner. This high-volume, low-average-check concept works for this location and has been a success since the day it opened.

Morris Nathanson Design's efforts produced a classic and created the look of an established restaurant, a place that has been around for a while. The familiar materials, along with the colorful art deco posters and blackboard menus create a warm, friendly, comfortable neighborhood atmosphere. It is a wonderful design because it fits the taste level of the customer and will never go out of style. It succeeds because the design matches the simple quality of the foodservice style without confusing the customer. It is a timeless design.

RALPHIE'S DINER

OWNERS

Ralphie's is owned by Hersh and Mike Pachino, proprietors of Hersh's Orchard Inn, one of Maryland's best restaurants. Mike Pachino is a graduate of Cornell University School of Hotel and Restaurant Administration.

DESIGNER

Martin E. Dorf of Dorf Associates, an architectural and interior design firm in New York City, designed Ralphie's. Dorf is an architect who has been involved with restaurant design for fifteen years and has produced several award-winning projects, including Caroline's Comedy Club and Restaurant, Bloomsbury, Bloom's, and Checker's Bar and Grill. He has also created several quick service concepts, including New York Fries, Haagen-Dazs Soft, and Market Street Café. In addition to his practice, he has lectured on restaurant design and has taught at Parson's School of Design in New York City.

SOURCES

ARCHITECT AND INTERIOR DESIGNER: Dorf Associates Interior Design Inc.
GENERAL CONTRACTOR: Riparius Construction
LIGHTING CONSULTANT: Carl Hillman & Associates
GRAPHIC DESIGN: Craig Carl Design
KITCHEN CONSULTANT: Thomas N. Pappas & Associates
PHOTOGRAPHER: Robert Creamer
CUSTOM BOOTHS, CHAIRS, TABLES, BARSTOOLS: L&B Products, Bronx, New York
CARPET: Charleston Carpets, Calhoun, Georgia
FLOOR AND COVE TILE: American Olean
PAINT: Benjamin Moore
WAINSCOT, TABLETOP LAMINATE: Nevamar
CUSTOM QUILTED STAINLESS WALLCOVERING: Riparius Construction, Timonium, Maryland
MARLITE CEILING PANELS: USG Interiors
DECORATIVE PENDANTS: Valley Lighting, Towson, Maryland
CUSTOM WALL SCONCES: Charles Flickenger Glass, Horbeck Metal, design by Dorf Associates
DESSERT CASE: Federal Industries, Wisconsin
CURVED CEILING FORMS: Pittcon Industries, Riverdale, Maryland
UPHOLSTERY: Douglas Industries, Illinois
METAL TRIM AND MOULDINGS: NY Metal Mouldings, Brooklyn, New York

HERSH PACHINO. PHOTOGRAPH © 1984 TADDER/BALTIMORE.

MIKE PACHINO.

MARTIN DORF. PHOTOGRAPH © MASEO UEDA

Ralphie's Diner is a 6,500 sq. ft. family style restaurant located on the ground level of a ten-story office building on Deereco Road in Timonium, Maryland, a suburb of Baltimore. It was named one of Maryland's best restaurants and has been busy since opening in 1989. It recently won an award from *Restaurant and Institutions* magazine.

Mike and Hersh Pachino both wanted an upscale casual dining concept that would appeal to a wide customer base, including families, couples, and young and elderly people. They brought photos to the Dorf Associates offices of several other similar concepts, and several of these concept sites were visited. It was determined that a diner concept could serve a wide audience. Several alternative themes for this project were discussed, and it was determined early on that Ralphie's should have a sense of permanence, quality, and fun. Martin Dorf convinced them that a 1950s diner with memorabilia on the walls could wear thin after a while and that a 1940s diner concept, complete with mahogany, fluted glass, and deco-style lighting fixtures would endure.

The Pachinos and Martin Dorf believed that a comfortable, fun, richly detailed space coupled with a modestly priced menu would be perceived as a great value. They wanted a space that the customers would not get tired of and would tell their friends about. It was important that each seat in the space was comfortable and had a sense of privacy, and that there was a sense of energy and excitement when one entered the space. It had to feel unique and special.

Ralphie's Diner is named after Ralphie Salvon, the former trainer of the Baltimore Orioles who loved food and people and was Hersh Pachino's friend. Hersh Pachino wanted Ralphie's to be a place that Ralphie himself would have enjoyed—a comfortable, fun, friendly space that served heaping portions of wonderful food to a wide audience.

Hersh and Mike Pachino stated that they needed 170 seats to make Ralphie's a financial success, and they wanted to combine a bar, soda fountain, retail take-out bakery and dessert section, and a dining area into one coherent environment.

The Pachinos had looked at several sites and decided on the one on Deereco Road because of the landlord's financial contribution and its proximity to major highways. In addition, it would be supported by several office and industrial uses at lunch and was conveniently situated as a destination location for residents in the surrounding communities. "It is not unusual for people to travel in their cars for 45 minutes to get here," says Mike Pachino.

Hersh Pachino's reputation as one of Maryland's best restaurateurs gave him some leverage in negotiating for the best location for Ralphie's Diner. The landlord wanted a seasoned operator for this space, since it would be the primary destination for lunch and dinner for the office tenants. The landlord contributed a substantial amount for the construction costs and felt that

THE "DINING CAR" EATING AREAS HAVE BOOTHS THAT OFFER PRIVACY AND COMFORT FOR THE ENTIRE FAMILY.
PHOTOGRAPH © ROBERT CREAMER.

Hersh Pachino's experience as a restaurateur would lead to a successful operation.

The success of Ralphie's Diner assisted in fully leasing the office building it is housed in. In fact, customers of Ralphie's have leased space in the building. "This area is developing rapidly as a very desirable business and residential community, and over the next several years, we see continued growth for Ralphie's," says Mike Pachino.

MENU DEVELOPMENT

Mike Pachino states, "A great deal of research and time went into developing the Ralphie's menu. We literally taste-tested hundreds of items before we felt they could be placed on the final menu, since we had the advantage of preparing and tasting these items at the Orchard Inn, our other restaurant, by serving them as specials to our customers. If these specials didn't sell, we knew not to have them on the menu. We felt that serving large portions at moderate prices would create a sense of value for our customers."

The menu has over 75 items, with more than 16 appetizers and 22 entrées plus salad, sandwich, and burger platters. Desserts include ice cream, fresh fruit, sundaes, and assorted cakes and pies that are also available from the take-home counter. The food style is American with upscale add-ons, in a variety that spans any taste, from simple burgers to baked Crab Imperial. "We have changed the menu three times in two years to adapt to changes in clientele," says Mike Pachino, "since we have seen an increase in young families with children.

"We have developed a good relationship with our purveyors, and our purchasing power is enhanced because of our volume and the fact that we own another restaurant. Our restaurants are successful and purveyors compete aggressively among themselves to deliver the best quality. In fact, one of the things that helped us at the beginning was negotiating not having to pay our first month's bills to our purveyors."

STAFF

Mike Pachino feels that the most difficult challenge is providing consistently excellent service. Wait staff are pleasant, friendly, helpful, and caring, and Ralphie's has built a reputation for a level of service that is appreciated by its customers.

Attaining this level of service wasn't easy, according to Mike Pachino. It took a lot of work. The labor pool is shrinking, and turnover is much higher than it used to be. Young wait staff aren't choosing this job as their lifelong career, and it is important to keep them motivated while they're with the restaurant. Mike Pachino says, "We work with them early on to overcome problems and don't give up on them, starting them off slowly with two tables, and letting them graduate slowly. Our training program starts with work in the kitchen, where they learn how it operates, and then they move to the front of the house after they pass a basic foodservice test.

"The upbeat atmosphere and the fact that we are always busy helps build morale and allows wait staff to make good tips. The generous size of the kitchen and the overall layout of the dining room alleviates a lot of tension."

RALPHIE'S DINER MENU.

BLUE PLATE *Specials*

THE MAIN EVENT

All entrees come with the vegetable du jour.

Ralphie never had it so good!

Meatloaf	6.25
with mashed potatoes and gravy, Marcie's favorite	
Hot Turkey	6.50
with mashed potatoes and gravy	
Hot Roast Beef	6.50
with mashed potatoes and gravy	
White Meatloaf	6.50
with mashed potatoes and gravy	
Chicken Pot Pie	5.95
don't burn your mouth!	
London Broil	6.75
sliced flank steak topped with mushroom sauce, and served with french fries	
Yankee Pot Roast	6.75
served with a potato pancake	

"You'll feel anything but blue once you've tasted our B.P. Specials."

Filet Mignon	12.95
Prime Sirloin of Beef	12.95
Chopped Steak Dinner	9.95
Fresh Fish of the Day	market price
prepared according to your specification, grilled, broiled, sauteed or blackened	
Broiled Stuffed Shrimp	18.95
Fresh Sea Scallops	9.95
prepared broiled or fried	
Shrimp Scampi	15.50
tender shrimp tastefully sauteed in a sauce of butter and garlic	
Crab Imperial	15.95
all jumbo lump crabmeat seasoned and baked to a golden brown	
Crab Cake Platter	15.50
we know you love them, so we give you two	
Chicken of the Day	priced daily
no fowl play here, just great chicken	

"Eat up, our chef worked really hard on this stuff."

FOUNTAIN *Favorites*

Soda	.95	Coffee or Tea	.95
Milk Shakes	2.50	Espresso	1.50
Malteds	2.75	"Cap Pachino"	1.95
Iced Tea	.95	Mineral Water	2.25
Assorted Fruit Juices	1.50	Tap Water	Free

Lotsa **PASTA**

Freeway Pasta	12.95
Linguine with a mix of fresh seafood	
Spaghetti with Meat Sauce	8.95
Linguine Primavera	10.95
linguine tossed with fresh vegetables in a light sauce of olive oil and Parmesan cheese	
Chicken Fettuccine Ricardo	10.95
our own version of a classic	
Personal Size Cheese Pizza	4.95
Made fresh to order	

Additional Toppings Available

You can pay the waitress or the cashier. We don't care just as long as you pay !

Happy **ENDINGS**

Assorted Cakes and Pies	priced daily
Ice Cream	2.25
Fresh Fruit	2.95
Ice Cream Sundaes	2.95

Wise old saying: "It's just as easy to love a rich dessert as it is to love a lite one."

Ralphie's Diner was built for a cost of $1.3 million, or approximately $200 per square foot. The space was entirely new and consisted of a concrete slab over a garage area and a metal deck and concrete ceiling. There was a sprinkler grid in the ceiling and a main sewer line located in the basement garage level.

It was stated in the landlord's work letter that provisions were made for exhaust to the roof, but on investigation, it was found that ductwork, sprinklers, fans, and controls had not been provided for exhaust or make-up air, and that only a vertical ten-story shaft had been provided. The installation of necessary exhaust items increased the budget considerably and was a source of further negotiation between the landlord and Ralphie's.

THE SODA FOUNTAIN CREATES ANOTHER DINING EXPERIENCE FOR SINGLE CUSTOMERS. PHOTOGRAPH © ROBERT CREAMER.

Dorf Associates provided an in-depth analysis of the budget after the concept was developed, along with a rendering and sample boards. This provided the landlord and Ralphie's with a realistic budget that reflected the scope of work and the level of finishes. It was more than what Hersh Pachino originally felt he wanted to spend, but he realized that the level of finishes necessary for this concept and the sheer size of the project could not be built for less than $200 a square foot.

Ralphie's took two months for design and construction documents, including kitchen, mechanical, and electrical components, and it took over five months to build.

Several millwork bids came back somewhat over budget, until a reputable millwork contractor who understood the detailing was found and was able to build the richly detailed bar, booths, and moulding economically.

Riparius Construction controlled all the subcontractors quite well, and foreman George Sipes was very easy to work with. Once the final price was determined, there weren't very many change orders; in fact, they amounted to less than 5 percent of the original budget.

Other richly detailed diners that had recently been built had cost $250 a square foot or more.

DESIGN CONCEPT

Ralphie's was designed to appeal to a wide audience, and it is important that families, businesspeople, teens, young, middle-aged, and elderly people feel comfortable here. In order to achieve this, Dorf Associates developed a palette of warm wood, burgundy upholstery, flutex glass, and black-and-white tile. These warm finishes coupled with deco shapes and forms in both the lighting fixtures, furnishings, details, and the architecture of the space contributed to a sense of casual elegance one would find on the Orient Express. The infusion of patterned, sparkly stainless steel and neon graphics added a touch of whimsy and energy to the space.

The entrance is alive and welcomes the customer with large, well-lit display cases filled with baked items and desserts and a cashier area that bustles with energy and contributes to the excitement and heightened expectations.

The two separate "dining cars" are defined with cove-lit vaulted ceiling wells and three large art deco pendant lighting fixtures. Within these well-defined spaces are booths surrounded with flutex glass and mahogany trim, while the ceiling over the booths is lowered to 8', creating a sense of enclosure and privacy. These "dining cars" are very much a part of the fun experience that keeps customers coming back.

The soda fountain area provides a totally different experience: there, diners can have meals and desserts at a counter or a booth for two people. The patterned stainless steel and the neon clock, along with the bright red sparkly vinyl on the stools and the sparkly laminate on the countertop, combine to create a fun environment.

The island bar area features an illuminated slab of marble that radiates light through the glasses filled with beer and adds a sense of elegance and drama to this section of the restaurant. The mirror and art deco wall sconces add further sparkle to this space.

In order to light the food so that it would sparkle and look more appetizing, we installed low-voltage accent lights over each table. Low-voltage MR-16 lamps were chosen because they produce less heat and the beam of light can be controlled so that it doesn't produce circles under people's eyes.

An inexpensive computerized dimming system was installed with four presets, including lunch, cocktail hour, dinner, and clean-up. This system cost $3,500, and it conserves energy while prolonging lamp life.

Ralphie's Diner is a vibrant, exciting, and fun place to be in. Part of this excitement is the tinkle of glasses and the noise. It is an essential part of the experience. We designed some of the areas to be quieter than others for people who are more sensitive to noise. Carpet insets and banquettes with high-density foam were installed in the dining area to reduce noise levels. The design of the curved vaulted ceilings assists in extending reverberation time, thus reducing abrasive sound.

Linear air conditioning diffusers were used to distribute air more evenly, eliminating drafts. These linear diffusers also were selected because they were compatible with the linear lines of the space. Electric heating elements were placed along the windows to eliminate condensation and cold drafts.

Floor materials, woodwork, stainless steel, and all other materials were selected to minimize maintenance. Mike Pachino says, "The restaurant still looks fresh three years after the opening."

The sense of romance, elegance, and fun all had to be accomplished with the lighting at

THE DESSERT DISPLAYS GREETS CUSTOMERS AS THEY ENTER AND SETS THE TONE FOR THE FUN EXPERIENCE THAT LIES AHEAD. PHOTOGRAPH © ROBERT CREAMER.

Ralphie's on a very tight budget. The wall sconce and pendant lighting fixture selections were very important to the overall image of the space. The wall sconces were custom-fabricated for less than $100 each, based on a design provided by Dorf Associates. The glass and brushed-aluminum enclosures were made by two different manufacturers and were assembled at the site, while the pendant fixtures were bought at a local lighting distributor for less than $500 apiece. Both of these lighting sources have incandescent lamps and provide a warm glow on people's faces. Their warm color and soft shapes attract the eye and provide a sense of style.

The vaulted ceilings over each "dining car" are illuminated with warm white fluorescent lamps and are dimmed with 90% neutral density filters, which slide over the surface of the lamp. In addition to the neutral density filter, a pink gel was added to soften and color the light in the vaults. The cost of dimming the fluorescent lamps mechanically would have been over $10,000.

SPACE PLANNING

In order to insure that there was enough room for the necessary amount of seats, Martin Dorf quickly developed a space plan that included the bar, bathrooms, retail/cashier area, dining rooms, soda fountain, service stations, and the kitchen.

The bathrooms needed approximately 450 sq. ft. and would have made the kitchen too small or reduced the amount of seating. Hersh Pachino negotiated for more space with the landlord, and we were able to locate the bathrooms in a corridor near the main lobby of the office building.

In order to minimize disturbing the facade of the newly constructed office building, the landlord decided to locate the entrance to Ralphie's at an existing fire corridor exit. The position for this entrance determined the location of the coat room, bar, and retail/cashier areas.

The main dining areas split into two "diner cars" approximately 15' wide by 45' long, and at the intersection of the two dining rooms, there is a semi-private area for larger parties of 6, 8, or 10 people. The island bar is located off the entrance to serve as a hangout and waiting area. This island bar

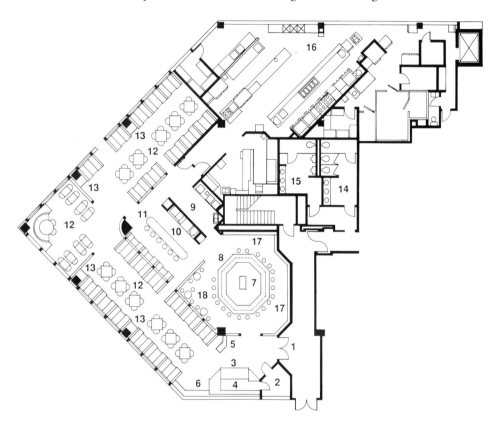

RALPHIE'S DINER FLOOR PLAN. COURTESY OF DORF ASSOCIATES. REFERENCE TABLE: 1. ENTRY; 2. COAT ROOM; 3. DESSERT DISPLAY; 4. CASHIER; 5. MAITRE D'; 6. WAITING AREA; 7. BAR; 8. SERVICE BAR; 9. WAITER'S STATION; 10. BEVERAGE STATION; 11. SODA FOUNTAIN; 12. DINING ROOM; 13. BUS STATIONS; 14. WOMEN'S BATHROOM; 15. MEN'S BATHROOM; 16. KITCHEN; 17. DRINK RAIL; 18. HIGH TOPS

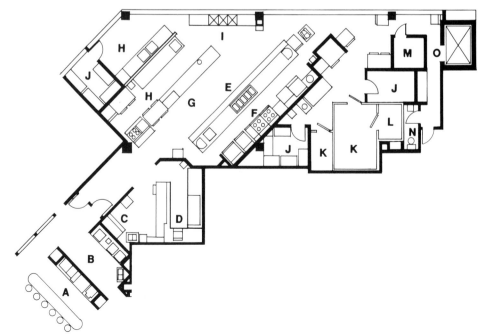

RALPHIE'S DINER KITCHEN PLAN. COURTESY OF DORF ASSOCIATES. REFERENCE TABLE: A. HOT BEVERAGES; B. WAITER'S STATION; C. ICE; D. DISHWASHING; E. HOT PICK-UP COUNTER; F. HOT LINE; G. COLD PICK-UP COUNTER; H. COLD PREP; I. POT SINKS; J. DRY STORAGE; K. WALK-IN REFRIGERATOR; L. FREEZER; M. OFFICE; N. EMPLOYEE'S BATHROOM; O. ELEVATOR FROM DOWNSTAIRS LOADING DOCK

seats 40, has standing room for 30 more at happy hour, and consumes less room than a straight bar.

In order to maximize seating capacity, booth sizes were set at 5'6" on center, approximately 6" smaller than the average booth. This reduced size allowed us to fit 16 more seats into the restaurant, with 4 more booths being added. At first, it seemed that the size of the seat would be uncomfortable. However, we worked with L&B, the booth manufacturer, to design a tapered back that proved to be quite comfortable.

The service bar is conveniently located near the waiter's station and close to the exit from the kitchen. Coffee, beverages, and desserts can be picked up at the soda fountain.

Two-foot by 3' bus stations house cups, saucers, flatware, napkins, coffee warmers, and a place for soiled dishes and are located strategically in the dining area. There is one bus station for every 50 customers.

The kitchen was located near the main sanitary waste line to avoid expensive trenching and long runs for waste lines, while floor drains were consolidated near the main sanitary waste line as well to minimize steel cuts. Deliveries are made at the garage level, and brought up by elevator to the kitchen storage area. The hot water heater and the refrigerator compressors are in a remote location in a separate room in the garage.

Ralphie's is accessible throughout its facility for the physically disabled. The 6,500 square feet of Ralphie's is located on one level as follows:

DINING ROOM: 1,730 sq. ft.
BAR: 642 sq. ft.
CASHIER/RETAIL, WAITING AREA: 308 sq. ft.
COAT ROOM: 56 sq. ft.
BATHROOMS: 427 sq. ft.
WAITER'S STATIONS: 88 sq. ft.
SODA FOUNTAIN: 263 sq. ft.
KITCHEN: 2,319 sq. ft.
OFFICE: 42 sq. ft.
DRY STORAGE: 132 sq. ft.
REFRIGERATED STORAGE: 135 sq. ft.
WARE WASHING: 180 sq. ft.

KITCHEN DESIGN

The kitchen was designed to produce high volume with abundant aisle space and room to work. Mike Pachino feels these comfortable working conditions encourage staff to stay longer at Ralphie's, contributing to consistently good food. There are three hot line cooks at lunch and four at dinner along with two salad and cold food cooks for each shift. Mike Pachino expedites personally four days a week to assure consistency and quality. "Sometimes I wish that we had more storage space for produce, and then I realize more frequent deliveries allow me to have more money in the bank than on the shelves," he says. He involved the cooks in the kitchen design decisions to insure smooth operation.

COST OF OPERATIONS

Ralphie's still serves over 850 meals a day to a wide audience of families, businesspeople, young singles, and middle-aged and elderly people. It has a low average check and provides great quality and value for its customers. Current operations are as follows:

SEATING CAPACITY: dining room, 166; bar, 30
AVERAGE COVERS: lunch, 350; dinner, 500
AVERAGE CHECK: lunch, $9; dinner, $13
LIQUOR AND BEER SALES: 10%
FOOD COST: 30%
LABOR COST: 32%
TOTAL STAFF: 75
YEARLY SALES: $4 million

Mike Pachino thrives on the challenge of being a restaurateur. He spends four days a week in the kitchen expediting and does most of the purchasing. One day he is a plumber, the next a lawyer, a maitre d', or an accountant. He works on the average twelve hours a day and is also raising a family. He does have a support system, which consists of his wife, Lisa, who handles front-of-the-house employees, and a solid management team.

He believes that "knowing your business and your customer is the key to success." His idea of a casual, upscale concept that provides value for a wide audience has proven very successful. His business and organizational skills, which he developed under his father, Hersh Pachino, at the Orchard Inn, have contributed greatly to the success of Ralphie's Diner.

The enduring design of Ralphie's Diner has wide appeal and is not going to go out of style. That enduring design coupled with good service and food at reasonable prices in a good location has made Ralphie's Diner one of the most popular restaurants in Maryland.

TRIBECA GRILL

OWNERS

Tribeca Grill is owned by Drew Nieporent and Robert DeNiro. Nieporent is a graduate of the Cornell University School of Hotel Administration and worked at La Grenouille, Le Perigord, Tavern on the Green, and Maxwell's Plum before opening his own critically acclaimed, three-star restaurant, Montrachet, in 1985.

DESIGNER

Tribeca Grill was designed by Lo Yi Chan, FAIA, of Prentice & Chan, Ohlhausen, Architects.

SOURCES

ARCHITECT: Prentice & Chan, Ohlhausen, Architects.
GENERAL CONTRACTOR: Cor Rep Construction Corp
KITCHEN EQUIPMENT: Gaul Construction
MILLWORK: Gaul Construction
BAR: Originally Jack Dempsey's Bar, then installed at Maxwell's Plum, rebuilt by Gaul Construction for Tribeca Grill
CARPET: SCS Systems Ltd.
FLOOR TILE: American Olean
LIGHTING: Artemide
PHOTOGRAPHER: Wolfgang Hoyt

ROBERT DENIRO, DON PINTABONA, DREW NIEPORENT.
PHOTOGRAPH © TRIBECA GRILL.

LO YI CHAN. PHOTOGRAPH
© JESSICA WICKHAM.

Tribeca Grill is an 8,000 sq. ft. full-service restaurant located in the Washington Market area on Franklin and Greenwich Streets in Manhattan. It was completed in 1990, and it serves delectable food and wine in a simple, understated environment that has become one of New York's favorite restaurants and is a hangout for people in the film industry.

Robert DeNiro had looked at several sites in Manhattan to locate a film center that could contain offices for his and other film production companies in addition to a restaurant. The cost of locating this film center in midtown Manhattan was prohibitive, and since he had lived in the Tribeca district for over ten years and liked the feeling of the neighborhood, he decided to locate the film center there. The building he finally selected had a great deal of character and suited DeNiro's vision for a film center that would act as a magnet for people in the industry. The restaurant would be a great place to dine and also a hangout for local residents, artists, writers, actors, and actresses, as well as businesspeople from midtown and Wall Street.

DeNiro, however, had no prior restaurant experience and approached Drew Nieporent, the owner of Montrachet, a well-known restaurant in Tribeca, to see if he would be interested in becoming involved in this new venture. DeNiro had been a frequent guest of Montrachet and was impressed with Nieporent's skill as a restaurateur. Drew Nieporent agreed to the proposed venture and felt confident that "this was a good location for a restaurant even though this area of Manhattan is not easy to get to. The building itself is very dynamic and is located on Greenwich Street, which is a fairly wide thoroughfare. This area has not yet been gentrified and still remains a 'genuine neighborhood,' with a mix of industrial, office, and residential uses."

Although this was DeNiro's restaurant, it had other celebrity investors, such as Bill Murray, Mikhail Baryshnikov, Lou Diamond Philips, Sean Penn, and Christopher Walken, so it was felt that advance publicity would draw customers to this location.

However, Drew Nieporent felt that once the publicity lost its initial capacity to draw customers, it was extremely important to establish a place where well-prepared food could be purchased at moderate prices, appealing to a wide audience. One of the models for Tribeca Grill, Nieporent says, was "the simple fish grill restaurants in San Francisco, where one can eat wonderfully prepared fish dishes at moderate prices in a place that looks like it has been there forever." Drew Nieporent also liked Stars, Jeremiah Tower's restaurant in San Francisco, because it was a grand café with a great deal of style, but was not overbearing.

Tribeca Grill had to be an unpretentious bar and grill, since anything else would seem out of place with this building, the area, and Robert DeNiro's personality.

THE SPACE SEEMS TO HAVE BEEN A RESTAURANT FOR MANY DECADES, AND THAT SENSE OF PLACE IS REFLECTED IN THE INTERIOR FINISHES.
PHOTOGRAPH © WOLFGANG HOYT.

Drew Nieporent says, "In addition to the simple fish grills in San Francisco, another restaurant that I had eaten in was in Paris, called La Cagouille. There you could also eat simply prepared grilled fish in unpretentious surroundings. This restaurant also served as a model for Tribeca Grill.

"Although fish is a key component of the restaurant, it is not the only item on the menu, and there are ten entrées on the menu without any specific regional influence. It is neither French, Italian, or American, but can best be described as crosscultural cuisine. There are several grilled items on the menu, including a grilled minestrone."

Don Pintabona, who gained experience at the River Café, was selected to be the chef at Tribeca Grill. He had experience in handling volume and trained with Drew Nieporent in Montrachet's kitchen. "People come expecting a steak and baked potato and are surprised at the quality of the food and the presentation," says Pintabona. This surprise increases the "perceived value" of the experience and encourages repeat patronage. The predominantly grilled and sautéed menu is inherently easy on waste, contributing to lower food costs.

In order to keep the menu fresh and current after the patina of the first year's success had worn off, Drew introduced some little touches such as home-made breadsticks and three kinds of spreads for the table.

TRIBECA GRILL
BRUNCH MENU.

BRUNCH

Homemade Granola with Fresh Fruit	7.
Arugula Salad with Bocconcini & Basil Oil	8.
Warm Potato and Garlic Sausage Salad	8.
Green Salad	7.
Daily Soup	7.
House Smoked Salmon with Celery & Fennel Brandade	10.
Assortment of Breads & Muffins	2. per person
Banana Stuffed French Toast, Maple Butter	14.
Smoked Ham, Muenster & Grilled Onion Omelette	13.
Poached Eggs Over Roast Beef Hash, Watercress Sauce	13.
Scrambled Eggs with Homemade Sage Sausage	10.
Hazelnut Waffles with Comice Pear Relish	14.
Homemade Tagliatelle with Roasted Peppers & Broccoli Rabe	16.
Chicken Piccata with Orzo & Artichokes	18.
Norwegian Salmon & Crabmeat Cakes, Bell Pepper Chutney	17.
Poached Chicken Salad with Avocado, Citrus Vinaigrette	17.
Grilled Market Available Fish, Warm Vinaigrette	19.
Red Bliss Potatoes with Carmelized Onions	4.
Homemade Sage Sausage	4.
Sticky Buns	4.
Creme Brulee	6.
Chocolate Torte	6.
Mascarpone Cream with Candied Cashews, Espresso Sauce	6.
Caramelized Peach with Almond Strudel & Vanilla Cream	6.
Selection of Fresh Fruit	6.
Homemade Ice Creams & Sorbets	6.

TriBeCa Grill	Chef, Don Pintabona	10/91

TriBeCa Grill Menu

Fried Oysters with Thai Marinated Vegetables	10.
Terrine of Grilled Vegetables	10.
Green Salad	7.
Daily Soup	8.
Endive, Watercress & Roquefort Salad	8.
Carpaccio of Tuna with Citrus Vinaigrette	12.
Arugula Salad with Bocconcini & Basil Oil	10.
Grilled Quail Salad with Sherry Shallot Vinaigrette	12.

Salmon   Mahi Mahi   Snapper   Market Available   21.

Choice of Preparation: *Grilled with a sweet corn succotash;*
Sauteed with lemon & herbs;
Roasted with warm vinaigrette

Homemade Cheese Ravioli with Roasted Tomatoes & Broccoli Rabe	16.
Lemon Tagliatelle with Sauteed Shrimp, New Zealand Clam Broth	19.
Roasted Chicken with Whipped Potatoes, Root Vegetables	18.
Grilled Rack of Lamb, Rosemary Essence, Provencal Vegetable Tart	24.
Game Special	26.
Grilled Filet Mignon with Roasted Garlic & Mascarpone Polenta	25.
Breast of Duck with Wild Mushroom Cannelloni	22.

Potato Pancakes "Vonnas"	5.
Whipped Potatoes	4.
Mascarpone Polenta	4.

Mascarpone Cream with Candied Cashews, Espresso Sauce	7.
Banana Tart with Milk Chocolate Malt Ice Cream	7.
Chocolate Torte	7.
Crisp Pear & Almond Tart with Vanilla Ice Cream	7.
Selection of Fresh Fruit	6.
Homemade Ice Creams & Sorbets	6.
Special	

Chef, Don Pintabona   11/91

Please refrain from cigar and pipe smoking.
A gratuity will be added to parties of 6 people or more.
All tables are re-booked 2 - 2 1/2 hours after reservation time

TRIBECA GRILL DINNER MENU.

Drew Nieporent interviews as many as thirty people for one job, and he feels that this is the key to the restaurant's success. Recently, he asked a prospective waitress for a resume and she answered, "Do you need to have a resume to be a waitress?" Nieporent is interested in people who view working in a restaurant as a serious commitment, not a hobby, and wants experienced people who have worked at other restaurants who still can be trained to work under his system. It is important to select key staff, such as chefs and managers, whose personalities are compatible with those of the owner, since tension is part of the restaurant business, and key personnel have to respect each other and get along.

Drew Nieporent states, "The way a space is laid out has a direct bearing on keeping staff employed for several years. Good kitchen design, along with an efficiently organized dining room, can make it a pleasant environment to work in. Since keeping the same staff for several years contributes to the consistency of the food and service, our kitchen is air conditioned for employee comfort."

Drew has established a detailed reservation system and strictly honors these reservations, so he has established good will with regular customers and has sacrificed very little in volume. His challenge was and is to control the crowd, and not to be consumed by success.

Drew Nieporent states, "The original budget for the restaurant was $1.3 million. The final construction budget was $1.9 million, and several items had to be eliminated from the project in order to control costs, including kitchen equipment, furniture, and millwork.

"The compressors for all refrigeration were remote in a central area on the roof, and while remoting the compressors where they can be cooled increases efficiency and extends their life, it can be costly. Elevators were originally planned for the space to convey physically disabled customers to the second floor bathrooms. Since this was a costly solution, a separate unisex bathroom was located on the ground floor for the physically disabled, while retaining the

THE "MAHOGANY BAR AS CENTERPIECE" IS THE FOCAL POINT AT TRIBECA GRILL. PHOTOGRAPH © WOLFGANG HOYT.

bathrooms upstairs. This allowed us to increase seating capacity downstairs."

Tribeca Grill was a complex project on three levels that required substantial improvements to the infrastructure of the building to make it suitable for a restaurant. Eighty-five percent of the budget was spent on general construction, plumbing, electrical, heating, air conditioning, kitchen exhaust, sprinklers, and kitchen equipment. Ten percent of the budget, or $170,000, was spent on millwork and furniture, the only elements the customer actually sees. The interior of this space is simple, direct, and without embellishments, reflecting Robert DeNiro's idea for an unpretentious bar and grill that seems always to have been there.

The budget figures cited below include overhead, profit, and general conditions, but they do not include architectural and engineering fees.

GENERAL CONSTRUCTION: total cost of $512,000 at $64.41 per sq. ft.
PLUMBING: $180,000 at $22.64
ELECTRICAL AND LIGHTING: $245,000 at $30.82
MECHANICAL: $402,000 at $50.37
SPRINKLERS: $35,000 at $4.40
KITCHEN EQUIPMENT: $182,000 at $22.89
MILLWORK (BAR AND BOOTHS): $91,000 at $11.44
FURNITURE: $82,000 at $10.31
TOTAL COST: $1,729,000 at $217.51 per sq. ft.

DESIGN CONCEPT

Lo Yi Chan states, "The design of the space is unpretentious and simple because the industrial quality of the building was seen as a positive influence and was not abandoned in the interior." Drew Nieporent adds, "In fact, the radiator pipes in the ceiling that were removed during demolition were reinstalled as a decorative feature, since Mr. DeNiro wanted a space where the decor didn't overshadow the people or the food."

The space seems to have been a restaurant for many decades, and that sense of place is reflected in the interior finishes. The walls are mostly exposed natural brick and green tongue-and-groove wainscoting, with artwork by Robert DeNiro, Sr., adorning the walls. The floors are a mixture of wood, tile, and carpet in the dining room, and a mahogany bar and a tall island back bar cabinet for liquor storage are the central features in the space. Drew Nieporent, who had worked with Warner

LeRoy at Maxwell's Plum, remembers how successful the "bar as centerpiece" concept was and felt Tribeca Grill should have as its focal point a large mahogany island bar. In fact, the bar is from the former Maxwell's Plum and was bought at an auction. Nieporent feels that "Tribeca Grill is a latter-day Maxwell's Plum in spirit, without the frou-frou, since the large expanses of windows create a grand café that bustles with energy."

Lo Yi Chan states, "The lighting in this space serves as a background for this warm palette of brick and wood and consists of simple pendant fixtures that provide general illumination and track fixtures that highlight the brick columns, artwork, and the bar."

The tables are covered with tablecloths with cloth napery. The china, glassware, and flatware are simple and elegant and serve as a background for the wonderful food presentation. Some of the glassware is hand-blown, and the china is from Germany, with a large peppermill at each table. Nieporent feels that what people touch and see reflects his attention to detail and reinforces the level of quality in food and service.

SPACE PLANNING

Tribeca Grill's main dining room seats 170 and is located on the first floor. It is essentially a square, with the bar as the focal point in the center, dividing the space into several intimate dining spaces. The main service area is integrated with the wine storage area and is one of the most popular places to dine. The maitre d' area is located to the left of the vestibule, with the coat area to the right. The maitre d' station was purposefully positioned to the left of the entrance in order to eliminate any barrier so that patrons could go directly to the bar. The square layout of the space makes it easy to provide service to any part of the dining room. The special function room on the second floor seats 150.

Tribeca Grill's 7,950 sq. ft. are located on three floors divided up as follows:

MAIN DINING AREA: 3,850 sq. ft.
MAIN KITCHEN (SECOND FLOOR): 800 sq. ft.
BASEMENT PREP AREA, STORAGE, OFFICES: 1,222 sq. ft.
BANQUET AREA, SPECIAL FUNCTION ROOM (SECOND FLOOR): 1,050 sq. ft.
BANQUET AREA KITCHEN (SECOND FLOOR): 515 sq. ft.

The finishing kitchen is 800 sq. ft., with the 20' hot line intersecting at right angles with the 8' *garde manger*. This layout is extremely efficient, because Don Pintabona, the chef, who acts as the expeditor, stands at the intersection of the hot and cold lines and has complete visual control of the kitchen. The computer stations are conveniently located at this intersection so that Pintabona knows when to fire an entrée, usually within 14 minutes after the appetizers have left the kitchen. The timing for firing the hot entrées is essential, since there are no heat lamps to keep the food warm.

Drew Nieporent feels that "heat lamps would compromise the quality of the food, since grilled and sautéed food loses its flavor and heat quickly if left under these lamps. Food should be brought to the customer piping hot, immediately after it's cooked. The elimination of these heat lamps and plate shelves allows better communication between the expeditor, the runners, and the line cooks, and

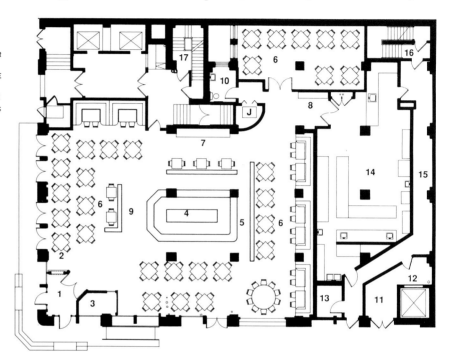

TRIBECA GRILL FIRST FLOOR PLAN. COURTESY OF PRENTICE CHAN OLHAUSEN. REFERENCE TABLE: 1. ENTRY; 2. MAITRE D'; 3. COAT ROOM; 4. BAR; 5. SERVICE BAR AND GLASS STORAGE; 6. DINING ROOMS; 7. WAITER'S COMPUTER STATION AND WINE DISPLAY; 8. BEVERAGE STATION, COFFEE, EXPRESSO; 9. WATER STATION; 10. UNISEX HANDICAPPED TOILET; 11. DELIVERY AREA; 12. SERVICE ELEVATOR TO BASEMENT AND SECOND FLOOR; 13. STEWARD'S OFFICE; 14. KITCHEN; 15. FIRE CORRIDOR; 16. SERVICE STAIRWAY TO BASEMENT AND SECOND FLOOR; 17. PUBLIC STAIRWAY TO BASEMENT AND BATHROOMS   .

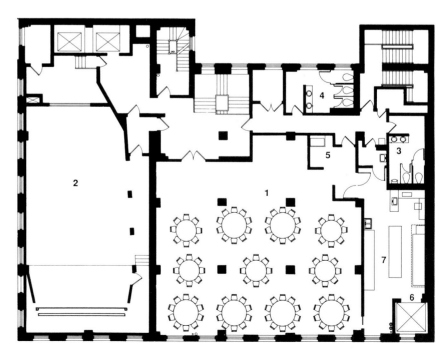

TRIBECA GRILL SECOND FLOOR PLAN. COURTESY OF PRENTICE CHAN OLHAUSEN. REFERENCE TABLE: 1. BANQUET/SPECIAL FUNCTIONS ROOM; 2. SCREENING ROOM/PART OF FILM CENTER; 3. MEN'S BATHROOM; 4. WOMEN'S BATHROOM; 5. WAITER'S STATION; 6. ELEVATOR; 7. KITCHEN

enables Don to have much more room to assemble and plate the food for each table on time."

Don Pintabona states, "This is an intense kitchen with 350 covers on a busy night, and each line cook has to fire the food in the right sequence in order for all the entrées to be ready a the same time. The elimination of the plate shelf lets me see what's going on so that I can expedite and control the line cooks at the same time. There are four people on the hot line, with two on the *garde manger*, and when things are hectic, I can assist in plating salads and appetizers while expediting because of the layout of the hot and cold lines. There are four runners who are extremely experienced and who assist in timing and plating the food. We don't use trays or covers, so two runners often serve one large table."

COST OF OPERATIONS

Drew prepared a conservative pro forma based on 170 seats. More seating could have been squeezed into the space, but Drew had a strong commitment to provide comfort for his guests. Tribeca Grill continues to serve great food at reasonable prices to a wide audience.

SEATING CAPACITY: dining room, 170; special function room, 150
AVERAGE COVERS: lunch, 170; dinner, 325
AVERAGE CHECK: lunch, $33; dinner, $40 dinner
LIQUOR AND WINE SALES: 28%
FOOD COST: 30%
LABOR COST: 28%
YEARLY SALES: $7 million

Tribeca Grill is a simple, unpretentious bar and grill that offers high quality food and service at affordable prices. Drew Nieporent's commitment to customers' comfort is reflected in his attention to every detail, from selection and training of staff to tabletop design, the food and wine served, and his reservation policy. In a word, Drew Nieporent personifies hospitality.

Don Pintabona's delectable, wonderfully prepared assortment of grilled, sautéed, or roasted fish, combined with great salads, appetizers, and other entrées are a delight.

Robert DeNiro's idea to create a film center combined with a simple bar and grill restaurant in the Tribeca area of Manhattan has become a great success.

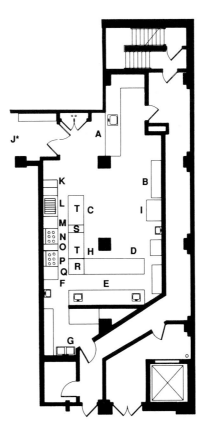

TRIBECA GRILL FIRST FLOOR KITCHEN PLAN. COURTESY OF PRENTICE CHAN OLHAUSEN. REFERENCE TABLE: A. DISHWASHING; B. POT WASHING; C. HOT PICK-UP; D. SALAD & DESSERT PICK-UP; E. GARDE MANGER; F. HOT LINE; G. PREP; H. EXPEDITOR; I. REACH-IN REFRIGERATOR; J. ICE MACHINE (SEE RESTAURANT PLAN); K. INGREDIENTS FOR FISH GRILL; L. FISH GRILL; M. HOT TOP FOR CHICKEN, DUCK, AND FISH SAUTÉE; N. 6-BURNER OVEN FOR DUCK, ROASTED CHICKEN, AND LOBSTER SAUTÉE; O. FRYOLATOR; P. 6-BURNER OVEN FOR PASTA SAUTÉE; Q. PASTA MACHINE; R. INGREDIENTS FOR LOBSTER AND PASTA SPECIALS; S. INGREDIENTS, STORAGE, AND UNDERCOUNTER TRAY HOLDERS; T. PLATING

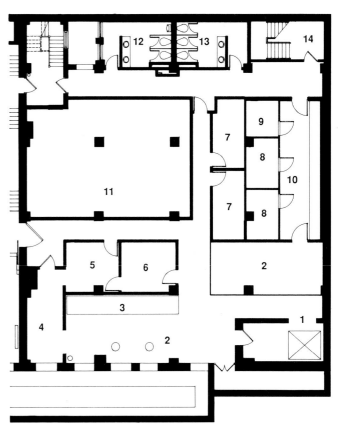

TRIBECA GRILL CELLAR PLAN. COURTESY OF PRENTICE CHAN OLHAUSEN. REFERENCE TABLE: 1. ELEVATOR FROM LOADING DOCK; 2. DRY STORAGE; 3. BEER COOLER; 4. WINE STORAGE; 5. LIQUOR STORAGE; 6. OFFICE; 7. MEN'S AND WOMEN'S LOCKERS; 8. WALK-IN REFRIGERATOR; 9. FREEZER; 10. PREP AREA; 11. STORAGE AREA FOR FILM CENTER; 12. MEN'S ROOM; 13. WOMEN'S ROOM; 14. SERVICE STAIRWAY FROM UPSTAIRS

UNION SQUARE CAFÉ

DANNY MEYER. PHOTOGRAPH © DIANE PADYS.

MICHAEL ROMANO. PHOTOGRAPH © LOU MANNA STUDIO.

LARRY BOGDANOW. PHOTOGRAPH © RANDI HALPERN.

Union Square Café is a 5,600 square-foot full-service restaurant located at 21 East Sixteenth Street in Manhattan. It was completed in 1985 and serves wonderfully prepared food in a timeless environment that has endured and prospered. It is many New Yorkers' favorite restaurant.

Danny Meyer wanted Union Square Café to be a restaurant where there was compatibility between the wine, the food, the decor, and the people. He hoped that twenty years hence, no one would look back and say that this restaurant had been designed in 1985, and he wanted a timeless space with warm materials that made people feel comfortable. Danny Meyer also wanted a restaurant that transmitted joy to his customers. When asked why he became a restaurateur, Danny Meyer said, "I don't think that there is a better medium to make people happy than the joys of the table.

"The concept for this restaurant began by asking myself an important question: What kind of guests are going to feed me the most joy? The menu items, the wine, and the design were developed to be compatible with the kind of guest I would be comfortable serving. I'm my favorite customer, I like good value, I like the feeling that the restaurant is on my side, they're not trying to rip me off. I like a restaurant where my server knows more than I do about the wine and food being served, not less than I do."

Several sites were evaluated before the site on Sixteenth Street was selected. At the time that Union Square was being planned there was a citywide trend toward large, wide-open grand café concepts, but Danny Meyer decided that he wanted an intimately scaled and civilized environment. This narrowed the field of potential sites considerably.

The Sixteenth Street site was selected because the rent was considerably lower than the market value for similar sites in Manhattan. Its proximity to the Greenmarket, a fruit and vegetable market in Union Square Park, was also a determining factor in selecting this site.

For the past forty-nine years, this site had been leased by Brownie's, a well-known health food restaurant, and it was assumed that much of the equipment, existing plumbing, electrical wiring, and ductwork could be reused. However, it turned out that almost everything had to be scrapped, adding to the total cost of the project. But even starting from scratch, the rent for this space was so far below market that it still made economic sense. Some of the existing equipment and fixtures were sold.

Another reason that this site was selected is that it had previously been a restaurant. It had already been approved under the pre-existing New York City Building Code, and without this prior approval, mezzanine use and bathroom accessibility would have been issues for concern. It proved more economical to build a restaurant in a location approved for earlier restaurant use.

Architect Larry Bogdanow and his associate Warren Ashworth were part of this site selection process before the lease was signed. The advice Bogdanow gave Meyer during this site selection process assisted in reducing the overall cost of the project. It is important to have a qualified restaurant architect review potential sites before signing a lease, since they can advise on code violations, utility deficiencies, and other factors that can lead to larger-than-expected construction costs.

The selection of this site was a bit of a gamble. Offices were just beginning to be renovated in

THE ENTRY WELCOMES THE CUSTOMER WITH ITS HIGH CEILINGS AND ARCHWAY, WHILE INSIDE, THE BAR IS THE SOUL AND ONE OF THE CIVILIZING FEATURES OF THE SPACE. PHOTOGRAPH © DANIEL EIFERT

this lower Fifth Avenue area. However, the major migration from uptown had not begun. Union Square Café was one of the pioneers in this area.

MENU DEVELOPMENT

Danny Meyer states, "The dinner menu always has ten entrées and fourteen appetizers, four of which are salads. We have daily specials that are repeated each week. For example, Tuesday is Black Angus ribbed steak for two, encouraging people to return on that day. The food is real, straightforward, and delicious, since I want the flavor of the food to be the most important factor, not the words on the menu or the presentation on the plate. I want people to bite into the steak and say, 'That's the best steak I have had in New York.'"

The food was inspired from Danny Meyer's travels through Italy, France, and the United States, and this eclectic and diverse menu has items like grilled marinated filet mignon of tuna and porchetta, a roast suckling pig.

Chef Michael Romano, who has been with the restaurant since 1988, changes the menu four times a year to match the seasonal changes in the availability of food and the changes in the weather. They taste-test each recipe along with the staff so that they can explain the ingredients to the customer. Meyer and Romano are vigilant about using farm-fresh ingredients of the season, grown by local producers situated virtually next door, at the Greenmarket. Danny Meyer says, "The diverse menu and the fact that each plate has a different garnish or vegetable accounts for higher-than-average food costs. However, this diversity and attention to detail is the heart and soul of this menu, encouraging customers to return."

Forty to 60 percent of the menu changes from year to year and season to season. Signature items, such as filet mignon of tuna, or incredibly tender fried calamari with spicy anchovy mayonnaise dipping sauce, are always served.

Danny Meyer has invested in an extensive wine cellar where over seventy selections of vintage wine from France, Italy, and California are served. He stores 30,000 bottles off-premises, and 5,000 in a 300 sq. ft. wine cellar in the basement.

STAFF

Danny Meyer says that "the biggest trick in staffing is to hire happy people who are naturally smart, naturally friendly; who, for one reason or another, bring a natural joy, which I do, to making other people happy. I learned maybe three years into this business that those are three things I am absolutely incapable of teaching anybody. We are, unfortunately, in an industry where most people are not choosing this as the way of their life. They're doing it because it's a good buck, it's a versatile schedule, and our country has had such a low common denominator of expectations for service, that almost anyone can do it, but that's not good enough. It's not good enough in this day and age, and it's certainly not good enough for this restaurant.

"We go through literally two to four hundred applications to find an employee, and I am talking about a very long and custom application that I have done for the restaurant, just to identify one person.

"At this point in an applicant's life, even though they may be pursuing a career in acting, or may be pursuing a career as an artist, we expect that they will derive pleasure from making other people happy. That is really all it takes.

Union Square Cafe

MAIN COURSES

Grilled Vegetables "Bagna Cauda" with Mashed Fagioli & Garlic Olive Oil	16.50
Steamed Striped Bass Fillet with Mushroom-Tarragon Vinaigrette and Spinach	19.50
Grilled Smoked Black Angus Shell Steak with Mashed Potatoes and Frizzled Leeks	23.50
Union Square Cafe's Grilled Marinated Fillet Mignon of Tuna with Braised Baby Bok Choy	24.00
Seared Monkfish "alla Milánese" with Roast Tomato Jus and a Salad of White Beans, Fennel & Radicchio	19.50
Baked Lobster "Shepherd's Pie" -- with Mushrooms, Spinach, Carrots and Lobster Sauce	23.00
Grilled Veal Lombatina with a Baked Zucchini, Eggplant and Parmigiano Tortino	22.50
Herb-Roasted Chicken with Creamy Polenta and Tomato-Sourdough "Panzanella"	18.50
Crisp Roasted Lemon-Pepper Duck with Spiced Pears & Three-Grain Pilaf	19.75

VEGETABLES AND CONDIMENTS

Hot Garlic Potato Chips	3.95
Sautéed Spinach with Lemon and Tuscan Olive Oil	4.95
Union Square Cafe's Mashed Turnips with Crispy Shallots	4.75
Creamy Polenta with Mascarpone, Toasted Walnuts & Crumbled Gorgonzola	4.50
Fagioli alla Toscana - Simmered White Beans with Savory Herbs, Tuscan Olive Oil and Pecorino	4.95
Bruschetta Rossa - Garlic-Rubbed Grilled Sourdough with Tomatoes, Basil and Tuscan Olive Oil	4.95
Creamy Mashed Potatoes with Crispy Leeks	4.25
Grilled Slices of Sweet Red Onion	2.95

SPECIALS TODAY

UNION SQUARE CAFÉ DINNER MENU.

"If someone gets great joy out of making somebody else happy, that's service. An act of service is the act of giving of yourself to somebody else. Then the food, the wine, where to place the silverware, how to repour the water, are all just props that we have. Those are the things that distinguish the restaurant business, but those are quite secondary, in my opinion. I think anybody is capable of learning how to carry a tray, or how to open a bottle of wine, but the chemistry must be right. Somebody needs to communicate to a table, nonverbally, that they're really enjoying doing that.

BUDGET

The total cost of this project was $750,000; $450,000 was spent on general construction,

---

Michael Romano
Executive Chef

Union Square Cafe

APPETIZERS

Risotto with Shredded Goose Confit, Radicchio, Red Wine and Parmigiano Reggiano	7.50
Homemade Spinach, Ricotta and Veal Ravioli with Tomatoes, Basil & Pecorino Romano	7.95
Farfalle "allo Zafferano" -- with Creamy Saffron Sauce, Chile Peppers and Sizzled Shrimp	8.50
Crostini "ai Fegatini" -- Chicken Liver-Sage Sourdough Toasts with Onion-Juniper Marmalade	6.95
Pepper-Crusted Yellowfin Tuna -- House-Smoked and Drizzled with Lemon and Tuscan Olive Oil	8.50
Escargots Simmered with Baby White Beans, Frisée, Prosciutto, Garlic and "Parsley Pesto"	7.95
Warm Terrine of Wild Mushrooms with Roasted Shallot-Hazelnut Vinaigrette	9.50
Union Square Cafe's Fried Calamari with Spicy Anchovy Mayonnaise	7.95

SALAD AND SOUP

"Creamless" Mushroom Soup with a Swirl of Porcini Oil	6.50
Union Square Cafe's Black Bean Soup with Lemon and a Shot of Australian Sherry	5.95
Red Oak Leaf and Bibb Lettuce Salad with Grated Gruyere and Dijon Vinaigrette	6.95
Union Square Cafe Greens Salad with Garlic Croutons and Sherry Vinaigrette	6.95
Baked Goat Cheese and Flageolet Salad with Frisée, Mâche & Fines Herbes	8.50
Arugula, Endive and Radicchio Salad with Mustard Vinaigrette	7.50

WEEKLY SPECIAL ENTREES

Monday:	Crisped Confit of Goose with Sautéed Potatoes and Haricots Verts	19.50
Tuesday:	Grilled Black Angus Rib Steak for Two with Spinach and Grilled Red Onions	24.00pp
Wednesday:	Porchetta Arrosta -- Roast Suckling Pig with Rosemary and Garlic, Served with Sautéed Greens and Herb-Roasted Potatoes	23.00
Thursday:	Spicy Chicken-Fried Venison Steak with Creamed Mustard, Mashed Potatoes & Wild Greens	19.75
Friday:	"Quenelles de Brochet" -- Steamed Freshwater Pike Dumplings with Basmati Rice, Sautéed Watercress and Lobster-Cognac Sauce	19.50
Saturday:	Grilled Marinated Lamb Chops with Ratatouille and Potato Gratin	22.50
Sunday:	Braised Lamb Shank with Roast Shallots, Wild Rice, Shiitakes and Cranberry Beans	19.50

Union Square Cafe • New York • (212) 243•4020

UNION SQUARE CAFÉ DINNER MENU.

which included walls, floors, ceilings, finishes, and furniture; $200,000 was spent on kitchen equipment and installation; and approximately $100,000 was spent on professional fees, lawyers' fees, and other preopening expenses.

The design process and construction documents took four months, while the construction of the restaurant, including Building Department approvals, took approximately four months.

The construction budget exceeded the original bid by approximately 15 percent owing to the fact that this was a renovation project. Structural steel reinforcement for openings in existing walls was needed after demolition was complete, and issues like this cannot be predicted before demolition.

Larry Bogdanow says that "some finishes were changed in order to reduce the budget. The original wainscoting was tongue-and-groove painted wood. Instead, painted Marlite was utilized." Danny Meyer wanted hand-fired Mexican terra cotta tile on the floor. Bogdanow explained that this was expensive, and very difficult to maintain, so an American-made machine-fired terra cotta tile was chosen instead.

Danny Meyer said, "Most restaurants fail because they are undercapitalized and aren't realistic about budgets and are unprepared to deal with budget overruns that are bound to happen in renovating an existing restaurant space. They never recover because they are indebted to contractors and the bank forever. These overruns are reflected in lower wages, causing staff problems, or higher prices that alter the perceived value of the restaurant.

"Union Square Café, with its budget overruns, was still built for much less than other comparable restaurants. The finishes and lighting selected reflect a sense of quality, but were not overly expensive. The budget was appropriate."

DESIGN CONCEPT

Danny Meyer had spent time vacationing and living in Italy, eating in and experiencing many restaurants there, and he had also visited many restaurants in the United States and worked in a few before formulating his idea for the style of restaurant he felt most comfortable in. He says, "I'm the guy toiling here; it needs to be comfortable for me, and the joy for me is the guests coming here and loving it too. Customers must feel welcome and sense that this restaurant is an extension of their home."

Larry Bogdanow states, "The natural materials for Union Square Café, including mahogany wood, antique pine, terra cotta tile, green

THE WARM MATERIALS AND LIGHT PAINTED WALLS SERVE AS A BACKGROUND FOR DANNY MEYER'S COLLECTION OF ARTWORK AND MURALS. PHOTOGRAPH © DANIEL EIFERT.

196

wainscoting, and off-white painted wall surfaces were selected to create a warm, timeless atmosphere. The high wood-beamed ceilings are reminiscent of scale, permanence, and warmth. The antique pine service stations were chosen to reflect Danny's attitude toward personalized service and hospitality.

"The warm materials and light painted walls serve as a background for Danny's collection of art and the murals. These pieces of art are colorful additions that reinforce the personal quality of this space."

The lighting in the space, like the artwork, is contemporary without being flashy. Surface mounted low-voltage quartz-halogen fixtures were used in the main dining area because the beams and ductwork above the ceiling prevented recessed lighting, and these fixtures add sparkle and look like small candles. The decorative pendant fixtures over the bar are soothing and create just enough energy for this bustling bar area. The remainder of the lights in the space are track fixtures that highlight artwork and architectural features, and they wash the wall with a warm glow. The subtle "warm glow" created by the reflection of light off the cream-colored walls is very flattering to skin tones, making people look good in this space, a key factor in the success of Union Square Café.

Although there is no carpet and many hard surfaces, customers can actually have conversations in this space. Fabric-wrapped acoustical panels were used in the mezzanine area and the front dining area with the 7' ceiling, while the wood beams in the bar and entry area assist in baffling sound.

SPACE PLANNING

Union Square Café's basement contains walk-in refrigerators/freezers, dry storage, a receiving area, a small steward's office, ice machines, and men's and employees' bathrooms and lockers. The ground level consists of the dining rooms, bar, kitchen, and ladies' bathroom. There is also a mezzanine dining room. Recently, a 1,000 square foot area has been built to house offices and employee changing rooms.

The entry into Union Square Café has high ceilings and an archway that welcomes the customer and creates a sense of arrival. There are three tables in this area and twelve seats that are used at lunch and for cocktails. This casual seating area can be seen from the street, setting the tone for the comfortable elegance associated with Union Square Café.

Once inside, after being greeted by the maitre d', customers are either brought to their tables or to the bar, where they can nibble on appetizers, have

THE INTIMATELY SCALED, SIMPLY DECORATED DINING AREAS SERVE AS A BACKGROUND FOR THE WONDERFUL FOOD. PHOTOGRAPH © DANIEL EIFERT.

drinks, or eat a full meal. This bar area represents 25 percent of the ground level and is the soul and one of the civilizing features of the space. It usually bustles with energy, and often single people prefer to eat there, read their newspapers, and converse with the bartender while observing everyone coming and going.

There are three distinct areas for dining: a low-ceiling intimate room that is a few steps down and to the left of the maitre d' area, a dining room in the rear of the restaurant that is equally intimate and features a large wall mural painted by Judy Rifka, and a popular mezzanine dining space overlooking the rear dining area. These intimately scaled dining areas create a personal sense of space so that each customer feels at home. This sense of warmth and comfort personifies Danny Meyer's commitment to the pleasures of the table.

Meyer says, "I opted for fewer seats than could actually fit in the space, and tables were spaced further apart to provide a comfortable environment. When you make a pro-guest decision, even if in the short term it doesn't add to the bottom line, it's the best decision one can make to assure a thriving business."

The space is approximately 5,600 square feet and is located on three levels. The ground floor is divided up as follows:

ENTRY AREA: 50 sq. ft.
DINING ROOMS: 2,000 sq. ft.
BAR: 400 sq. ft.
KITCHEN: 1,000 sq. ft.
SERVICE AREAS: 80 sq. ft.
COAT ROOM: 50 sq. ft.
LADIES BATHROOM: 50 sq. ft.

The mezzanine level is divided up as follows:

DINING AREA: 250 sq. ft.
OFFICES, CHANGING ROOM: 1,000 sq. ft.

The basement is divided up as follows:

WINE CELLAR: 300 sq. ft.
REFRIGERATED AND DRY STORAGE: 450 sq. ft.
MEN'S BATHROOM: 50 sq. ft.

KITCHEN DESIGN

The kitchen at Union Square Café has evolved over the years to adapt to the popularity of the restaurant. Michael Romano states, "There are two seatings, sometimes three, at dinner where we serve 250 to 300 covers, and since the kitchen is somewhat small, we have to rely on careful timing to alleviate crowding. We've added needed space to the kitchen by building an addition in a

UNION SQUARE CAFÉ FIRST FLOOR PLAN. COURTESY OF UNION SQUARE CAFÉ. REDRAWN BY LORRAINE KNAPP. REFERENCE TABLE: 1. ENTRY; 2. RECEIVING; 3. INFORMAL DINING; 3A. RECEPTION; 4. BAR; 5. SERVICE BAR; 6. WAITER'S STATION/WATER; 7. STAIRWAY TO MEN'S BATHROOM; 8. COAT ROOM; 9. DINING AREAS; 10. LADIES' BATHROOM; 11. OUTDOOR DISPLAY; 12. KITCHEN; 13. STAIRWAY TO DOWNSTAIRS STORAGE AREA; 14. SPIRAL STAIR TO OFFICES AND EMPLOYEE LOCKERS ABOVE; 15. STAIRWAY TO MEZZANINE DINING

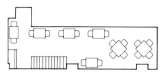

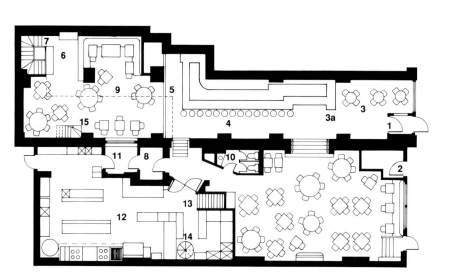

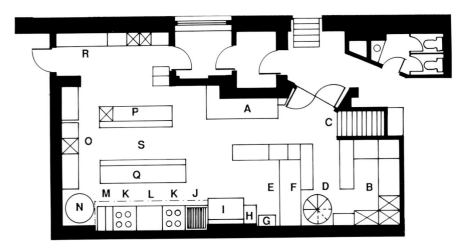

UNION SQUARE CAFÉ KITCHEN PLAN.
COURTESY OF UNION SQUARE CAFÉ.
REDRAWN BY LORRAINE KNAPP.
REFERENCE TABLE: A. WAITER'S
STATION/COFFEE STATIONS;
B. DISHWASHING; C. STORAGE AND
OFFICES; D. SPIRAL STAIR TO OFFICES
ABOVE; E. PASTRY PREP; F. PASTRY
TABLE; G. SINK; H. 2-BURNER
STOVE; I. CONVECTION OVEN; J. GRILL
WITH OVEN BELOW; K. OVEN WITH
SALAMANDER ABOVE; L. FLAT TOP
WITH CONVECTION OVEN BELOW;
M. FRYERS; N. 50 GALLON STEAM
KETTLE; O. PREP AREA; P. COLD
STATION; Q. HOT STATION;
R. REFRIGERATOR; S. EXPEDITOR

courtyard that contains salad prep sinks and upright refrigerators. We moved the dishwashing area where there once was an office and installed a spiral staircase to access the offices on the mezzanine level. Pastries are made next to the spiral stair in this area.

"The sous chef or I expedite between the *garde manger* and the hot plating counter, where we have visual control over both areas. There are three people on the hot line, two on the *garde manger*, and two in the pastry area. The runners stop right past a smaller waiter's station awaiting plates to be handed to them, since it's too small an area between the *garde manger* and the hot line.

"The timing of all entrées being served at each table is crucial, since all dishes must reach the customers at the same time, piping hot. Each entrée's cooking time varies and the expeditor must orchestrate the firing sequence in order to avoid one item getting cold, since it can't just be reheated and would have to be cooked again, adding to food costs. We fire our entrées ten minutes after each appetizer leaves the kitchen."

Danny Meyer states, "The small kitchen and its tight configuration have to some extent restricted us to a simpler menu."

COST OF OPERATIONS

Danny Meyer prepared an initial, conservative pro forma analysis assuming three-quarters of a turn on seating at lunch and one and a quarter at dinner with a lower average check. He had not anticipated the extent of wine sales at first and is now proud of his extensive wine cellar. Union Square Café continues to serve a wide audience and is still one of New York's favorite restaurants. His cost of operations are as follows:

SEATING CAPACITY: dining areas, 130; bar, 12
AVERAGE COVERS: lunch, 160; dinner 190-260
AVERAGE CHECK: lunch, $28; dinner, $44
LIQUOR AND WINE SALES: 28%
FOOD COST: 35%
LABOR COST: 35%
TOTAL EMPLOYEES: 72
RENT: 4%
YEARLY SALES: N.A.

Union Square Café's enduring success for over six years is owed in large part to Danny Meyer's commitment to quality. He wanted a restaurant where wonderful-tasting, imaginative food and wine are paired with caring service in a warm civilized atmosphere. All of the decisions he has made, including the menu, staff selection, and interior design, reflect this commitment to quality and attention to detail. Although he rarely sits down to eat at Union Square Café, Danny Meyer is his own most demanding customer, and he treats everyone as though it were himself he was serving.

His first chef, Ali Barker, and his current chef, Michael Romano, share this love for the joys of the table, and this is quite evident when the food is brought to the table by the caring and intelligent wait staff.

Larry Bogdanow was able to translate Danny Meyer's vision into this warm, intimately scaled, and civilized environment. The construction costs were managed well and did not leave Meyer with unmanageable debt. This timeless environment, like good red wine, is improving with age.

ARCADIA

OWNERS

Arcadia is owned by Anne Rosenzweig and Ken Aretsky. An innovative chef, consultant, and restaurateur, Anne Rosenzweig began in a very different arena. Graduating from Columbia University with a degree in anthropology, Rosenzweig spent several years doing field work in Africa and Nepal. During this time, she became interested in food and its preparation, and on her return to the United States, she chose cooking for her next career.

Anne Rosenzweig began her basic training as an unpaid apprentice in several New York restaurants. In 1981, she became a chef at Vanessa in Greenwich Village, where she was lauded for her originality and creativity. After leaving Vanessa, she worked as a consultant to several New York restaurants. In 1985, Rosenzweig opened Arcadia in Manhattan. Acclaim from reviewers and diners came almost immediately.

Anne Rosenzweig gives a good deal of time to several charities, including the United Way, Meals on Wheels, and the Entropy Trust, of which she is a founder. She has lectured and taught around the country.

An active member of the American Institute of Wine and Food, Rosenzweig is on the board of the New York chapter. She was listed in the *Cook's Magazine Who's Who of Cooking in America* for 1987 and is currently working on a new cookbook.

DESIGNER

Arcadia was designed by Randolph R. Croxton, AIA, founding partner of Croxton Collaborative, Architects. Entering into its fourteenth year, the firm has pursued a multidisciplined practice of interior design, architecture, and urban planning. The eighteen-person firm, which is located in a renovated 1880s carriage house in New York City, has received numerous awards for its work.

SOURCES

ARCHITECT: Randolph R. Croxton, AIA, Croxton Collaborative

LIGHTING CONSULTANTS: Incorporated Consultants Ltd.

STRUCTURAL ENGINEERS: Richard H. Balser & Associates

FOODSERVICE CONSULTANTS: Skolodz & Associates Ltd., Bayville, New York

MECHANICAL ENGINEERS: Pavane Associates, Bayside, New York

PHOTOGRAPHER: Otto Baitz

LIGHTING: Edison Price

CHAIRS: Stendig

BARSTOOLS: Beaver Furniture

BAR: Theo J. Svalgard, Inc.

UPHOLSTERY: Lee Jofa

CHINA: Bauscher

FLATWARE: D. J. Industries

GLASSWARE: Cristallerie Zweisel

MURAL: Paul Davis

ANNE ROSENZWEIG.

RANDOLPH R. CROXTON.

Arcadia is a 2,600 sq. ft. restaurant that seats fifty people and is located on East Sixty-second Street near Madison Avenue in Manhattan. It was completed in 1985, and it is considered one of New York's best restaurants, serving flavorful, inventive, regional food, using seasonal ingredients in a comfortably elegant environment.

The development of Arcadia went through several iterations before being realized. Before Anne Rosenzweig became involved, Ken Aretsky and his partners had determined that this restaurant should be a comfortable, refined dining experience.

In 1984, when this concept was developed, several large, noisy restaurants had recently been built to serve the burgeoning yuppie population. Rosenzweig and Aretsky felt that they wanted to open a restaurant for "grown-ups." They both felt that there still was a market demand for a comfortable, formal, intimate restaurant that served well-prepared, inventive regional food.

Anne Rosenzweig states, "I thought elegance, style, and formality were appropriate as an alternative to informal 'theatrical' dining. When people dress up to come to a restaurant, their expectations are heightened; it's a special event. They can't wait to eat the food. We also tried, however, to temper this sense of formality with a relaxed and comfortable feeling. It was very important that people feel welcome and special so that they would come two times a week for lunch and dinner, not only on their birthdays or anniversaries."

Arcadia is committed to the idea of hospitality. Rosenzweig feels that "the customer must feel welcome the minute they come in the door. Each

TO ACCOMPLISH A TIMELESS QUALITY, THE ENTRANCE PIVOT DOORS, THE BAR, AND THE SCREEN SERVE AS HANDMADE DISTINCTIVE HEIRLOOMS. PHOTOGRAPH © OTTO BAITZ.

customer is greeted, 'Hello, Mr. Smith' or 'Mrs. Smith.' It makes them feel special and cared-for. We also send something special to the table; something not on the menu. Arcadia or the arcadian retreat is an idealized special place that is serene, comfortable, and beautiful. It's a place where the guest is pampered with inventive, bountiful, flavorful food and gracious service. I hope that each guest feels well-cared-for, satiated, relaxed, and pleased after the meal."

Ken Aretsky had looked at several locations for his still-undefined restaurant concept. He decided on the Upper East Side because the affluent residential neighborhood could support his notion of a formal dining establishment. It was also within walking distance from several large hotels and office buildings. The location on Sixty-second Street near Madison was very

desirable, since it had previously been occupied by a restaurant. It is difficult in New York to construct a restaurant in a building that was occupied by a different use. Changing from one use to another is often not permitted in certain residential zones.

Since a kitchen, prep space, and some area for storage were already in place, it was assumed that it would be less expensive to build in this location. This, in fact, turned out not to be the case. The partners were able to purchase the net lease on the entire building, thus reducing the overall operating expenses. Arcadia occupies the basement and first floor of this 16' by 100' brownstone.

Ultimately, this truly beautiful urban setting proved to be a perfect location for Arcadia. The "home-away-from-home" concept seems to fit into its surroundings as though it had always been part of the neighborhood. It is real, and not pretentious.

MENU DEVELOPMENT

Arcadia serves the style of food Anne Rosenzweig calls "innovative American," for which she has become well known. She takes proven classics and gives them unexpected twists. It is hearty food with rural roots and urban polish. She has written *The Arcadia Seasonal Mural and Cookbook*, in which she published some of the recipes she created for the restaurant.

Rosenzweig states that the most important element in her food is flavor. "Flavor comes before anything else. Without flavor, it's absolutely meaningless, I don't care how good the food looks. Contrast between hot and cold, textures and flavors, is also very important to me. We always have a protein, a starch, and a vegetable. You may not see it or realize it when you're eating, like a TV dinner with compartments, but at the end of the meal, you're satisfied.

"We change a menu four times a year, to match the seasons. Certain ingredients are truly at their best at harvest. They smell and taste better. I am constantly inventing new dishes each season to delight my customers. My specials are consumed within two hours after they're announced. Customers trust this menu and can't wait to try new seasonal varieties. There are no flowery words describing the menu items.

warm chocolate bread pudding with brandy custard
strawberry shortcake with strawberry ice cream
warm apple charlotte with sticky caramel sauce
fresh fruit with pineapple sorbet
espresso/brownie sundae with peanut brittle
warm pear crumble with lemon curd ice cream

espresso decaf espresso 2.00
cappuccino, decaf cappuccino 2.50

dessert wines by the glass:

Sauternes - Raymond Lafon 1981	$10.
Essencia / Elysium - Andrew Quady 1989	$5.
Bonny Doon - vin de glacière - muscat canelli 1986	$7.
Fonseca bin 27	$8.
Graham's 20 year tawny	$12.
Graham's 1977 vintage port	$

by the bottle:
Gainey vineyards - late harvest johannisberg riesling 1989 $32. ½ bottle
Bonny Doon - vin de glacière - semillon ½ bottle $25.

please no cigar or pipe smoking

ARCADIA DESSERT MENU.

smoked salmon & potato tart on greens
squash & carrot soup with beet crème fraîche
arcadian caesar salad with arugula & brioche croutons
buckwheat fried oysters with oyster remoulade
seared foie gras sandwich with pear / cranberry chutney
field salad with fresh herb vinaigrette
corn cakes with crème fraîche & caviars $5.00

---

crispy roast chicken with potato / zucchini pancakes & plum compote
chimney smoked lobster with tarragon butter & celery root $7.00
grilled limousin rib-eye with straw potato fries
pan poached salmon with saffron, basmati rice & snow peas
mustard crisped crab cakes on an acorn squash ratatouille
roast cod with roasted beets and savoy cabbage

prix fixe $55.

It is simply stated, and if the customer needs an explanation, the staff is eager to provide information on how the dish is prepared.

"The food is served in bountiful portions, and is well-seasoned. It is sincere, inventive food that uses seasonal ingredients from the Hudson River valley. These natural ingredients are sources of inspiration and allow me to experiment with flavors, textures, and contrast. The food is personal, and is nurtured to please the customer's palate."

STAFF

Anne Rosenzweig states that "the high level of service, attention to detail, and the sense of welcome that starts at the door are the elements that have contributed to our success. I spend a great deal of time interviewing prospective service personnel to determine if they have caring personalities. Each member of our staff must have a genuine, caring concern for the customer. If they don't have that, all the training in the world won't matter.

"Arcadia's reputation was built on the idea of hospitality. I tell my staff all the time at our regular meetings that making each customer feel special is the single most important element. We have the most beautiful and largest fresh flowers in town on the tables, and use the finest crystal, flatware, and china. I try when I can to come out into the dining room to greet customers and to bring something special to their tables. However, I feel it's very essential for me to be in the kitchen nurturing the food.

"We have two meetings a day where I try to make everyone enthusiastic about the food. I explain the recipes and involve everyone in the process of inventing the recipes. Most of my staff stay with me for several years. Some have been with me since we opened.

"The kitchen is very comfortable, and my five wait staff have no more than twenty covers each. No one is overburdened. We have life and disability insurance. We also have a major medical and dental plan, along with a pension and profit-sharing plan. There are also paid vacations for all staff."

BUDGET

"Most items were planned for," according to Rosenzweig, "but there were items that went way over budget, especially electrical, plumbing, and mechanical issues related to the kitchen. It seems inevitable that restaurant budgets will always be exceeded. We had to borrow additional funds to pay for the overruns. Adding the one-story kitchen addition cost much more than we thought. The cost for this project was approximately $500,000, not including preopening expenses."

According to Arcadia's architect, Randy Croxton, it took approximately three months to provide design and construction drawings for the final Arcadia concept. The restaurant took over six months to complete and was delayed because the building was in a historic district.

DESIGN CONCEPT

Anne Rosenzweig wanted an elegant, formal, comfortable, and relaxed space with a high level of finishes to serve as a setting for her food. The basic space planning and some of the finishes were selected prior to her becoming a partner. Randy Croxton states that Rosenzweig selected the final color palette for the space and changed the theme of the mural that was installed in the main dining area: "Anne provided the emotional content for the space and made it a personal statement. She raised the level of finishes a notch to achieve an interior that would have a timeless quality. We both wanted a classic space that would not overpower the customer with stylistic forms and colors. The design should defer to the food and people in the space. It was important that the space look like it had always been there and twenty years hence, no one would comment that this restaurant was designed in 1985. The design must endure and serve as a classic background for the food and wine.

"To accomplish this timeless quality, I designed the entrance pivot doors, the bar, and the screen to serve as handmade, distinctive heirlooms. These richly detailed ox-blood mahogany pieces establish a level of finishes that one would find in an elegant residence. They also established a sense of permanence and quality. The entrance and bar area floors are tongue-and-groove hardwood, while the dining area is carpeted. The ceiling and walls are painted an off-white color. The intimate scale of the windowpanes in the entrance doors creates a friendly sense of welcome." Rosenzweig adds, "This is the perfect space for the kind of food that I create."

Anne Rosenzweig felt that there must be compatibility between her personal attention to food and service and the personal handmade quality of the space. The previous restaurant was a claustrophobic space with heavy wrought-iron chandeliers and candelabra. In order to overcome this closed-in feeling, Randy Croxton created a space-expanding, indirectly lighted mural that followed a continuous sweeping arc surrounding the entire dining area. This mural was placed to fall within standing or seated eye-level, and it was more intensely lighted than any other vertical surface in order to create the illusion that the 8'-high ceiling was higher. The tall mahogany screen, which is the only element to rise full-height to the ceiling, also creates this illusion of height.

Since Arcadia has a low sheetrock ceiling in the entire space and hardwood floors in the bar area, needed additional materials to prevent from being noisy. The thick carpet and banquettes absorb sound and make it acoustically comfortable.

Rosenzweig states, "We looked into alternative acoustical treatments and determined that they were so unattractive that I'd rather have some noise. Because Arcadia is a small space, people themselves absorb sound when the space is full. Sound tends to reverberate up front when there are few people.

"We close down one week every year to paint and touch up. Every two years, we reupholster the banquettes and change the carpet. Because the space is small, every nick, spot, and ding is noticeable. We are committed to the idea that this restaurant should be as spotless as one's home when guests are being entertained."

Lighting: Randy Croxton feels the most important space-expanding element is the recessed continuous cove light that illuminates the mural. This glow of light simulates sunlight, allowing the rich colors of the mural to blossom. This imitation of sunlight gives depth to the mural, thus expanding the room. This light also provides a warm glow throughout the dining room, making everyone look wonderful.

A SPACE-EXPANDING INDIRECTLY LIGHTED MURAL FOLLOWS A CONTINUOUS SWEEPING ARC SURROUNDING THE ENTIRE DINING ROOM.
PHOTOGRAPH © OTTO BAITZ.

The food and tablecloths are lit with appropriately spaced recessed low-voltage lighting. "I purposely chose not to add more objects like wall sconces or ceiling fixtures, since they would have made the space seem smaller. This is a very simple bold lighting scheme that works with the form and scale of the space," says Croxton.

Randy Croxton describes the building as a typical long and narrow New York brownstone with low ceilings. It was only 16' wide by 100' long without the kitchen addition. Croxton felt that the transition from the street to the dining room was important, and he designed an entry hall space where guests could be greeted.

He felt that this entry hall space should be separated from the main dining space so that there would be a natural progression of arrival, procession, and destination. The dining room would feel that much more special when perceived as a separate room when standing at the maitre d' station in the entry hall space. He felt that if the dining room continued all the way to the front of the space, people near the entry would not feel comfortable. Both Anne and Ken felt strongly that the space should not be carved into two spaces because it was too small to begin with. They also felt that customers seated in the front of the restaurant would not feel as important as those seated in the main dining space. Randy was able to create the sense of definition between the two functions without literally dividing the two areas. This was accomplished with the hand-

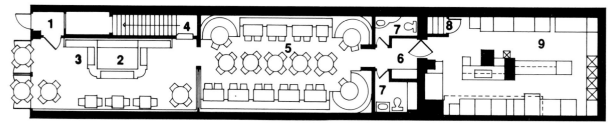

ARCADIA FIRST FLOOR PLAN. COURTESY OF CROXTON COLLABORATIVE.
REFERENCE TABLE: 1. ENTRY; 2. BAR; 3. MAITRE D'; 4. COAT AREA; 5. DINING AREA; 6. WAITER STATION; 7. BATHROOMS; 8. STAIRWAY TO BASEMENT/STORAGE AND PREP; 9. KITCHEN

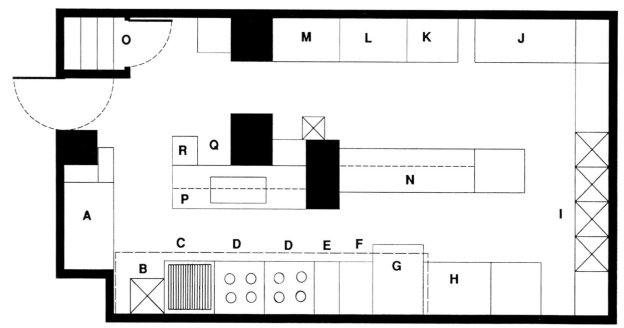

ARCADIA KITCHEN PLAN. COURTESY OF CROXTON COLLABORATIVE. REDRAWN BY LORRAINE KNAPP.
REFERENCE TABLE: A. MISE EN PLACE FOR GRILL STATION; B. PREP SINK; C. GRILL; D. 4-BURNER STOVE W/OVEN; E. FRYER; F. WORK TABLE; G. CONVECTION OVEN; H. PASTRY PREP; I. POT WASHING; J. DISHWASHING; K. ICE MACHINE; L. COFFEE; M. BREAD; N. GARDE MANGER/PLATING; O. STAIRWAY TO BASEMENT; P. PLATING; Q. EXPEDITOR; R. GARNISHES

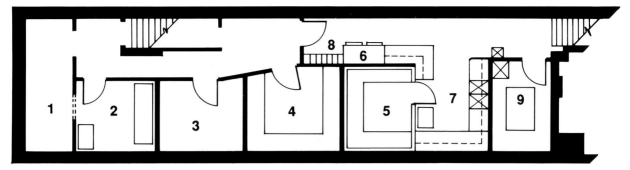

ARCADIA BASEMENT PLAN. COURTESY OF CROXTON COLLABORATIVE. REDRAWN BY LORRAINE KNAPP.
REFERENCE TABLE: 1. CHUTE FROM SIDEWALK; 2. RECEIVING; 3. OFFICE; 4. DRY STORAGE; 5. WALK-IN REFRIGERATOR; 6. FREEZERS; 7. PREP AREA;
8. EMPLOYEE'S LOCKERS; 9. MECHANICAL ROOM

carved wood screen in the center of the space. This tall screen also made the space seem much larger. The bar was placed in the entry hall area for guests waiting for tables. Pivot doors open at the entrance in warmer months, allowing tables and chairs to be placed outdoors.

DINING AREA: 1,000 sq. ft.
GROUND LEVEL KITCHEN: 600 sq. ft.
BASEMENT KITCHEN AND STORAGE: 1,000 sq. ft.

KITCHEN DESIGN

The space for the kitchen in the restaurant that preceded Arcadia was, according to Anne Rosenzweig, "tiny and had to be expanded. This created an expensive and difficult situation, since the only way to do this was to build a new one-story extension on the back of the building.

"The kitchen that was ultimately designed and built works extremely well. It's extremely space-efficient, allowing us to cram every necessary piece of equipment into a long and narrow space. The only problem is the big column between the hot and cold lines. It's difficult to talk and to see the person preparing appetizers and desserts when I'm standing at the hot line. There are two people on the hot line, and one person at the *garde manger*. I control all the expediting and plating, shuttling around the column between the hot and cold lines. We have one waiter/runner and five waiters for fifty seats."

Deliveries are received at the sidewalk and are sent to the basement storage area by way of a chute. The basement has a dry storage section, a large walk-in refrigerator, reach-in and walk-in freezers, a preprep area, and employee's lockers and bathrooms.

COST OF OPERATIONS

Arcadia serves a loyal, affluent clientele, has received two stars from the *New York Times*, and is many New Yorkers' favorite restaurant. Anne prides herself on being a sound businesswoman. She enjoys it almost as much as cooking. She says, "There are literally hundreds of issues I juggle every day, including labor and food costs, breakage, utility costs, and operating expenses. I work fourteen hours a day, and I relax on the five-minute cab ride home at night." Arcadia's cost of operations are as follows:

SEATING CAPACITY: dining room, 50
AVERAGE COVERS: lunch, 75; dinner, 100
AVERAGE CHECK: lunch, $35; dinner, $65
LIQUOR AND WINE SALES: 22%
FOOD COST: 30%
TOTAL YEARLY SALES: $3 million

Arcadia's success can be summarized in one word: hospitality. Anne Rosenzweig's wonderfully inventive food, using fresh, seasonal ingredients, is served in a soothing, relaxed, and intimately scaled atmosphere by an attentive caring staff. Her commitment to quality, her ability to motivate her staff, and her strong business sense have contributed to Arcadia's success.

Randy Croxton's timeless, carefully executed design reinforces the commitment to quality by utilizing richly detailed materials to create a comfortable environment. His utilization of space-expanding forms and lighting make this very small restaurant seem much larger.

Arcadia is a restaurant that is truly committed to the pleasures of the table, where the concept of hospitality is at its zenith.

GULF COAST AND TORTILLA FLATS

In 1982, a group of people with a need to focus their energies on a new kind of project got together. This group included Jay Savulich and Sherry Delamarter, who were in television production; Barry Secular, who had been a minor league ball player; and Zeet Peabody (a.k.a. Bart Walker), an artist who had had some prior restaurant experience. (There was an ex-bicycle messenger in the original group, but he left because things didn't move quickly enough for him.) This group formed individual corporations that included the same key players to own and operate Gulf Coast and Tortilla Flats, as well as two other Manhattan restaurants, Sugar Reef and the Cowgirl Hall of Fame.

These two restaurants are popular hangouts where regional food is served in abundant portions at bargain prices. They are both very successful.

Gulf Coast is a 2,000 sq. ft. full-service restaurant seating ninety people. It is located on West Twelfth and West streets in Manhattan. It was completed in 1984 and serves down-home New Orleans-style southern cooking in an environment reminiscent of restaurants found in that part of the country. It is a popular hangout and has endured for many years.

Tortilla Flats is a 1,500 sq. ft. full-service restaurant seating sixty-five people. It is located in Manhattan on West Twelfth and Washington streets, one block away from Gulf Coast. It was completed in 1983 and serves Texas-style Mexican food in a simply decorated, fun

GULF COAST IS A PLACE WITH SOUL THAT LOOKS LIKE IT HAS ALWAYS BEEN THERE. PHOTOGRAPH © JAY SAVULICH.

environment. It has been and still is a popular hangout that also has endured.

In 1983, a group of people with almost no prior restaurant experience were looking for something else to do. They wanted to open a very different kind of restaurant that would be an alternative to the uptown, expensive, white tablecloth establishments.

Tortilla Flats would be a place where young people could hang out and eat inexpensive Mexican food in the kind of place one would find in Texas. The goal was to see how little capital would be needed to open up a restaurant, and there was no thought given to how much money could be made. Jay Savulich says, "It was like the Little Rascals opening up a restaurant."

The restaurant was successful, as Savulich puts it, "partly because there was a simple idea executed for very little money and because people wanted inexpensive, unpretentious dining. It was dumb luck. It was not an organized business plan that led to success; it was a bunch of people who had a gut feeling that this concept was the right thing to do."

At its inception, Tortilla Flats was supposed to be a kind of sleepy, typical Mexican hangout that you might find in any border town. Instead, it became a vibrant, popular nightspot where Andy Warhol, Bianca Jagger, and Calvin Klein would hang out. For three years, it was one of New York's most popular places. People danced on the tables till dawn.

Tortilla Flats was previously a restaurant. Jay Savulich and his partners cleaned the floors, walls, and bar, hung decorative elements on the walls, and opened. It was not expected that this place would last more than a few years. It is still going strong.

Gulf Coast was opened in 1984 to accommodate the spill-over from Tortilla Flats.

The location for Tortilla Flats was chosen because it was previously a restaurant and didn't need a large investment for renovation. The partners lived and worked in the neighborhood and had a gut feeling for what could work on this corner. This area known as the Far West Village was the home of artists, writers, and just-arrived young people who needed inexpensive apartments. The recession in 1982 hit the Texas panhandle quite hard and spurred the migration of many Texans to the Big Apple. Tortilla Flats was an inexpensive alternative for them to uptown dining.

Both of Tortilla Flats and Gulf Coast fit their locations. They are situated among affordable housing converted from industrial buildings and the meat market next to the Hudson River. These locations are considered off-beat, and so is the food and decor of the restaurants. People have to want to come down here to eat. It's not the kind of restaurant you would stumble upon.

There was no specific target market when Tortilla Flats and Gulf Coast were opened. Local residents and people from the West Village were the first customers. Young professionals from Wall Street followed, and then both restaurants drew from Manhattan, New Jersey, and the outer boroughs. Tourists from the south heard about the food and also came.

MENU DEVELOPMENT

Jay Savulich says that consistency is the most important part of keeping their restaurants successful. He gives an example of how important a certain type of Worcestershire sauce is to particular menu items. In order to keep food costs down, he and his partners searched for a less expensive sauce, but found after experimenting with these sauces that the food wasn't the same. Coleslaw and crackers are brought to table before every meal. That adds to the food cost, but if that was taken away, regular customers would rebel.

Jay Savulich states, "The food for Gulf Coast has its origins in Louisiana, Texas, and Mississippi. The recipes were conceived from many visits to restaurants in these states. The partners tasted the dishes they liked, took notes, asked how they were prepared, mixed in a few ideas of their own, and created the menu items. The food is real. It is what we remember eating in Louisiana, Texas, or Florida or what we imagine it would be like.

"The original menu at Gulf Coast had ten items on it, while the menu at Tortilla Flats had eight items. The menus were limited in order to provide quality items consistently, but menu items were later added at the request of regular customers. People would ask, 'How come you don't have chicken-fried steak?'

"The foodservice concept was a hit from the start and didn't need much modification. That came as a shock to everyone. The chef contributes to success by continuing to make the original items the same way. That can be quite a challenge.

<u>FROM THE GULF COAST GRILL</u> (all items cooked to order over a mesquite wood fire, please be patient)

<u>FRESH FISH</u> all of our grilled fish dishes are served with today's green vegetable and our lemon dill rice

PEPPERED REDFISH FILLET coated with our hot & spicy three pepper mixture 14.95

TUNA LOIN STEAK please let us know how you want it cooked 14.95

PEPPERED TUNA STEAK coated with our hot & spicy three pepper mixture 15.95

FRESH WATER SALMON STEAK served with a tarragon cream sauce 15.95

SHRIMP FAJITA KEBOBS lime marinated shrimp, peppers and onions served with a spicy chipotle pepper sauce 12.95

<u>GRILLED MEATS</u> served with buttery mashed potatoes and todays vegetable

TEXAS SIZED RIB EYE STEAK at least 3/4 pound of prime beef please tell us how you want it cooked 15.95

PEPPERED RIB EYE STEAK coated with our hot& spicy three pepper mixture please tell us how you want it cooked 16.95

GRILLED STEAK FAJITAS boneless lime marinated beef strips served with grilled flour tortillas, lettuce and tomato add sour cream for.95¢ 12.95

CENTER CUT PORK CHOPS seared and smoking off the grill, a best seller 9.75

PORK CHOPS CAJUN STYLE our famous chops lightly dusted with our three pepper mixture and skinny dipping in a mint jalapeno jelly 10.75

<u>CHICKEN</u>

MESQUITE GRILLED 1/2 CHICKEN our most popular dinner, simple and delicious, served with buttery mashed potatoes 9.95 and today's green vegetable

CHICKEN FAJITAS strips of boneless chicken breast, peppers and onions marinated in lime juice and served with grilled flour 12.95 tortillas, lettuce and tomato (add sour cream fpr 95¢)

<u>VEGETABLE GARDEN KEBOB</u> peppers, tomatoes, mirliton, zucchini, onions, carrots and okra grilled and served with a spicy 9.45 chipotle pepper sauce over rice

<u>FLASH FRIED FAVORITES</u>

BUTTERFLYED MISSISSIPPI CATFISH farm bred corn fed whole catfish, corn battered and served with jalapeno hushpuppies & a green vegetable 11.95

LOUISIANA OYSTER PLATTER whole oysters bathed in a new orlean's italian breading and served with a spicy remoulade sauce, jalapeno hush 13.95 puppies and a green vegetable

CHICKEN FRIED STEAK west texas traditional pounded beef steak, flour battered and smothered with home style cream gravy, with buttery mashed potatoes and a green vegetable 10.95

<u>SIDE DISHES</u>

JALAPENO HUSHPUPPIES	deep fried corn balls with spicy pepper bits	2.95
BUTTERMILK BISCUITS	home made fluffy baked biscuits with butter and honey	3.95
BOWL OF RED BEANS	just the beans, cooked fresh every day	3.50
BOWL OF WHITE RICE	what can we say if you want it we got it	1.95
SIDE OF APPLESAUCE	.95	
SIDE OF SOUR CREAM	.95	

<u>DESSERT</u> ask your waitperson about the gulf coast's fabulous world of fresh made pies from the special board $3.95 per slice

GULF COAST MENU.

<u>DESSERTS</u>

ASK YOUR WAITPERSON ABOUT THE GULF COAST'S FABULOUS WORLD OF FRESH-MADE PIES AND OTHER DESSERTS FROM THE SPECIAL BOARD ○○○○○

○○○○○ TODAY'S PIES 3.95/SLICE

COFFEES OF THE WORLD

American Regular	1.50
New Orleans Community w/ Chickory	1.50
Decaffeinated French Roast	1.50
Mexican Coffee (with Kahlua)	4.00
Spanish Coffee (with Brandy & Kahlua)	4.00
Irish Coffee (with Irish Whisky)	3.50

ICED TEA 1.50
Tea 1.50   Sodas 1.50

NOW SERVING →

OUR COFFEE IS SO GOOD
We always drink it *Ourselves!*

SATURDAY 11:30 3:30

BRUNCH
sunday 11:30 3:30

GULF COAST ACTIONWEAR

T-SHIRTS: two sided 100% cotton white shirts with full color logo
NO POCKET $11/WITH POCKET $12 (Small, Med.,Large,X-Large)
SPECIAL LOUISIANA MAP DESIGN $12 (Large,X-Large)

TANK TOPS: 100% cotton white shirt with full color logo one side (Large, X-Large) $9

POLO SHIRTS: 100% cotton Lacoste type golf shirts with embroidered logo $22
WHITE or TURQUOISE color (Med., Large and X-Large)

GULF COAST HATS: 100% cotton baseball style hat with embroidered logo $13
WHITE, BLACK , GREY, MINT AND BLUE One size adjustable

we now take RESERVATIONS all sizes ~ private parties

■ *see our new drink menu for your favorite cocktail* ■

COME HEAR OUR
FREE LIVE MUSIC
EVERY TUESDAY WITH
? Call for lineups
(212) 206·1588

try our new place~
Cowgirl
HALL OF FAME
BAR · B · Q
519 HUDSON ST NYC 10014 212·633·1133

RESERVED
for vacation fun!

• GULF COAST
12 St. & W. Side Hwy
N.Y.C. 206-8790

• SUGAR REEF
92 2nd Ave. (bet. 5 & 6th Sts.)
N.Y.C. 477-8754

• TORTILLA FLATS
Cor. 12 St. & Washington St.
N.Y.C. 243-1053 •

GULF COAST DESSERT MENU.

TORTILLA FLATS

THINGS IN BOWLS

TORTILLA SOUP - CHICKEN & TOMATO SOUP WITH CHUNKS OF CHICKEN,
AVOCADO, STRIPS OF CORN TORTILLA & CHEESE 3.95

BLACK BEAN SOUP - CLASSIC RECIPE WITH A DASH OF SHERRY 3.75

CHILE CON CARNE - LOTS OF BEEF WITH GRATED CHEDDAR
CUP 2.75   BOWL . . . 4.50

CHILE CON QUESO - AUTHENTIC MEXICAN CHEESE DIP MADE FROM TWO
CHEESES, TWO CHILES AND ONIONS SERVED WITH CHIPS 4.95

APPETIZERS

NACHOS - CORN TORTILLA PIECES SMOTHERED WITH BEANS, CHEDDAR &
JALAPENO PEPPERS 3.25
NACHOS WITH BEEF OR CHICKEN ADD $ 1.00

QUESADILLA - SOFT FLOUR TORTILLA FOLDED AND FILLED WITH CHEDDAR &
JALEPENO PEPPERS 3.25

QUESADILLA CON FRIJOLES NEGROS (BLACK BEANS) - AS ABOVE WITH BEANS . . . 3.75

CHALUPAS - WHOLE CORN TORTILLA TOPPED WITH REFRIED BEANS, CHEDDAR
AND GUACAMOLE 3.95

GUACAMOLE AND TORTILLA CHIPS - MADE FRESH DAILY FROM WHOLE
AVOCADOS 4.25

THREE TAMALES - HAND MADE CORN ROLLS FILLED WITH BEEF, COVERED
WITH CORN HUSK AND TIED WITH A COTTON STRING 2.95   OR 6 FOR . . 5.50

ENSALADA DE LA CASA - AVOCADO, RED ONION, RED & GREEN PEPPERS, CUKES,
LETTUCE & TOMATO SERVED IN A DEEP FRIED FLOUR TORTILLA SHELL
WITH OUR JALAPENO HOUSE DRESSING 5.95

QUESADILLA GRANDE - OUR JUMBO APPETIZER OF FLOUR TORTILLA STACK
FILLED WITH CHICKEN, CHEDDAR, LETTUCE, TOMATOES & JALAPENOS
TOPPED WITH A DASH OF GUACAMOLE 6.75

ALL ITEMS ABOVE ARE A LA CARTE. IF YOU WOULD LIKE A BASKET OF CHIPS AND
A BOWL OF SALSA TO ACCOMPANY THERE IS AN ADDITIONAL CHARGE: CHIPS AND
HOME MADE SALSA 1.00

PLATOS GRANDE/MAIN COURSES

COMBINATION PLATES: ENCHILADAS - (BEEF, CHEESE OR CHICKEN)
TACOS   - (BEEF OR CHICKEN)
BURRITOS   - (BEEF, CHICKEN, REFRIED OR
TOSTADAS   - BLACK BEAN)

WITH REFRIED BEANS, MEXICAN RICE, LETTUCE & TOMATO
ONE ITEM: . . . 6.50   TWO ITEMS: . . . 7.95   ADD GUACAMOLE: . . . 1.25 PER ITEM

CARNITAS BURRITOS - TWO FLOUR TORTILLAS FILLED WITH SHREDDED PORK
GRILLED WITH RED SALSA, WITH MEXICAN RICE AND REFRIED BEANS 7.95

TACOS AL PASTOR - BITE-SIZED PORK TACOS YOU MAKE YOURSELF W/MINI
SOFT CORN TORTILLAS, ONIONS AND GREEN CHILE SALSA, RICE + BEANS . . 8.75

CARNITAS COLORADO - TWO SHREDDED PORK BURRITOS GRILLED WITH A
HOT RANCHEROS SAUCE, WITH MEXICAN RICE AND REFRIED BEANS 8.75

BLANCHITOS - TWO CHICKEN ENCHILADAS FILLED WITH SOUR CREAM, ONION
AND CHEDDAR, COVERED WITH A WHITE SAUCE AND MUNSTER CHEESE,
WITH RICE AND BEANS 8.95

MOLE ENCHILADAS - TWO CHEESE OR CHICKEN COVERED WITH OUR DARK
CHILE AND BITTERSWEET CHOCOLATE PUREE, WITH RICE AND BEANS 8.95

ENCHILADAS VERDE - TWO CHICKEN ENCHILADAS COVERED WITH A GREEN
CHILE SALSA AND WHITE CHEESE, MEXICAN RICE AND REFRIED BEANS 8.95

CHIMICHANGAS - TWO DEEP FRIED CHICKEN BURRITOS SERVED WITH SOUR
CREAM AND GUACAMOLE, LETTUCE + TOMATO GARNISH 8.95

POLLO MOLE - BONELESS CHICKEN BREAST COVERED WITH A DARK CHILE,
TOASTED PEANUT AND CHOCOLATE SAUCE SERVED WITH MEXICAN
RICE AND REFRIED BEANS 9.50

POLLO VERDE - BONELESS CHICKEN BREAST COVERED WITH A GREEN CHILE
AND TOMATILLO SAUCE, WITH MEXICAN RICE AND REFRIED BEANS 9.50

OVER

The chef also is in charge of finding ingredients that have consistent quality, while keeping food costs down. New food items come from each partner and not from the chef. This allows each of them to have control over the concept."

Tortilla Flats never had a review. Gulf Coast got generally favorable reviews. Sugar Reef got fantastic reviews the first month it was open. Savulich admits, "I never thought I would own and operate restaurants that would be reviewed. Now I feel I live and die by these reviews. The challenge is, how do you live up to the good review when it happens. Will the kitchen be uncomfortably hot when the cook has to prepare 200 dinners to satisfy this new demand? Will he quit? Will the staff be capable of serving more customers after a good review? Will there be enough space to accommodate more people?"

Jay Savulich feels that "a restaurant needs to be open at least two months before it can work out the bugs." The worst thing that can happen is getting a rave review after a few days. The challenge to live up to the advance hype could spell disaster.

STAFF

One reason why Jay Savulich feels that the restaurants are successful is the way that the staff is treated. "Staff tend to stay for years at our restaurants, and regular patrons see familiar faces and feel at home."

Jay Savulich works about fifty hours a week and surrounds himself with people that work with him and not for him. He tries to find wait staff and support personnel that are smart, well-groomed, and intrinsically want to be in the restaurant business. He doesn't want people who want to work in a restaurant as a hobby, nor does he want professional restaurant people. This makes it hard to find staff. They go through at least forty interviews before they select someone for a position.

Savulich states that "originally, the partners split up the responsibility of running the restaurants by zones, where one was responsible for the food and kitchens for all the restaurants, while one was responsible for accounting, taxes, and insurance, and another partner was responsible

for future business development. This structure proved to be very inefficient. Now each partner has control over each restaurant.

"Restaurants that are operated by the owner directly have a much better chance of succeeding than those that are run by a management team. The restaurants that I enjoy are owner-managed. I can feel it when I am in a restaurant that's run by employees and not the owner."

BUDGET

The budget for Tortilla Flats was $35,000. This included mostly cleaning, painting, decoration, and inventory. The rent in 1983 was $3,700 per month. It took one month of nights and weekends to fix up.

The budget for Gulf Coast was considerably more. It was $175,000, owing to problems with the existing structure. Steel reinforcement was needed to increase the second floor's capacity to support people because it had previously been a residence. The ground floor was rotting and had to be replaced, and it took a month to open downstairs and a year to open the second floor.

Savulich says, "We would never take over another existing building that was used for another purpose and build a restaurant, because it is much too expensive and is much more than originally estimated. When we open our next restaurant, we will take over an already-built space and adapt it to suit our needs. We would never build a restaurant from scratch in a new space because it is too expensive for the type of business we do. Our maximum capital expenditure on a restaurant is $150,000. The restaurant business is fraught with risk, and we're successful because we're not in business to lose other people's money. We will only risk what we can internally afford. Banks would not loan us money because of the high risk, so we used that problem and turned it around to our advantage. It allowed us out of necessity to invest only the money we could afford.

"No matter how meticulously the budgets for each restaurant were planned, they were exceeded by a significant amount, and compromises had to be made concerning finishes and equipment to keep the budgets from getting out of hand.

TORTILLA FLATS MENU.

GULF COAST PRESENTS SOUTHERN COOKING IN AN ENVIRONMENT REMINISCENT OF RESTAURANTS FOUND IN NEW ORLEANS. PHOTOGRAPH © JAY SAVULICH.

TORTILLA FLATS LOOKS LIKE A PLACE THAT COULD BELONG ANYWHERE ALONG THE MEXICAN BORDER. PHOTOGRAPH © JAY SAVULICH.

"One of the reasons these restaurants have been successful is that we were able to see a return on our investments quickly. If we had borrowed the money and hadn't been a hit from the start, investors might have changed the concept before it had a chance to make it.

"If a lot of investors were asking for returns on their investments quickly, the restaurants would have been run a lot more conservatively at the outset. This conservative approach might have killed the concept before it had a chance to become a hit."

DESIGN CONCEPT

Both Tortilla Flats and Gulf Coast look like they have always been there. They're the kind of place you hear about, eat at, and wonder where they've been all your life. They fit their locations and feel genuine, not contrived. They're the kind of place you would find on the Mississippi River or in a small border town. They have great appeal because they are perceived as "real" places that do not put any demands on your behavior. You can roll up your sleeves, have a beer and a "mess o' catfish," and have a great time.

Gulf Coast features flowered vinyl upholstered booths, the kind Jay Savulich saw on trips to Florida. They were not chosen to be cute, funny, or campy. They are real.

All the partners truly believe in places like this. Each of them had memories of places that had real soul. They all felt that if they had places of their own, they would have to have that kind of soul. Each of their restaurants is planned and designed by the partners. They do not hire designers. Architects are hired to provide Building Department drawings.

THE TABLE TOPS HAVE POSTCARDS LAMINATED TO THEIR SURFACES WITH A PLASTIC FINISH OVER THEM. PHOTOGRAPH © JAY SAVULICH.

The interior design and the foodservice concept were born together. One could not succeed without the other. Both Gulf Coast and Tortilla Flats look like the kind of place in which you could have the kind of food that is served. That's what makes them so memorable.

At Gulf Coast, the tabletops have postcards laminated to the surface with a plastic finish over them. The ceilings are made of corrugated metal. The walls are finished with painted wood wainscoting and are decorated with beer signs, memorabilia, and other unknown artwork. Colored bare-bulb lighting is strung over tables.

Tortilla Flats is handled in much the same way, only it looks like a place that could have been anywhere along the Mexican border.

SPACE PLANNING

Gulf Coast's 2,000 sq. ft. is spread out over two levels as follows:

KITCHEN: 500 sq. ft.

DINING ROOM: 500 sq. ft.

BAR: ground floor, 500 sq. ft.; second level, 400 sq. ft.

BATHROOMS: ground floor, 50 sq. ft.; second level, 50 sq. ft.

STORAGE (SECOND-LEVEL): 200 sq. ft.

COST OF OPERATIONS

There was no formal business plan or pro forma analysis prepared for Tortilla Flats or Gulf Coast. When they first opened, rent was low, business was great, and the cash register never stopped ringing.

The rent at Gulf Coast is now $13,000 a month. Jay Savulich says that rent should never be more than 10% of gross sales. He likes to negotiate rent at 5% or 6% at the start and have it escalate to no more than 10% after several years.

All of the restaurants were funded through operating capital. Bank loans have not been needed because no more was invested than could be afforded by the partners.

Although rent has gone up considerably, as have labor costs, the average check has not increased dramatically to offset the rise in overhead, as this would destroy the concept.

Customers have always perceived that they were receiving great value at both Tortilla Flats and Gulf Coast, and this is still the case today. The cost of operations at Gulf Coast are:

SEATING CAPACITY: 90
AVERAGE COVERS: dinner, 180
AVERAGE CHECK: $27
LIQUOR AND BEER SALES: 31%
FOOD COST: 31%
LABOR COST: 31%
TOTAL EMPLOYEES: 30
YEARLY SALES: $1.1 million

The cost of operations at Tortilla Flats are:

SEATING CAPACITY: winter, 65; summer, 90
AVERAGE COVERS: lunch, N.A.; dinner, 143
AVERAGE CHECK: lunch, $7; dinner, $18
LIQUOR AND BEER SALES: 42%
FOOD COST: 28%
LABOR COST: 31%

TOTAL EMPLOYEES: 25
YEARLY SALES: $1 million

Tortilla Flats and Gulf Coast, as well as Sugar Reef and The Cowgirl Hall of Fame, are successful restaurants because each of them is a genuine place that offers wonderfully prepared food in unpretentious, fun environments at reasonable prices.

The partners invested their money in the original Tortilla Flats and built the other restaurants with the profits. This financial freedom allowed them to have control over the menu and interior design.

All of the partners had a singular vision about how these restaurants should look and what food would be served. They all believed strongly that each of these places should provide value and quality in settings that have a soul. The customer knows what to expect in these places, and keeps coming back to hang out, eat wonderful food, and have a good time.

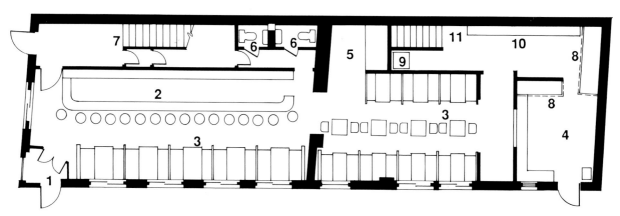

GULF COAST FIRST FLOOR PLAN. COURTESY OF JAY SAVULICH. REDRAWN BY LORRAINE KNAPP.
REFERENCE TABLE: 1. ENTRY; 2. BAR; 3. DINING AREA; 4. KITCHEN PREP AREA; 5. WAITER'S STATION; 6. BATHROOMS; 7. TO UPSTAIRS DINING; 8. HOT LINE; 9. REFRIGERATOR; 10. DISH AND POT WASHING; 11. UP TO SECOND FLOOR STORAGE AND DINING AREA

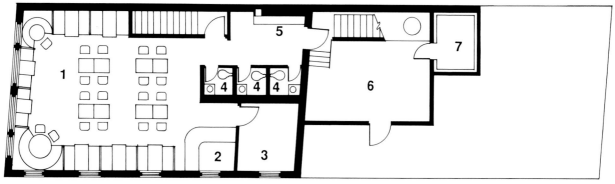

GULF COAST SECOND FLOOR PLAN. COURTESY OF JAY SAVULICH. REDRAWN BY LORRAINE KNAPP.
REFERENCE TABLE: 1. DINING; 2. BAR; 3. OFFICE; 4. BATHROOMS; 5. WAITER'S STATION; 6. DRY STORAGE; 7. WALK-IN REFRIGERATOR

APPENDIX

The implications for restaurateurs of the Americans with Disabilities Act of 1990 (ADA) is described in the Eastern Paralyzed Veteran's Association's (EPVA) handbook, *Understanding the Americans with Disabilities Act*, which provides the basis for the following information. The ADA gives civil rights protection to individuals with disabilities, similar to the protections provided to individuals on the basis of race, sex, national origin, and region. The ADA guarantees equal opportunity for individuals with disabilities in the areas of employment, state and local government services, public transportation, privately operated transportation available to the public, places of public accommodation, and telephone services offered to the general public. Some believe that because of the widespread physical barriers the ADA will cause to be removed, it is the most far-reaching civil rights law ever enacted.

The basis for the ADA is that during the past two decades, educational and vocational training opportunities for individuals with disabilities have greatly improved, while employment opportunities in the private sector and access to places of public accommodation, including restaurants, have not improved. Enforcement of the ADA in the years ahead should enable disabled individuals to realize the heretofore elusive goal of full participation in American society.

The key employment provisions of the ADA began on July 26, 1992. Employers with twenty-five or more employees are now prohibited from discriminating against qualified individuals with a disability in all of the following areas: job application procedures hiring, advancement or discharge of employees, employee compensation, job training, and other terms, conditions, and privileges of employment

Beginning on July 26, 1994, the prohibition of discrimination in employment against qualified individuals with disabilities is expanded to cover employers with fifteen or more employees. Types or forms of prohibited discrimination in employment include: denying employment solely on the basis of the need to make "reasonable accommodation" to the disability of a qualified applicant; not making "reasonable accommodation" to the disability of the qualified employee, unless such accommodation would impose an "undue hardship" on the employer.

Making "reasonable accommodation" to the disability of a qualified applicant or employee is generally regarded as a key to the successful employment of persons with severe disabling conditions. The ADA defines "reasonable accommodation" as efforts that may include: making existing facilities used by employees accessible to disabled individuals; job restructuring; part-time or modified work hours; reassignment to a vacant position; acquisition or modification of equipment or devices; appropriate adjustment or modifications of examinations, training materials, or policies; the provision of qualified readers or interpreters; other similar accommodations for individuals with disabilities.

"Undue hardship" means an action requiring significant difficulty or expense, and the ADA includes a number of factors for consideration in determining if a "reasonable accommodation" actually constitutes an "undue hardship" on the employer, such as the nature and cost of the accommodation, the financial resources of the employer, the impact of such accommodations on the financial resources of the employer, or other factors.

Restaurants, bars, or other establishments serving food or drink are among the private entities considered "public accommodations" for purposes of the ADA, if the operations of such entities affect commerce.

Concerning the new construction of places of public accommodation and commercial facilities, such new construction must be accessible in facilities for first occupancy after January 26, 1993. Concerning alterations in places of public accommodation and commercial facilities, both the altered portion of the facility and the path of travel to the altered area, including bathrooms, telephones, and drinking fountains must be rendered accessible, as long as the cost of modifying the path of travel, bathrooms, telephones, and drinking fountains is not disproportionate to the overall cost of the alteration project. Elevators are not required in places of public accommodation and commercial facilities that are less than three stories or that have less than 3,000 sq. ft. per story, unless the building is a shopping center, a shopping mall, or the professional office of a health care provider.

In the provisions of the Revenue Reconciliation Act of 1990 (RRC), Congress adopted an important new tax credit for barrier removal in existing buildings to specifically comply with the requirements of the ADA. Effective for expenditures paid or incurred after November 5, 1990, Section 44 of the IRS code allows an eligible small business to elect a nonrefundable tax credit equal to 50 percent of the amount of the eligible access expenditures for any tax year between $250 and $10,250. Consequently, the maximum amount of the credit for any taxable year is $5,000.

An eligible small business is defined as any person (term includes corporation) that: had gross receipts (reduced by returns and allowances) for the preceding taxable year that did not exceed $1 million or had no more than thirty full-time employees, and elects the application of the disabled access credit for the tax year. An employee is considered full-time if such employee is employed at least 30 hours per week for 20 or more calendar weeks in the tax year.

Eligible access expenditures specifically include amounts paid or incurred: for the purpose of removing architectural, communication, physical, or transportation barriers that prevent a business from being accessible to, or usable by, individuals with disabilities; to provide qualified interpreters or other effective means of making aurally delivered materials available to individuals with hearing impairments; to provide qualified readers, taped texts, and other effective methods of making visually delivered materials available to individuals with visual impairments; to acquire or modify equipment or devices for individuals with disabilities; or to provide other similar services, modifications, materials, or equipment.

The Section 44 tax credit can be elected in more than one taxable year, provided that eligible access expenditures were paid by an eligible small

business; however, if the Section 44 credit is elected in a taxable year, no deduction or credit is allowed for access improvements under any other IRS Code provision (e.g. Section 190 of the IRS Code. The RRA reduced the maximum allowable amount of the Section 190 deduction from $35,000 to $15,000, effective since 1991.)

Restaurants that must comply with provisions of the ADA may need to remove certain architectural and transportation barriers in order to comply with ADA. Under section 190 of the IRS code, an annual tax deduction of up to $15,000 each year may be taken by any taxpayer who removes barriers to disabled individuals in a place where a business or trade is conducted. This applies only to the removal of barriers at existing places of business or trade. Design areas that are covered include: grading; walks; parking lots; ramps; entrances; doors and doorways; stairs; floors; toilet rooms; water fountains; public telephones; elevators; controls; identification; warning signals; hazards; international symbol of accessibility; additional standards for rail facilities; and standards for fuses.

An additional provision in the Section 190 regulations covers other barrier removals, which may include a substantial barrier to the access or use of a facility or public transportation vehicle; a barrier to one or more major classes of such individuals (such as blind or deaf persons or persons using wheelchairs); and, the removal of such barrier being accomplished without creating any new barrier that significantly impairs access to or use of the facility or vehicle. This provision of the Section 190 regulations is meant to cover other barrier removals that are not covered specifically in the regulations. For example, if the barrier removal is covered in a local code section governing provisions for physically handicapped persons, it would be an eligible expense under this provision of Section 190.

The ADA requires that certain new design standards for accessibility are to be prepared by the U.S. Architectural and Transportation Barriers Compliance Board. Further, the ADA requires compliance with the Uniform Federal Accessibility Standards (UFAS) if certain implementing regulation time frames are not met by other federal agencies. It is recommended that businesses that remove barriers in existing facilities to qualify for the Section 190 tax deduction follow design specifications in the UFAS or an equivalent local standard.

BIBLIOGRAPHY

Baraban, Regina S., and Joseph F. Durocher. *Successful Restaurant Design*. New York: Van Nostrand Reinhold, 1989.

BOCA. *National Building Code: 1990*. 11th ed. Illinois: Building Officials and Code Administrators, International, 1989.

de Chiara, Joseph, and John Callender. *Time-Saver Standards for Building Types*. 2d ed. New York: McGraw-Hill, 1980.

Dannenberg, Linda. *Paris Bistro Cooking*. New York: Clarkson Potter, 1991.

Hirshorn, Paul, and Steven Izenour. *White Towers*. Cambridge, Mass.: MIT Press, 1979.

Hoke, John Ray, Jr., ed. *Ramsey/Sleeper Architectural Graphic Standards*. 8th ed. New York: John Wiley & Sons, 1988.

Lang, Jenifer Harvey, ed. *Larousse Gastronomique*. New York: Crown Publishers, 1988.

Langdon, Philip. *Orange Roofs, Golden Arches: The Architecture of American Chain Restaurants*. New York: Alfred A. Knopf, 1986.

Lathrop, James K., ed. *Life Safety Code Handbook*. 3d ed. Massachusetts: National Fire Protection Association, 1985.

Understanding the Americans with Disabilities Act. 2d printing. Eastern Paralyzed Veterans Association, 1991.

INDEX